The

Ethnicity

Reader

The
Ethnicity
Reader

*Nationalism, Multiculturalism
and Migration*

MONTSERRAT GUIBERNAU
AND
JOHN REX

Polity Press

Copyright © this collection Polity Press 1997.

First published in 1997 by Polity Press in association with Blackwell Publishers Ltd.

2 4 6 8 10 9 7 5 3 1

Editorial office:
Polity Press
65 Bridge Street
Cambridge CB2 1UR, UK

Marketing and production:
Blackwell Publishers Ltd
108 Cowley Road
Oxford OX4 1JF, UK

Published in the USA by
Blackwell Publishers Inc.
Commerce Place
350 Main Street
Malden, MA 02148, USA

A CIP catalogue record for this book is available from the British Library.

Library of Congress Cataloging-in-Publication Data

The ethnicity reader : nationalism, multiculturalism, and migration
 [edited by] Montserrat Guibernau and John Rex.
      p.   cm.
   Includes index.
   ISBN 0-7456-1922-3 (hardcover). — ISBN 0-7456-1923-1 (pbk.)
   1. Ethnicity.   2. Ethnic relations.   3. Nationalism.
4. Multiculturalism.   I. Guibernau i Berdún, M. Montserrat (Maria
Montserrat)   II. Rex, John.
GN495.6.E8935   1997
305.8—dc21
                                                                        97-23201
                                                                        CIP

Typeset in 10 on 12 pt Stempel Garamond
by Ace Filmsetting Ltd, Frome, Somerset
Printed in Great Britain by TJ International, Padstow, Cornwall

This book is printed on acid-free paper.

Contents

vi   *Contents*

Editors' note

Omissions from the material as originally published are indicated by ellipses within square brackets, thus: [...]. Where a paragraph or more has been excluded, there is a line space above and below such ellipses. All others are as in the original publication. Apart from minor amendments (e.g. capitalization and British rather than American spellings), the few editorial interventions necessitated by publishing these essays in a single volume also appear in square brackets.

Acknowledgements

We owe an enormous debt to Tony Giddens for actively supporting this project from the beginning. His comments and advice have been of vital importance.

Among those who have helped us in the preparation of this book we would like to give especial thanks to Gill Motley, Pamela Thomas, Julia Harsant, Sue Pope, Ruth Thackeray, Rose Goodwin and Claudette Brennan. Particular thanks are due to John B. Thompson, Zig Layton-Henry and Daniéle Joly for their help and encouragement.

The editors and publishers wish to thank the following for permission to use copyright material: The University of California Press for material from Roth & Wittich (eds/trans), *Max Weber, Economics and Society*, 2 vols, © 1978 The Regents of the University of California (original German publication by J. C. B. Mohr (Paul Siebeck) Tübingen); Blackwell Publishers for material from Anthony D. Smith, *The Ethnic Origin of Nations*, © (1986) Anthony D. Smith; Pluto Press for material from Thomas Hylland Eriksen, *Ethnicity and Nationalism* (1993); Verso for material from Benedict Anderson, *Imagined Communities* (1983); Blackwell Publishers and Cornell University Press for material from Ernest Gellner, *Nations and Nationalism* © Ernest Gellner 1983; Cambridge University Press for material from E. J. Hobsbawm, *Nations and Nationalism since 1780 (Canto 1990)* © (1990, 1992) Cambridge University Press; Princeton University Press for material from M. E. Brown (ed.), *Ethnic Conflict and International Security* © 1993 Princeton University Press; Macmillan Press Ltd and St Martin's Press for material by W. Harvey Cox, in Catterall & McDougall (eds), *The Northern Ireland Question in British Politics* (1996) © P. Catterall and S. McDougall; C. Hurst & Co. (Publishers) Ltd for material from Christopher Bennett, *Yugoslavia's Bloody Collapse: Causes, Course and Consequences* (1995); Institute for Public Policy Research for the chapter (James McCormick and Wendy Alexander, 'Firm Foundations: securing the Scottish Parliament' [here 'Scotland: towards devolution']) from *The*

State and the Nations: Politics of Devolution, © IPPR 1996; *Scottish Affairs* for the article by Michael Keating 'Canada and Quebec: Two Nationalisms in the Global Age' (1995); Sage Publications for material from Franke Wilmer, *The Indigenous Voice in World Politics* (1993); Centre for Research in Ethnic Relations for 'The Concept of a Multicultural Society', by John Rex, *Occasional Papers in Ethnic Relations No. 3*, CRER, 1985; L. Kuper and M. Smith for material from *Pluralism in Africa*, University of California Press, 1969; Oxford University Press for material from Will Kymlicka, *Multicultural Citizenship,* © Will Kymlicka 1995; Avebury Publishing Ltd for material by F. Radtke from Rex and Drury (eds), *Ethnic Mobilization in a Multicultural Society* (1994); The Population Council for material from Douglas S. Massey *et al.*, 'Theories of International Migration: A Review and Appraisal' [here 'Causes of migration'] in *Population and Development Review*, vol. 19, no. 3 (September 1993), pp. 431–63; *Innovation: The European Journal of Social Science* for material by John Rex from vol. 7, no. 3 (1994), pp. 207–17; The University of Chicago Press for the article 'Diasporas' by J. Clifford in *Current Anthropology*, vol. 9, no. 3 (1994), pp. 302–38; Polity Press and Michel Wieviorka for material by Michel Wieviorka in Rattansi and Westwood (eds), *Racism, Modernity and Identity* © 1994 Michel Wieviorka; Beacon Press for material from *Turning Back* © 1995 by Stephen Steinberg; Éditions La Découverte for material from 'Class Racism' in Étienne Balibar and Immanuel Wallerstein, *Race, nation, class, les identités ambiguës* © La Découverte 1988.

Every effort has been made to trace the copyright holders, but if any have been inadvertently overlooked, the publishers will be pleased to make the necessary arrangements at the first opportunity.

Introduction

THE GROWING IMPORTANCE OF THE CONCEPT OF ETHNICITY

The term ethnicity became increasingly crucial in the social sciences in the 1960s, a period marked by the consolidation of the process of decolonization in Africa and Asia as numerous new nation states were created. Anti-colonial and anti-racist arguments contributed to the generation of a new vocabulary in which the term 'ethnicity' was used by sociologists and others, as Spoonley has suggested, to acknowledge 'the *positive* feelings of belonging to a cultural group' (Spoonley [1988] 1993).

In more recent years, since the collapse of the Communist regimes, more negative aspects of ethnicity have come to the fore. The notion of 'ethnic cleansing' in the former Yugoslavia brought the very idea of ethnicity into political disrepute. However much a sense of shared ethnicity created positive feelings of belonging to an in-group, it seemed to imply total hostility and genocide towards neighbouring out-groups.

An additional reason for an increasing use of the term ethnicity was the coming to northern Europe of immigrants from post-colonial societies and from dependent economies. Their presence in the European Union was seen by many as constituting a political problem, a cultural problem and an identity problem. Moreover, since some of these immigrants would move on to North America, they were seen as constituting transnational communities with less than a complete commitment to the nation states in whose territory they had first settled. In North America, while many European immigrants had been assimilated over a period of more than a century, there now appeared two problems: that of assimilating new immigrants coming directly or indirectly from Asia, Africa and Latin America; and that of integrating black or African-American residents descended in part from a slave population and coming out of a semi-colonial plantation economy.

Whether it was viewed in positive or negative terms, however, one thing was clear. Ethnic bonding and ethnic identity were becoming more important for sociology and social psychology than mere biological descent or class. While gender differences were, it is true, given increasing prominence, their study always vied with the study of ethnicity.

In Part I of this collection we have included essays dealing with the relation between the concept of ethnicity and those of the nation, nationalism and the nation state. In Part II the essays deal with transnational migrant communities and the constitution of multicultural societies.

THE THEORY OF NATIONALISM AND THE CONCEPT OF ETHNICITY

The new emphasis upon ethnicity posed important problems for the theory of nations and nationalism. Theory in this area dealt with the nation in its eighteenth- and nineteenth-century European forms: the modern nation was seen in rational terms as part of the modernizing project of industrial societies. It was now increasingly recognized, however, that, far from resting solely on this rationalizing base, the nation state might be held together emotionally by bonds not unlike ethnic ones and would at the same time generate opposition and resistance by subordinated ethnic nations.

In attempting to grapple with this new intellectual situation sociologists could gain little from the classical sociological tradition. Marxism seemed to regard ethnicity as a form of false consciousness which would be replaced in due course by a consciousness of shared and opposed interests, while the tradition of Tönnies ([1887] 1963) and Durkheim (1933) was more concerned with the contrast between traditional and modern society, understanding the latter in terms of the concepts of '*Gesellschaft*' and 'organic solidarity'.

The one classical theorist who did find space for a consideration of the ethnic concept was Max Weber, who sought, within the limitations of his own time, to conceptualize it in contrast to the notions of class, status and party. Weber called ethnic groups 'those human groups that entertain a subjective belief in their common descent because of similarities of physical type or of customs or of both, or because of memories of colonisation or migration' (Weber [1922] 1968: 389). This is an attempt at a comprehensive definition and it will be useful to draw attention to some of its implications.

In the first place it is clear that Weber distinguished ethnic groups from 'races' conceived in biological terms. It is not biological difference alone that constitutes an ethnic group, 'common customs' are also a factor. However, it is not simply having physical or cultural characteristics that is important but rather the subjective perception of these characteristics, both by those who share them and by those who react to them.

Secondly, Weber did not believe that shared ethnicity of itself leads to group formation. It only facilitates group formation, particularly in the political sphere. It is political community, however it is organized, which appeals to shared ethnicity and brings it into action. Yet, once ethnic groups have been constituted politically in this way, the belief in common ethnicity 'tends to persist even after the disintegration of the political community, unless drastic differences in the custom, physical type, or, above all, language exist among its members' (Weber [1922] 1968: 389). Clearly, then, Weber saw united political action as central to the dynamic of ethnicity.

Thirdly, as a consequence, Weber had a strong sense of the role of history in shaping ethnic groups, which he perceived as having memories of a common past, attachment to a clearly demarcated territory and certain traditions or ways of life. All of these elements may survive for a long time in the collective consciousness of peoples who may have lost the political institutions which used to represent them, or may have migrated or been forced to migrate and become inhabitants and even citizens of nation states controlled by others. These are factors involved in the nationalisms of subordinate and minority groups which act as a counterweight to the incorporative rationalizing processes of the modern state.

Weber, it will be noted, did recognize the experience of migration in the history and consciousness of ethnic nations. Such a reference to the migration experience is at odds with the sense of belonging which the nation states in lands of present settlement may seek to encourage or impose. This is also a factor of central importance among immigrant communities in contemporary Europe and it is a theme to which we return in our discussion of 'multiculturalism' later in this introduction.

Fourthly, Weber recognized that ethnicity serves to delimit 'social circles' which are not identical with 'endogenous connubial groups'. What happens, however, is that some of the characteristics of such groups are attributed through myths and symbols to wider social circles. This, indeed, is the essence of the constitution of a so-called '*ethnie*'. Symbols are used to stand in for the presence of actual kin.

These issues are of some importance in such countries as contemporary Germany, where Germanness is thought to be based upon the *jus sanguinis*. In these cases the subjective belief is that what unites Germans is not a shared culture but a unity of descent, a unity of blood. It matters little that this cannot really exist after centuries of intermarriage with those among whom they have settled. What is important is a myth through which the ethnic community has attributed to its sense of unity some of the characteristics of the small 'endogamous connubial group'.

One factor which must be taken into account in any discussion of ethnicity is the difference between the ethnicity claimed by the people themselves and that attributed to them by others. In either case the perception of ethnicity will rest not upon some scientific sociological truth but on subjective

interpretation. Moreover, the subjective interpretations of the difference between groups may vary enormously in attitude to what group members think
about themselves and how they are regarded by others. Those who classify them
from the outside may do so in terms of particular aspects of physical appearance
or culture, while different criteria may be applied in classifying themselves.

A point which is sometimes made is that the term 'ethnic group' may be used
only to classify minorities and inferiors, whereas majority and dominant
groups do not see themselves as ethnic at all. Thus, in Britain, the term 'ethnic
minorities' is used to refer primarily to non-white immigrants, while in some
other countries the term refers to such groups as the Australian Aborigines, the
Sami in the Scandinavian countries, Roma or Gypsies, or the First Nations
(Native Americans) of North America who seek to live outside the modern
economy and polity, although sometimes seeking to develop their economic
resources for their own advantage.

A further problem for the theory of ethnicity is posed by the use of the term
'ethnic identity'. Identity is both a psychological and a sociological term. It
may provide 'a definition, an interpretation of the self that establishes what and
where the person is in both social and psychological terms' (Guibernau 1996:
72). On the one hand it helps the individual to produce order in his or her own
individual life. On the other it helps to place that individual within a group or
involves 'identification' with a collectivity. Both of these forms of identity may
be accomplished through the use of symbols. These two aspects of identity vary
independently of each other. As Anthony Cohen put it, 'ethnicity has come to
be regarded as a mode of action and of representation: it refers to a decision
people make to depict themselves or others symbolically as the bearers of a
certain cultural identity' (Cohen 1994: 119); but 'the apparently monolithic or
generalised character of ethnicity at the collective level [...] does not preempt
the continual reconstruction of ethnicity at a personal level' (Cohen 1994: 120).
Others have pointed to the fact that acceptance of multiple identifications at a
collective level does not mean a loss of identity at an individual and psychological level. It is simply a fact of human existence that human beings live within,
and identify with, a multiplicity of groups according to occasion, without
becoming individually psychologically disturbed; such disturbance, however,
might occur among a minority.

The social dimensions of identity and identification may, as we have argued,
be either chosen or imposed. Political communities of all shapes and sizes have
sought to instil in their members a sentiment of belonging and a belief in a
common destiny. Around the late eighteenth century and the early nineteenth,
a process was initiated by which old loyalties to the lord or the monarch were
replaced by loyalty to the nation. The nation thus became an emotionally
charged object and nationalism emerged as an ideology centred upon the
sentiment of belonging to a particular community and the subsequent desire to
see it flourish and develop.[1] The nation state was created as a political institution with a territorial base which utilized the doctrine of nationalism in its

foundational moment to generate a common culture and a sense of belonging among its members. Most of these nation states had a multinational character since they were established through dynastic unions and by conquest and annexations. Once the nation state was created, however, whether out of one nation or as a multinational or imperial entity, it actively promoted the cultural homogenization of its members and even appealed to a new common ethnicity which had to be constructed in a symbolic manner.

In the mid-nineteenth century the Romantic movement brought about the idea that cultural difference mainly expressed through linguistic diversity was valuable and had to be preserved. Such an assertion prompted the emergence of cultural movements (such as the Catalan *Renaixença*) to defend minority cultures struggling to survive within nation states; the latter were trying to expand an official culture and language which did not take account of – or sometimes actively pursued the eradication of – minority cultures and languages, perceived as a threat to the integrity of the state. Some of these initially cultural movements of resistance would turn into nationalist movements, vindicating the rights of nations once absorbed into nation states to exist and develop their own cultures and languages. They would then become nations without states claiming the right to decide about their political future.

The concepts of ethnicity and nationalism imply a certain commonality among members of a group, the ethnic group in one case, the nation in the other; these are constructed symbolically and presuppose the existence of boundaries which separate one group from another. In fact they both emphasize minimal differences between the members of certain groups. The nation predicates continuity with the past and common descent and this is how ethnicity is brought into nationalism.

The belief in the uniformity and the ancestral origins of a community which considers itself a natural grouping is not, however, a feature which defines all nationalisms. Greenfeld (1992) has made a useful distinction between 'ethnic' and 'civic' nationalism. Civic nationalism is identical with citizenship, and, in this case, 'nationality is at least in principle open and voluntaristic, it can sometimes be acquired'. Ethnic nationalism believes nationality 'to be inherent – one can neither acquire it if one does not have it, nor change it if one does; it has nothing to do with individual will, but constitutes a genetic characteristic' (Greenfeld 1992: 11). Common ethnicity is not a constant in all nationalisms; more than that, ethnicity is in no way conducive to nationality. According to Greenfeld, 'the population of the United States of America, the identity of which is unmistakably national and which undoubtedly possesses a well-developed sense of uniqueness, is a case in point: it has no "ethnic" characteristics because its population is not an "ethnic community" ' (Greenfeld 1992: 13).

The appeal to common ethnicity in terms of a common cultural identity, which may or may not have a direct link with common descent, is often invoked by political leaders as a factor of social cohesion. In doing this, they reflect the force of the belief in a common ethnicity, or, in the case of nationalism, the power of the idea of belonging to the same nation. Ethnicity and nationalism may be latent for years and suddenly re-emerge with unexpected vigour, as has happened in the former Soviet Republics. In fact they are useful tools in periods of ideological vacuum. After the demise of communism, nationalism became a prominent alternative in a set of countries lacking a democratic tradition and unused to competing diverse political ideologies. At present nationalism is showing afresh its capacity to bring together people from different social and cultural backgrounds. Billig argues that 'nationalism, far from being an intermittent mood in established nations, is the endemic condition'. He uses the term 'banal nationalism' 'to cover the ideological habits which enable the established nations of the West to be reproduced' (Billig 1995: 6).

A shared ethnicity is sometimes made a condition of establishing membership of particular nations. In these cases nationalism adopts an ethnic character and, depending upon the political ideologies to which nationalism is attached, it might lead to violence and xenophobia. On the other hand, it might adopt what could be called a Durkheimian outlook, following the principle that nations may somehow become the vehicle of the human ideal, insofar as they assume that their main task is not to expand by extending their borders, but to improve the level of their members morality (Giddens 1987: 201; Durkheim [1973]: 101). The connection between ethnicity and violence stems from the idea that those who do not belong should be treated as potential or actual enemies. Discrimination and the annihilation of the different follow from this assumption and are exemplified in nazism, fascism and other movements using 'ethnic cleansing' as a policy against selected strangers.

The meaning of ethnicity is not exhausted by its relation with violence. The appeal to a common ethnicity which emphasizes commonality of culture is actively defended by nationalist movements struggling for self-determination. This is the case in nations without states such as Catalonia, Quebec or Scotland: the larger states in which they are contained are usually reluctant to recognize their own multinational character. The plea for self-determination was also crucial in the Wilsonian dispensation of 1918 which was later involved in the process of decolonization of European empires in Asia and Africa. Nations without states continue to struggle for self-determination, their various political scenarios depending upon the political will of the state within which they are included.

In Part I we have sought to bring together extracts which deal with the relation of ethnicity to nationalism. This is important because much of the theorization of nations, the nation state and nationalism has been modernist in its emphasis and has underplayed not only the need of even the nation state to find a basis for emotional and moral attachment for its members but the fact that, in their modernizing projects, these nation states met ethnic resistance. We would hope that the extracts included here illustrate some of the complexity of the engagement of ethnicity with nationalism.

ETHNICITY, MIGRATION AND MULTICULTURALISM

Part II deals with the notion of multicultural societies and with the relation of transnational migrant communities to the nation state. To some extent this suggests that two separate problematics have developed, one concerned with ethnicity and nationalism, the other with ethnicity and migration. Another view is that these two problematics have a common root in a more general theory of ethnicity from which both may be thought to branch.

Some of these theoretical issues are covered in John Rex's discussion of 'The concept of a multicultural society'. Rex suggests that the theory of ethnicity has necessarily to address the problems raised by the notion of primordial ethnicity on the one hand and that of 'instrumental' or 'situational' ethnicity on the other. The notion of primordiality is a questionable one if it suggests inexplicable forms of bonding and social relationships. The task of social science may, indeed, be precisely to explain what appears inexplicable. A consideration of Geertz's attempt (Geertz 1963) to define primordiality shows that it can be deconstructed and shown to refer to a primary form of community or *Gemeinschaft*, as that term is used by Tönnies ([1887] 1963). Such a community is based upon kinship, neighbourhood, shared language and beliefs about the supernatural and some narrative or myth of the group's origin. It involves an intense feeling of belonging together, and, in the sense in which the term is used by Durkheim, of sacredness (Durkheim 1915).

Fredrik Barth, who is generally thought to be the proponent of the instrumental or situational theory of ethnicity, however, raises the important question of where the boundaries of such groups might lie. One of the problems of the primordial theory is that some of the component elements of a primary community stretch beyond the bounds of a small community. Barth therefore goes on to argue that the boundaries considered to constitute and define an ethnic group or community depend upon the purpose in hand. Who is and who is not a Pathan in the North-West Frontier Province of Pakistan depends upon what the particular group calling itself Pathan is doing.

If this holds even in relation to small-scale communities, it does so even more when an attempt is made to claim the features of intense belonging and sacredness for much larger groups, or, as they are sometimes called, *ethnies*. Much argument in the theory of ethnicity is about the constitution of such groups. We need not accept, as the theory of primordiality would suggest, that they are simply 'given'. Rather they must be seen as constituted to serve particular purposes, whether unconsciously by all the members of the *ethnie*, or by leaders who use the appeal to ethnicity to serve their own purposes.

One purpose which the *ethnie* may serve is to seek to assert its political control or sovereignty over a territory, and, when this occurs, the *ethnie* becomes an ethnic nation. It is not, however, the only possible purpose to which ethnic bonding might be applied. It might, for instance, refer to the formation of classes and status groups, or, of even greater importance for our purposes here, to the formation of transnational migrating communities (Rex 1991 and 1996).

One tendency in the theory of ethnicity has been to treat these communities as quasi-nations, or, emphasizing their spread across different territories, as 'diasporas' with an ideology of 'diasporic nationalism'. This, however, can be misleading if the term diaspora is taken, in its narrow sense, as referring to a group which has been dispersed from its historic home by some traumatic experience and wishes to return there. It is more acceptable if it is used more loosely to refer to any internationally dispersed ethnic group, whether or not it has nationalist aspirations.

The selection of papers in Part II is based upon the assumption that instead of using ethnicity as the basis of bonding in a group laying claim to a territory, it can be used in the process of migration to unite members of a group in their migration project. In order to clarify the nature of migrating groups it is necessary to place them within the framework of migration theory, which should be as important to the theory of ethnicity as the theory of nationalism and ethnic nationalism. Since, however, migration theory has been developed on an interdisciplinary basis by political economists, political theorists, anthropologists and sociologists, it becomes necessary to draw the threads together to show what such theories mean for the constitution of migrating groups.

One very important point which has to be understood in any theory of ethnicity, as mentioned above, is that ethnicity often has a dual nature. On the one hand there is the ethnicity which the members of a group claim and feel for themselves; on the other there is the ethnicity which is attributed to them by others. There is also the more complex possibility that the claimed or felt ethnicity of group members may be shaped by that which is attributed to them by others.

The others with whom a migrant ethnic group has to engage are often the agents of a nation state. Such a nation state may be of the modernizing kind as described in Gellner's theory (Gellner 1983), or it may be the agent of a dominant ethnic group. In either case it is very likely to be corrosive of subordinate ethnicity, as it is of class and other solidarities. Another possibility is that the nation state may define itself as 'multicultural' or 'multi-ethnic' and this is a possibility which must also be explored, especially in Europe and North America, where a number of societies have defined themselves in this way. There is, in fact, in most modern industrial and post-industrial societies, a conflict and tension between the principle of a unified nation and a multicultural one (Rex and Drury 1994; Rex 1996).

The notion of a multicultural society is sometimes confused with that of a plural one, but unfortunately the concept of the plural society has been developed to analyse the nature of colonial and post-colonial societies rather than those which are modern, industrial and democratic, though it is also true that something called 'pluralism' is a virtuous feature of these more democratic societies. The concept of multiculturalism may then be used to refer to features which are both democratic and egalitarian and those which are antidemocratic and hierarchical. It therefore becomes necessary to sort out the differences between malign and virtuous pluralism and malign and virtuous forms of multiculturalism as judged by the standards of modern democracy.

A similar debate to that developed around these themes by anthropologists and sociologists has occurred among political philosophers who have reflected on the nature of a liberal society. Such a society is generally built around the concept of individual human rights and it has had to extend itself to take account of group rights. This has been a very important theme in recent political philosophy, particularly in the work of such writers as Charles Taylor (Taylor 1992). Unfortunately in such writings, which are on a very abstract level, insufficient distinction is made between the problems of the nationality of subordinate nations, as in Quebec, and the problem of the treatment of immigrant minorities. What a sociology of ethnicity and nationalism therefore needs is a theory which takes account of both multinationality and of multiculturalism as a policy concerned with the position of minorities who have no aspiration to statehood in their land of settlement.

It should be added here that there is also a socialist or social democratic view of these problems: the modern state is seen not as simply following the logic of promoting human rights but as having emerged from a conflict of interests (largely class interests) which have been reconciled through the institutions of the welfare state. For social democrats the problem is that of the compatibility of the normal institutions of the welfare state and institutions set up especially for handling minority problems.

Much of the writing which exists on ethnicity concerns itself with the problem of minorities within nation states and it is quite right that this should be so. There is, however, an increasing concern in sociology with looking at all problems from an angle wider than that of the nation state. Thus Immanuel Wallerstein sought to transcend a narrow nation-based viewpoint by developing a theory of 'world systems' (Wallerstein 1974), and, much more commonly today, a new dominant approach is that of 'globalization'. These viewpoints probably overplay the notion that the nation state is no longer important; in our selection of essays we have sought to reflect both those which still concern themselves with the internal structures of the nation state and those based upon a world systems or globalization outlook. Arguably, moreover, our concern with transnational communities reflects our belief that the study of such communities represents a too much neglected part of the theory of globalization.

To return to the theme of attributed ethnicity, we have also thought it necessary to include studies which deal with what are generally referred to as 'racism' and 'xenophobia' or simply with ideologies of 'exclusion'. These all deal with an analysis of the reasons offered for treating ethnic minorities as inferiors.

The theoretical discussion above is illustrated by the readings included in this collection. Part I deals with themes related to ethnicity and nationalism, Part II with migration, transnational communities and multicultural societies.

Chapter 1 contains three essays: a discussion of the concept of an ethnic group by Max Weber; Anthony D. Smith's analysis of the structure and persistence of *ethnies* which are essential to the understanding of the emergence of nations in the modern era; and Thomas Hylland Eriksen's account of the different uses of the term ethnicity, relating it to the concepts of race and nation.

In chapter 2, Benedict Anderson defines the nation as an 'imagined community' and stresses the role of print capitalism in contributing to the generation of a common national consciousness. Ernest Gellner connects nationalism with industrialism, arguing that nationalism is based upon the modern need for a standard culture instilled by the state and shared by all of its citizens. Eric Hobsbawm questions the strength of nationalism as a political ideology and provides an evaluation of its role after the rejection of Communism in 1989.

Chapter 3 is concerned with the connection between ethnicity and violence. Michael E. Brown considers the possible causes and consequences of ethnic conflict, taking account of the very large number of refugees likely to result from ethnic confrontations. W. Harvey Cox offers a detailed account of the events unfolding in Northern Ireland from the Hillsborough Agreement in 1985 onwards. The final essay in this chapter is by Christopher Bennett, who reflects on the experience of ethnic cleansing in the former Yugoslavia.

Part I concludes with a chapter that relates ethnicity to securing the right of peoples to self-determination and the use of peaceful means to attain this goal. Montserrat Guibernau analyses the content of contemporary Catalan nationalism and evaluates the future of nations without states in the context of a united Europe. James McCormick and Wendy Alexander consider the main problems and implications of the creation of a devolved Scottish Parliament which would alter the present political structure of Britain. Michael Keating writes about the development of both Canadian and Québecois identity in the light of an increasingly powerful Québecois nationalism in an age of globalization. Franke Wilmer discusses First Nations (Native Americans) in the USA and analyses their use of the concept of nation when applied to them.

Discussions of multiculturalism and migration begin in chapter 5 with an essay by John Rex setting out the ideal of multiculturalism as it has come to be discussed in Europe. This is followed by Leo Kuper's essay on the plural society and the contrast between the malign and unequal form of pluralism developed under colonialism and the sort of pluralism thought to be virtuous in a modern democratic society. This leads naturally to the topic of citizenship in multicultural societies, represented in chapter 6 by an extract addressing the need to rethink the liberal tradition from Will Kymlicka's book *Multicultural Citizenship*. Frank-Olaf Radtke discusses the problems of grafting a multicultural apparatus on to the institutions of what he calls 'the social democratic welfare state'. Radtke writes with the case of Frankfurt particularly in mind.

Chapter 7 deals with the nature of migrant communities. The essay by Douglas S. Massey and his colleagues brings together theories from a number of disciplines and addresses the reasons for the initiation of migration as well as the structures through which it comes to be sustained. This forms an essential background to John Rex's analysis of the structure of transnational migrant communities. This is followed by an essay entitled 'Diasporas': its author, the anthropologist James Clifford, recognizes the value of the term but also acknowledges its limitations if used in a narrow sense. Clifford also clarifies the nature of other structures and groupings which differ from, even though they overlap with, true diasporas.

In chapter 8 we have included three essays on the various negative ways in which minorities can be viewed or even excluded, as in European and North American society. These reflect a number of different disciplines and theoretical and ideological trends. Michel Wieviorka writes about racism and anti-racism in France from the viewpoint of the theory of social movements, developing some of the ideas of Alain Touraine. Stephen Steinberg looks at the United States experience and argues that the movement to win civil rights for American blacks (now called African-Americans) reached its high point when the Johnson administration secured their legal and political rights. Subsequently, he claims, the perception gained ground that legal rights were not enough, but that this in turn led to two tendencies, one arguing that affirmative action must continue, the other that something had to be done to alter the nature of the African-American family and community. In his view much American sociology has wrongly supported the second position. Finally Étienne Balibar discusses how ideologies of nationalism and racism have come to compete with the ideology of Marxism based upon analysis of class.

In a more comprehensive Reader we would have felt it necessary to include case studies dealing with the reconstitution of a range of post-colonial societies which are still undergoing change. The existing essays on plural societies, such as that by Leo Kuper (a South African by birth), do, however, cover the important theoretical issues inherent in understanding these societies rather more satisfactorily than would a snapshot case study of their contemporary situation. We have not attempted to adjudicate all the views represented here. In any case we could not easily do so, since we have shown the issue of ethnicity to be many-faceted. We would hope, however, that our introduction and our selection of readings will contribute to the advancement of the study of Ethnic Relations and that our readers and students will be encouraged to read in full the works from which we have sought to choose representative extracts.

MONTSERRAT GUIBERNAU
JOHN REX

NOTE

1 For a detailed analysis of nation formation in the Middle Ages see Llobera (1994); for a complete study of the process of nation-state formation see Giddens (1985).

REFERENCES

Barth, F. (1969), *Ethnic Groups and Boundaries*, Allen and Unwin, London.
Billig, M. (1995), *Banal Nationalism*, Sage, London.
Cohen, A. P. (1994), *Self-Consciousness: An Alternative Anthropology of Identity*, Routledge, London.
Durkheim, E. (1915), *The Elementary Forms of Religious Life*, Allen and Unwin, London.
Durkheim, E. (1933), *The Division of Labour in Society*, Free Press, Glencoe, Illinois.
Durkheim, E. (1973), 'Pacifisme et Patriotisme' (translated by N. Layne) in *Sociological Inquiry*, Vol. 43, No. 2, pp. 99–103.
Geertz, C. (1963), *Old Societies and New States*, Free Press, New York.
Gellner, E. (1983), *Nations and Nationalism*, Blackwell, Oxford.
Giddens, A. (1985), *The Nation-State and Violence*, Polity Press, Cambridge.
Giddens, A. (1987), *Durkheim on Politics and the State*, Fontana Paperbacks, London.
Greenfeld, L. (1992), *Nationalism: Five Roads to Modernity*, Harvard University Press, Cambridge, Mass.
Guibernau, M. (1996), *Nationalisms: The Nation-State and Nationalism*, Polity Press, Cambridge.
Llobera, J. R. (1994), *The God of Modernity*, Berg, Oxford.
Rex, J. (1991), *Ethnic Identity and Ethnic Mobilisation in Britain*, Research Monograph No. 5, Centre for Research in Ethnic Relations, University of Warwick, Coventry.
Rex, J. (1996), *Ethnic Minorities in the Modern Nation State*, Macmillan, London and Basingstoke.
Rex, J. and Drury, B. (1994), *Ethnic Mobilisation in a Multi-Cultural Britain*, Avebury, Aldershot.
Spoonley, P. ([1988] 1993), *Racism and Ethnicity*, Oxford University Press, Oxford.
Taylor, C. (1992), *Multi-Culturalism and the Politics of Recognition*, Princeton University Press, Princeton.
Tönnies, F. ([1887] 1963), *Community and Society* (translated by C. P. Loomis), Harper and Row, New York.
Wallerstein, I. (1974), *The Modern World System*, Academic Press, New York.
Weber, M. ([1922] 1968), *Economy and Society*, University of California Press, Los Angeles.

Part I

Ethnicity and Nationalism

1 The Concept of Ethnicity

What is an ethnic group?
MAX WEBER

'RACE' MEMBERSHIP

A [particularly] problematic source of social action [...] is 'race identity': common inherited and inheritable traits that actually derive from common descent. Of course, race creates a 'group' only when it is subjectively perceived as a common trait: this happens only when a neighbourhood or the mere proximity of racially different persons is the basis of joint (mostly political) action, or conversely, when some common experiences of members of the same race are linked to some antagonism against members of an *obviously* different group. The resulting social action is usually merely negative: those who are obviously different are avoided and despised or, conversely, viewed with superstitious awe. Persons who are externally different are simply despised irrespective of what they accomplish or what they are, or they are venerated superstitiously if they are too powerful in the long run. In this case antipathy is the primary and normal reaction. However, this antipathy is shared not just by persons with anthropological similarities, and its extent is by no means determined by the degree of anthropological relatedness; furthermore, this antipathy is linked not only to inherited traits but just as much to other visible differences.

If the degree of objective racial difference can be determined, among other things, purely physiologically by establishing whether hybrids reproduce themselves at approximately normal rates, the subjective aspects, the reciprocal racial attraction and repulsion, might be measured by finding out whether sexual relations are preferred or rare between two groups, and whether they are carried on permanently or temporarily and irregularly. In all groups with a developed 'ethnic' consciousness the existence or absence of intermarriage (*connubium*) would then be a normal consequence of racial attraction or segregation. Serious research on the sexual attraction and repulsion between different ethnic groups is only incipient, but there is not the slightest doubt that racial factors, that means, common descent, influence the incidence of sexual relations and of marriage, sometimes decisively. However, the existence of several million mulattos in the United States speaks clearly against the assumption of a 'natural' racial antipathy, even among quite different races. Apart from the laws against biracial marriages in the southern states, sexual relations between the two races are now abhorred by both sides, but this development began only with the Emancipation and resulted from the Negroes' demand for equal civil rights. Hence this abhorrence on the part of the Whites is socially determined by the previously sketched tendency toward the monopolization of social power and honour, a tendency which in this case happens to be linked to race.

The *connubium* itself, that means, the fact that the offspring from a permanent sexual relationship can share in the activities and advantages of the father's political, economic or status group, depends on many circumstances. Under undiminished patriarchal powers [. . .] the father was free to grant equal rights to his children from slaves. Moreover, the glorification of abduction by the hero made racial mixing a normal event within the ruling strata. However, patriarchal discretion was progressively curtailed with the monopolistic closure [. . .] of political, status or other groups and with the monopolization of marriage opportunities; these tendencies restricted the *connubium* to the offspring from a permanent sexual union within the given political, religious, economic and status group. This also produced a high incidence of inbreeding. The 'endogamy' of a group is probably everywhere a secondary product of such tendencies, if we define it not merely as the fact that a permanent sexual union occurs primarily on the basis of joint membership in some association, but as a process of social action in which only endogamous children are accepted as full members. (The term 'sib endogamy' should not be used: there is no such thing unless we want to refer to the levirate marriage and arrangements in which daughters have the right to succession, but these have secondary, religious and political origins.) 'Pure' anthropological types are often a secondary consequence of such closure; examples are sects (as in India) as well as pariah peoples, that means, groups that are socially despised yet wanted as neighbours because they have monopolized indispensable skills.

Reasons other than actual racial kinship influence the degree to which blood relationship is taken into account. In the United States the smallest admixture of Negro blood disqualifies a person unconditionally, whereas very considerable admixtures of Indian blood do not. Doubtlessly, it is important that Negroes appear aesthetically even more alien than Indians, but it remains very significant that Negroes were slaves and hence disqualified in the status hierarchy. The conventional *connubium* is far less impeded by anthropological differences than by status differences, that means, differences due to socialization and upbringing (*Bildung* in the widest sense of the word). Mere anthropological differences account for little, except in cases of extreme aesthetic antipathy.

THE BELIEF IN COMMON ETHNICITY: ITS MULTIPLE SOCIAL ORIGINS AND THEORETICAL AMBIGUITIES

The question of whether conspicuous 'racial' differences are based on biological heredity or on tradition is usually of no importance as far as their effect on mutual attraction or repulsion is concerned. This is true of the development of endogamous conjugal groups, and even more so of attraction and repulsion in other kinds of social intercourse, i.e., whether all sorts of friendly, companionable, or economic relationships between such groups are established easily and on the footing of mutual trust and respect, or whether such relationships are established with difficulty and with precautions that betray mistrust.

The more or less easy emergence of social circles in the broadest sense of the word (*soziale Verkehrsgemeinschaft*) may be linked to the most superficial features of historically accidental habits just as much as to inherited racial characteristics. That the different custom is not understood in its subjective meaning since the cultural key to it is lacking, is almost as decisive as the peculiarity of the custom as such. But [. . .] not all repulsion is attributable to the absence of a 'consensual group'. Differences in the styles of beard and hairdo, clothes, food and eating habits, division of labour between the sexes, and all kinds of other visible differences can, in a given case, give rise to repulsion and contempt, but the actual extent of these differences is irrelevant for the emotional impact, as is illustrated by primitive travel descriptions, the Histories of Herodotus or the older prescientific ethnography. Seen from their positive aspect, however, these differences may give rise to consciousness of kind, which may become as easily the bearer of group relationships as groups ranging from the household and neighbourhood to political and religious communities are usually the bearers of shared customs. All differences of customs can sustain a specific sense of honour or dignity in their practitioners. The original motives or reasons for the inception of different habits of life are forgotten and the contrasts are then perpetuated as conventions. In this manner, any group can create customs, and it can also effect, in certain circumstances very decisively, the selection of anthropological types. This it can do by providing favourable chances of survival and reproduction for certain hereditary qualities and traits. This holds both for internal assimilation and for external differentiation.

Any cultural trait, no matter how superficial, can serve as a starting point for the familiar tendency to monopolistic closure. However, the universal force of imitation has the general effect of only gradually changing the traditional customs and usages, just as anthropological types are changed only gradually by racial mixing. But if there are sharp boundaries between areas of observable styles of life, they are due to conscious monopolistic closure, which started from small differences that were then cultivated and intensified; or they are due to the peaceful or warlike migrations of groups that previously lived far from each other and had accommodated themselves to their heterogeneous conditions of existence. Similarly, strikingly different racial types, bred in isolation, may live in sharply segregated proximity to one another either because of monopolistic closure or because of migration. We can conclude then that similarity and contrast of physical type and custom, regardless of whether they are biologically inherited or culturally transmitted, are subject to the same conditions of group life, in origin as well as in effectiveness, and identical in their potential for group formation. The difference lies partly in the differential instability of type and custom, partly in the fixed (though often unknown) limit to engendering new hereditary qualities. Compared to this, the scope for assimilation of new customs is incomparably greater, although there are considerable variations in the transmissibility of traditions.

Almost any kind of similarity or contrast of physical type and of habits can induce the belief that affinity or disaffinity exists between groups that attract or repel each other. Not every belief in tribal affinity, however, is founded on the resemblance of customs or of physical type. But in spite of great variations in this area, such a belief can exist and can develop group-forming powers when it is buttressed by a memory of an actual migration, be it colonization or individual migration. The persistent effect of the old ways and of childhood reminiscences continues as a source of native-country sentiment (*Heimatsgefühl*) among emigrants even when they have become so thoroughly adjusted to the new country that return to their homeland would be intolerable (this being the case of most German-Americans, for example).

In colonies, the attachment to the colonists' homeland survives despite considerable mixing with the inhabitants of the colonial land and despite profound changes in tradition and hereditary type as well. In case of political colonization, the decisive factor is the need for political support. In general, the continuation of relationships created by marriage is important, and so are the market relationships, provided that the 'customs' remained unchanged. These market relationships between the homeland and the colony may be very close, as long as the consumer standards remain similar, and especially when colonies are in an almost absolutely alien environment and within an alien political territory.

The belief in group affinity, regardless of whether it has any objective foundation, can have important consequences especially for the formation of a political community. We shall call 'ethnic groups' those human groups that entertain a subjective belief in their common descent because of similarities of physical type or of customs or both, or because of memories of colonization and migration; this belief must be important for the propagation of group formation; conversely, it does not matter whether or not an objective blood relationship exists. Ethnic membership (*Gemeinsamkeit*) differs from the kinship group precisely by being a presumed identity, not a group with concrete social action, like the latter. In our sense, ethnic membership does not constitute a group; it only facilitates group formation of any kind, particularly in the political sphere. On the other hand, it is primarily the political community, no matter how artificially organized, that inspires the belief in common ethnicity. This belief tends to persist even after the disintegration of the political community, unless drastic differences in the custom, physical type, or, above all, language exist among its members.

This artificial origin of the belief in common ethnicity follows the [...] pattern [...] of rational association turning into personal relationships. If rationally regulated action is not widespread, almost any association, even the most rational one, creates an overarching communal consciousness; this takes the form of a brotherhood on the basis of the belief in common ethnicity. As late as the Greek city state, even the most arbitrary division of the polis became for the member an association with at least a common cult and often a common fictitious ancestor. The twelve tribes of Israel were subdivisions of a political community, and they alternated in performing certain functions on a monthly basis. The same holds for the Greek tribes (*phylai*) and their subdivisions: the latter, too, were regarded as units of common ethnic descent. It is true that the original division may have been induced by political or actual ethnic differences, but the effect was the same when such a division was made quite rationally and schematically, after the break-up of old groups and relinquishment of local cohesion, as it was done by Cleisthenes. It does not follow, therefore, that the Greek polis was actually or originally a tribal or lineage state, but that ethnic fictions were a sign of the rather low degree of rationalization of Greek political life. Conversely, it is a symptom of the greater rationalization of Rome that its old schematic subdivisions (*curiae*) took on religious importance, with a pretence to ethnic origin, to only a small degree.

The belief in common ethnicity often delimits 'social circles', which in turn are not always identical with endogamous connubial groups, for greatly varying numbers of persons may be encompassed by both. Their similarity rests on the belief in a specific 'honour' of their members, not shared by the outsiders, that is, the sense of 'ethnic honour' (a phenomenon closely related to status honour, which will be discussed later). These few remarks must suffice at this point. A specialized sociological study of ethnicity would have to make a finer distinction between these concepts. [...]

Groups, in turn, can engender sentiments of likeness which will persist even after their demise and will have an 'ethnic' connotation. The political community in particular can produce such an effect. But most directly, such an effect is created by the *language group*, which is the bearer of a specific 'cultural possession of the masses' (*Massenkulturgut*) and makes mutual understanding (*Verstehen*) possible or easier.

Wherever the memory of the origin of a community by peaceful secession or emigration ('colony', *ver sacrum*, and the like) from a mother community remains for some reason alive, there undoubtedly exists a very specific and often extremely powerful sense of ethnic identity, which is determined by several factors: shared political memories or, even more importantly in early times, persistent ties with the old cult, or the strengthening of kinship and other groups, both in the old and the new community, or other persistent relationships. Where these ties are lacking, or once they cease to exist, the sense of ethnic group membership is absent, regardless of how close the kinship may be.

Apart from the community of language, which may or may not coincide with objective, or subjectively believed, consanguinity, and apart from common religious belief, which is also independent of consanguinity, the ethnic differences that remain are, on the one hand, aesthetically conspicuous differences of the physical appearance (as mentioned before) and, on the other hand and of equal weight, the perceptible differences in the *conduct of everyday life*. Of special importance are precisely those items which may otherwise seem to be of small social relevance, since when ethnic differentiation is concerned it is always the conspicuous differences that come into play.

Common language and the ritual regulation of life, as determined by shared religious beliefs, everywhere are conducive to feelings of ethnic affinity, especially since the intelligibility of the behaviour of others is the most fundamental presupposition of group formation. But since we shall not consider these two elements in the present context, we ask: what is it that remains? It must be admitted that palpable differences in dialect and differences of religion in themselves do not exclude sentiments of common ethnicity. Next to pronounced differences in the economic way of life, the belief in ethnic affinity has at all times been affected by outward differences in clothes, in the style of housing, food and eating habits, the division of labour between the sexes and between the free and the unfree. That is to say, these things concern one's conception of what is correct and proper and, above all, of what affects the individual's sense of honour and dignity. All those things we shall find later on as objects of specific differences between status groups. The conviction of the excellence of one's own customs and the inferiority of alien ones, a conviction which sustains the sense of ethnic honour, is actually quite analogous to the sense of honour of distinctive status groups.

The sense of ethnic honour is a specific honour of the masses (*Massenehre*), for it is accessible to anybody who belongs to the subjectively believed community of descent. The 'poor white trash', i.e., the property-less and, in the absence of job opportunities, very often destitute white inhabitants of the southern states of the United States of America in the period of slavery, were the actual bearers of racial antipathy, which was quite foreign to the planters. This was so because the social honour of the 'poor whites' was dependent upon the social *déclassement* of the Negroes.

And behind all ethnic diversities there is somehow naturally the notion of the 'chosen people', which is merely a counterpart of status differentiation translated into the plane of horizontal co-existence. The idea of a chosen people derives its popularity from the fact that it can be claimed to an equal degree by any and every member of the mutually despising groups, in contrast to status differentiation which always rests on subordination. Consequently, ethnic repulsion may take hold of all conceivable differences among the notions of propriety and transform them into 'ethnic conventions'.

Besides the previously mentioned elements, which were still more or less closely related to the economic order, conventionalization [. . .] may take hold of such things as a hairdo or style of beard and the like. The differences thereof have an 'ethnically' repulsive effect, because they are thought of as symbols of ethnic membership. Of course, the repulsion is not always based merely on the 'symbolic' character of the distinguishing traits. The fact that the Scythian women oiled their hair with butter, which then gave off a rancid odour, while Greek women used perfumed oil to achieve the same purpose, thwarted – according to an ancient report – all attempts at social intercourse between the aristocratic ladies of these two groups. The smell of butter certainly had a more compelling effect than even the most prominent racial differences, or – as far as I could see – the 'Negro odour', of which so many fables are told. In general, racial qualities are effective only as limiting factors with regard to the belief in common ethnicity, such as in the case of an excessively heterogeneous and aesthetically unaccepted physical type; they are not positively group-forming.

Pronounced differences of custom, which play a role equal to that of inherited physical type in the creation of feelings of common ethnicity and notions of kinship, are usually caused, in addition to linguistic and religious differences, by the diverse economic and political conditions of various social groups. If we ignore cases of clear-cut linguistic boundaries and sharply demarcated political or religious communities as a basis of differences of custom – and these in fact are lacking in wide areas of the African and South American continents – then there are only gradual transitions of custom and no immutable ethnic frontiers, except those due to gross geographical differences. The sharp demarcations of areas wherein ethnically relevant customs predominate, which were not conditioned either by political or economic or religious factors, usually came into existence by way of migration or expansion, when groups of people that had previously lived in complete or partial isolation from each other and became accommodated to heterogeneous conditions of existence came to live side by side. As a result, the obvious contrast usually evokes, on both sides, the idea of blood disaffinity (*Blutsfremdheit*), regardless of the objective state of affairs.

It is understandably difficult to determine in general – and even in a concrete individual case – what influence specific ethnic factors (i.e., the belief in a blood relationship, or its opposite, which rests on similarities, or differences, of a person's physical appearance and style of life) have on the formation of a group.

There is no difference between the ethnically relevant customs and customs in general, as far as their effect is concerned. The belief in common descent, in combination with a similarity of customs, is likely to promote the spread of the activities of one part of an ethnic group among the rest, since the awareness of ethnic identity furthers imitation. This is especially true of the propaganda of religious groups.

It is not feasible to go beyond these vague generalizations. The content of joint activities that are possible on an ethnic basis remains indefinite. There is a corresponding ambiguity of concepts denoting ethnically determined action, that means, determined by the belief in blood relationship. Such concepts are *Völkerschaft, Stamm* (tribe), *Volk* (people), each of which is ordinarily used in the sense of an ethnic subdivision of the following one (although the first two may be used in reversed order). Using such terms, one usually implies either the existence of a contemporary political community, no matter how loosely organized, or memories of an extinct political community, such as they are preserved in epic tales and legends; or the existence of a linguistic or dialect group; or, finally, of a religious group. In the past, cults in particular were the typical concomitant of a tribal or *Volk* consciousness. But in the absence of the political community, contemporary or past, the external delimitation of the group was usually indistinct. The cult communities of Germanic tribes, as late as the Burgundian period (sixth-century AD), were probably rudiments of political communities and therefore pretty well defined. By contrast, the Delphic oracle, the undoubted cultic symbol of Hellenism, also revealed information to the barbarians and accepted their veneration, and it was an organized cult only among some Greek segments, excluding the most powerful cities. The cult as an exponent of ethnic identity is thus generally either a remnant of a largely political community which once existed but was destroyed by disunion and colonization, or it is – as in the case of the Delphic Apollo – a product of a *Kulturgemeinschaft* brought about by other than purely ethnic conditions, but which in turn gives rise to the belief in blood relationship. All history shows how easily political action can give rise to the belief in blood relationship, unless gross differences of anthropological type impede it.

TRIBE AND POLITICAL COMMUNITY: THE DISUTILITY OF THE NOTION OF 'ETHNIC GROUP'

The tribe is clearly delimited when it is a subdivision of a polity, which, in fact, often establishes it. In this case, the artificial origin is revealed by the round numbers in which tribes usually appear, for example, the previously mentioned division of the people of Israel into twelve tribes, the three Doric *phylai* and the various *phylai* of the other Hellenes. When a political community was newly established or reorganized, the population was newly divided. Hence the tribe is here a political artefact, even though it soon adopts the whole symbolism of blood relationship and particularly a tribal cult. Even today it is not rare that political artefacts develop a sense of affinity akin to that of blood relationship. Very schematic constructs such as those states of the United States that were made into squares according to their latitude have a strong sense of identity; it is also not rare that families travel from New York to Richmond to make an expected child a 'Virginian'.

Such artificiality does not preclude the possibility that the Hellenic *phylai*, for example, were at one time independent and that the polis used them schematically when they were merged into a political association. However, tribes that existed before the polis were either identical with the corresponding political groups which were subsequently associated into a polis; and in this case they were called *ethnos*, not *phyle* or, as it probably happened many times, the politically unorganized tribe, as a presumed 'blood community', lived from the memory that it once engaged in joint political action, typically a single conquest or defence, and then such political memories constituted the tribe. Thus, the fact that tribal consciousness was primarily formed by common political experiences and not by common descent appears to have been a frequent source of the belief in common ethnicity.

Of course, this was not the only source: common customs may have diverse origins. Ultimately, they derive largely from adaptation to natural conditions and the imitation of neighbours. In practice, however, tribal consciousness usually has a political meaning: in case of military danger or opportunity, it easily provides the basis for joint political action on the part of tribal members or *Volksgenossen* who consider one another as blood relatives. The eruption of a drive to political action is thus one of the major potentialities inherent in the rather ambiguous notions of tribe and people. Such intermittent political action may easily develop into the moral duty of all members of tribe or people (*Volk*) to support one another in case of a military attack, even if there is no corresponding political association; violators of this solidarity may suffer the fate of the (Germanic, pro-Roman) sibs of Segestes and Inguiomer – expulsion from the tribal territory – even if the tribe has no organized government. If the tribe has reached this stage, it has indeed become a continuous political community, no matter how inactive in peacetime, and hence unstable, it may be. However, even under favourable conditions the transition from the habitual to the customary and therefore obligatory is very fluid. All in all, the notion of 'ethnically' determined social action subsumes phenomena that a rigorous sociological analysis – as [I] do not attempt it here – would have to distinguish carefully: the actual subjective effect of those customs conditioned by heredity and those determined by tradition; the differential impact of the varying content of custom; the influence of common language, religion and political action, past and present, upon the formation of customs; the extent to which such factors create attraction and repulsion, and especially the belief in affinity or disaffinity of blood; the consequences of this belief for social action in general, and specifically for action on the basis of shared custom or blood relationship, for diverse sexual relations, etc. – all of this would have to be studied in detail. It is certain that in this process the collective term 'ethnic' would be abandoned, for it is unsuitable for a really rigorous analysis. However, we do not pursue sociology for its own sake and therefore limit ourselves to showing briefly the diverse factors that are hidden behind this seemingly uniform phenomenon.

The concept of the 'ethnic' group, which dissolves if we define our terms exactly, corresponds in this regard to one of the most vexing, since emotionally charged concepts: the *nation*, as soon as we attempt a sociological definition.

NATIONALITY AND CULTURAL PRESTIGE

The concept of 'nationality' shares with that of the 'people' (*Volk*) – in the 'ethnic' sense – the vague connotation that whatever is felt to be distinctively common must derive from common descent. In reality, of course, persons who consider themselves members of the same nationality are often much less related by common descent than are persons belonging to different and hostile nationalities. Differences of nationality may exist even among groups closely related by common descent, merely because they have different religious persuasions, as in the case of Serbs and Croats. The concrete reasons for the belief in joint nationality and for the resulting social action vary greatly.

Today, in the age of language conflicts, a shared common language is pre-eminently considered the normal basis of nationality. Whatever the 'nation' means beyond a mere 'language group' can be found in the specific objective of its social action, and this can only be the *autonomous polity*. Indeed, 'nation state' has become conceptually identical with 'state' based on common language. In reality, however, such modern nation states exist next to many others that comprise several language groups, even though these others usually have one official language. A common language is also insufficient in sustaining a sense of national identity (*Nationalgefühl*). [. . .] Aside from the examples of the Serbs and Croats, this is demonstrated by the Irish, the Swiss and the German-speaking Alsatians; these groups do not consider themselves as members, at least not as full members, of the 'nation' associated with their language. Conversely, language differences do not necessarily preclude a sense of joint nationality: the German-speaking Alsatians considered themselves – and most of them still do – as part of the French 'nation', even though not in the same sense as French-speaking nationals. Hence there are qualitative degrees of the belief in common nationality.

Many German-speaking Alsatians feel a sense of community with the French because they share certain customs and some of their 'sensual culture' (*Sinnenkultur*) [. . .] and also because of common political experiences. This can be understood by any visitor who walks through the museum in Colmar, which is rich in relics such as tricolors, *pompier* and military helmets, edicts by Louis Philippe and especially memorabilia from the French Revolution; these may appear trivial to the outsider, but they have sentimental value for the Alsatians. This sense of community came into being by virtue of common political and, indirectly, social experiences which are highly valued by the masses as symbols of the destruction of feudalism, and the story of these events takes the place of the heroic legends of primitive peoples. *La grande nation* was the liberator from feudal servitude, she was the bearer of civilization (*Kultur*), her language was *the* civilized language; German appeared as a dialect suitable for everyday communication. Hence the attachment to those who speak the language of civilization is an obvious parallel to the sense of community based on common language, but the two phenomena are not identical; rather, we deal here with an attitude that derives from a partial sharing of the same culture and from shared political experiences.

Until a short time ago most Poles in Upper Silesia had no strongly developed sense of Polish nationality that was antagonistic to the Prussian state, which is based essentially on the German language. The Poles were loyal if passive 'Prussians', but they were not 'Germans' interested in the existence of the *Reich*; the majority did not feel a conscious or a strong need to segregate themselves from German-speaking fellow-citizens. Hence, in this case there was no sense of nationality based on common language, and there was no *Kulturgemeinschaft* in view of the lack of cultural development.

Among the Baltic Germans we find neither much of a sense of nationality amounting to a high valuation of the language bonds with the Germans, nor a desire for political union with the *Reich*; in fact, most of them would abhor such a unification. However, they segregate themselves rigorously from the Slavic environment, and especially from the Russians, primarily because of status considerations and partly because both sides have different customs and cultural values which are mutually unintelligible and disdained. This segregation exists in spite of, and partly because of, the fact that the Baltic Germans are intensely loyal vassals of the Tsar and have been as interested as any 'national' Russian (*Nationalrusse*) in the predominance of the Imperial Russian system, which they provide with officials and which in turn maintains their descendants. Hence, here too we do not find any sense of nationality in the modern meaning of the term (oriented towards a common language and culture). The case is similar to that of the purely proletarian Poles: loyalty towards the state is combined with a sense of group identity that is limited to a common language group within this larger community and strongly modified by status factors. Of course, the Baltic Germans are no longer a cohesive status group, even though the differences are not as extreme as within the white population of the American South.

Finally, there are cases for which the term nationality does not seem to be quite fitting; witness the sense of identity shared by the Swiss and the Belgians or the inhabitants of Luxemburg and Liechtenstein. We hesitate to call them 'nations', not because of their relative smallness – the Dutch appear to us as a nation – but because these neutralized states have purposively forsaken power. The Swiss are not a nation if we take as criteria common language or common literature and art. Yet they have a strong sense of community despite some recent disintegrative tendencies. This sense of identity is not only sustained by loyalty towards the body politic but also by what are perceived to be common customs (irrespective of actual differences). These customs are largely shaped by the differences in social structure between Switzerland and Germany, but also all other big and hence militaristic powers. Because of the impact of bigness on the internal power structure, it appears to the Swiss that their customs can be preserved only by a separate political existence.

The loyalty of the French Canadians towards the English polity is today determined above all by the deep antipathy against the economic and social structure, and the way of life, of the neighbouring United States; hence membership in the Dominion of Canada appears as a guarantee of their own traditions.

This classification could easily be enlarged, as every rigorous sociological investigation would have to do. It turns out that feelings of identity subsumed under the term 'national' are not uniform but may derive from diverse sources: differences in the economic and social structure and in the internal power structure, with its impact on the customs, may play a role, but within the German *Reich* customs are very diverse; shared political memories, religion, language and finally, racial features may be sources of the sense of nationality. Racial factors often have a peculiar impact. From the viewpoint of the Whites in the United States, Negroes and Whites are not united by a common sense of nationality, but the Negroes have a sense of American nationality at least by claiming a right to it. On the other hand, the pride of the Swiss in their own distinctiveness, and their willingness to defend it vigorously, is neither qualitatively different nor less widespread than the same attitudes in any 'great' and powerful 'nation'. Time and again we find that the concept 'nation' directs us to political power. Hence, the concept seems to refer – if it refers at all to a uniform phenomenon – to a specific kind of pathos which is linked to the idea of a powerful political community of people who share a common language, or religion, or common customs, or political memories; such a state may already exist or it may be desired. The more power is emphasized, the closer appears to be the link between nation and state. This pathetic pride in the power of one's own community, or this longing for it, may be much more widespread in relatively small language groups such as the Hungarians, Czechs or Greeks than in a similar but much larger community such as the Germans 150 years ago, when they were essentially a language group without pretensions to national power.

Structure and persistence of ethnie
ANTHONY D. SMITH

[. . .] *Ethnie* (ethnic communities) may [. . .] be defined as named human populations with shared ancestry myths, histories and cultures, having an association with a specific territory and a sense of solidarity. I shall try to show that such communities have been widespread in all eras of history, at least since the onset of the Bronze Age in the Middle East and Aegean, when written records appear to recount communal exploits and chronicle ethnic vicissitudes, and that they still characterize many areas of the globe and are to be found even in the most modernized states of the industrialized world. I am not claiming that they have constituted the main mode of socio-cultural organization, let alone the sole one, even in pre-modern eras; only that they have been at least as important as other forms of organization and culture, and that we therefore neglect them at our peril. Even today they remain of significance in several culture-areas, notably Africa and parts of Asia, but also in the [former] Soviet Union, Europe and North America. Nor would I claim that ethnicity, let alone *ethnie*, have been continuous, even if invisible. That would smack of the 'perennialism', even 'primordialism', which has been rejected. Instead, I hope to show that *ethnie* (different ones, usually) have emerged and re-emerged at different periods in several continents and culture-areas right up to the modern era; and that ethnicity has remained as a socio-cultural 'model' for human organization and communication from the early third millennium BC until today, even if not every 'society' has followed this model of organization. In other words, while making no claims for its universality, I am arguing for the widespread and chronic, if intermittent, appearance and persistence of this phenomenon. The paradox of ethnicity is its mutability in persistence, and its persistence through change.

[. . .]

In identifying the 'bases' of ethnicity in the localism and nostalgia of a sedentary agrarian existence, in the organization and sectarianism of religious communities, and in the mobilization, myths and communal locations of interstate warfare, we do not mean to imply anything about the archaic origins of *ethnie*. While a combination of these factors might, in given cases, lie at the root of their formation, it cannot account for the initial cultural difference – of religion, customs, language, institutions, colour and the like – from which *ethnie* can emerge or be constructed. The origins of ethnic differentiation itself are shrouded in obscurity, even if the veil is lifted in a few cases, particularly in more recent times. But, then, the modern act of classifying populations as *ethnie* is itself modelled on the ubiqitous presence and longevity of other ethnic communities, which we nowadays take for granted. The original 'tower of Babel' which allowed and encouraged the formation of *ethnie* cannot be elucidated from our meagre records. At the point where written history begins, in the mid-third millennium BC, *ethnie* are already in evidence, and named culture-communities appear as historical actors.

What can be explained, through the factors outlined above – and no doubt others – is the extraordinary persistence and resilience of ethnic ties and sentiments, once formed, as well as the processes by which 'ethnic categories' become crystallized and integrated as genuine 'ethnic communities'. For the durability, or chronic recurrence, of these 'bases' of ethnic persistence ensures their continuous self-awareness, as well as their significance for the identities and loyalties of their members. What has not yet been ascertained is the optimal degree and combination of these and other bases and factors – optimal, that is, for the salience and survival of a given *ethnie* or for ethnicity in general. Perhaps, too, in different areas and periods, such combinations of factors will vary with the development of the particular ethnic community. Well-formed *ethnie*, for example, may no longer need the cement of peasant mores and territorial nostalgia, or the mobilizing effects of interstate warfare; commercially located diasporas or trading maritime city-state confederations can survive and flourish as selfconscious *ethnie* through their religious and literary cultures and arts, even in the absence of other bases, once their sense of community has become well crystallized. Alternatively, elements of organized religious culture and community may be subordinated to the needs of a warrior or knightly aristocratic *ethnie* engaged in the defence of its territorial space, and acting, as did the Hungarian knights, as the *antemurale* bulwark of a Christendom threatened by Mongol and Ottoman steppe nomads. Again, however, such 'recombinations' of bases and factors only operate in cases of well-formed ethnicity and where the typical format and structure of the *ethnie* has operated for a few generations.

But, what is this 'typical' format and structure of *ethnie*? An 'ideal-typical' picture of pre-modern ethnic communities (allowing for significant variations) would, I think, include the following elements:

1 A large mass of peasants and artisans in villages and small market towns, subject to various restrictions on their freedom (corvée labour, serfdom, ghettoization, caste) and wedded to local 'folk cultures' (vernaculars, legends, rural customs and rites, dress, dance and music, crafts) influenced loosely by the nearest Great Traditions;

2 A small urban stratum of competing elites in the main towns – rulers and their courts, bureaucrats, noble landowners, military leaders – monopolizing wealth and political power, and centred loosely on an administrative capital and core area, and patronizing specialist trading and artisan client strata;

3 A tiny stratum of priests/monks and scribes claiming a monopoly of the community's belief-system, ritual and educational services, and acting as transmitters and conduits of its symbolism between the various urban elites and between them and the peasants and rural artisans, thereby seeking to incorporate the various Little Traditions of the latter into the central Great Tradition of which they act as guardians and agents of socialization;

4 A fund of myths, memories, values and symbols, often encoded, which express and explain the community's perceptions of itself, its origins, development and destiny, and its place in the cosmic order; all of these being manifested in a round of ceremonies, rites, artefacts and laws which bind the community to its celestial pantheon and its homeland;

5 Processes of communication, transmission and socialization of the store of myths, memories, values and symbols among both urban elites and their specialist clients, and where necessary outwards and downwards to the dependent peasantry; using mainly temple ritual and worship, dissemination of the precepts and morals of sacred texts, the use of symbols in art, architecture and dress, the elaboration of oral traditions, ballads, epics and hymns, but also the promulgation of legal codes and edicts, some rudimentary rote learning in local schools for selected members of various strata, and the use of military service and public works labour forces.

In constructing such an 'ideal-type' *ethnie*, we leave open the question of the degree of penetration of ethnic myth and symbolism among non-urban strata [. . .]. For the present, it suffices that most of the urban strata are 'touched', in varying degrees by the forms and content of ethnic symbolic funds, and hence that they are open to one or more priestly monopolies of symbolic and mythic communication and transmission. [. . .] The role of priests and scribes is, in many ways, pivotal both as custodians of the ethnic fund and as transmission belts and conduits; indeed, in some instances, what we grasp as religious competition may equally well be understood as ethnic competition for the monopoly of symbolic domination and communication in a given population, whose 'ethnic' profile is as much *shaped* by priestly and scribal activities as it is reinforced. This is not to say that other agencies of ethnic socialization do not exist, and are of no importance. The role of polities themselves can, on occasion, be crucial, both in their civilian and military roles. Equally important is the family network, especially in ensuring the failure or success of ethnic socialization processes, something that ethnic leaders themselves fully comprehend; here the role of local aristocratic leaders and their families in spreading, by example and precept, the store of ethnic symbolism in the areas of their influence, is crucial.

There is, however, one important distinction that needs to be made in considering the structure and pervasiveness of ethnic communities in pre-modern eras, the distinction between ethnic polities and ethnic minorities which are incorporated into a wider polity. If the *ethnie* in question constitutes a majority of the population of the polity, if, for example, it constitutes a patrimonial kingdom or forms the core of a wider agrarian empire, then its ethnic myths and symbols will reflect the elements of political domination and kingship, and its conduits of ethnic communication will include officials, judges and officers alongside the priests and scribes which are common to all pre-modern ethnic communication. They will diffuse, along with other myths of origins and ancestry, myths of kingship and nobility, of royal lineage and political domination, as part of the ethnic fund, and the symbolism of the community will reflect the centrality of this political experience. Such was undoubtedly the case in ancient Egypt. The ruler became a god, his court, nobility and bureaucracy reflected Pharaonic patronage and glory, and royalty was placed at the apex of Memphite and Theban priestly mythologies. Despite some regionalism, the unique ecology of the Nile valley helped to diffuse the symbols of Pharaonic religion and royalty by a whole series of propaganda devices in artefacts and genres of painting, sculpture, pottery and jewellery, as well as royal and priestly inscriptions in the great temples and royal and noble tombs. During the more centralized periods of the three Kingdoms, Pharaoh and priests joined forces, with one brief exception, to expand their influence and incorporate every expression of rural regionalism and every peasant tradition from the Delta to Aswan; and the peculiar geography of the area enabled a greater degree of ethnic homogeneity to develop, despite internal breakdowns and external invasions (by Hyksos, Sea Peoples, Assyrians and Persians), than anywhere else in the ancient world, with the possible exception of the Jews. What characterized the content of both ethnic symbolism and ethnic social structure was exactly this identity between the ethnic community of Egyptians and the dynastic state.

In the case of incorporated *ethnie*, or ethnic 'minorities', on the other hand, no such identity was present. Here the ideal of a political kingdom and dynastic state is replaced by that of the ethnic homeland or territory of belonging. The Israelite tribes before their periods of unified monarchy, as well as afterwards; the Sumerian city states before their unification by the dynasty of Agade and the third dynasty of Ur; the Phoenician and Greek city states; the early Swiss cantons; and, later, the various subjugated eastern European ethnic communities like the Serbs, Croats, Bulgarians, Greeks, Czechs and Slovaks; all relied for their sense of solidarity and continuity upon a real or alleged tie with an ancestral homeland and memories of a glorious past on its soil. Here, any burgeoning sense of ethnic unity expressed in political terms sprang, not from any pretensions of royalty or the impact of a conquest state and its dynastic rule, but from the pooling of more local loyalties in the face of common enemies and from a more or less vivid myth of common origins and common culture. Thus, in ancient Sumer and Akkad, the competing city states had their own *ensi* (lord), gods, temples and priesthoods; though there was a ceremonial centre at Nippur, it seems to have had no power to regulate inter-city conflicts and resist marauding tribes from the desert or marcher regions. There was no other political agent of unity until Sargon's conquests; but this did not impede a growing cultural unity, based on common language and religious myths and rituals, a common script and literature, common building styles and arts, and common irrigation techniques. It was just such a religio-linguistic-literary unity on which the Third Dynasty of Ur and later the Amorite dynasty of Babylon could capitalize in their quests for a measure of political unification, even when Akkadian replaced Sumerian as the language of commerce, diplomacy and literature, and even when the Babylonian Marduk became the chief god in the Mesopotamian pantheon.

[. . .] This difference between ethnic polities and divided and incorporated *ethnie* [left its] mark on the types of *mythomoteur* and modes of social penetration characteristic of the two types of *ethnie*. For the present, we need only note how both kinds of *ethnie* reveal otherwise similar structures and cultural features, and how frequently both are found in the historical record. For, whether politicized or not, whether as patrimonial kingdom or tribal confederation or city-state amphictyony, ethnic communities can be found playing active roles in human society and culture in most parts of the globe from at least the early Bronze Age, when writing first appears in the Near East, *c.*3000 BC. Whether, indeed, *ethnie* antedated this era is hard to say. Pottery styles in Mesopotamia and Egypt during the fifth and fourth millennia BC suggest a succession of cultures, like the Halaf and al-Ubaid on the lower Tigris, but, in the absence of written records or archaeological evidence, we have no means of ascertaining whether this stylistic succession expresses the presence of new ethnic migrations. Perhaps this period saw the formation of 'ethnic categories' with their separate myths of ancestry, memories, religions and languages, as successive waves of migrants settled in fertile riverine zones. But it was with the emergence of the first city states and patrimonial kingdoms in the early third millennium BC, and the first use of bronze weaponry in interstate warfare, that we find a growing sense of a more-than-local ethnic consciousness and sentiment, notably among the Egyptians and Sumerians.

Certainly, from the later third millennium BC, a succession of states based on a core ethnic community – Elamites, Amorites, Kushites, Canaanites, as well as Egyptians and Sumerians – appear in the historical records of the Near East, along with other communities whose political framework is far more tenuous, if it existed at all – peoples like the Guti or Lullubi, or the 'Harappans' – all of whom flourished in the period 2300–1700 BC. At this time, polities and *ethnie* do not often coincide; the more usual pattern is that of city states uniting temporarily because of common culture or religion in the face of a general threat, or of confederations of tribes seeking to expand their influence or dominate cities or districts, as it appears the Aryan tribes did in the early second millennium BC when they fanned out from Afghanistan and Central Asia into the Indus valley and the Punjab, and gradually subjugated the darker-skinned indigenous Dasa of the Harappan civilization. There is, at this stage, little ethnic cohesion or intense ethnic sentiments, except perhaps among the long-settled Egyptians and Sumerians.

By the later second millennium BC, more *ethnie* appear and evince greater self-awareness and cohesion. Apart from the Hittites and Mitannian Hurrians, Kassites, 'Minoans', Mycenaeans, Philistines, Arameans, Phoenicians, Assyrians and Canaanites are active for several centuries, some of them patrimonial kingdoms (Hittites, Mitanni, Kassites, Assyrians) built usually over an excluded and conquered indigenous population, some peaceful or warring city kingdoms ('Minoans', Mycenaeans, Philistines, Phoenicians) and some tribal confederations (Arameans, Canaanites) who infiltrate and set up their own city kingdoms. The degree of ethnic unity or consciousness varies, but to judge by the biblical record of the Philistines and Syrian Arameans, it was greater than in earlier periods. We may surmise that the greater degree of interstate rivalry and communications during the Tell-el-Amarna period (fourteenth century BC), may have brought cultures and communities into more direct contact, and heightened their self-awareness through juxtaposition with neighbours and enemies.

Certainly, from this time until the great expansion of China and Rome in the late first millennium BC, ethnicity became of greater political importance and cultural salience. Both Hebraic and classical cultures reveal the growing role of *ethnie* in social life, as in the Books of Ruth and Jonah and the earlier Books of Kings, the histories of Herodotus and Xenophon and the *Persae* of Aeschylus. In Assyrian and Persian friezes, in Greek sculpture, as in later Egyptian art, there is a growing awareness of foreigners and their alien customs. In the Assyrian practice of deportations of the ruling elites and whole cities of conquered states and peoples, there are the first signs of an awareness of the force of cultural and historic bonds in sustaining resistance to imperial rule.

Since this early period, *ethnie* have vied or colluded with other forms of community – of city, class, religion, region – in providing a sense of identity among populations and in inspiring in them a nostalgia for their past and its traditions. In periods of grave crisis, it has even been able to arouse in them powerful sentiments of anger and revenge for what were seen as attacks upon a traditional lifestyle and identity. For the most part, however, *ethnie* have provided foci of identification with ancestors and thereby a means of confronting death, especially violent death at the hands of enemies. By invoking a collective name, by the use of symbolic images of community, by the generation of stereotypes of the community and its foes, by the ritual performance and rehearsal of ceremonies and feasts and sacrifices, by the communal recitation of past deeds and ancient heroes' exploits, men and women have been enabled to bury their sense of loneliness and insecurity in the face of natural disasters and human violence by feeling themselves to partake of a collectivity and its historic fate which transcends their individual existences.

The evidence for the pervasiveness and ubiquity of ethnicity exists not only in the presence of such names, images, stereotypes, rituals and recitations, but in the very differences of styles in dress and coiffure, in crafts and furnishings, in tombs, temples and palaces, in the portrayal of the human figure, in

characteristic use of metals and jewels, pottery and woodwork, in the depic-
tions of activities and personages that have survived, as much as in the languages
and scripts, laws and customs that differentiate human populations at all
periods everywhere. All of these materials furnish rich evidence of ethnic
differentiation and cultural identity, even if they cannot tell us how far a
community felt itself to be unique and cohesive, and how deeply its fund of
myths, memories, values and symbols had penetrated the social hierarchy.
They may, however, by their durability, suggest something of the persistence
of ethnicity, its ability to withstand change and absorb outside influences,
particularly if they can be allied to more conventional written records. Though
not all cultural differences reflect ethnic differentiation, much less ethnic
community (*ethnie*), the persistence over centuries of separate styles attached
to particular peoples in certain areas does point to the longevity and widespread
incidence of *ethnie* in all periods. Along with polities, religious organizations
and class, ethnicity provides one of the central axes of alignment and division
in the pre-modern world, and one of the most durable.

Ethnicity, race and nation
THOMAS HYLLAND ERIKSEN

[. . .]

'Ethnicity seems to be a new term', state Nathan Glazer and Daniel Moynihan
(1975: 1), who point to the fact that the word's earliest dictionary appearance
is in the *Oxford English Dictionary* in 1972. Its first usage is attributed to the
American sociologist David Riesman in 1953. The word 'ethnic', however, is
much older. It is derived from the Greek *ethnos* (which in turn derived from the
word *ethnikos*), which originally meant heathen or pagan. It was used in this
sense in English from the mid-fourteenth century until the mid-nineteenth
century, when it gradually began to refer to 'racial' characteristics. In the
United States, 'ethnics' came to be used around the Second World War as a
polite term referring to Jews, Italians, Irish and other people considered
inferior to the dominant group of largely British descent. None of the founding
fathers of sociology and social anthropology – with the partial exception of
Max Weber – granted ethnicity much attention.

Since the 1960s, ethnic groups and ethnicity have become household words
in Anglophone social anthropology, although, as Ronald Cohen (1978) has
remarked, few of those who use the terms bother to define them. I shall examine

a number of approaches to ethnicity. Most of them are closely related, although they may serve different analytical purposes. All of the approaches agree that ethnicity has something to do with the *classification of people* and *group relationships*.

In everyday language the word ethnicity still has a ring of 'minority issues' and 'race relations', but in social anthropology it refers to aspects of relationships between groups which consider themselves, and are regarded by others, as being culturally distinctive. Although it is true that 'the discourse concerning ethnicity tends to concern itself with subnational units, or minorities of some kind or another' (Chapman *et al.*, 1989: 17), majorities and dominant peoples are no less 'ethnic' than minorities. [. . .]

ETHNICITY, RACE AND NATION

A few words must be said initially about the relationship between ethnicity and 'race'. The term race has deliberately been placed within inverted commas in order to stress that it has dubious descriptive value. Whereas it was for some time common to divide humanity into four main races, modern genetics tends not to speak of races. There are two principal reasons for this. First, there has always been so much interbreeding between human populations that it would be meaningless to talk of fixed boundaries between races. Second, the distribution of hereditary physical traits does not follow clear boundaries. In other words, there is often greater variation within a 'racial' group than there is systematic variation between two groups.

Concepts of race can nevertheless be important to the extent that they inform people's actions; at this level, race exists as a cultural construct, whether it has a 'biological' reality or not. Racism, obviously, builds on the assumption that personality is somehow linked with hereditary characteristics which differ systematically between 'races', and in this way race may assume sociological importance even if it has no 'objective' existence. Social scientists who study race relations in Great Britain and the United States need not themselves believe in the existence of race, since their object of study is the social and cultural relevance of the *notion* that race exists. If influential people in a society had developed a similar theory about the hereditary personality traits of red-haired people, and if that theory gained social and cultural significance, 'redhead studies' would for similar reasons have become a field of academic research, even if the researchers themselves did not agree that redheads were different from others in a relevant way. In societies where ideas of race are important, they may therefore be studied as part of local discourses on ethnicity.

Should the study of race relations, in this meaning of the word, be distinguished from the study of ethnicity or ethnic relations? Pierre van den Berghe

(1983) does not think so, but would rather regard 'race' relations as a special case of ethnicity. Others, among them Michael Banton (1967), have argued the need to distinguish between race and ethnicity. In Banton's view, race refers to the categorization of people, while ethnicity has to do with group identification. He argues that ethnicity is generally more concerned with the identification of 'us', while racism is more oriented to the categorization of 'them'. However, ethnicity can assume many forms, and since ethnic ideologies tend to stress common descent among their members, the distinction between race and ethnicity is a problematic one, even if Banton's distinction between groups and categories can be useful. I shall not, therefore, distinguish between race relations and ethnicity. Ideas of 'race' may or may not form part of ethnic ideologies, and their presence or absence does not seem to be a decisive factor in interethnic relations.

Discrimination on ethnic grounds is spoken of as 'racism' in Trinidad and as 'communalism' in Mauritius, but the forms of imputed discrimination referred to can be nearly identical. On the other hand, it is doubtless true that groups who 'look different' from majorities or dominating groups may be less liable to become assimilated into the majority than others, and that it can be difficult for them to escape from their ethnic identity if they wish to. However, this may also hold good for minority groups with, say, an inadequate command of the dominant language. In both cases, their ethnic identity becomes an imperative status, an ascribed aspect of their personhood from which they cannot escape entirely. Race or skin colour as such is not the decisive variable in every society.

The relationship between the terms ethnicity and nationality is nearly as complex as that between ethnicity and race. Like the words ethnic and race, the word nation has a long history, and has been used with a variety of different meanings in English. We shall refrain from discussing these meanings here, and will concentrate on the sense in which nation and nationalism are used analytically in academic discourse. Like ethnic ideologies, nationalism stresses the cultural similarity of its adherents and, by implication, it draws boundaries *vis-à-vis* others, who thereby become outsiders. The distinguishing mark of nationalism is by definition its relationship to the state. A nationalist holds that political boundaries should be coterminous with cultural boundaries, whereas many ethnic groups do not demand command over a state. When the political leaders of an ethnic movement make demands to this effect, the ethnic movement therefore by definition becomes a nationalist movement. Although nationalisms tend to be ethnic in character, this is not necessarily the case. [. . .]

ETHNICITY AND CLASS

The term ethnicity refers to relationships between groups whose members consider themselves distinctive, and these groups may be ranked hierarchically within a society. It is therefore necessary to distinguish clearly between ethnicity and social class.

In the literature of social science, there are two main definitions of classes. One derives from Karl Marx, the other from Max Weber. Sometimes elements from the two definitions are combined.

The Marxist view of social classes emphasizes economic aspects. A social class is defined according to its relationship to the productive process in society. In capitalist societies, according to Marx, there are three main classes. First, there is the capitalist class or bourgeoisie, whose members own the means of production (factories, tools and machinery and so on) and buy other people's labour-power (employ them). Second, there is the petit-bourgeoisie, whose members own means of production but do not employ others. Owners of small shops are typical examples. The third and most numerous class is the proletariat or working class, whose members depend upon selling their labour-power to a capitalist for their livelihood. There are also other classes, notably the aristocracy, whose members live by land interest, and the lumpenproletariat, which consists of unemployed and underemployed people – vagrants and the like.

Since Marx's time in the mid-nineteenth century, the theory of classes has been developed in several directions. Its adherents nevertheless still stress the relationship to property in their delineation of classes. A further central feature of this theory is the notion of class struggle. Marx and his followers held that oppressed classes would eventually rise against their oppressors, overthrow them through a revolution, and alter the political order and the social organization of labour. This, in Marx's view, was the chief way in which societies evolved.

The Weberian view of social classes, which has partly developed into theories of social stratification, combines several criteria in delineation classes, including income, education and political influence. Unlike Marx, Weber did not regard classes as potential corporate groups; he did not believe that members of social classes necessarily would have shared political interests. Weber preferred to speak of 'status groups' rather than classes.

Theories of social class always refer to systems of social ranking and distribution of power. Ethnicity, on the contrary, does not necessarily refer to rank; ethnic relations may well be egalitarian in this regard. Still, many polyethnic societies are ranked according to ethnic membership. The criteria for such ranking are nevertheless different from class ranking: they refer to imputed cultural differences or 'races', not to property or achieved statuses.

There may be a high *correlation* between ethnicity and class, which means that there is a high likelihood that persons belonging to specific ethnic groups also belong to specific social classes. There can be a significant interrelationship between class and ethnicity, both class and ethnicity can be criteria for rank, and ethnic membership can be an important factor in class membership. Both class differences and ethnic differences can be pervasive features of societies, but they are not one and the same thing and must be distinguished from one another analytically.

[. . .]

FROM TRIBE TO ETHNIC GROUP

There has been a shift in Anglophone social anthropological terminology concerning the nature of the social units we study. While one formerly spoke of 'tribes', the term 'ethnic group' is nowadays much more common. This switch in terminology implies more than a mere replacement of one word with another. Notably, the use of the term 'ethnic group' suggests contact and interrelationship. To speak of an ethnic group in total isolation is as absurd as to speak of the sound from one hand clapping. By definition, ethnic groups remain more or less discrete, but they are aware of – and in contact with – members of other ethnic groups. Moreover, these groups or categories are in a sense *created* through that very contact. Group identities must always be defined in relation to that which they are not – in other words, in relation to non-members of the group.

The terminological switch from 'tribe' to 'ethnic group' may also mitigate or even transcend an ethnocentric or Eurocentric bias which anthropologists have often been accused of promoting covertly. When we talk of tribes, we implicitly introduce a sharp, qualitative distinction between ourselves and the people we study; the distinction generally corresponds to the distinction between modern and traditional or so-called primitive societies. If we instead talk of ethnic groups or categories, such a sharp distinction becomes difficult to maintain. Virtually every human being belongs to an ethnic group, whether he or she lives in Europe, Melanesia or Central America. There are ethnic groups in English cities, in the Bolivian countryside and in the New Guinea highlands. Anthropologists themselves belong to ethnic groups or nations. Moreover, the concepts and models used in the study of ethnicity can often be applied to modern as well as non-modern contexts, to Western as well as non-Western societies. In this sense, the concept of ethnicity can be said to bridge two important gaps in social anthropology: it entails a focus on dynamics rather than statics, and it relativizes the boundaries between 'Us' and 'Them', between moderns and tribals.

WHAT IS ETHNICITY?

When we talk of ethnicity, we indicate that groups and identities have developed in mutual contact rather than in isolation. But what is the nature of such groups?

When A. L. Kroeber and Clyde Kluckhohn investigated the various meanings of 'culture' in the early 1950s they found about 300 different definitions. Although Ronald Cohen is correct in stating that most of those who write on ethnicity do not bother to define the term, the extant number of definitions is already high – and it is growing. Instead of going through the various definitions of ethnicity here, I will point out significant differences between theoretical viewpoints as we go along. As a starting-point, let us examine the recent development of the term as it is used by social anthropologists.

The term 'ethnic group' has come to mean something like 'a people'. But what is 'a people'? Does the population of Britain constitute a people, does it comprise several peoples (as Nairn, 1977, tends to argue), or does it rather form part of a Germanic, or an English-speaking, or a European people? All of these positions may have their defenders, and this very ambiguity in the designation of peoples has been taken on as a challenge by anthropologists. In a study of ethnic relations in Thailand, Michael Moerman (1965) asks himself: 'Who are the Lue?' The Lue were the ethnic group his research focused on, but when he tried to describe who they were – in which ways they were distinctive from other ethnic groups – he quickly ran into trouble. His problem, a very common one in contemporary social anthropology, concerned the boundaries of the group. After listing a number of criteria commonly used by anthropologists to demarcate cultural groups, such as language, political organization and territorial contiguity, he states: 'Since language, culture, political organization, etc., do not correlate completely, the units delimited by one criterion do not coincide with the units delimited by another' (Moerman, 1965: 1215). When he asked individual Lue what were their typical characteristics, they would mention cultural traits which they in fact shared with other, neighbouring groups. They lived in close interaction with other groups in the area; they had no exclusive livelihood, no exclusive language, no exclusive customs, no exclusive religion. Why was it appropriate to describe them as an ethnic group? After posing these problems, Moerman was forced to conclude that '[s]omeone is Lue by virtue of believing and calling himself Lue and of acting in ways that validate his Lueness' (Moerman 1965: 1219). Being unable to argue that this 'Lueness' can be defined with reference to objective cultural features or clear-cut boundaries, Moerman defines it as an *emic category of ascription*.[1] This way of delineating ethnic groups has become very influential in social anthropology.

Does this imply that ethnic groups do not necessarily have a distinctive culture? Can two groups be culturally identical and yet constitute two different ethnic groups? [. . .] At this point we should note that, contrary to a widespread commonsense view, cultural difference between two groups is not the decisive feature of ethnicity. Two distinctive, endogamous groups, say, somewhere in New Guinea, may well have widely different languages, religious beliefs and even technologies, but that does not necessarily mean that there is an ethnic relationship between them. For ethnicity to come about, the groups must have a minimum of contact with each other, and they must entertain ideas of each other as being culturally different from themselves. If these conditions are not fulfilled, there is no ethnicity, for ethnicity is essentially an aspect of a relationship, not a property of a group. This is a key point. Conversely, some groups may seem culturally similar, yet there can be a socially highly relevant (and even volatile) interethnic relationship between them. This would be the case of the relationship between Serbs and Croats following the break-up of Yugoslavia, or of the tension between coastal Sami and Norwegians. There may also be considerable cultural variation within a group without ethnicity. Only in so far as cultural differences are perceived as being import-ant, and are made socially relevant, do social relationships have an ethnic element.

Ethnicity is an aspect of social relationship between agents who consider themselves as culturally distinctive from members of other groups with whom they have a minimum of regular interaction. It can thus also be defined as a social identity (based on a contrast *vis-à-vis* others) characterized by meta-phoric or fictive kinship. When cultural differences regularly make a difference in interaction between members of groups, the social relationship has an ethnic element. Ethnicity refers both to aspects of gain and loss in interaction, and to aspects of meaning in the creation of identity. In this way it has a political, organizational aspect as well as a symbolic one.

Ethnic groups tend to have myths of common origin and they nearly always have ideologies encouraging endogamy, which may nevertheless be of highly varying practical importance.

'KINDS' OF ETHNIC RELATIONS?

This very general and tentative definition of ethnicity lumps together a great number of very different social phenomena. My relationship with my Pakistani greengrocer has an ethnic aspect; so, it could be argued, do the war in former Yugoslavia and 'race riots' in American cities. Do these phenomena have anything interesting in common, justifying their comparison within a single conceptual framework? The answer is both yes and no.

One of the contentions from anthropological studies of ethnicity is that there may be mechanisms of ethnic processes which are relatively uniform in every interethnic situation: to this effect, we can identify certain shared formal properties in all ethnic phenomena.

On the other hand, there can be no doubt that the substantial social contexts of ethnicity differ enormously, and indeed that ethnic identities and ethnic organizations themselves may have highly variable importance in different societies, for different individuals and in different situations. We should nevertheless keep in mind that the point of anthropological comparison is not

necessarily to establish similarities between societies; it can also reveal important differences. In order to discover such differences, we must initially possess
some kind of measuring stick, a constant or a conceptual bridgehead, which can
be used as a basis of comparison. If we first know what we mean by ethnicity,
we can then use the concept as a common denominator for societies and social
contexts which are otherwise very different. The concept of ethnicity can in this
way not only teach us something about similarity, but also about differences.

Although the concept of ethnicity should always have the same meaning lest
it ceases to be useful in comparison, it is inevitable that we distinguish between
the social contexts under scrutiny. Some interethnic contexts in different
societies are very similar and may seem easily comparable, whereas others
differ profoundly. In order to give an idea of the variation, I shall briefly
describe some typical empirical foci of ethnic studies, some kinds of ethnic
groups, so to speak. This list is not exhaustive.

1 Urban ethnic minorities. This category would include, among others,
non-European immigrants in European cities and Hispanics in the United
States, as well as migrants to industrial towns in Africa and elsewhere. Research
on immigrants has focused on problems of adaptation, on ethnic discrimination from the host society, racism, and issues relating to identity management
and cultural change. Anthropologists who have investigated urbanization in
Africa have focused on change and continuity in political organization and
social identity following migration to totally new settings. Although they have
political interests, these ethnic groups rarely demand political independence or
statehood, and they are as a rule integrated into a capitalist system of production and consumption.

2 Indigenous peoples. This word is a blanket term for aboriginal inhabitants
of a territory, who are politically relatively powerless and who are only partly
integrated into the dominant nation state. Indigenous peoples are associated
with a non-industrial mode of production and a stateless political system. The
Basques of the Bay of Biscay and the Welsh of Great Britain are not considered
indigenous populations, although they are certainly as indigenous, technically
speaking, as the Sami of northern Scandinavia or the Jívaro of the Amazon
basin. The concept 'indigenous people' is thus not an accurate analytical one,
but rather one drawing on broad family resemblances and contemporary
political issues.

3 Proto-nations (so-called ethnonationalist movements). These groups,
the most famous of ethnic groups in the news media of the 1990s, include
Kurds, Sikhs, Palestinians and Sri Lankan Tamils, and their number is growing.
By definition, these groups have political leaders who claim that they are
entitled to their own nation state and should not be 'ruled by others'. These
groups, short of having a nation state, may be said to have more substantial

characteristics in common with nations than with either urban minorities or indigenous peoples. They are always territorially based; they are differentiated according to class and educational achievement, and they are large groups.

4 Ethnic groups in 'plural societies'. The term 'plural society' usually designates colonially created states with culturally heterogeneous populations (Furnivall 1948; M. G. Smith, 1965). Typical plural societies would be Kenya, Indonesia and Jamaica. The groups that make up the plural society, although they are compelled to participate in uniform political and economic systems, are regarded as (and regard themselves as) highly distinctive in other matters. In plural societies, secessionism is usually not an option and ethnicity tends to be articulated as group competition. [. . .]

The definition of ethnicity proposed earlier would include all of these 'kinds' of group, no matter how different they are in other respects. Surely, there are aspects of politics (gain and loss in interaction) as well as meaning (social identity and belonging) in the ethnic relations reproduced by urban minorities, indigenous peoples, proto-nations and the component groups of plural societies alike. Despite the great variations between the problems and substantial characteristics represented by the respective kinds of group, the term ethnicity may, in other words, meaningfully be used as a common denominator for them.

NOTE

1 In the anthropological literature, the term *emic* refers to 'the native's point of view'. It is contrasted with *etic*, which refers to the analyst's concepts, descriptions and analyses. The terms are derived from phonemics and phonetics.

REFERENCES

Banton, Michael (1967), *Race Relations*. London: Tavistock.
Berghe, Pierre L. van den (1983), 'Class, race and ethnicity in Africa'. *Ethnic and Racial Studies*, vol. 6(2), pp. 221–36.
Chapman, Malcolm, Maryon McDonald and Elizabeth Tonkin (1989), 'Introduction: History and social anthropology' in Elizabeth Tonkin, Maryon McDonald and Malcolm Chapman (eds) *History and Ethnicity*, pp. 1–21. London: Routledge.
Cohen, Ronald (1978), 'Ethnicity: Problem and focus in anthropology'. *Annual Review of Anthropology*, vol. 7, pp. 379–404.
Furnivall, J. S. (1948), *Colonial Policy and Practice: A Comparative Study of Burma and Netherlands India*. Cambridge: Cambridge University Press.
Glazer, Nathan and Daniel P. Moynihan (eds) (1975), *Ethnicity: Theory and Experience*. Cambridge, Mass.: Harvard University Press.
Kroeber, A. L. and Clyde Kluckhohn (1952), *Culture: A Critical Review of Concepts and Definitions*. Cambridge, Mass.: Harvard University Press.

Moerman, Michael (1965), 'Who are the Lue?: Ethnic identification in a complex civilization'. *American Anthropologist*, vol. 67, pp. 1215–29.
Nairn, Tom (1977), *The Break-up of Britain*. London: New Left Books.
Smith, M. G. (1965), *The Plural Society of the British West Indies*. London: Sangster's.

2 Ethnicity and Nationalism

The nation and the origins of national consciousness
BENEDICT ANDERSON

[. . .]

Nationality, or, as one might prefer to put it in view of that word's multiple significations, nation-ness, as well as nationalism, are cultural artefacts of a particular kind. To understand them properly we need to consider carefully how they have come into historical being, in what ways their meanings have changed over time, and why, today, they command such profound emotional legitimacy. I will be trying to argue that the creation of these artefacts towards the end of the eighteenth century was the spontaneous distillation of a complex 'crossing' of discrete historical forces; but that, once created, they became 'modular', capable of being transplanted, with varying degrees of self-consciousness, to a great variety of social terrains, to merge and be merged with a correspondingly wide variety of political and ideological constellations. I will also attempt to show why these particular cultural artefacts have aroused such deep attachments.

CONCEPTS AND DEFINITIONS

Before addressing the questions raised above, it seems advisable to consider briefly the concept of 'nation' and offer a workable definition. Theorists of nationalism have often been perplexed, not to say irritated, by these three paradoxes:

1 The objective modernity of nations to the historian's eye vs. their subjective antiquity in the eyes of nationalists;

2 The formal universality of nationality as a socio-cultural concept – in the modern world everyone can, should, will 'have' a nationality, as he or she 'has' a gender – vs. the irremediable particularity of its concrete manifestations, such that, by definition, 'Greek' nationality is *sui generis*;

3 The 'political' power of nationalisms vs. their philosophical poverty and even incoherence.

In other words, unlike most other -isms, nationalism has never produced its own grand thinkers: no Hobbeses, Tocquevilles, Marxes or Webers. This 'emptiness' easily gives rise, among cosmopolitan and polylingual intellectuals, to a certain condescension. Like Gertrude Stein in the face of Oakland, one can rather quickly conclude that there is 'no there there'. It is characteristic that even so sympathetic a student of nationalism as Tom Nairn can nonetheless write that: ' "Nationalism" is the pathology of modern developmental history, as inescapable as "neurosis" in the individual, with much the same essential ambiguity attaching to it, a similar built-in capacity for descent into dementia, rooted in the dilemmas of helplessness thrust upon most of the world (the equivalent of infantilism for societies) and largely incurable' (Nairn 1977: 359).

Part of the difficulty is that one tends unconsciously to hypostasize the existence of Nationalism-with-a-big-N – rather as one might Age-with-a-capital-A – and and then to classify 'it' as *an* ideology. (Note that if everyone has an age, Age is merely an analytical expression.) It would, I think, make things easier if one treated it as if it belonged with 'kinship' and 'religion' rather than with 'liberalism' or 'fascism'.

In an anthropological spirit, then, I propose the following definition of the nation: it is an imagined political community – and imagined as both inherently limited and sovereign.

It is *imagined* because the members of even the smallest nation will never know most of their fellow-members, meet them, or even hear of them, yet in the minds of each lives the image of their communion. Renan referred to this imagining in his suavely back-handed way when he wrote that 'Or l'essence d'une nation est que tous les individus aient beaucoup de choses en commun, et aussi que tous aient oublié bien des choses' (Renan 1947: 892). With a certain ferocity Gellner makes a comparable point when he rules that 'Nationalism is not the awakening of nations to selfconsciousness: it invents nations where they do not exist' (Gellner 1964: 169). The drawback to this formulation, however, is that Gellner is so anxious to show that nationalism masquerades under false pretences that he assimilates 'invention' to 'fabrication' and 'falsity' rather than to 'imagining' and 'creation'. In this way he implies that 'true' communities exist which can be advantageously juxtaposed to nations. In fact, all communities larger than primordial villages of face-to-face contact (and perhaps even these) are imagined. Communities are to be distinguished, not by their falsity/genuineness, but by the style in which they are imagined. Javanese villagers have always known that they are connected to people they have never seen, but these ties were once imagined particularistically – as indefinitely stretchable nets of kinship and clientship. Until quite recently, the Javanese language had no word meaning the abstraction 'society'. We may today think of the French aristocracy of the *ancien régime* as a class; but surely it was imagined this way only very late. To the question 'Who is the Comte de X?' the normal answer would have been not 'a member of the aristocracy' but 'the lord of X', 'the uncle of the Baronne de Y' or 'a client of the Duc de Z'.

The nation is imagined as *limited* because even the largest of them, encompassing perhaps a billion living human beings, has finite, if elastic, boundaries, beyond which lie other nations. No nation imagines itself coterminous with mankind. The most messianic nationalists do not dream of a day when all the members of the human race will join their nation in the way that it was possible, in certain epochs, for, say, Christians to dream of a wholly Christian planet.

It is imagined as *sovereign* because the concept was born in an age in which Enlightenment and Revolution were destroying the legitimacy of the divinely ordained, hierarchical dynastic realm. Coming to maturity at a stage of human history when even the most devout adherents of any universal religion were inescapably confronted with the living *pluralism* of such religions, and the allomorphism between each faith's ontological claims and territorial stretch, nations dream of being free, and, if under God, directly so. The gage and emblem of this freedom is the sovereign state.

Finally, it is imagined as a *community* because, regardless of the actual inequality and exploitation that may prevail in each, the nation is always conceived as a deep, horizontal comradeship. Ultimately it is this fraternity that makes it possible, over the past two centuries, for so many millions of people, not so much to kill, as willingly to die for such limited imaginings.

These deaths bring us abruptly face to face with the central problem posed by nationalism: what makes the shrunken imaginings of recent history (scarcely more than two centuries) generate such colossal sacrifices? I believe that the beginnings of an answer lie in the cultural roots of nationalism.

THE ORIGINS OF NATIONAL CONSCIOUSNESS

If the development of print-as-commodity is the key to the generation of wholly new ideas of simultaneity, still, we are simply at the point where communities of the type 'horizontal-secular, transverse-time' become possible. Why, within that type, did the nation become so popular? The factors involved are obviously complex and various. But a strong case can be made for the primacy of capitalism.

At least 20 million books had already been printed by 1500, signalling the onset of Benjamin's 'age of mechanical reproduction'. If manuscript knowledge was scarce and arcane lore, print knowledge lived by reproducibility and dissemination. If, as Febvre and Martin believe, possibly as many as 200 million volumes had been manufactured by 1600, it is no wonder that Francis Bacon believed that print had changed 'the appearance and state of the world'.

One of the earlier forms of capitalist enterprise, book publishing felt all of capitalism's restless search for markets. The early printers established branches all over Europe: 'in this way a veritable "international" of publishing houses, which ignored national [sic] frontiers, was created' (Febvre and Martin 1976: 122). And since the years 1500–1550 were a period of exceptional European prosperity, publishing shared in the general boom. More than at any other time it was a great industry under the control of wealthy capitalists. Naturally, booksellers were primarily concerned to make a profit and to sell their products, and consequently they sought out first and foremost those works which were of interest to the largest possible number of their contemporaries.

The initial market was literate Europe, a wide but thin stratum of Latin-readers. Saturation of this market took about 150 years. The determinative fact about Latin – aside from its sacrality – was that it was a language of bilinguals. Relatively few were born to speak it and even fewer, one imagines, dreamed in it. In the sixteenth century the proportion of bilinguals within the total population of Europe was quite small; very likely no larger than the proportion in the world's population today, and – proletarian internationalism notwithstanding – in the centuries to come. Then and now the vast bulk of mankind is monoglot. The logic of capitalism thus meant that once the elite Latin market was saturated, the potentially huge markets represented by the monoglot masses would beckon. To be sure, the Counter-Reformation encouraged a temporary resurgence of Latin publishing, but by the mid-seventeenth century the movement was in decay, and fervently Catholic libraries replete. Meanwhile, a Europe-wide shortage of money made printers think more and more of peddling cheap editions in the vernaculars.

The revolutionary vernacularizing thrust of capitalism was given further impetus by three extraneous factors, two of which contributed directly to the rise of national consciousness. The first, and ultimately the least important, was a change in the character of Latin itself. Thanks to the labours of the Humanists in reviving the broad literature of pre-Christian antiquity and spreading it through the print market, a new appreciation of the sophisticated stylistic achievements of the ancients was apparent among the trans-European intelligentsia. The Latin they now aspired to write became more and more Ciceronian, and, by the same token, increasingly removed from ecclesiastical and everyday life. In this way it acquired an esoteric quality quite different from that of Church Latin in medieval times. For the older Latin was not arcane because of its subject-matter or style, but simply because it was written at all, i.e. because of its status as *text*. Now it became arcane because of what was written, because of the language-in-itself.

Second was the impact of the Reformation, which, at the same time, owed much of its success to print capitalism. Before the age of print, Rome easily won every war against heresy in western Europe because it always had better internal lines of communication than its challengers. But when in 1517 Martin Luther nailed his theses to the chapel door in Wittenberg, they were printed up in German translation, and within fifteen days [had been] seen in every part of the country. In the two decades 1520–40 three times as many books were published in German as in the period 1500–1520, an astonishing transformation to which Luther was absolutely central. His works represented no less than one third of *all* German-language books sold between 1518 and 1525. Between 1522 and 1546, a total of 430 editions (whole or partial) of his biblical translations appeared. [. . .] In effect, Luther became the first best-selling author *so known*. Or, to put it another way, the first writer who could 'sell' his *new* books on the basis of his name.

Where Luther led, others quickly followed, opening the colossal religious propaganda war that raged across Europe for the next century. In this titanic 'battle for men's minds', Protestantism was always fundamentally on the offensive, precisely because it knew how to make use of the expanding vernacular print market being created by capitalism, while the Counter-Reformation defended the citadel of Latin. The emblem for this is the Vatican's *Index Librorum Prohibitorum* – to which there was no Protestant counterpart – a novel catalogue made necessary by the sheer volume of printed subversion. Nothing gives a better sense of this siege mentality than François I's panicked 1535 ban on the printing of *any* books in his realm – on pain of death by hanging! The reason for both the ban and its unenforceability was that by then his realm's eastern borders were ringed with Protestant states and cities producing a massive stream of smugglable print. To take Calvin's Geneva alone: between 1533 and 1540 only forty-two editions were published there, but the numbers swelled to 527 between 1550 and 1564, by which latter date no fewer than forty separate printing presses were working overtime.

The coalition between Protestantism and print capitalism, exploiting cheap popular editions, quickly created large new reading publics – not least among merchants and women, who typically knew little or no Latin – and simultaneously mobilized them for politico-religious purposes. Inevitably, it was not merely the Church that was shaken to its core. The same earthquake produced Europe's first important non-dynastic, non-city states in the Dutch Republic and the Commonwealth of the Puritans. (François I's panic was as much political as religious.)

Third was the slow, geographically uneven, spread of particular vernaculars as instruments of administrative centralization by certain well-positioned would-be absolutist monarchs. Here it is useful to remember that the universality of Latin in medieval western Europe never corresponded to a universal political system. The contrast with Imperial China, where the reach of the mandarinal bureaucracy and of painted characters largely coincided, is instructive. In effect, the political fragmentation of western Europe after the collapse of the Western Empire meant that no sovereign could monopolize Latin and make it his-and-only-his language-of-state, and thus Latin's religious authority never had a true political analogue.

The birth of administrative vernaculars pre-dated both print and the religious upheaval of the sixteenth century, and must therefore be regarded (at least initially) as an independent factor in the erosion of the sacred imagined community. At the same time, nothing suggests that any deep-seated ideological, let alone proto-national, impulses underlay this vernacularization where it occurred. The case of 'England' – on the north-western periphery of Latin Europe – is here especially enlightening. Prior to the Norman Conquest, the language of the court, literary and administrative, was Anglo-Saxon. For the next century and a half virtually all royal documents were composed in Latin. Between about 1200 and 1350 this 'state' Latin was superseded by Norman French. In the mean time, a slow fusion between this language of a foreign ruling class and the Anglo-Saxon of the subject population produced Early English. The fusion made it possible for the new language to take its turn, after 1362, as the language of the courts – and for the opening of parliament. Wycliffe's vernacular *manuscript* Bible followed in 1382. It is essential to bear in mind that this sequence was a series of 'state', not 'national', languages; and that the state concerned covered at various times not only today's England and Wales, but also portions of Ireland, Scotland *and France*. Obviously, huge elements of the subject populations knew little or nothing of Latin, Norman French, or Early English. Not until almost a century *after* Early English's political enthronement was London's power swept out of 'France'.

On the Seine, a similar movement took place, if at a slower pace. As Bloch wrily puts it, 'French, that is to say a language which, since it was regarded as merely a corrupt form of Latin, took several centuries to raise itself to literary dignity' (Bloch 1961: 98), only became the official language of the courts of justice in 1539, when François I issued the Edict of Villers-Cotterêts (Seton-Watson 1977: 48). In other dynastic realms Latin survived much longer – under the Habsburgs well into the nineteenth century. In still others, 'foreign' vernaculars took over: in the eighteenth century the languages of the Romanov court were French and German.

In every instance, the 'choice' of language appears as a gradual, unselfconscious, pragmatic, not to say haphazard development. As such, it was utterly different from the selfconscious language policies pursued by nineteenth-century dynasts confronted with the rise of hostile popular linguistic-nationalisms. One clear sign of the difference is that the old administrative languages were *just that*: languages used by and for officialdoms for their own inner convenience. There was no idea of systematically imposing the language on the dynasts' various subject populations. Nonetheless, the elevation of these vernaculars to the status of languages-of-power, where, in one sense, they were competitors with Latin (French in Paris, [Early] English in London), made its own contribution to the decline of the imagined community of Christendom.

At bottom, it is likely that the esotericization of Latin, the Reformation, and the haphazard development of administrative vernaculars are significant, in the present context, primarily in a negative sense – in their contributions to the dethronement of Latin and the erosion of the sacred community of Christendom. It is quite possible to conceive of the emergence of the new imagined national communities without any one, perhaps all, of them being present. What, in a positive sense, made the new communities imaginable was a half-fortuitous, but explosive, interaction between a system of production and productive relations (capitalism), a technology of communications (print), and the fatality of human linguistic diversity.

The element of fatality is essential. For whatever superhuman feats capitalism was capable of, it found in death and languages two tenacious adversaries. Particular languages can die or be wiped out, but there was and is no possibility of man's general linguistic unification. Yet this mutual incomprehensibility was historically of only slight importance until capitalism and print created monoglot mass reading publics.

While it is essential to keep in mind an idea of fatality, in the sense of a *general* condition of irremediable linguistic diversity, it would be a mistake to equate this fatality with that common element in nationalist ideologies which stresses the primordial fatality of *particular* languages and their association with *particular* territorial units. The essential thing is the *interplay* between fatality, technology and capitalism. In pre-print Europe, and, of course, elsewhere in the world, the diversity of spoken languages, those languages that for their speakers were (and are) the warp and woof of their lives, was immense; so immense, indeed, that had print capitalism sought to exploit each potential oral vernacular market, it would have remained a capitalism of petty proportions. But these varied idiolects were capable of being assembled, within definite limits, into print-languages far fewer in number. The very arbitrariness of any system of signs for sounds facilitated the assembling process. (At the same time, the more ideographic the signs, the vaster the potential assembling zone. One can detect a sort of descending hierarchy here from algebra through Chinese and English, to the regular syllabaries of French or Indonesian.) Nothing served to 'assemble' related vernaculars more than capitalism, which, within the limits imposed by grammars and syntaxes, created mechanically reproduced print-languages, capable of dissemination through the market.

These print-languages laid the bases for national consciousnesses in three distinct ways. First and foremost, they created unified fields of exchange and communications below Latin and above the spoken vernaculars. Speakers of the huge variety of Frenches, Englishes or Spanishes, who might find it difficult or even impossible to understand one another in conversation, became capable of comprehending one another via print and paper. In the process, they gradually became aware of the hundreds of thousands, even millions, of people in their particular language-field, and at the same time that *only those* hundreds of thousands, or millions, so belonged. These fellow-readers, to whom they were connected through print, formed, in their secular, particular, visible invisibility, the embryo of the nationally imagined community.

Second, print capitalism gave a new fixity to language, which in the long run helped to build that image of antiquity so central to the subjective idea of the nation. As Febvre and Martin remind us, the printed book kept a permanent form, capable of virtually infinite reproduction, temporally and spatially. It was no longer subject to the individualizing and 'unconsciously modernizing' habits of monastic scribes. Thus, while twelfth-century French differed markedly from that written by Villon in the fifteenth, the rate of change slowed decisively in the sixteenth. 'By the 17th century languages in Europe had generally assumed their modern forms' (Febvre and Martin 1976: 319). To put it another way, for now three centuries these stabilized print-languages have been gathering a darkening varnish; the words of our seventeenth-century forebears are accessible to us in a way that his twelfth-century ancestors were not to Villon.

Third, print capitalism created languages-of-power of a kind different from the older administrative vernaculars. Certain dialects inevitably were 'closer' to each print-language and dominated their final forms. Their disadvantaged cousins, still assimilable to the emerging print-language, lost caste, above all because they were unsuccessful (or only relatively successful) in insisting on their own print form. 'North-western German' became Platt Deutsch, a largely spoken, thus substandard German, because it was assimilable to print-German in a way that Bohemian spoken Czech was not. High German, the King's English, and, later, Central Thai, were correspondingly elevated to a new politico-cultural eminence. (Hence the struggles in late twentieth-century Europe for certain 'sub-'nationalities to change their subordinate status by breaking firmly into print – and radio.)

It remains only to emphasize that in their origins, the fixing of print-languages and the differentiation of status between them were largely unself-conscious processes resulting from the explosive interaction between capitalism, technology and human linguistic diversity. But as with so much else in the history of nationalism, once 'there', they could become formal models to be imitated, and, where expedient, consciously exploited in a Machiavellian spirit. Today, the Thai government actively discourages attempts by foreign missionaries to provide its hill-tribe minorities with their own transcription-systems and to develop publications in their own languages: the same government is largely indifferent to what these minorities *speak*. The fate of the Turkic-speaking peoples in the zones incorporated into today's Turkey, Iran, Iraq and the [former] USSR is especially exemplary. A family of spoken languages, once everywhere assemblable, thus comprehensible, within an Arabic ortho-graphy, has lost that unity as a result of conscious manipulations. To heighten Turkish-Turkey's national consciousness at the expense of any wider Islamic identification, Atatürk imposed compulsory romanization. The Soviet authorities followed suit, first with an anti-Islamic, anti-Persian compulsory romanization, then, in Stalin's 1930s, with a Russifying compulsory Cyrillicization.

We can summarize the conclusions to be drawn from the argument thus far by saying that the convergence of capitalism and print technology on the fatal diversity of human language created the possibility of a new form of imagined community, which in its basic morphology set the stage for the modern nation. The potential stretch of these communities was inherently limited, and, at the same time, bore none but the most fortuitous relationship to existing political boundaries (which were, on the whole, the highwater marks of dynastic expansionisms).

Yet it is obvious that while today almost all modern self-conceived nations – and also nation states – have 'national print-languages', many of them have these languages in common, and in others only a tiny fraction of the population 'uses' the national language in conversation or on paper. The nation states of Spanish America or those of the 'Anglo-Saxon family' are conspicuous examples of the first outcome; many ex-colonial states, particularly in Africa, of the second. In other words, the concrete formation of contemporary nation states is by no means isomorphic with the determinate reach of particular print-languages. To account for the discontinuity-in-connectedness between print-languages, national consciousnesses and nation states, it is necessary to turn to the large cluster of new political entities that sprang up in the Western hemisphere between 1776 and 1838, all of which selfconsciously defined themselves as nations, and, with the interesting exception of Brazil, as (non-dynastic) republics. For not only were they historically the first such states to emerge on the world stage, and therefore inevitably provided the first real models of what such states should 'look like', but their numbers and contemporary births offer fruitful ground for comparative enquiry.

REFERENCES

Bloch, Marc (1961), *Feudal Society*. Chicago: University of Chicago Press (2 vols, translated by I. A. Manyon).

Febvre, Lucien, and Henri-Jean Martin (1976), *The Coming of the Book. The Impact of Printing, 1450–1800*. London: New Left Books (translation of *L'Apparition du livre*. Paris: Albin Michel. 1958).

Gellner, Ernest (1964), *Thought and Change*. London: Weidenfeld and Nicholson.

Nairn, Tom (1977), *The Break-up of Britain*. London: New Left Books.

Renan, Ernest (1947–61), 'Qu'est-ce qu'une nation?' In *Oeuvres Complètes*. Paris: Calmann-Lévy, vol. I, pp. 887–906.

Seton-Watson, Hugh (1977), *Nations and States. An Enquiry into the Origins of Nations and the Politics of Nationalism*. Boulder, Colo.: Westview Press.

Nationalism as a product of industrial society
ERNEST GELLNER

Nationalism is primarily a political principle, which holds that the political and the national unit should be congruent.

Nationalism as a sentiment, or as a movement, can best be defined in terms of this principle. Nationalist *sentiment* is the feeling of anger aroused by the violation of the principle, or the feeling of satisfaction aroused by its fulfilment. A nationalist *movement* is one actuated by a sentiment of this kind.

There is a variety of ways in which the nationalist principle can be violated. The political boundary of a given state can fail to include all the members of the appropriate nation; or it can include them all but also include some foreigners; or it can fail in both these ways at once, not incorporating all the nationals and yet also including some non-nationals. Or again, a nation may live, unmixed with foreigners, in a multiplicity of states, so that no single state can claim to be *the* national one.

But there is one particular form of the violation of the nationalist principle to which nationalist sentiment is quite particularly sensitive: if the rulers of the political unit belong to a nation other than that of the majority of the ruled, this, for nationalists, constitutes a quite outstandingly intolerable breech of political propriety. This can occur either through the incorporation of the national territory in a larger empire, or by the local domination of an alien group.

In brief, nationalism is a theory of political legitimacy, which requires that ethnic boundaries should not cut across political ones, and, in particular, that ethnic boundaries within a given state – a contingency already formally excluded by the principle in its general formulation – should not separate the power-holders from the rest.

The nationalist principle can be asserted in an ethical, 'universalistic' spirit. There could be, and on occasion there have been, nationalists-in-the-abstract, unbiased in favour of any special nationality of their own, and generously preaching the doctrine for all nations alike: let all nations have their own political roofs, and let all of them also refrain from including non-nationals under it. There is no formal contradiction in asserting such non-egoistic nationalism. As a doctrine it can be supported by some good arguments, such as the desirability of preserving cultural diversity, of a pluralistic international political system, and of the diminution of internal strains within states.

In fact, however, nationalism has often not been so sweetly reasonable, nor so rationally symmetrical. It may be that, as Immanuel Kant believed, partiality, the tendency to make exceptions on one's own behalf or one's own case, is *the* central human weakness from which all others flow; and that it infects national sentiment as it does all else, engendering what the Italians under

Mussolini called the *sacro egoismo* of nationalism. It may also be that the political effectiveness of national sentiment would be much impaired if nationalists had as fine a sensibility to the wrongs committed by their nation as they have to those committed against it.

But over and above these considerations there are others, tied to the specific nature of the world we happen to live in, which militate against any impartial, general, sweetly reasonable nationalism. To put it in the simplest possible terms: there is a very large number of potential nations on earth. Our planet also contains room for a certain number of independent or autonomous political units. On any reasonable calculation, the former number (of potential nations) is probably much, *much* larger than that of possible viable states. If this argument or calculation is correct, not all nationalisms can be satisfied, at any rate at the same time. The satisfaction of some spells the frustration of others. This argument is further and immeasurably strengthened by the fact that very many of the potential nations of this world live, or until recently have lived, not in compact territorial units but intermixed with each other in complex patterns. It follows that a territorial political unit can only become ethnically homogeneous, in such cases, if it either kills, or expels, or assimilates all non-nationals. Their unwillingness to suffer such fates may make the peaceful implementation of the nationalist principle difficult.

These definitions must, of course, like most definitions, be applied with common sense. The nationalist principle, as defined, is not violated by the presence of *small* numbers of resident foreigners, or even by the presence of the occasional foreigner in, say, a national ruling family. Just how many resident foreigners or foreign members of the ruling class there must be before the principle is effectively violated cannot be stated with precision. There is no sacred percentage figure, below which the foreigner can be benignly tolerated, and above which he becomes offensive and his safety and life are at peril. No doubt the figure will vary with circumstances. The impossibility of providing a generally applicable and precise figure, however, does not undermine the usefulness of the definition.

STATE AND NATION

Our definition of nationalism was parasitic on two as yet undefined terms: state and nation.

Discussion of the state may begin with Max Weber's celebrated definition of it, as that agency within society which possesses the monopoly of legitimate violence. The idea behind this is simple and seductive: in well-ordered societies, such as most of us live in or aspire to live in, private or sectional violence is illegitimate. Conflict as such is not illegitimate, but it cannot rightfully be resolved by private or sectional violence. Violence may be applied only by the central political authority, and those to whom it delegates this right. Among the various sanctions of the maintenance of order, the ultimate one – force – may be applied only by one special, clearly identified, and well-centralized, disciplined agency within society. That agency or group of agencies *is* the state.

The idea enshrined in this definition corresponds fairly well with the moral intuitions of many, probably most, members of modern societies. Nevertheless, it is not entirely satisfactory. There are 'states' – or, at any rate, institutions which we would normally be inclined to call by that name – which do not monopolize legitimate violence within the territory which they more or less effectively control. A feudal state does not necessarily object to private wars between its fief-holders, provided they also fulfil their obligations to their overlord; or again, a state counting tribal populations among its subjects does not necessarily object to the institution of the feud, as long as those who indulge in it refrain from endangering neutrals on the public highway or in the market. The Iraqi state, under British tutelage after the First World War, tolerated tribal raids, provided the raiders dutifully reported at the nearest police station before and after the expedition, leaving an orderly bureaucratic record of slain and booty. In brief, there are states which lack either the will or the means to enforce their monopoly of legitimate violence, and which, nonetheless remain, in many respects, recognizable 'states'.

Weber's underlying principle does, however, seem valid *now*, however strangely ethnocentric it may be as a general definition, with its tacit assumption of the well-centralized Western state. The state constitutes one highly distinctive and important elaboration of the social division of labour. Where there is no division of labour, one cannot even begin to speak of the state. But not any or every specialism makes a state: the state is the specialization and concentration of order maintenance. The 'state' is that institution or set of institutions specifically concerned with the enforcement of order (whatever else they may also be concerned with). The state exists where specialized order-enforcing agencies, such as police forces and courts, have separated out from the rest of social life. They *are* the state.

Not all societies are state-endowed. It immediately follows that the problem of nationalism does not arise for stateless societies. If there is no state, one obviously cannot ask whether or not its boundaries are congruent with the limits of nations. If there are no rulers, there being no state, one cannot ask whether they are of the same nation as the ruled. When neither state nor rulers exist, one cannot resent their failure to conform to the requirements of the principle of nationalism. One may perhaps deplore statelessness, but that is another matter. Nationalists have generally fulminated against the distribution of political power and the nature of political boundaries, but they have seldom if ever had occasion to deplore the absence of power and of boundaries altogether. The circumstances in which nationalism has generally arisen have not normally been those in which the state itself, as such, was lacking, or when its reality was in any serious doubt. The state was only too conspicuously present. It was its boundaries and/or the distribution of power, and possibly of other advantages, within it which were resented.

This in itself is highly significant. Not only is our definition of nationalism parasitic on a prior and assumed definition of the state: it also seems to be the case that nationalism emerges only in milieux in which the existence of the state is already very much taken for granted. The existence of politically centralized units, and of a moral-political climate in which such centralized units are taken for granted and are treated as normative, is a necessary though by no means a sufficient condition of nationalism.

By way of anticipation, some general historical observations should be made about the state. Mankind has passed through three fundamental stages in its history: the pre-agrarian, the agrarian, and the industrial. Hunting and gathering bands were and are too small to allow the kind of political division of labour which constitutes the state; and so, for them, the question of the state, of a stable specialized order-enforcing institution, does not really arise. By contrast, most, but by no means all, agrarian societies have been state-endowed. Some of these states have been strong and some weak, some have been despotic and others law-abiding. They differ a very great deal in their form. The agrarian phase of human history is the period during which, so to speak, the very existence of the state is an option. Moreover, the form of the state is highly variable. During the hunting-gathering stage, the option was not available.

By contrast, in the post-agrarian, industrial age there is, once again, no option; but now the *presence*, not the absence of the state is inescapable. Paraphrasing Hegel, once none had the state, then some had it, and finally all have it. The form it takes, of course, still remains variable. There are some traditions of social thought – anarchism, Marxism – which hold that even, or especially, in an industrial order the state is dispensable, at least under favourable conditions or under conditions due to be realized in the fullness of time. There are obvious and powerful reasons for doubting this: industrial societies are enormously large, and depend for the standard of living to which they have become accustomed (or to which they ardently wish to become accustomed) on an unbelievably intricate general division of labour and co-operation. Some of this co-operation might under favourable conditions be spontaneous and need no central sanctions. The idea that all of it could perpetually work in this way, that it could exist without any enforcement and control, puts an intolerable strain on one's credulity.

So the problem of nationalism does not arise when there is no state. It does not follow that the problem of nationalism arises for each and every state. On the contrary, it arises only for *some* states. It remains to be seen which ones do face this problem.

THE NATION

The definition of the nation presents difficulties graver than those attendant on the definition of the state. Although modern man tends to take the centralized state (and, more specifically, the centralized national state) for granted, nevertheless he is capable, with relatively little effort, of seeing its contingency, and of imagining a social situation in which the state is absent. He is quite adept at visualizing the 'state of nature'. An anthropologist can explain to him that the tribe is not necessarily a state writ small, and that forms of tribal organization exist which can be described as stateless. By contrast, the idea of a man without a nation seems to impose a far greater strain on the modern imagination. Chamisso, an *emigré* Frenchman in Germany during the Napoleonic period, wrote a powerful proto-Kafkaesque novel about a man who lost his shadow: though no doubt part of the effectiveness of this novel hinges on the intended ambiguity of the parable, it is difficult not to suspect that, for the author, the Man without a Shadow was the Man without a Nation. When his followers and acquaintances detect his aberrant shadowlessness they shun the otherwise well-endowed Peter Schlemiehl. A man without a nation defies the recognized categories and provokes revulsion.

Chamisso's perception – if indeed this is what he intended to convey – was valid enough, but valid only for one kind of human condition, and not for the human condition as such anywhere at any time. A man must have a nationality as he must have a nose and two ears; a deficiency in any of these particulars is not inconceivable and does from time to time occur, but only as a result of some disaster, and it is itself a disaster of a kind. All this seems obvious, though, alas, it is not true. But that it should have come to *seem* so very obviously true is indeed an aspect, or perhaps the very core, of the problem of nationalism. Having a nation is not an inherent attribute of humanity, but it has now come to appear as such.

In fact, nations, like states, are a contingency, and not a universal necessity. Neither nations nor states exist at all times and in all circumstances. Moreover, nations and states are not the *same* contingency. Nationalism holds that they were destined for each other; that either without the other is incomplete, and constitutes a tragedy. But before they could become intended for each other, each of them had to emerge, and their emergence was independent and contingent. The state has certainly emerged without the help of the nation. Some nations have certainly emerged without the blessings of their own state. It is more debatable whether the normative idea of the nation, in its modern sense, did not presuppose the prior existence of the state.

What then is this contingent, but in our age seemingly universal and normative, idea of the nation? Discussion of two very makeshift, temporary definitions will help to pinpoint this elusive concept.

1 Two men are of the same nation if and only if they share the same culture, where culture in turn means a system of ideas and signs and associations and ways of behaving and communicating.

2 Two men are of the same nation if and only if they *recognize* each other as belonging to the same nation. In other words, *nations maketh man*; nations are the artefacts of men's convictions and loyalties and solidarities. A mere category of persons (say, occupants of a given territory, or speakers of a given language, for example) becomes a nation if and when the members of the category firmly recognize certain mutual rights and duties to each other in virtue of their shared membership of it. It is their recognition of each other as fellows of this kind which turns them into a nation, and not the other shared attributes, whatever they might be, which separate that category from non-members.

Each of these provisional definitions, the cultural and the voluntaristic, has some merit. Each of them singles out an element which is of real importance in the understanding of nationalism. But neither is adequate. Definitions of culture, presupposed by the first definition, in the anthropological rather than the normative sense, are notoriously difficult and unsatisfactory. It is probably best to approach this problem by using this term without attempting too much in the way of formal definition, and looking at what culture *does*.

[. . .]

NATIONALISM AND INDUSTRIALIZATION

If cognitive growth presupposes that no element is indissolubly linked *a priori* to any other, and that everything is open to rethinking, then economic and productive growth requires exactly the same of human activities and hence of human roles. Roles become optional and instrumental. The old stability of the social role structure is simply incompatible with growth and innovation. Innovation means doing new things, the boundaries of which cannot be the same as those of the activities they replace. No doubt most societies can cope with an occasional redrawing of job specifications and guild boundaries, just as a football team can experimentally switch from one formation to another, and yet maintain continuity. One change does not make progress. But what happens when such changes themselves are constant and continuous, when the persistence of occupational change itself becomes the one permanent feature of a social order?

When this question is answered, the main part of the problem of nationalism is thereby solved. Nationalism is rooted in a *certain kind* of division of labour, one which is complex and persistently, cumulatively changing.

High productivity, as Adam Smith insisted so much, requires a complex and refined division of labour. Perpetually growing productivity requires that this division be not merely complex, but also perpetually, and often rapidly, changing. This rapid and continuous change both of the economic role system itself and of the occupancy of places within it, has certain immediate and profoundly important consequences. Men located within it cannot generally rest in the same niches all their lives; and they can only seldom rest in them, so to speak, over generations. Positions are seldom (for this and other reasons) transmitted from father to son. Adam Smith noted the precariousness of bourgeois fortunes, though he erroneously attributed stability of social station to pastoralists, mistaking their genealogical myths for reality.

The immediate consequence of this new kind of mobility is a certain kind of egalitarianism. Modern society is not mobile because it is egalitarian; it is egalitarian because it is mobile. Moreover, it has to be mobile whether it wishes to be so or not, because this is required by the satisfaction of its terrible and overwhelming thirst for economic growth.

A society which is destined to a permanent game of musical chairs cannot erect deep barriers of rank, of caste or estate, between the various sets of chairs which it possesses. That would hamper the mobility, and, given the mobility, would indeed lead to intolerable tensions. Men can tolerate terrible inequalities, if they are stable and hallowed by custom. But in a hectically mobile society, custom has no time to hallow anything. A rolling stone gathers no aura, and a mobile population does not allow any aura to attach to its stratification. Stratification and inequality do exist, and sometimes in extreme form; nevertheless they have a muted and discreet quality, attenuated by a kind of gradualness of the distinctions of wealth and standing, a lack of social distance and a convergence of lifestyles, a kind of statistical or probabilistic quality of the differences (as opposed to the rigid, absolutized, chasm-like differences typical of agrarian society), and by the illusion or reality of social mobility.

That illusion is essential, and it cannot persist without at least a measure of reality. Just how much reality there is in this appearance of upward and downward mobility varies and is subject to learned dispute, but there can be no reasonable doubt that it does have a good deal of reality: when the system of roles itself is changing so much, the occupants of positions within it cannot be, as some left-wing sociologists claim, tied to a rigid stratificational system. Compared with agrarian society, this society is mobile and egalitarian.

But there is more than all this to the egalitarianism and mobility engendered by the distinctively industrial, growth-oriented economy. There are some additional subtler traits of the new division of labour, which can perhaps best be approached by considering the difference between the division of labour in an industrial society and that of a particularly complex, well-developed agrarian one. The *obvious* difference between the two is that one is more stable and the other is more mobile. In fact, one of them generally wills itself to be stable, and the other wills itself to be mobile; and one of them pretends to be more stable than social reality permits, while the other often claims more mobility, in the interest of pretending to satisfy its egalitarian ideal, than its real constraints actually permit. Nevertheless, though both systems tend to exaggerate their own central features, they do indeed markedly posses the trait they claim as their own when contrasted with each other: one is rigid, the other mobile. But if that is the obvious contrast, what are the subtler features which accompany it?

Compare in detail the division of labour in a highly advanced agrarian society with that of an average industrial one. Every kind of function, for instance, now has at least one kind of specialist associated with it. Car mechanics are becoming specialized in terms of the make of car they service. The industrial society will have a larger population, and probably, by most natural ways of counting, a larger number of different jobs. In *that* sense, the division of labour has been pushed much further within it.

But by some criteria, it may well be that a fully developed agrarian society actually has the more complex division of labour. The specialisms within it are more distant from each other than are the possibly more numerous specialisms of an industrial society, which tend to have what can only be described as a mutual affinity of style. Some of the specialisms of a mature agrarian society will be extreme: they will be the fruits of lifelong, very prolonged and totally dedicated training, which may have commenced in early youth and required an almost complete renunciation of other concerns. The achievements of craft and art production in these societies are extremely labour- and skill-intensive, and often reach levels of intricacy and perfection never remotely equalled by anything later attained by industrial societies, whose domestic arts and decorations, gastronomy, tools and adornments are notoriously shoddy.

Notwithstanding their aridity and sterility, the scholastic and ritual complexity mastered by the schoolmen of a developed agrarian society is often such as to strain the very limits of the human mind. In brief, although the peasants, who form the great majority of an agrarian society, are more or less mutually interchangeable when it comes to the performance of the social tasks which are normally assigned to them, the important minority of specialists within such societies are outstandingly complementary to each other; each one of them, or each group of them, is dependent on the others and, when sticking to its last, its specialism, quite incapable of self-sufficiency.

It is curious that, by contrast, in industrial society, notwithstanding its larger number of specialisms, the distance between specialists is far less great. Their mysteries are far closer to mutual intelligibility, their manuals have idioms which overlap to a much greater extent, and retraining, though sometimes difficult, is not generally an awesome task.

So, quite apart from the presence of mobility in the one case and stability in the other, there is a subtle but profound and important qualitative difference in the division of labour itself. Durkheim was in error when he in effect classed advanced pre-industrial civilizations and industrial society together under the single heading of 'organic solidarity', and when he failed to introduce properly this further distinction within the wider category of organic solidarity or of complementary division of labour. The difference is this: the major part of training in industrial society is *generic* training, not specifically connected with the highly specialized professional activity of the person in question, and *preceding* it. Industrial society may by most criteria be the most highly specialized society ever; but its educational system is unquestionably the *least* specialized, the most universally standardized, that has ever existed. The same kind of training or education is given to all or most children and adolescents up to an astonishingly late age. Specialized schools have prestige only at the end of the educational process, if they constitute a kind of completion of a prolonged previous unspecialized education; specialized schools intended for a younger, earlier intake have negative prestige.

Is this a paradox, or perhaps one of those illogical survivals from an earlier age? Those who notice the 'gentlemanly' or leisure-class elements in higher education have sometimes supposed so. But, although some of the frills and affectations attached to higher education may indeed by irrelevancies and survivals, the central fact – the pervasiveness and importance of generic, unspecialized training – is conjoined to highly specialized industrial society not as a paradox, but as something altogether fitting and necessary. The kind of specialization found in industrial society rests precisely on a common foundation of unspecialized and standardized training.

A modern army subjects its recruits first to a shared generic training, in the course of which they are meant to acquire and internalize the basic idiom, ritual and skills common to the army as a whole; and only subsequently are the recruits given more specialized training. It is assumed or hoped that every properly trained recruit can be retrained from one specialism to another without too much loss of time, with the exception of a relatively small number of very highly trained specialists. A modern society is, in this respect, like a modern army, only more so. It provides a very prolonged and fairly thorough training for all its recruits, insisting on certain shared qualifications: literacy, numeracy, basic work habits and social skills, familiarity with basic technical and social skills. For the large majority of the population the distinctive skills involved in working life are superimposed on the basic training, either on the job or as part of a much less prolonged supplementary training; and the assumption is that anyone who has completed the generic training common to the entire population can be retrained for most other jobs without too much difficulty. Generally speaking, the additional skills required consist of a few techniques that can be learned fairly quickly, plus 'experience', a kind of familiarity with a milieu, its personnel and its manner of operation. This may take a little time to acquire, and it is sometimes reinforced by a little protective mystique, but seldom really amounts to very much. There is also a minority of genuine specialists, people whose effective occupancy of their posts really depends on very prolonged additional training, and who are not easily or at all replaceable by anyone not sharing their own particular educational background and talent.

The ideal of universal literacy and the right to education is a well-known part of the pantheon of modern values. It is spoken of with respect by statesmen and politicians, and enshrined in declarations of rights, constitutions, party programmes and so forth. So far, nothing unusual. The same is true of representative and accountable government, free elections, an independent judiciary, freedom of speech and assembly, and so on. Many or most of these admirable values are often and systematically ignored in many parts of the world, without anyone batting an eyelid. Very often, it is safe to consider these phrases as simple verbiage. Most constitutions guaranteeing free speech and elections are as informative about the societies they allegedly define as a man saying 'Good morning' is about the weather. All this is well known. What is so very curious, and highly significant, about the principle of universal and centrally guaranteed education, is that it is an ideal more honoured in the observance than in the breach. In this it is virtually unique among modern ideals; and this calls for an explanation. Professor Ronald Dore has powerfully criticized this tendency, particularly among developing societies, of overrating formal 'paper' qualifications, and no doubt it has harmful side effects. But I wonder whether he fully appreciates the deep roots of what he castigates as the Diploma Disease. We live in a world in which we can no longer respect the informal, intimate transmission of skills, for the social structures within which such transmission could occur are dissolving. Hence the only kind of knowledge we can respect is that authenticated by reasonably impartial centres of learning, which issue certificates on the basis of honest, impartially administered examinations. Hence we are doomed to suffer the Diploma Disease.

All this suggests that the kind of education described – universal, standardized, and generic – *really* plays some essential part in the effective working of a modern society, and is not merely part of its verbiage or self-advertisement. This is in fact so. To understand what that role is, we must, to borrow a phrase from Marx (though not perhaps in the sense in which he used it), consider not merely the mode of production of modern society, but above all its mode of *reproduction*.

SOCIAL GENETICS

The reproduction of social individuals and groups can be carried out either on the one-to-one or on-the-job principle, or by what may be called the centralized method. There are, of course, many mixed and intermediate ways of doing this job, but their consideration can best be postponed until after the discussion of these two extreme, as it were polar, possibilities.

The one-to-one, on-the-job method is practised when a family, kin unit, village, tribal segment or similar fairly small unit takes the individual infants born into it, and by allowing and obliging them to share in the communal life, plus a few more specific methods such as training, exercises, precepts, *rites de passage* and so forth, eventually turns these infants into adults reasonably similar to those of the preceding generation; and in this manner the society and its culture perpetuate themselves.

The centralized method of reproduction is one in which the local method is significantly complemented (or in extreme cases, wholly replaced) by an educational or training agency which is distinct from the local community, and which takes over the preparation of the young human beings in question, and eventually hands them back to the wider society to fulfil their roles in it, when the process of training is completed. An extreme version of this system developed a high degree of perfection and effectiveness in the Ottoman empire, when under the *devshirme* and janissary systems, young boys, either secured as a tax obligation from conquered populations, or purchased as slaves, were systematically trained for war and administration and, ideally, wholly weaned and separated from their families and communities of origin. A less total version of this system was and in part still is practised by the British upper class, with its reliance on boarding schools from an early age. Variants of this system can on occasion be found even in relatively simple, preliterate agrarian societies.

Societies consisting of sub-communities can be divided into those in which the sub-communities can, if necessary, reproduce themselves without help from the rest of society, and those in which mutual complementarity and interdependence are such that they cannot do this. Generally speaking, the segments and rural communities of agrarian society *can* reproduce themselves independently. The anthropological concept of a segmentary society contains precisely this idea: the 'segment' is simply a smaller variant of the larger society of which it is a part, and can do on a smaller scale everything done by the larger unit.

Furthermore, one must distinguish between economic and educational self-sufficiency, in the sense of capacity for self-reproduction. The ruling strata of an agrarian society are, of course, dependent on a surplus drawn from the rest of society, but they may nevertheless be educationally quite self-sufficient. Various other kinds of non-self-sufficiency can also be engendered by social rules, such as those which make communities dependent on external ritual specialists, or on the supply of brides from outside. Here we are concerned with educational, not economic capacity for group self-reproduction. There are numerous complex, mixed and intermediate forms of group reproduction. When feudal lords send their sons as half-trainees, half-hostages to the local court, when masters accept apprentices who are not their sons, and so forth, we are obviously in the presence of such mixed systems.

Generally speaking, the situation in agrarian society seems to be this: the great majority of the population belongs to self-reproducing units, such as in effect educate their young on the job, in their stride, as part and parcel of the general business of living, without relying much or at all on any kind of educational specialist. A minority of the population receives specialized training. The society will contain one or more strata of full-time educators, who both reproduce themselves by taking on apprentices, and perform part-time services for the rest of the community: ritual, therapeutic, admonitory, secretarial, and so on. It may be useful to distinguish between one-to-one, intra-community training, and call it acculturation, and specialized *exo-training* (on the analogy of exogamy), which calls for skills outside the community, and call that education proper.

A very important stratum in literate agrarian society are the clerks, those who can read and transmit literacy, and who thus form one of the classes of specialists in that society. They may or may not form a guild or be incorporated in an organization. As, generally speaking, writing soon transcends its purely technical use in record-keeping, and acquires moral and theological significance, the clerks or clerics are almost invariably far more than mere grapho-technicians. It is not just writing, but what is written that counts, and, in agrarian society, the ratio of the sacred to the profane, within the realm of the written, tends to be heavily weighted in favour of the first. So the writers and readers are specialists and yet more than specialists; they are both part of a society, and claim to be the voice of the whole of it. Their specialism *says* something, something special, more so perhaps than that of the woodcarvers and other designers, and much more than that of the tinkers.

Specialists are often feared and despised in this kind of society. The clerics may be viewed ambivalently, but in the main their standing is rather high. They are both specialists and a part of society among others, and yet also, as stated, claim to be the voice of the totality. They are in an inherently paradoxical situation. Logicians possess, in their armoury of allegedly deep and significant puzzles, the Problem of the Barber: in a village, all men can be divided into those who shave themselves, and those who are shaved by the barber. But what of the barber himself? Is he a self-shaver, or one of the barber-shaved? In this form, let us leave it to the logicians. But the clerics are somewhat in the barber's situation. They reproduce their own guild by training entrants, but they also give a bit of training or provide services for the rest of society. Do they or do they not shave themselves? The tension and its problems (and they are not just logical) are with them, and they are not easily resolved.

In the end, modern society resolves this conundrum by turning *everyone* into a cleric, by turning this potentially universal class into an effectively universal one, by ensuring that everyone without exception is taught by it, that exo-education becomes the universal norm, and that no-one, culturally speaking, shaves himself. Modern society is one in which no sub-community, below the size of one capable of sustaining an independent educational system, can any longer reproduce itself. The reproduction of fully socialized individuals itself becomes part of the division of labour, and is no longer performed by sub-communities for themselves.

That is what developed modern societies are like. But why *must* this be so? What fate impels them in this direction? Why, to repeat the earlier question, is this one ideal, that of universal literacy and education, taken with this most unusual, untypical seriousness?

Part of the answer has already been given, in connection with the stress on occupational mobility, on an unstable, rapidly changing division of labour. A society whose entire political system, and indeed whose cosmology and moral order, is based in the last analysis on economic growth, on the universal incremental Danegeld and the hope of a perpetual augmentation of satisfactions, whose legitimacy hinges on its capacity to sustain and satisfy this expectation, is thereby committed to the need for innovation and hence to a changing occupational structure. From this it follows that certainly between generations, and very often within single lifespans, men must be ready for reallocation to new tasks. Hence, in part, the importance of the generic training, and the fact that the little bit extra of training, such as is attached to most jobs, doesn't amount to too much, and is moreover contained in manuals intelligible to all possessors of the society's generic training. (While the little bit extra seldom amounts to much, the shared and truly essential generic core is supplied at a rather high level, not perhaps when compared with the intellectual *peaks* of agrarian society, but certainly when placed alongside its erstwhile customary average.)

But it is not only mobility and retraining which engender this imperative. It is also the *content* of most professional activities. Work, in industrial society, does not mean moving matter. The paradigm of work is no longer ploughing, reaping, thrashing. Work, in the main, is no longer the manipulation of things, but of meanings. It generally involves exchanging communications with other people, or manipulating the controls of a machine. The proportion of people at the coal-face of nature, directly applying human physical force to natural objects, is constantly diminishing. Most jobs, if not actually involving work 'with people', involve the control of buttons or switches or levers which need to be *understood*, and are explicable, once again, in some standard idiom intelligible to all comers.

For the first time in human history, explicit and reasonably precise communication becomes generally, pervasively used and important. In the closed local communities of the agrarian or tribal worlds, when it came to communication, context, tone, gesture, personality and situation were everything. Communication, such as it was, took place without the benefit of precise formulation, for which the locals had neither taste nor aptitude. Explicitness and the niceties of precise, rule-bound formulation were left to lawyers, theologians or ritual specialists, and were parts of their mysteries. Among intimates of a close community, explicitness would have been pedantic and offensive, and is scarcely imaginable or intelligible.

Human language must have been used for countless generations in such intimate, closed, context-bound communities, whereas it has only been used by schoolmen and jurists, and all kinds of context-evading conceptual puritans, for a very small number of generations. It is a very puzzling fact that an institution, namely human language, should have this potential for being used as an 'elaborate code', in Basil Bernstein's phrase, as a formal and fairly context-free instrument, given that it had evolved in a milieu which in no way called for this development, and did not selectively favour it if it manifested itself. This puzzle is on a par with problems such as that posed by the existence of skills (for example, mathematical ability) which throughout most of the period of the existence of humanity had no survival value, and thus could not have been in any direct way produced by natural selection. The existence of language suitable for such formal, context-liberated use is such a puzzle; but it is also, clearly, a fact. This potentiality, whatever its origin and explanation, happened to be there. Eventually a kind of society emerged – and it is now becoming global – in which this potentiality really comes into its own, and within which it becomes indispensable and dominant.

To sum up this argument: a society has emerged based on a high-powered technology and the expectancy of sustained growth, which requires both a mobile division of labour, and sustained, frequent and precise communication between strangers involving a sharing of explicit meaning, transmitted in a standard idiom and in writing when required. For a number of converging reasons, this society must be thoroughly exo-educational: each individual is trained by specialists, not just by his own local group, if indeed he has one. Its segments and units – and this society is in any case large, fluid, and in comparison with traditional, agrarian societies very short of internal structures – simply do not possess the capacity or the resources to reproduce their own personnel. The level of literacy and technical competence, in a standardized medium, a common conceptual currency, which is required of members of this society if they are to be properly employable and enjoy full and effective moral citizenship, is so high that it simply *cannot* be provided by the kin or local units, such as they are. It can only be provided by something resembling a modern 'national' educational system, a pyramid at whose base there are primary schools, staffed by teachers trained at secondary schools, staffed by university-trained teachers, led by the products of advanced graduate schools. Such a pyramid provides the criterion for the minimum size for a viable political unit. No unit too small to accommodate the pyramid can function properly. Units cannot be *smaller* than this. Constraints also operate which prevent them being too large, in various circumstances; but that is another issue.

The fact that sub-units of society are no longer capable of self-reproduction, that centralized exo-education is the obligatory norm, that such education complements (though it does not wholly replace) localized acculturation, is of the very first importance for the political sociology of the modern world; and its implications have, strangely enough, been seldom understood or appreciated or even examined. At the base of the modern social order stands not the executioner but the professor. Not the guillotine, but the (aptly named) *doctorat d'état* is the main tool and symbol of state power. The monopoly of legitimate education is now more important, more central than is the monopoly of legitimate violence. When this is understood, then the imperative of nationalism, its roots, not in human nature as such, but in a certain kind of now pervasive social order, can also be understood.

Contrary to popular and even scholarly belief, nationalism does not have any very deep roots in the human psyche. The human psyche can be assumed to have persisted unchanged through the many, many millennia of the existence of the human race, and not to have become either better or worse during the relatively brief and very recent age of nationalism. One may not invoke a *general* substrate to explain a *specific* phenomenon. The substrate generates many surface possibilities. Nationalism, the organization of human groups into large, centrally educated, culturally homogeneous units, is but one of these, and a very rare one at that. What is crucial for its genuine explanation is to identify its specific roots. It is these specific roots which alone can properly explain it. In this way, specific factors are superimposed on to a shared universal human substrate.

The roots of nationalism in the distinctive structural requirements of industrial society are very deep indeed. This movement is the fruit neither of ideological aberration, nor of emotional excess. Although those who participate in it generally, indeed almost without exception, fail to understand what it is that they do, the movement is nonetheless the external manifestation of a deep adjustment in the relationship between polity and culture which is quite unavoidable.

THE AGE OF UNIVERSAL HIGH CULTURE

Let us recapitulate the general and central features of industrial society. Universal literacy and a high level of numerical, technical and general sophistication are among its functional prerequisites. Its members are and must be mobile, and ready to shift from one activity to another, and must possess that generic training which enables them to follow the manuals and instructions of a new activity or occupation. In the course of their work they must constantly communicate with a large number of other men, with whom they frequently have no previous association, and with whom communication must consequently be explicit, rather than relying on context. They must also be able to communicate by means of written, impersonal, context-free, to-whom-it-may-concern type messages. Hence these communications must be in the same shared and standardized linguistic medium and script. The educational system which guarantees this social achievement becomes large and is indispensable, but at the same time it no longer possesses monopoly of access to the written word: its clientele is co-extensive with the society at large, and the replaceability of individuals within the system by others applies to the educational machine at least as much as to any other segment of society, and perhaps more so. Some very great teachers and researchers may perhaps be unique and irreplaceable, but the average professor and schoolmaster can be replaced from outside the teaching profession with the greatest of ease and often with little, if any, loss.

What are the implications of all this for the society and for its members? The employability, dignity, security and self-respect of individuals, typically, and for the majority of men now hinges on their *education*; and the limits of the culture within which they were educated are also the limits of the world within which they can, morally and professionally, breathe. A man's education is by far his most precious investment, and in effect confers his identity on him. Modern man is not loyal to a monarch or a land or a faith, whatever he may say, but to a culture. And he is, generally speaking, gelded. The Mamluk condition has become universal. No important links bind him to a kin group; nor do they stand between him and a wide, anonymous community of culture.

The obverse of the fact that a school-transmitted culture, not a folk-transmitted one, alone confers his usability and dignity and self-respect on industrial man, is the fact that nothing else can do it for him to any comparable extent. It would be idle to pretend that ancestry, wealth or connections are unimportant in modern society, and that they are not on occasion even sources of pride to their beneficiaries; all the same, advantages secured in these ways are often explained away and are viewed at best ambivalently. It is interesting to ask whether the pervasive work ethic has helped to produce this state of affairs, or whether, on the contrary, it is a reflection of it. Drones and rentiers persist, of course, but they are not very conspicuous, and this in itself is highly significant. It is an important fact that such privilege and idleness as survive are now discreet, tending to prefer obscurity to display, and needing to be uncovered by eager researchers bent on unmasking the inequality which lurks underneath the surface.

It was not so in the past, when idle privilege was proud and brazen, as it persists in being in some surviving agrarian societies, or in societies which continue to uphold the ethos of pre-industrial life. Curiously enough, the notion of conspicuous waste was coined by a work-oriented member of a work-addicted society, Thorsten Veblen, scandalized by what he saw as the survivals from a pre-industrial, predatory age. The egalitarian, work- and career-oriented surface of industrial society is as significant as its inegalitarian hidden depths. Life, after all, is lived largely on the surface, even if important decisions are on occasion made deep down.

The teacher class is now in a sense more important – it is indispensable – and in another sense much less so, having lost its monopoly of access to the cultural wisdom enshrined in scripture. In a society in which everyone is gelded by indentification with his professional post and his training, and hardly anyone derives much or any security and support from whatever kin links he may have, the teaching clerics no longer possess any privileged access to administrative posts. When everyone has become a Mamluk, no special mamluk class predominates in the bureaucracy. At long last the bureaucracy can recruit from the population at large, without needing to fear the arrival of dozens of cousins as unwanted attachments of each single new entrant.

Exo-socialization, education proper, is now the virtually universal norm. Men acquire the skills and sensibilities which make them acceptable to their fellows, which fit them to assume places in society, and which make them 'what they are', by being handed over by their kin groups (normally nowadays, of course, their nuclear family) to an educational machine which alone is capable of providing the wide range of training required for the generic cultural base. This educational infrastructure is large, indispensable and expensive. Its maintenance seems to be quite beyond the financial powers of even the biggest and richest organizations within society, such as the big industrial corporations. These often provide their personnel with housing, sports and leisure clubs, and so forth; they do not, except marginally and in special circumstances, provide schooling. (They may subsidize school bills, but that is another matter.) The organization man works and plays with his organization, but his children still go to state or independent schools.

So, on the one hand, this educational infrastructure is too large and costly for any organization other than the biggest one of all, the state. But at the same time, though only the state can sustain so large a burden, only the state is also strong enough to control so important and crucial a function. Culture is no longer merely the adornment, confirmation and legitimation of a social order which was also sustained by harsher and coercive constraints; culture is now the necessary shared medium, the life-blood or perhaps rather the minimal shared atmosphere, within which alone the members of the society can breathe and survive and produce. For a given society, it must be one in which they can *all* breathe and speak and produce; so it must be the *same* culture. Moreover, it must now be a great or high (literate, training-sustained) culture, and it can no longer be a diversified, locality-tied, illiterate little culture or tradition.

But some organism must ensure that this literate and unified culture is indeed being effectively produced, that the educational product is not shoddy and substandard. Only the state can do this, and, even in countries in which important parts of the educational machine are in private hands or those of religious organizations, the state does take over quality control in this most important of industries, the manufacture of viable and usable human beings. That shadow state dating back to the time when European states were not merely fragmented but socially weak – the centralized Church – did put up a fight for the control of education, but it was in the end ineffectual, unless the Church fought on behalf of an inclusive high culture and thereby indirectly on behalf of a new nationalist state.

Time was when education was a cottage industry, when men could be made by a village or clan. That time has now gone, and gone forever. (In education, small can now be beautiful only if it is covertly parasitic on the big.) Exo-socialization, the production and reproduction of men outside the local intimate unit, is now the norm, and must be so. The imperative of exo-socialization is the main clue to why state and culture *must* now be linked, whereas in the past their connection was thin, fortuitous, varied, loose, and often minimal. Now it is unavoidable. That is what nationalism is about, and why we live in an age of nationalism.

REFERENCES

Dore, R. (1976), *The Diploma Disease*, London: Allen & Unwin.
Goody, J., ed. (1968), *Literacy in Traditional Societies*, Cambridge: Cambridge University Press.

An anti-nationalist account of nationalism since 1989
ERIC HOBSBAWM

Since [. . .] early 1990 more new nation states have been formed, or are in the process of formation, than at any time in this century. The break-up of the USSR and Yugoslavia have so far added sixteen to the number of internationally recognized sovereign entities, and there is no immediately foreseeable limit to the further advance of national separatism. All states are today officially 'nations', all political agitations are apt to be against foreigners, whom practically all states harry and seek to keep-out. It may therefore seem wilful blindness to [include here] some reflections on the *decline* of nationalism as a vector of historical change, compared with its role in the century from the 1830s to the end of the Second World War.

It would indeed be absurd to deny that the collapse of the Soviet Union and the regional and international system of which, as one super power, it was a pillar for some forty years marks a profound, and probably permanent, historical change, whose implications are, at the time of writing [1992], entirely obscure. However, they introduce *new* elements into the history of nationalism only insofar as the break-up of the USSR in 1991 went far beyond the (temporary) break-up of Tsarist Russia in 1918–20, which was largely confined to its European and transcaucasian regions. For, basically, the 'national questions' of 1989–92 are not new. They belong overwhelmingly to the traditional home of national causes, Europe. There is so far no sign of serious political separatism in the Americas, at least south of the US–Canadian border. There is little sign that the Islamic world, or at least the rising fundamentalist movements within it, are concerned with multiplying state frontiers. They want to return to the true faith of the founders. In fact, it is hard to see how separatism could interest them as such. Separatist agitations (largely terrorist) are clearly shaking corners of the South Asian sub-continent, but so far (except for the secession of Bangladesh) the successor states have held together. In fact, the post-colonial national regimes not only in this region still overwhelmingly accept the nineteenth-century traditions of nationalism, both liberal and revolutionary-democratic. Gandhi and the Nehrus, Mandela and Mugabe, the late Zulfikhar Bhutto and Bandaranaike, and, I would wager, the imprisoned leader of Burma (Myanmar), Ms Aung-San Su Xi, were or are not nationalists in the sense of Landsbergis and Tudjman. They are or were on exactly the same wavelength as Massimo d'Azeglio: nation-builders not nation-splitters.

Many more post-colonial African states may collapse into chaos and disorder, as has recently happened to some; including – though one hopes not – South Africa. Yet it is to stretch the sense of words to see the collapse of Somalia or Ethiopia as being brought about by the inalienable right of peoples to form independent sovereign nation states. Friction between ethnic groups and conflicts, often bloody ones, between them, are older than the political programme of nationalism, and will survive it.

In Europe the outburst of separatist nationalism has even more specific historical roots in the twentieth century. The eggs of Versailles and Brest Litowsk are still hatching. Essentially the permanent collapse of the Habsburg and Turkish empires and the short-lived collapse of the Tsarist Russian empire produced the same set of national successor-states with the same sort of problems, insoluble in the long run, except by mass murder or forced mass migration. The explosive issues of 1988–92 were those created in 1918–21. Czechs were then yoked to Slovaks for the first time, and Slovenes (formerly Austrian) with Croats (once the military frontier against the Turks) and – across a millennium of divergent history, with the Serbs who belonged to Orthodoxy and the Ottoman empire. The doubling of Romania's size produced friction between its component nationalities. The victorious Germans set up three small Baltic nation states for which there was no historical precedent at all, and – at least in Estonia and Latvia – no noticeable national demand. They were maintained in being by the Allies as part of the 'quarantine belt' against Bolshevist Russia. At the moment of Russia's greatest weakness, German influence encouraged the setting up of an independent Georgian and Armenian state, and the British the autonomy of oil-rich Azerbaijan. Transcaucasian nationalism (if such a term is not too strong for the grassroots anti-Armenian resentment of the Azeri Turks) had not been a serious political issue before 1917: the Armenians were, for obvious reasons, worried about Turkey rather than Moscow, the Georgians supported a nominally Marxist all-Russian party (the Mensheviks) as their national party. However, unlike the Habsburgs and the Ottoman empire, the multinational Russian empire survived for another three generations, thanks to the October Revolution and Hitler. Victory in the Civil War eliminated the possibility of Ukrainian separatism, and the recovery of Transcaucasia eliminated local nationalisms, though – since it was achieved partly through negotiations with Kemalist Turkey – it left a few sensitive issues for future nationalist resentment, notably the problem of the Armenian enclave of Mountain Karabakh in Azerbaijan. In 1939–40 the USSR in practice recovered all that Tsarist Russia had lost, except for Finland (which had been allowed to secede peacefully by Lenin) and former Russian Poland.

The simplest way to describe the apparent explosion of separatism in 1988–92 is thus as 'unfinished business of 1918–21'. Conversely, ancient and deep-seated national questions which actually seemed dangerous to European chanceries *before* 1914, have not proved explosive. It was not 'the Macedonian Question', well known to scholars as leading to battles between rival experts in a half-dozen fields at international congresses, which provoked the collapse of Yugoslavia. On the contrary, the Macedonian People's Republic did its best to stay out of the Serb-Croat imbroglio, until Yugoslavia was actually collapsing, and all its components, in sheer self-defence, had to look after themselves. (Characteristically enough, its official recognition has been hitherto sabotaged by Greece, which had annexed large parts of Macedonian territory in 1913.) Similarly, the only part of Tsarist Russia which contained a genuine national movement before 1917, though not a separatist one, was Ukraine. Yet Ukraine remained relatively quiet while Baltic and Caucasian republics demanded secession, remained under the control of the local Communist Party leadership, and did not resign itself to separation until after the failed coup of August 1991 destroyed the USSR.

Moreover, the definition of 'the nation' and its aspirations which, paradoxically, Lenin shared with Woodrow Wilson, automatically created the fracture lines along which multinational units constructed by communist states were to break, just as the colonial frontiers of 1880–1950 were to form the state frontiers of post-colonial states, there being no others available. (Most of their inhabitants did not know what frontiers were, or took no notice of them.) In the Soviet Union we can go further: it was the communist regime which deliberately set out to *create* ethno-linguistic territorial 'national administrative units', i.e. 'nations' in the modern sense, where none had previously existed or been thought of, as among the Asian Muslim peoples – or, for that matter, the Bielorussians. The idea of Soviet Republics based on Kazakh, Kirghiz, Uzbek, Tajik and Turkmen 'nations' was a theoretical construct of Soviet intellectuals rather than a primordial aspiration of any of those Central Asian peoples (G. Smith 1990: 215, 230, 262).

The idea that these peoples, whether because of 'national oppression' or Islamic consciousness, were putting the Soviet system under the intolerable strain which led to its collapse seems to be merely another expression for some Western observers' justified horror of the Soviet system and their belief that it could not last long. In fact, Central Asia remained politically inert until the collapse of the Union, except for some pogroms of the national minorities whom Stalin had tended to banish into those remote regions. Such nationalism as is developing in those republics is a post-Soviet phenomenon.

The changes in and after 1989 were thus essentially not due to national tensions, which remained under effective control even where they genuinely existed, as in Poland and among the Yugoslav peoples, so long as central party operated, but primarily to the decision of the Soviet regime to reform itself, and in doing so (a) to withdraw military support from its satellite regimes, (b) to undermine the central command and authority structure which allowed it to operate, and consequently also (c) to undermine the foundations of even the independent communist regimes in Balkan Europe. Nationalism was the beneficiary of these developments but not, in any serious sense, an important factor in bringing them about. Hence, indeed, the universal amazement at the sudden collapse of the eastern regimes, which had been entirely unexpected, even in Poland, where a deeply unpopular regime had shown that it could keep a massively organized opposition movement under control for almost a decade.

One has only to compare the German unifications of 1871 and 1990 to note the differences. The first was seen as the long-awaited achievement of an objective which, in one way or another, was the central concern of everyone interested in politics in the German lands, even those who wanted to resist it. [. . .] But until the autumn of 1989 none of the major parties in the Federal Republic had paid more than lip-service to the creation of a single German state for many years. This was not only because it was obviously not practicable until Gorbachev made it so, but because nationalist organizations and agitations were politically marginal. Nor did the desire for German unity motivate the political opposition in the DDR, or the ordinary East Germans, whose mass exodus precipitated the collapse of the regime. No doubt, among all their doubts and uncertainties about the future, most Germans welcome the unifi-cation of the two Germanies, but its very suddenness, and the patent lack of serious preparation for it, demonstrate that, whatever the public rhetoric, it was the by-product of unexpected events outside Germany.

As for the USSR, it collapsed not, as some Sovietologists had predicted, under its internal national tensions (Carrère d'Encausse 1978 and 1990), undeniable as these were, but under its economic difficulties. *Glasnost*, which the reform-communist leadership of the country regarded as a necessary condition of *perestroika*, reintroduced freedom of debate and agitation and also weakened the centralized command system on which both regime and society rested. The failure of *perestroika*, i.e. the growing deterioration of living conditions for ordinary citizens, undermined faith in the all-Union government made responsible for it, and indeed encouraged or even imposed regional and local solutions to problems. It is safe to say that before Gorbachev no Soviet republic envisaged secession from the USSR except the Baltic states, and even there independence was then obviously a dream. Nor can it be argued that only fear and coercion kept the USSR together, though it undoubtedly helped to stop ethnic and communal tensions in mixed regions from degenerating into mutual violence, as they have subsequently done. Indeed, in the long Brezhnev era local and regional autonomy was by no means illusory. Moreover, as the Russians never ceased to complain, most of the other republics were rather better off than the inhabitants of the RSFSR. The national disintegration of the USSR, and incidentally of its constituent republics, almost all effectively multinational, is plainly more the consequence of events in Moscow than their cause.

Paradoxically, the case for nationalist movements with the power to undermine existing regimes is rather stronger in the West, where such agitations disrupt some of the most ancient nation states: the United Kingdom, Spain, France, even in a more modest way Switzerland, not to mention Canada. Whether complete secession of Quebec, Scotland or some other region will actually take place is at present (1992) a matter for speculation. Outside the former Euro-Soviet red belt, successful secessions since the Second World War are extremely rare, and peaceful separations virtually unknown. Nevertheless, the possible secession of Scotland or Quebec can today be discussed as a realistic possibility, which it was not twenty-five years ago.

[. . .]

The anguish and disorientation which finds expression in this hunger to belong, and hence in the 'politics of identity' – not necessarily national identity – is no more a moving force of history than the hunger for 'law and order' which is an equally understandable response to another aspect of social disorganization. Both are symptoms of sickness rather than diagnoses, let alone therapy. Nevertheless, they create the illusion of nations and nationalism as an irresistibly rising force ready for the third millennium. This force is further exaggerated by the semantic illusion which today turns all states officially into 'nations' (and members of the United Nations), even when they are patently not. Consequently, all movements seeking territorial autonomy tend to think of themselves as establishing 'nations' even when this is plainly not the case; and all movements for regional, local or even sectional interests against central power and state bureaucracy will, if they possibly can, put on the national costume, preferably in its ethnic-linguistic styles. Nations and nationalism therefore appear more influential and omnipresent than they are. Aruba plans to break away from the rest of the Netherlands West Indies, because it does not like to be yoked to Curaçao. Does that make it a nation? Or Curaçao, or Surinam, which is already a member of the United Nations? The Cornish are fortunate to be able to paint their regional discontents in the attractive colours of Celtic tradition, which makes them so much more viable, even though it leads some of them to reinvent a language not spoken for 200 years, and even though the only popular public tradition with genuine roots in the county is Wesleyan Methodism. They are luckier than, say, Merseyside, which can mobilize in defence of the equally or more hard-hit local interests only the memory of the Beatles, of generations of Scouse comedians, and the proud tradition of its rival football teams, while taking care to keep away from anything that reminds its inhabitants too obviously of the divisive colours Orange and Green. Merseyside cannot blow a national trumpet. Cornwall can. But are the situations which produce discontent in one area substantially different from those which do so in the other?

In fact, the rise of separatist and ethnic agitations is partly due to the fact that, contrary to common belief, the principle of state-creation since the Second World War, unlike that after the First, had nothing to do with Wilsonian national self-determination. It reflected three forces: decolonization, revolution and, of course, the intervention of outside powers.

Decolonization meant that, by and large, independent states were created out of existing areas of colonial administration, within their colonial frontiers. These had, obviously, been drawn without any reference to, or sometimes even without the knowledge of, their inhabitants and therefore had no national or even proto-national significance for their populations; except for colonial-educated and Westernized native minorities of varying, but generally exigous, size. Alternatively, where such territories were too small and scattered, as in many colonized archipelagos, they were combined or broken up according to convenience or local politics. Hence the constant, and eventually often vain, calls of the leaders of such new states to surmount 'tribalism', 'communalism', or whatever forces were made responsible for the failure of the new inhabitants of the Republic of X to feel themselves to be primarily patriotic citizens of X rather than members of some other collectivity.

In short, the appeal of most such 'nations' and 'national movements' was the opposite of the nationalism which seeks to bond together those deemed to have common ethnicity, language, culture, historical past, and the rest. In effect it was *internationalist*. The internationalism of the leaders and cadres of national liberation movements in the Third World is more obvious where such movements played a leading part in the liberation of their countries than where countries were decolonized from above, for the post-independence breakdown of what previously operated, or seemed to operate, as a united movement of 'the people' is more dramatic. Sometimes, as in India, the unity of the movement has already cracked before independence.

More commonly, soon after independence tensions develop between the component parts of the independence movement (e.g. in Algeria, Arabs and Berbers), between peoples actively involved in it and those not, or between the emancipated non-sectional secularism of the leaders and the feelings of the masses. However, while the cases where multi-ethnic and multi-communal states have fractured, or are close to breaking, naturally attract most attention – the partition of the Indian sub-continent in 1947, the splitting of Pakistan, the demands for Tamil separatism in Sri Lanka – it should never be forgotten that these are special cases in a world where multi-ethnic and multi-communal states are the norm. What was written almost thirty years ago remains substantially true: 'Countries including many language and culture groups, like most African and Asian ones, have not split up, and those taking in only part of a single language group, like the Arab ones and North Africa, have ... not united' (Kautsky 1962: 35).

The intervention of outside powers, finally, has obviously been non-nationalist in both motivation and effect, except by pure accident. This is so evident that it does not require illustration. However, so also has been the impact of social revolution, though rather less effectively. Social revolutionaries have been keenly aware of the force of nationalism, as well as ideologically committed to national autonomy, even when it is not actually wanted, as among the Lusatian Slavs, whose language is slowly retreating, in spite of the admirable efforts of the German Democratic Republic during its period of independent existence to foster it. The *only* form of constitutional arrangements which socialist states have taken seriously since 1917 are formulas for national federation and autonomy. While other constitutional texts, where they existed at all, have for long periods been purely national, national autonomy has never ceased to have a certain operational reality. However, inasmuch as such regimes do not, at least in theory, identify with any of their constituent nationalities and regard the interests of each of them as secondary to a higher common purpose, they are non-national.

Hence, as we can now see in melancholy retrospect, it was the great achievement of the communist regimes in multinational countries to limit the disastrous effects of nationalism within them. The Yugoslav revolution succeeded in preventing the nationalities within its state frontiers from massacring each other almost certainly for longer than ever before in their history, though this achievement has now unfortunately crumbled. The USSR's potential for national disruption, so long kept in check (except during the Second World War), is now patent. In fact, the 'discrimination' or even 'oppression' against which champions of various Soviet nationalities abroad used to protest, was far less than the consequences of the withdrawal of Soviet power. Official Soviet anti-semitism, which has undoubtedly been observable since the foundation of the state of Israel in 1948, must be measured against the rise of popular anti-semitism since political mobilization (including that of reactionaries) became permitted again, not to mention the massacre of Jews on a considerable scale *by local elements* in the Baltic states and Ukraine as the Germans marched in but *before the systematic German killing of Jews began*. Indeed, it may be argued that the current wave of ethnic or mini-ethnic agitations is a response to the overwhelmingly non-ethnic and non-nationalist principles of state formation in the greater part of the twentieth-century world. However, this does not mean that such ethnic reactions provide in any sense an alternative principle for the political restructuring of the world in the twenty-first century.

A third observation confirms this. 'The nation' today is visibly in the process of losing an important part of its old functions, namely that of constituting a territorially bounded 'national economy' which formed a building-block in the larger 'world economy', at least in the developed regions of the globe. Since the Second World War, but especially since the 1960s, the role of 'national economies' has been undermined or even brought into question by the major transformations in the international division of labour, whose basic units are transnational or multinational enterprises of all sizes, and by the corresponding development of international centres and networks of economic transactions which are, for practical purposes, outside the control of state governments. The number of *intergovernmental* international organizations grew from 123 in 1951 through 280 in 1972 to 365 in 1984; the number of international *non-governmental* organizations from 832 through 2173 in 1972, more than doubling to 4615 in the next twelve years (Held 1988: 15). Probably the only functioning 'national economy' of the late twentieth century is the Japanese.

Nor have the old (developed) 'national economies' been replaced as the major building-blocks of the world system only by larger associations or federations of 'nation states' such as the European Economic Community, and collectively controlled international entities like the International Monetary Fund, even though the emergence of these is also a symptom of the retreat of the world of 'national economies'. Important parts of the system of international transactions, such as the Eurodollar market, are outside any control whatever.

All this has, of course, been made possible both by technological revolutions in transport and communication, and by the lengthy period of free movements of the factors of production over a vast area of the globe which has developed since the Second World War. This has also led to the massive wave of international and intercontinental migration, the largest since the decades before 1914, which has, incidentally, both aggravated inter-communal frictions, notably in the form of racism, and made a world of national territories 'belonging' exclusively to the natives who keep strangers in their place, even less of a realistic option for the twenty-first century than it was for the twentieth. At present we are living through a curious combination of the technology of the late twentieth century, the free trade of the nineteenth, and the rebirth of the sort of interstitial centres characteristic of world trade in the Middle Ages. City states like Hong Kong and Singapore revive, extraterritorial 'industrial zones' multiply inside technically sovereign nation states like Hanseatic Steelyards, and so do offshore tax-havens in otherwise valueless islands whose only function is, precisely, to remove economic transactions from the control of nation states. The ideology of nations and nationalism is irrelevant to any of these developments.

This does not mean that the economic functions of states have been diminished or are likely to fade away. On the contrary, in both capitalist and non-capitalist states they have grown, in spite of a tendency in both camps to encourage private or other non-state enterprise in the 1980s. Quite apart from the continued importance of state direction, planning and management even in countries dedicated in theory to neo-liberalism, the sheer weight of what public revenue and expenditure represent in the economies of states, but above all their growing role as agents of substantial redistributions of the social income by means of fiscal and welfare mechanisms, have probably made the national state a more central factor in the lives of the world's inhabitants than before. National economies, however, undermined by the transnational economy, co-exist and intertwine with it. However, except for the most self-sealed at one end – and how many of these are left after even Burma appears to consider re-entering the world? – and perhaps Japan at the other extreme, the old 'national economy' is not what it was. Even the USA, which in the 1980s still seemed sufficiently vast and dominant to deal with its economic problems without taking any notice of anyone else, at the end of that decade became aware that it 'had ceded considerable control over its economy to foreign investors . . . [who] now hold the power to help keep the US economy growing, or to help plunge it into recession' (*Wall Street Journal*, 5 December 1988: 1). As for all small and practically all medium-sized states their economies had plainly ceased to be autonomous, insofar as they had once been so.

Another observation also suggests itself. The basic political conflicts which are likely to decide the fate of the world today have little to do with nation states, because for half a century there has not existed an international state system of the nineteenth-century European type.

Politically the post-1945 world was bi-polar, organized round two super-powers which may just be describable as jumbo-sized nations, but certainly not as parts of an international state system of the nineteenth-century or pre-1939 type. At most, third-party states, whether aligned with a superpower or non-aligned, could act as a brake on superpower action, though there is no strong evidence that they did so to much effect. Moreover, as far as the USA was concerned – but vestigially this was probably also true of the USSR before the Gorbachev era – the basic conflict was ideological, the triumph of the 'right' ideology being equated with the supremacy of the appropriate superpower. Post-1945 world politics were basically the politics of revolution and counter-revolution, with national issues intervening only to underline or disturb the main theme. Admittedly this pattern broke down in 1989 when the USSR ceased to be a superpower; and indeed the model of a world divided by the October Revolution had ceased to have much relation to the realities of the late twentieth century for some time before then. The immediate result was to leave the world without any international system or principle of order, even though the remaining superpower attempted to impose itself singlehanded as the global policeman, a role probably beyond its, or any other single state's, economic and military power.

There is thus at present no system at all. That ethnic-linguistic separation provides no sort of basis for a stable, in the short run even for a roughly predictable, ordering of the globe is evident in 1992 from the merest glance at the large region situated between Vienna and Trieste in the west, and Vladivostock in the east. All maps for one fifth of the world's surface are uncertain and provisional. And the only thing clear even about its cartographic future is that it will depend on a handful of major players outside the region, except for Russia (which is likely to remain a political entity of some substance). They are major players precisely because they have not so far been disrupted by separatist agitations: Germany, Turkey, Iran, China, Japan and – at one remove – the USA.

For a new 'Europe of nations', and still more a 'world of nations', would not even create an ensemble of independent and sovereign states. In military terms the independence of small states depends on an international order, whatever its nature, which protects them against rapacious stronger neighbours, as the Middle East immediately demonstrated after the ending of the superpower balance. Until a new international system emerges at least a third of the existing states – those with populations of two and a half million or less – have no effective guarantees of independence. The establishment of several additional small states would merely increase the number of insecure political entities. And when such a new international system emerges, the small and the weak will have as little real role in it as Oldenburg or Mecklenburg-Schwerin had over the politics of the German Federation in the nineteenth century. Economically, as we have seen, even much more powerful states depend on a global economy over which they have no control and which determines their internal affairs. A Latvian or Basque 'national' economy separate from some larger entity of which it forms a part is as meaningless a concept as a Parisian economy considered in separation from France.

The most that could be claimed is that small states are today economically no less viable than larger states, given the decline of the 'national economy' before the transnational one. It may also be argued that 'regions' constitute more rational sub-units of large economic entities like the European Community than the historic states which are its official members. Both observations are correct, in my view, but they are logically unconnected. West European separatist nationalisms like the Scottish, Welsh, Basque or Catalan are today in favour of bypassing their national governments by appealing directly to Brussels as 'regions'. However, there is no reason to suppose that a smaller state *ipso facto* forms more of an economic region than a larger one (say Scotland than England) and conversely there is no reason why an economic region should *ipso facto* coincide with a potential political unit constituted according to ethnic-linguistic or historic criteria. Moreover, when separatist small-nation movements see their best hope in establishing themselves as sub-units of a larger politico-economic entity (in this case the European Community) they are in practice abandoning the classical aim of such movements, which is to establish independent and sovereign nation states.

However, the case against *Kleinstaaterei* today, at least in its ethnic-linguistic form, is not only that it provides no solution for the actual problems of our day, but that, insofar as it has the power to carry out its policies, it makes these problems more difficult. Cultural freedom and pluralism at present are almost certainly better safeguarded in large states which know themselves to be plurinational and pluricultural than in small ones pursuing the ideal of ethnic-linguistic and cultural homogeneity.

[. . .]

As I have suggested, 'nation' and 'nationalism' are no longer adequate terms to describe, let alone to analyse, the political entities described as such, or even the sentiments once described by these words. It is not impossible that nationalism will decline with the decline of the nation state, without which being English or Irish or Jewish, or a combination of all these, is only one way in which people describe their identity among the many others which they use for this purpose, as occasion demands. It would be absurd to claim that this day is already near. However, I hope it can at least be envisaged. After all, the very fact that historians are at least beginning to make some progress in the study and analysis of nations and nationalism suggests that, as so often, the phenomenon is past its peak. The owl of Minerva which brings wisdom, said Hegel, flies out at dusk. It is a good sign that it is now circling round nations and nationalism.

REFERENCES

Carrère d'Encausse, H. (1978), *L'Empire éclaté*, Paris: Flammarion.
Carrère d'Encausse, H. (1990), *La Gloire des nations, ou La Fin de l'empire sovietique*, Paris: Fayard; translated (1993) as *The End of the Soviet Empire: The Triumph of the Nations*, New York: Basic Books.
Held, David (1988), 'Farewell nation state', *Marxism Today*, December, p. 15.
Kautsky, John H. (1962), 'An essay in the politics of development' in *Political Change in Underdeveloped Countries: Nationalism and Communism*, ed. John. H. Kautsky, New York and London: Wiley.
Smith, Graham, ed. (1990), *The Nationalities Question in the Soviet Union*, London and New York: Longman.

3 Ethnicity and Violence

Causes and implications of ethnic conflict
MICHAEL E. BROWN

Expectations were too high. The Cold War generated great tension, but also exceptional stability – at least as far as Europe was concerned. When the Cold War ended, many people assumed that international tensions would be reduced, but that stability would be retained – perhaps even extended to previously troubled parts of the world. Learned commentators spoke of 'the end of history'. Presidents suggested that the great powers would work together to create a 'New World Order'. Many people expected, inferring too much from the international community's response to the Iraqi invasion of Kuwait, that effective international action would be taken in the future to prevent conflicts from breaking out and to resolve those that did. Many people seemed to think that the end of the Cold War marked the advent of the millennium.

These great expectations – which could only have been generated by wilfully ignoring the many ethnic conflicts around the world that have raged for years, even decades – have been dashed. People have been stunned by both the breadth and depth of the ethnic conflicts that are now taking place in many regions. The war in Bosnia-Herzegovina has received the most attention in the West because of the intense coverage it has received from the Western media, but equally if not more horrific conflicts are under way in Afghanistan, Angola, Armenia, Azerbaijan, Burma, Georgia, India, Indonesia, Liberia, Sri Lanka, Sudan and Tajikistan. Other trouble spots abound – Bangladesh, Belgium, Bhutan, Burundi, Estonia, Ethiopia, Guatemala, Iraq, Latvia, Lebanon, Mali, Moldova, Niger, Northern Ireland, Pakistan, the Philippines, Romania, Rwanda, South Africa, Spain and Turkey, for example – and the prospects for ethnic conflict in Russia and China cannot be dismissed.

Expectations about the willingness and ability of outside powers to prevent and resolve ethnic conflicts have also been dampened. European and American leaders have agonized over the conflict in Bosnia, trying to decide if genocidal acts and threats to outside interests have created either moral or strategic imperatives for intervention. Except for providing some small measure of humanitarian assistance, no action was taken as cities were bombed and civilians slaughtered. The possibility that Western powers will intervene in other ethnic conflicts, where their interests are even less engaged and where media attention is less intense, is remote.

This [essay examines] the causes and implications of ethnic conflict, as well as the recommendations that have been put forward to minimize the potential for instability and violence. [. . .] It begins with a brief discussion of some basic definitional issues, in an effort to sharpen an understanding of the parameters of the term 'ethnic conflict'. Second, it examines alternative explanations of the causes of ethnic conflict, focusing in turn on systemic, domestic and perceptual explanations. Third, it analyses the regional and international implications of ethnic conflicts, arguing that one must distinguish among the effects of three basic kinds of conflict outcomes: peaceful reconciliation, peaceful separation, and ethnic war. This last, it is argued, can affect the strategic interests and moral calculations of the outside world in seven important ways. This essay concludes with a discussion of recommendations that have been developed to prevent or dampen ethnic conflicts, focusing in particular on steps outside powers and the international community could take in this regard.

DEFINITIONS

The term 'ethnic conflict' is often used loosely, to describe a wide range of intrastate conflicts that are not, in fact, ethnic in character. The conflicts in Somalia, for example, is occasionally referred to as an ethnic conflict even though Somalia is the most ethnically homogenous country in Africa. The conflict in Somalia is not between rival ethnic groups, but between rival gangs, clans and warlords, all of whom belong to the same ethnic group.

This inquiry consequently begins with some definitions. According to Anthony Smith, an 'ethnic community' is 'a named human population with a myth of common ancestry, shared memories, and cultural elements; a link with a historic territory or homeland; and a measure of solidarity' (A. D. Smith, in Brown 1993: 28–9). Six criteria must be met, therefore, before a group can be called an ethnic community. First, the group must have a name for itself. This is not trivial; a lack of a name reflects an insufficiently developed collective identity. Second, the people in the group must believe in a common ancestry. This is more important than genetic ties, which may exist, but are not essential. Third, the members of the group must share historical memories, often myths or legends passed from generation to generation by word of mouth. Fourth, the group must have a shared culture, generally based on a combination of language, religion, laws, customs, institutions, dress, music, crafts, architecture, even food. Fifth, the group must feel an attachment to a specific piece of territory, which it may or may not actually inhabit. Sixth and last, the people in a group have to think of themselves as a group in order to constitute an ethnic community; that is, they must have a sense of their common ethnicity. The group must be self-aware.

At the risk of stating the obvious, an 'ethnic conflict' is a dispute about important political, economic, social, cultural or territorial issues between two or more ethnic communities. Some ethnic conflicts involve little or no violence. The struggle of French Canadians within Quebec to win more autonomy from the Canadian government is a case in point; Czechoslovakia's 'velvet divorce' is another. Tragically, other ethnic conflicts involve full-scale military hostilities and unspeakable levels of savagery, as seen in Angola, Bosnia, the Caucasus and elsewhere.

Two points should be kept in mind about these definitions. First, although Smith's conception of ethnic communities is a broad one – it would include many groups defined in terms of religious and tribal distinctions – many domestic disputes and civil wars are not ethnic in character. The war between the Sendero Luminoso and the Peruvian government, for example, is primarily political and ideological in nature, as is the continuing struggle between the Khmer Rouge and other factions in Cambodia; Cambodian persecution of ethnic Vietnamese is another matter, however. The problems in Georgia with South Ossetian and Abkhazian separatists are ethnic in nature; the struggle for power in Tblisi among various Georgian factions is not. The Burmese military's repression of Karen, Kachin, Naga and Rohingya insurgents is an ethnic conflict; its suppression of the democracy movement in the country as a whole has other political motivations.

Second, many ethnic conflicts start out as domestic disputes, but become interstate conflicts when outside powers become involved. In some cases, trouble spills over into neighbouring countries. In others, neighbouring powers intervene in domestic disputes to protect the interests of their ethnic brethren. Disinterested powers may intervene in ethnic wars, which often involve attacks on civilian populations, for humanitarian reasons. For these and other reasons that will be discussed in more detail below, ethnic conflicts often become internationalized.

CAUSES

The conventional wisdom among journalists and policy-makers is that ethnic conflicts have sprung up in eastern Europe, the former Soviet Union, and elsewhere because the collapse of authoritarian rule has made such conflicts possible. The 'lid' on ancient rivalries, it is said, has been taken off, and long-suppressed grievances are now being settled. Scholars generally agree that this conventional wisdom offers an inadequate explanation of the causes of ethnic conflict. It fails to explain why conflicts have broken out in some places, but not others, and it fails to explain why some ethnic disputes are more violent than others. In short, this single-factor explanation cannot account for significant variation in the incidence and intensity of ethnic conflict.

Serious academic studies of the causes of ethnic conflict develop explanations at three main levels of analysis: the systemic level, the domestic level, and the perceptual level.

Systemic explanations

Systemic explanations of ethnic conflict focus on the nature of the security systems in which ethnic groups operate and the security concerns of these groups. The first and most obvious systemic prerequisite for ethnic conflict is that two or more ethnic groups must reside in close proximity. This condition is met in many parts of the world. As David Welsh observes, 'Of the approximately 180 states that exist today, fewer than 20 are ethnically homogenous, in the sense that minorities account for less than 5 percent of the population.'

The second systemic prerequisite for ethnic conflict is that national, regional, and international authorities must be too weak to keep groups from fighting and too weak to ensure the security of individual groups. As Barry Posen explains, in systems where there is no sovereign – that is, where anarchy prevails – individual groups have to provide for their own defence. They have to worry about whether neighbouring groups pose security threats and whether threats will grow or diminish over time. The problem groups face is that, in taking steps to defend themselves – mobilizing armies and deploying military forces – they often threaten the security of others. This, in turn, can lead neighbouring groups to take actions that will diminish the security of the first group. This is the security dilemma. Groups are often unaware of, or insensitive to, the impact their actions will have on others. In other cases, they are aware of this problem, but act anyway because they feel compelled to address what they see as imminent security threats. This, of course, is the situation in eastern Europe and the former Soviet Union today. Imperial 'sovereigns' have disappeared, and individual groups have to provide for their own defence.

According to Posen, instabilities develop when either of two conditions hold. First, when offensive and defensive military forces are hard to distinguish, groups cannot signal their defensive intentions by the kinds of military force they deploy. Forces deployed for defensive purposes will have offensive capabilities and will therefore be seen as threatening by others. Second, if offensive military operations are more effective than defensive operations, due to the nature of military technology or the kinds of capability that are available, groups will adopt offensive military postures, and they will have powerful incentives to launch pre-emptive attacks in political crises.

Posen argues that these conditions are often generated when empires collapse and ethnic groups suddenly have to provide for their own security. First, under these circumstances, offensive and defensive forces are generally hard to distinguish. The military hardware available to newly independent ethnic groups is often unsophisticated from a technological standpoint, so defences are based on infantry. Whether or not these forces are effective is essentially a function of the number, cohesiveness and motivation of the troops in the field. Not surprisingly, newly independent ethnic groups often have large numbers of highly motivated, like-minded volunteers on which to draw. Cohesive, well-motivated infantries have inherent offensive capabilities against similarly configured forces, however, so they will inevitably be seen as threatening by other newly independent ethnic groups. This, in turn, will serve as a stimulus to military mobilization elsewhere.

Second, Posen argues that when empires break up, ethnic geography frequently creates situations that favour the offence over the defence. In some cases, ethnic groups will effectively surround 'islands' of people from other groups. Defending these islands in the event of hostilities is generally quite difficult: all are vulnerable to blockades and sieges, and some are simply indefensible. Often, groups will try to expel pockets of minorities from their territory. The offence has tremendous tactical advantages in these 'ethnic cleansing' operations; even small, lightly armed forces can generate tremendous amounts of terror in attacks on civilians. Posen is careful to note that ethnic geography is a variable, not a constant: some ethnic islands are large, economically autonomous, and militarily defensible; others could be reinforced by nearby brethren. In short, ethnic geography can be stabilizing or destabilizing. In some cases, groups will be able to defend themselves and their brethren. In many cases, however, the offence will have the upper hand, and stability will be tenuous.

Posen identifies two other factors that have to be taken into account in analyses of the prospects for ethnic stability. First, windows of opportunity and vulnerability will be created because newly independent groups will develop state structures at different rates. Groups that are further along in developing states and deploying military forces will have powerful incentives to go on the offensive – expelling minorities, rescuing islands of brethren, launching preventive attacks against potential adversaries – before rival groups are able to defend themselves or launch offensives of their own. Second, the presence of nuclear weapons will affect stability in important ways: nuclear weapons make infantries less important, they make defence easier, and they can prevent windows of vulnerability from opening up. In the hands of a status quo power, nuclear weapons could enhance stability.

Domestic explanations

Other explanations of ethnic conflict focus on factors that operate primarily at the domestic level: the effectiveness of states in addressing the concerns of their constituents, the impact of nationalism on interethnic relations, and the impact of democratization on interethnic relations.

Jack Snyder argues that people look to states to provide security and promote economic prosperity. Nationalism, he maintains, reflects the need to establish states capable of achieving these goals. Thus, it is not surprising that nationalism has flared up in parts of eastern Europe and the former Soviet Union, where state structures have weakened or collapsed altogether. New state structures have been, or are in the process of being, established, but in many cases they are not yet able to provide for the security and well-being of their constituents. In some cases, ethnic minorities feel persecuted by the new states in which they find themselves. More generally, many in eastern Europe and the former Soviet Union feel that they are not being adequately protected from unregulated markets. Inflation and unemployment are high, and economic prospects are often grim. Ethnic minorities frequently find themselves being blamed for these economic difficulties.

These problems are compounded by the fact that, when state structures are weak, nationalism is likely to be based on ethnic distinctions, rather than the idea that everyone who lives in a country is entitled to the same rights and privileges. As Snyder explains: 'By its nature, nationalism based on equal and universal citizenship rights within a territory depends on a framework of laws to guarantee those rights, as well as effective institutions to allow citizens to give voice to their views. Ethnic nationalism, in contrast, depends not on institutions, but on culture.' It is not surprising, therefore, that there are strong currents of ethnic nationalism in eastern Europe and the former Soviet Union, where state structures and political institutions have diminished capacities, and in those parts of the developing world where state structures and political institutions are inherently fragile.

The emergence of ethnic nationalism makes some form of ethnic conflict almost inevitable. The rise of ethnic nationalism in one group will be seen as threatening by others and will lead to the development of similar sentiments elsewhere. This will sharpen distinctions between groups, make it more likely that minority groups will be persecuted and more likely that ethnic minorities will demand states of their own. Secessionist crusades might be launched – and opposed. Ethnic nationalism will also make it easier for groups to field large, highly motivated armies. This will lead others to be more vigilant and to build up their own military forces. This, in turn, can make pre-emptive attacks or preventive war between neighbouring groups more likely.

Other scholars – such as Donald Horowitz (1985), Arend Lijphart (1990), Renée de Nevers and David Welsh (both in Brown 1993) – have examined the impact that democratization and other domestic political factors have on the prospects for ethnic conflict. Democratization, scholars agree, is particularly problematic in multi-ethnic societies. It often exacerbates existing ethnic problems.

Much depends on the level of ethnic tension when the democratization process begins, according to de Nevers (in Brown 1993). If the old regime was an extension of a minority ethnic group that suppressed demographically larger groups, then ethnic problems will complicate negotiations over new political arrangements from the very beginning. If the old regime exacerbated ethnic problems by engaging in forced assimilation, forced relocation, ethnic expulsion or extermination campaigns, then the democratization process is likely to be both highly problematic and emotionally charged; many ethnic problems will be on the agenda. If, on the other hand, the old regime drew from all major ethnic groups in a fairly representative way and pursued comparatively benign policies towards the ethnic groups under its sway, ethnic issues will probably play a less prominent role in negotiations over new arrangements. These negotiations, in turn, will be more likely to resolve those ethnic problems that do exist.

A second factor in the equation, de Nevers argues, is the relative size of the ethnic groups in the country. If one group is substantially larger than the others, then it is more likely that the majority group will be able to dominate discussions about new political arrangements and that minority interests will be neglected. If negotiations are between two or more groups of roughly equal size, however, it is more likely that all groups' core concerns will be addressed. Third, if the opposition to the old regime was led by only one or two groups and if the old regime itself was an extension of another, the country's political system could easily fragment along ethnic lines as the democratization process unfolds. Ethnic tensions would intensify correspondingly. If, on the other hand, the opposition to the old regime emanated from all major ethnic groups in that society, these groups will have a co-operative foundation on which to build when they begin their discussions on new political arrangements. Fourth, if the military is loyal to a single ethnic group, rather than the state, then the prospects for managing ethnic conflict are not good. If the military is loyal to the state, however, the prospects are substantially better.

Finally, de Nevers points out that different kinds of democratization processes pose different problems for the management of ethnic conflict. If the fall of the old regime comes about suddenly, negotiations on new political arrangements will be conducted in great haste. Ethnic problems are more likely to be ignored, and power struggles, perhaps along ethnic lines, are more likely to take place. The euphoria experienced as the old regime passes from the scene might produce a moment of national unity, but this moment will not endure if underlying problems are neglected. If the demise of the old regime takes place over a period of months or even years, opposition leaders will have more time to address ethnic problems when they go about devising new political institutions and processes. They will also have more of an opportunity to develop a broad-based political alliance, and ethnic leaders will have a stronger co-operative foundation on which to build. One of the keys to minimizing ethnic conflict during democratic transitions, de Nevers maintains, is addressing ethnic problems early in the transition process. If ethnic grievances can be anticipated and dealt with early, ethnic conflicts are more likely to be prevented or at least mitigated.

A number of other domestic factors also affect the prospects for ethnic conflict. One problem, as Horowitz and Welsh point out, is the tendency in multi-ethnic societies for political parties to be organized along ethnic lines. When this happens, party affiliations are a reflection of ethnic identity rather than political conviction. Political systems organized along these lines contain few independent voters, individuals who might cast votes for different parties in different elections. Under these circumstances, elections are mere censuses, and minority parties have no chance of winning power. In countries where parties are organized along ethnic lines and where winner-take-all elections are conducted – not uncommon in many parts of the world – democratic forms might be observed, but minorities remain essentially powerless, victims of a 'tyranny of the majority'.

A related problem is the tendency in multi-ethnic societies for opportunistic politicians to appeal to communal, ethnic and nationalistic impulses. This is often an effective way of mobilizing support and winning elections. Along the way, ethnic minorities are often blamed for many of society's ills; ethnic bashing and scapegoating are common features of electoral politics in many parts of the world. In many multi-ethnic societies, especially those coming out from under years or decades of authoritarian rule, political accommodation and compromise are alien principles. This, along with a lack of familiarity with and interest in coalition-building, undermines the prospects for ethnic rap-prochement and the development of broad-based political communities. The mass media are often used for partisan and propagandistic purposes in ways that further damage interethnic relations.

Finally, many countries have inadequate constitutional safeguards for minority rights. Even in places where minority rights guarantees exist on paper, they are often inadequately enforced. In short, constitutional and political reforms are needed in many places to address important ethnic grievances.

Perceptual explanations

Some explanations of ethnic conflict focus on the false histories that many ethnic groups have of themselves and others. As Posen and Snyder point out (both in Brown 1993), these histories are not subjected to dispassionate, scholarly scrutiny because they are usually passed from generation to genera-tion by word of mouth. These stories become part of a group's lore. They tend to be highly selective in their coverage of events and not unbiased in their interpretation of these events. Distorted and exaggerated with time, these histories present one's own group as heroic, while other groups are demonized. Grievances are enshrined, and other groups are portrayed as inherently vicious and aggressive. Group members typically treat these ethnic myths as received wisdom.

It is not surprising, therefore, that the oral histories of groups involved in an intense rivalry tend to be mirror images of each other. Serbs, for example, see themselves as heroic defenders of Europe and they see Croats as belligerent thugs; Croats see themselves as valiant victims of oppression and Serbs as congenital aggressors. Under such circumstances, the slightest provocation on either side simply confirms deeply held systems of belief and provides the justification for a retaliatory response. Incendiary perceptions such as these, especially when they are held by both parties in a rivalry – which is generally the case – make conflict hard to avoid and even harder to limit. These kinds of belief and perception create tremendous escalatory pressures. The fact that opportunistic politicians use, propagate and embellish these myths compounds the problem.

These problems are particularly pronounced in countries that have experienced long stretches of authoritarian rule. Authoritarian regimes invariably suppress ethnic histories and, in an effort to create their own political myths, manipulate historical facts to suit their own purposes. Furthermore, authoritarian regimes fail to promote objective historical inquiry or scholarly standards of evidence in political discourse. Therefore, it is no surprise that the pernicious effects of ethnic mythology are especially pronounced today in eastern Europe and the former Soviet Union.

Explaining the causes of ethnic conflict

If political science was as advanced as the physical sciences, it might be possible to integrate these systemic, domestic and perceptual factors in an overarching theory of the causes of ethnic conflict. Sadly, that is not possible. It is not yet clear what conditions are necessary and sufficient for the initiation of ethnic hostilities, nor is there a rigorous understanding of why some conflicts are more intense than others. Perhaps this is because, as Albert Einstein once remarked, politics is like physics, only harder.

However, it is possible to delineate some systemic conditions that are *necessary* for ethnic conflict to occur. First, two or more ethnic groups must reside in close proximity. Second, national, regional and international authorities must be too weak to keep groups from fighting and too weak to ensure the security of individual groups. It is far from clear, however, that the presence of these and other systemic factors by themselves will be *sufficient* for ethnic conflict to break out. It seems more likely that systemic conditions will make conflict possible – and some of the systemic factors analysed by Posen might even make it highly probable – but in most cases factors operating at the domestic and perceptual levels will have to be taken into account as well. More effort needs to be put into integrating explanations across these levels of analysis, as Posen and Snyder have begun to do. Equally important, more effort needs to be put into developing testable propositions about the incidence and intensity of ethnic conflict, as Posen, Snyder, Welsh, de Nevers and others have done.

IMPLICATIONS

What are the implications of ethnic conflicts for outside powers and the international community in general? The answer to this question depends on the type of conflict and its course. Three broad types of ethnic conflict outcomes can be identified: peaceful reconciliation, peaceful separation, and war. In other words, groups might agree to live together, agree to live apart, or fight for control of the situation.

Ethnic reconciliation

In some cases, the ethnic groups involved in a dispute may stay associated with each other under some sort of overarching political and legal framework, although they may devise new constitutional arrangements to address specific concerns and grievances. Often, more local autonomy and more explicit minority rights guarantees will be incorporated into new schemas. Austria, Belgium and Switzerland operate under federal arrangements of various kinds that have been altered in various ways without recourse to violence. The onset of democratization provided the occasion for negotiations on more autonomy for Catalans, Galicians and Basques in Spain. Disputes between the Indian government, on the one hand, and Naga, Mizo and Gharo separatists, on the other, were resolved when internal statehood was granted to the latter. Negotiations between Quebec and the other Canadian provinces about Quebec's constitutional status have been continuing for years; whether new, mutually acceptable constitutional arrangements can be devised remains an unresolved issue, however.

When ethnic groups are able to resolve their differences peacefully, ethnic conflicts pose comparatively few problems for outside powers because the international status quo is, by and large, maintained. In cases in which negotiations are the main conduit for conflict resolution, the international community may be able to help mediate disputes, devise minority rights guarantees, and suggest possible constitutional changes. When these internal negotiations are completed, outside powers may have to devise new trading arrangements with newly autonomous regional actors, but little else would change as far as the outside world is concerned.

Ethnic separation

In other cases, groups may be unable to devise new constitutional arrangements that are satisfactory to all concerned. They may consequently decide to
dissolve existing legal ties. In some cases – the break-up of the Soviet Union and
the separation of Czechoslovakia into separate, independent republics – this
process might involve comparatively little bloodshed. Velvet divorces are
likely to be rare, however, because ethnic geography is generally complicated
and because many groups will see fragmentation as a threat to their identity,
their regional influence, and their place in world affairs.

Be that as it may, cases such as these pose several problems for the international community. Specifically, cases such as these disrupt the international
status quo in at least six respects. First, what were previously internal borders
will have to be accepted and respected as international borders. Second, outside
powers will have to decide if and when to extend diplomatic recognition to the
new political entities. If diplomatic recognition is extended, outside powers
will have to decide how to go about establishing and exchanging diplomatic
missions with the new states. Third, outside powers will have to decide if and
when to extend membership in regional and international organizations – such
as the Conference on Security and Cooperation in Europe (CSCE), the
Organization of African Unity (OAU), the Council of Europe (COE), the
European Community (EC), the International Monetary Fund (IMF), the
General Agreement on Tariffs and Trade (GATT) and the United Nations
(UN).

Fourth, international treaties signed by the defunct state will have to be
reformulated. For example, the first Strategic Arms Reduction Treaty
(START I), signed by the United States and the Soviet Union in July 1991,
had to be revised in 1992 to take into account the demise of the Soviet Union;
Soviet strategic nuclear weapons were deployed in four republics – Russia,
Ukraine, Kazakhstan, and Belarus – each of which had to be made a party to
the agreement. In general, outside powers will want to receive assurances from
new states that they will uphold the treaties and commitments undertaken by
the defunct state, with reasonable allowances for the political and economic
circumstances in which the new states find themselves. Fifth, new commercial
and financial relationships will have to be developed with the new states.
Decisions will have to be made about granting most favoured nation trading
status to new states and about providing economic, financial and technical
assistance to these states. Sixth, outside powers will have to assess the implications of these developments for regional stability and the international balance
of power. These implications could be momentous indeed, as they were in the
case of the break-up of the Soviet Union. At a practical level, outside powers
will have to decide how these developments will affect their defence postures
and alliance commitments, and how they will respond to requests from new
states for security guarantees and membership in existing military alliances.

Several eastern European states and several republics of the former Soviet Union have expressed an interest in joining the North Atlantic Treaty Organization (NATO), for example.

Many of these issues will come up before negotiations between the disputing groups have been completed. Outside powers, therefore, will be under great pressure to make the right decisions at the right time. If they fail to do so, they may find that they have disrupted the negotiating process and made war more likely.

The break-up of the Russian Federation, a possibility that cannot be ruled out, would present special problems for the international community. Although Russia's future is particularly murky, it is at least conceivable that economic collapse and ethnically based secessionist movements could lead to the disintegration of the Russian Federation. Bashkortostan, Chechnia, Kalmyk, Tatarstan, Tyumen and Yakutsia (now Sakha) have been lobbying for – and some have already received – substantial amounts of autonomy from Moscow. Should this process lead to the fragmentation of Russia and the collapse of the Russian military, effective control of Russia's 25,000 strategic and tactical nuclear weapons and 40,000 agent tons of chemical weapons could be lost, along with control of Russia's extensive nuclear weapons establishment. Should this occur, international efforts to control the transfer of assembled nuclear weapons, nuclear weapon components, nuclear weapon technology, fissile material, technical expertise and chemical weapon stockpiles would suffer a cataclysmic setback. National and international security policies would have to be radically overhauled as a result.

Ethnic war

In many cases, antagonistic ethnic groups will not be able to agree on new constitutional arrangements or a peaceful separation. Many ethnic disputes consequently become violent, some escalating into all-out interethnic wars. The objectives of the combatants will of course vary from case to case. A minority group might insist on seceding and establishing an independent state of its own; it might demand an independent state within a confederation of states; it might insist on an independent political entity within a new federal structure; it might want more political, economic, cultural or administrative autonomy within existing institutional arrangements; or it might be satisfied with democratic reforms aimed at the implementation of a consociational democracy, ethnic power-sharing or simply more equitable representation. Groups of roughly equal size and power might fight about similar issues or control of the state. Majority groups might fight to retain or extend their influence and position in the rest of the country.

In some cases, those seeking more autonomy are defeated, and central authorities are successful in imposing their own conception of order on the vanquished, as in the case of Tibet. Cases such as these have few direct effects on the international community because the international status quo is unchanged. The issue that is added to the international agenda is whether or not outside powers want to exert pressure on the winner to respect the rights of the loser. In other cases, secessionist groups are successful in breaking away and establishing states of their own, as in Bangladesh, Eritrea and Slovenia, for example. Once this process is completed, the implications for the international community are similar to those for peaceful separation, with the added complication that outside assistance will probably be needed to help the combatants recover from the effects of war. In still other cases, neither party is able to win on the battlefield, and the conflict degenerates into a stalemate. This is the situation today in Angola, Cyprus, Kashmir, Lebanon and Sri Lanka, for example, where neither political nor military solutions are in sight. It is not yet clear how other conflicts – in Afghanistan, Bosnia, the Caucasus, Liberia and Tajikistan, for example – will eventually play out.

Why should outside powers care about ethnic wars? Why should they even think about intervening in these potential quagmires? The short answer to these questions is that some ethnic conflicts create moral imperatives for intervention, and some threaten the strategic interests of outside powers and the international community as a whole. Specifically, ethnic wars can affect the outside world in seven respects.

ETHNIC WARS AND CIVILIAN SLAUGHTER Ethnic wars almost always involve deliberate, systematic attacks on civilians. Why is this so? First, ethnic conflicts are rarely high-technology affairs. They are usually fought by recently formed or recently augmented militias composed of ordinary citizens. A group's civilian population, therefore, is the well spring of its military power; it is the group's main source of military manpower and an essential source of economic and logistical support. Civilian populations are attacked to weaken the military resources on which adversaries can draw. Second, militarily weak groups will have strong incentives to conduct guerrilla campaigns and launch terrorist attacks against soft, high-value targets – cities, towns and villages – in an attempt to force powerful adversaries into acquiescence. Third, the civilian populations of warring groups are often intermingled. When battle lines exist, they often cut through cities, towns, even neighbourhoods. Civilians are inevitably killed under such circumstances. Fourth, ethnic conflicts are often fought for control of particular pieces of territory. To secure complete territorial control, militias seek to drive out civilians from other groups: intimidating, threatening, evicting, assassinating, raping, massacring and commiting genocide along the way. Many ethnic conflicts involve forced expulsions and systematic slaughter of civilians, now known as ethnic cleansing.

Why should outside powers care about civilian slaughter in distant lands? One reason is that it poses a direct challenge to important international norms of behaviour, the maintenance and promotion of which is in the interest of the international community as a whole. The international community has tried to distinguish between combatants and noncombatants in formulating rules and laws about the conduct of war; it will find its distinctions and norms hard to sustain in the long run if it allows them to be trampled in ethnic conflicts, in which civilians are attacked not just indiscriminately, but deliberately and systematically. Another reason for caring about – and taking action against – civilian slaughter is that tolerating it is morally diminishing. The savagery in Bosnia, it could be argued, has been proscribed by the Genocide Convention. If so, the international community has a moral obligation – as well as a legal right – to intervene.

ETHNIC WARS AND REFUGEES Ethnic conflicts often generate staggering numbers of refugees, precisely because they typically involve systematic attacks on civilian populations. It has been estimated, for example, that 100,000 Hindus have fled their homes because of the war in Kashmir, and an equal number of South Ossetians have become refugees as a result of their conflict with Georgia. The war between Armenia and Azerbaijan has generated an estimated 500,000 refugees, and 600,000 people – roughly one-quarter of the total population – have been displaced by the war in Liberia. Conflict in the former Yugoslavia has uprooted an estimated 3 million people, 600,000 of whom have fled the Balkans altogether. In addition, huge numbers of refugees have been generated by the ethnic conflicts in Bhutan, Burma, Cambodia, Ethiopia, Iraq, Sri Lanka, Sudan and Tajikistan.

Refugee problems, especially of this magnitude, affect the outside world in several ways. First, offering sanctuary to refugees can invite military reprisal, thereby drawing the host country into the conflict. Often, fighters mingle with refugee populations, using refugee camps for rest, recuperation and recruitment. Second, if refugees flee to neighbouring countries where large numbers of their ethnic brethren live, their plight can lead their compatriots to become more involved in the original conflict, thereby widening the war. Third, refugees impose tremendous economic costs on host states. Large numbers of impoverished people have to be housed and fed for long and sometimes indefinite periods of time. Fourth, refugees can be seen as potential threats to the cultural identity of host states, especially when refugee communities are large and when they establish their own schools, newspapers, cultural organizations and places of worship. Fifth, refugees can become political forces in host countries, particularly regarding foreign policy issues relating to their homeland. Some host governments worry that refugee communities will turn against them if they pursue uncongenial policies. Sixth and last, when refugee problems pose threats to 'international peace and security', as they often do, the United Nations has a right, if not an obligation, to consider intervening in the crisis.

ETHNIC WARS AND WEAPONS OF MASS DESTRUCTION The proliferation of nuclear weapons and other weapons of mass destruction has added a new dimension to ethnic conflicts: the possibility, however remote, that these weapons could be used in interstate or intrastate ethnic wars. Both India and Pakistan have nuclear and chemical weapon capabilities, and tensions between the two have risen to high levels on more than one occasion in recent years. One of the main sources of tension between the two is India's claim that Pakistan is supporting Kashmiri separatists and Pakistan's claim that India is supporting Sindh insurgents. India and Pakistan are also involved in a prolonged, bitter battle over the Siachen Glacier and their northern border. Russia and Ukraine both have nuclear weapons stationed on their territory, although the latter does not yet have operational control of the weapons on its soil. Although military hostilities between the two are unlikely at present, they cannot be ruled out for the future.

Another possibility is that central authorities could use weapons of mass destruction against would-be secessionists in desperate attempts to maintain the integrity of their states. China has both nuclear and chemical weapon capabilities, and the current regime in Beijing would presumably use every means at its disposal to prevent Tibet, Xinxiang or Inner Mongolia from seceding, which many in these nominally autonomous regions would like to do. Iran has chemical weapon capabilities and is trying to develop or acquire nuclear weapon capabilities. One suspects that Tehran would not rule out using harsh measures to keep Azeris in north-western Iran from seceding, should they become inclined to push this course of action. It is not inconceivable that Russian, Indian and Pakistani leaders could be persuaded to take similar steps in the face of national collapse.

Use of nuclear or chemical weapons in any of these situations would undermine international taboos about the use of weapons of mass destruction and, thus, would be detrimental to international non-proliferation efforts, as well as international security in general. Although the possibility that a state would use weapons of mass destruction against its citizens might appear remote, it cannot be dismissed altogether: the Iraqi government used chemical weapons in attacks on Kurdish civilians in the 1980s.

ETHNIC WARS AND CHAIN REACTION EFFECTS Ethnic conflicts can spread in a number of ways. If a multi-ethnic state begins to fragment and allows some ethnic groups to secede, other groups will inevitably press for more autonomy, if not total independence. This is happening in the former Soviet Union, where fourteen republics successfully broke away from Moscow. Now, other groups want to redefine their relationships with the Russian Federation; as noted earlier, Bashkortostan, Chechnia, Kalmyk, Tatarstan, Tyumen and Yakutsia (now Sakha) have been lobbying for – and some have already received – substantial amounts of autonomy from Moscow. India is fighting tenaciously to retain control of Kashmir because it fears that Kashmiri secession would be the first step in a process that would lead to disintegration of perhaps the most heterogenous state in the world. The view in Delhi, a view not unsupported by logic and history, is that fragmentation is easier to prevent than control.

Other problems are created when state A fragments, allowing B to secede and form its own state. A minority group in B might attempt to secede from B. If it has ethnic ties to A, it might prefer to be associated with its brethren in A. When Croatia seceded from Yugoslavia, for example, Serbs in Croatia attempted to secede from Croatia to maintain ties with Serbs in what was left of Yugoslavia. Similarly, when Georgia seceded from the Soviet Union, South Ossetians attempted to secede from Georgia and pressed for union with their Ossetian brethren in Russia. Other problems are created when the minority group in question has a distinct ethnic identity. It might want its own state, C, either because it fears persecution or simply because establishing an independent state appears to be within the realm of the possible. When Moldova seceded from the Soviet Union, for example, the Gagauz attempted to secede from Moldova and form their own state.

Many of these chain reactions have been accompanied by extremely high levels of violence. This has important international implications and not just because fragmentation and violence can combine to create chaos. The more worrisome prospect, at least from the West's viewpoint, is that fragmentation, violence and chaos in and around Russia could provide a useful pretext for hard-liners in Moscow to seize power. A hard-line regime might then deploy large numbers of troops in unstable parts of Russia. This, in turn, might lead Moscow to attempt to reassert control over unstable neighbouring states. This would inevitably lead to interstate war, and it would constitute a breach of Moscow's pledge not to use military force to resolve international disputes. Developments of this kind, were they to take place, would have profound implications for Moscow's relations with the West and for international security in general, for all the obvious reasons.

Another kind of chain reaction effect is more indirect: successful secessions in one part of the world could inspire secessionist movements in others. The growth of international telecommunications capabilities and international media networks makes these 'demonstration effects' increasingly potent.

ETHNIC WARS AND NEIGHBOURING POWERS Neighbouring powers can become involved in ethnic wars in a variety of ways. First, if state A fragments, allowing B to secede and form its own state, a minority group in B might attempt to secede from B and join with its brethren in C. When Azerbaijan seceded from the Soviet Union, for example, Armenians in Nagorno-Karabakh pushed forward with their demand to secede from Azerbaijan and join Armenia.

Second, when minority groups are persecuted, their brethren in neighbouring states might come to their defence. If Serbia took steps to drive ethnic Albanians from Kosovo, for example, Albania might try to defend them. The war in the Balkans could consequently spread. Many in Moscow argue that Russia should come to the aid of ethnic Russians who are being denied their political and economic rights in Estonia and Latvia. In many cases, of course, those who come to the defence of their brethren have ulterior motives in mind – absorption and expansion. Many believe that Belgrade's assistance to Serbs in Croatia and Bosnia, for example, is part of a blatant campaign to create a 'Greater Serbia'. Similarly, Delhi believes that Pakistani support for Kashmiri insurgents in India reflects Islamabad's desire to control more of Kashmir.

Third, the establishment of new, ethnically defined states might create pressures in neighbouring states for more autonomy or outright independence. As John Chipman points out (in Brown 1993), the creation of an independent Azerbaijani state has worried Iran, which has a large Azeri population. Similarly, the creation of an independent Kazakhstan has troubled China: China fears that Kazakhs in China's Xinxiang Province might try to develop ties with their newly independent brethren or agitate for more autonomy. Similarly, India feared that a federal solution to the conflict in Sri Lanka would give more autonomy to Tamils there than India was willing to grant to Tamils living in the Indian state of Tamil Nadu.

Fourth, if an ethnic group spread over two (or more) states is persecuted in one, the group as a whole could become more nationalistic and militant. This, in turn, could lead to trouble with central authorities in other states. Iraqi persecution of its Kurdish population, for example, has intensified Kurdish sensitivities and, along with the creation of large numbers of Kurdish refugees, has led to increased agitation in Turkey.

Finally, in some cases, states might take advantage of ethnic troubles in neighbouring states to further their own strategic and political ends. Indian support for Sindh separatists in Pakistan, for example, is at least in part motivated by a desire to weaken a regional rival and create another lever in Indian-Pakistani relations.

ETHNIC WARS AND DISTANT INTERESTS In some cases, the interests of distant powers will be affected by ethnic conflicts. In 1990, for example, the United States sent military forces into Liberia to rescue US citizens trapped and endangered by the conflict there. France and Belgium sent forces into Rwanda in 1990 for the same reason. In other cases, states intervene to protect or promote broader strategic and political interests. Saudi Arabia, for example, has tried to contain Iranian influence by opposing Shi'a factions and the Persian-speaking Tajiks in the Afghan civil war; it has thrown its weight behind fundamentalist Pashtuns instead. Although unlikely at the moment, it is possible that intensified ethnic warfare in Iraq in the future could lead Western powers to intervene in an effort to safeguard the Kirkuk oil fields in the north, on Kurdish lands, and the Rumaila oil fields in the south, where large numbers of Shi'a live.

ETHNIC WARS AND INTERNATIONAL ORGANIZATIONS Finally, ethnic wars affect outside powers because they can undermine the credibility of regional and international security organizations. Among its functions, the CSCE is supposed to help European powers anticipate, prevent and resolve European conflicts. One of the reasons for preserving NATO, it is often said, is that it helps to maintain stability in Europe. Neither of these organizations has played an effective role in the Yugoslav crisis, which can only diminish their viability and long-term prospects. Similarly, Bosnian Serb defiance of UN Security Council resolutions and UN humanitarian initiatives, a prominent feature of the Yugoslav crisis, will inevitably impede the development of the United Nations' peacemaking and peacekeeping capabilities. This, in turn, will have an impact on the prospect for ethnic violence and international conflict in general: just as effective intervention would bolster the credibility of international action and possibly have a deterrent effect elsewhere, ineffective intervention has a demonstration effect of its own.

More generally, casual defiance of international norms of behaviour – with respect to minority rights and the use of force, for example – will undercut principles that the international community would do well to maintain and extend. In short, ethnic wars can undermine the long-term ability of outside powers to preserve international order.

RECOMMENDATIONS

What, if anything, can outside powers do to minimize the potential for ethnic violence? The conventional wisdom among many journalists and policy-makers is that there is little outsiders can do because these conflicts are driven by implacable ancient hatred. Their implicit policy recommendation, as Snyder points out, is to steer clear and let conflicts play themselves out. In fact, the causes of ethnic conflict are complex. A number of variables affect the probability and intensity of ethnic conflict, and some of these variables are manipulable; that is, they can be influenced by outside powers.

Jenonne Walker (in Brown 1993) argues persuasively that the best course of action is to address ethnic problems early, before concrete disputes materialize and violence erupts. If ethnic conflicts are easier to prevent than resolve, then the first question to be considered should be: what can outside powers usefully do to ease tensions between and among potentially hostile ethnic groups?

At the systemic level, as Posen argues, groups worry about immediate, imminent and potential security threats. One of the keys to dampening the potential for ethnic violence, therefore, is to address these security concerns. This will not be easy, however. Providing arms to a group, thus enhancing its ability to protect itself, will often increase its offensive military capacities. This, in turn, will be seen as threatening by others. Providing arms to several rival groups in an attempt to establish a balance of power will be problematic as well. Vague security commitments from outsiders who do not have much at stake will not be particularly credible. Security commitments will be more credible

– and, therefore, more effective – if an ethnic war would have important security implications for powerful outside actors.

At the domestic level, three main avenues are open. First, as Snyder suggests, outside powers should help groups develop effective states. This will dampen nationalism in general and ethnic nationalism in particular. Therefore, international economic initiatives should be framed with these overriding political objectives in mind; imposing harsh economic medicine on groups already in turmoil could weaken fragile state structures and trigger a nationalistic backlash. Similarly, outside powers should be careful not to bully groups in turmoil, as this could also weaken already fragile states.

Second, outside powers can help groups develop more representative political institutions. Welsh explains: 'No salient group should be prohibited from a share of effective power. Political institutions should be designed to ensure that minorities are proportionately represented in parliaments and bureaucracies and that their interests – political, cultural and economic – are heeded.' Ideally, governments would be based on broad coalitions. To achieve this, winner-take-all elections should be proscribed. In addition to playing an advisory role, outside powers can help shape political institutions and processes in troubled countries by withholding diplomatic recognition and economic assistance from those who retain or advance unrepresentative schemas.

Third, outside powers should insist that cultural diversity be respected, even nourished, in multi-ethnic states. At a minimum, outside powers should insist that discrimination against minorities be prohibited. All ethnic groups should be equal before the law. All should have the same political and economic rights and opportunities. All should be entitled to worship as they see fit. As far as possible, ethnic groups should be allowed to use their own languages in schools, bureaucracies, parliaments and courts. Legal mechanisms for redress of grievances should be established if they do not already exist.

In December 1992 the UN General Assembly passed a Declaration on the Rights of Persons Belonging to National or Ethnic, Religious and Linguistic Minorities that outlined the international community's views on these issues. However, as Kathleen Newland points out (in Brown 1993), this declaration, like other UN human rights instruments, contains no implementation or enforcement provisions. On the whole, Newland maintains the UN human rights regime is weak. To improve the situation, outside powers and the United Nations should do more to help states draft effective minority rights safeguards. They should develop more effective capabilities to detect minority rights violations and be more aggressive in deploying monitors in potentially troubled areas. Indeed, deploying monitors might help deter violations in the first place. In addition, outside powers should withhold diplomatic recognition, economic assistance, and membership in regional and international organizations from new states until they develop effective minority rights safeguards. Trial memberships in regional and international institutions should be granted in cases in which the prospects for minorities are uncertain.

Finally, outside powers should impose sanctions – diplomatic, economic, even military – on states that fail to grant and protect these rights. In short, outside powers should do more to help develop and enforce minority rights standards and utilize more effectively the considerable leverage they all too often squander.

At the perceptual level, outside powers should try to help ethnic groups develop better histories of each other. Posen suggests that oral histories should be openly discussed with other groups and assessed by disinterested parties. Where possible, competing versions of events should be reconciled. This process should involve outsiders, including academics and representatives from non-governmental organizations. Obviously, as Posen points out, a few conferences will not undo 'generations of hateful politicized history, bolstered by reams of more recent propaganda'. However, these exercises would cost little and, therefore, should be tried.

What should outside powers do if preventive measures fail, violence erupts and an ethnic war breaks out? Under what conditions should outside powers intervene in such a war? Drawing on the arguments developed by Robert Cooper and Mats Berdal (in Brown 1993), five conditions should be met before action is taken. First, there should be either a strategic or moral imperative for action. Second, those contemplating intervention should have clear political objectives. If military forces are to be used, political objectives must be translatable into clear military objectives. Third, one must have options – diplomatic, political, economic, military – that will lead to the attainment of one's objectives. Fourth, one must be willing and able to persevere in the face of adversity. Ethnic wars tend to be both long-lasting and intense: warring groups are highly motivated because, in many cases, they believe their existence is on the line. If outsiders are to impose their will on such combatants, they will have to be determined. Multinational or international efforts, therefore, must be based on a strong, sustainable political consensus; legitimization in the form of strong backing from the UN Security Council is extremely important in this regard. Fifth, before one intervenes in an ethnic war, one should identify the circumstances that would lead one to withdraw. These are general guidelines, to be sure, but policy-makers need to keep such considerations in mind when they contemplate intervening in ethnic wars. Discrete decisions should be made one way or the other; otherwise, leaders run the risk of gradually becoming involved in conflicts about which they care little and can do less.

In contemplating intervention in ethnic wars, it is important to note that diplomatic efforts are unlikely to be successful unless they are backed by the threat of economic and military sanctions. It is also important to note that military operations will be more effective at keeping combatants apart than bringing people together. Military interventions, by themselves, will not resolve the underlying strategic, political and perceptual problems that propel ethnic conflicts. The key to true conflict resolution is the development of civil societies in genuine political communities. That, however, is something about which the international community still has much to learn – and not just in conjunction with ethnic conflict.

REFERENCES

Brown, Michael E., ed. (1993), *Ethnic Conflict and International Security*, Princeton University Press, Princeton.
Horowitz, Donald (1985), *Ethnic Groups in Conflict*, University of California Press, Berkeley.
Lijphart, Arend (1990), 'The Power-Sharing Approach', in *Conflict and Peacemaking in Multiethnic Societies*, Lexington Books, Lexington, Mass., pp. 491–509.
Smith, A. D. (1986), *The Ethnic Origins of Nations*, Basil Blackwell, Oxford.

Conflict in Northern Ireland
W. HARVEY COX

When the Downing Street Declaration was issued by Messrs Major and Reynolds on 15 December 1993, it was, to the day, eight years and one month since their predecessors had signed the Anglo-Irish Agreement at Hillsborough. The Agreement's proclaimed aims were those of 'promoting peace and stability in Northern Ireland; helping to reconcile the two major traditions in Ireland; creating a new climate of friendship and cooperation between the people of the two countries; and improving cooperation in combatting terrorism.'

HILLSBOROUGH – UNIONISM SAYS NO

Any assessment at, for instance, the fifth anniversary of its signing would have had to conclude that it had largely been a failure. Its main achievement had simply been survival. It had proved, as its framers had intended, unsinkable by any unionist or republican opposition. It set up nothing internal to Northern Ireland, unlike in 1974, that anyone there could 'bring down'. But it had not, to that date, perceptibly advanced the cause of peace and stability, or reconciled the two traditions in Ireland. It may have furthered, somewhat, the lesser of the four initial objectives, but as for the major ones, in the short run at least it actually set those back. The statistics of violence told a story in themselves. In the three years to 31 December 1985 there were 195 deaths in Northern Ireland due to the political conflict; in the three years from 1 January 1986 there were 247. (In 1991, indeed, the annual toll reached 94, the highest since 1982.) The years after the Agreement saw the Provisional IRA engage in some of its most spectacular offensive actions, such as the bombs at Enniskillen on 8 November 1987, at Deal on 22 September 1989, the murder of Ian Gow, MP and Thatcher confidant, on 30 July 1990, and a widening campaign on the European mainland, including the abortive would-be bombing at Gibraltar on 6 March 1988.

But the most important feature of the aftermath of the Agreement was its rejection by the unionist community.

[. . .]

But, despite massive demonstrations, the unionist reaction was striking less for its intensity than its unanimity. Opinion polls showed Protestant support for the Agreement at about 8 per cent and opposition at 75–80 per cent (different polls). [. . .]

Support for the Agreement among Catholics was not as strong as opposition to it clearly was among Protestants. One poll, for the BBC, showed 54 per cent Catholic approval, but as much as 35 per cent who didn't know or had no clear view. Clearly, Catholics had little reason actively to disapprove of something intended for their benefit, but would naturally want to wait and see whether it actually would be so. Meanwhile the obvious discomfiture of Protestants with the Agreement was its own incentive to Catholics to derive at least qualified satisfaction from the introduction of the Republic's Government into the governing process of Northern Ireland, in however limited a way. Some years on, the Northern Irish Catholic community had observably made great advances. [. . .] but, as with so much else to do with the Agreement, it would be impossible to quantify how much change to attribute to it; most would have happened anyway.

On the other hand, the Agreement, while advancing the cause of peace in Northern Ireland very little, did serve other key purposes of the two signatory governments. The Irish Government gained a foothold in the constitutional machinery of Northern Ireland for the first time, and ensured that it would be a player in any future negotiations, however distant these might be. It is arguable that the complex of negotiations of the 1990s could not have got off the ground without the intergovernmental framework laid down at Hillsborough. On a more immediate level, the Secretariat at Maryfield enabled the Irish Government to keep more closely in touch with the governing process in Northern Ireland, and to articulate, through the Inter-Governmental Conference, the preoccupations and needs of the nationalist community. The British gained a permanent collaborator in the management of Northern Ireland. Tensions between the two governments were not absent in the post-1985 period (e.g. extradition, on which the Republic was slow to deliver, was one running sore) but the Conference, and Maryfield, did appear to be a means of speeding up the healing process when tensions arose. The British also secured a lessening of the international opprobrium which their handling of Northern Ireland had earned; especially, for some years, American opinion was more muted. Finally, there were improvements in cross-border security co-operation, showing itself in arms finds if not in shared intelligence.

[. . .]

The paradox of the Anglo-Irish Agreement was that for several years it appeared to have become in itself the most immediate obstacle to the achievement of its own proclaimed purposes. To a degree the implication of Hillsborough was the turning upside down of 1973–4, by starting at the intergovernmental level and then, in time, moving on to local power-sharing, with an 'Irish dimension' already in place. But this was no more palatable to unionists than Sunningdale had been in 1973–4. Now they were refusing to consider talks on power-sharing or any other constitutional development until the Agreement was removed. This was a recipe for stalemate, unless and until the unionists were to climb down and accept, *de facto*, the hated Agreement. In 1912–14 and again in 1974, the unionist community had been prepared to fight a government taking a route they detested. On this occasion the Agreement was not sufficiently tangible a threat, and 'fight' not a sufficiently plausible or effective response. Hence the main actual response: sullen impotence. By the late 1980s the indications were that the unionist community, though disliking the Agreement and its provisions as always, were prepared to live with it, especially as, self-evidently, the more lurid prophecies as to its meaning for the Union had not been realized, and it had changed little enough on the day-to-day level. The *Garda Siochana* was still not directing the traffic in Newry, let alone Donegall Square. In 1987 the unionist community showed signs of recovery from the shock of the Agreement; some of them were now thrashing around for ways forward either within or without it. The Ulster Defence Association produced its *Common Sense* report in January 1987, advocating a power-sharing devolved administration but without any Irish dimension; while in July 1987 a think-tank of three younger Unionist leaders, McCusker, Robinson and Millar, came up with the *Task Force* report also advocating talks to produce a devolved power-sharing government. This was unacceptable to the two Unionist party leaders, though they did enter talks about talks with the government, in which they continued to insist on the suspension of the Agreement as a prerequisite for political progress. Shortly after the failure of the *Task Force* report one of its principal authors, Frank Millar, left politics altogether for journalism, a sign of the failure of unionism, under its then leadership and in its current predicament, to offer hope to newer generations within its ranks. (At the same time John Cushnahan, leader of the Alliance Party, resigned from Northern Irish politics for similar reasons, though he became a *Fine Gael* MEP for Munster in June 1989.) In a similar vein of seeking a way out was the establishment of Conservative constituency associations in Northern Ireland in 1989. The Conservatives had some initial success in North Down, capturing six council seats in May 1989, but secured a meagre 2.9 per cent in May 1990 in the Upper Bann by-election.

BROOKE'S INITIATIVE

We might date, crudely, the end of the post-Hillsborough phase and the beginning of a new one, leading to the Downing Street Declaration of December 1993, with the arrival of Peter Brooke as the new Secretary of State on 24 July 1989. Involved neither in the negotiation nor the selling of the Anglo-Irish Agreement, a new Secretary of State for a new decade was well placed to make a fresh attempt to move things on. [. . .]

Brooke observed [. . .] that the Provisional IRA could not be defeated militarily, and that he would not rule out talks with *Sinn Féin* after violence had ended. The government would be 'imaginative'. This was welcomed by the (Social Democrat and Labour Party) and by *Sinn Féin*, though not by Unionist politicians. For a time, Brooke was almost a figure of fun (in a thoroughly unfunny situation), a kind of elderly political Wooster. He was, reputedly, a clever man; if so, part of his cleverness lay in concealment of this behind a mask, almost, of well-meaning naivety.

Observers, already in a mood of puzzlement about Brooke, reacted with some surprise to his announcement, in a speech at Bangor on 9 January 1990, that he had found 'common ground' between the constitutional parties in Northern Ireland, such as to encourage him to believe there could be inter-party talks about 'workable and acceptable arrangements for the exercise of devolved powers'. [. . .] On 5 July 1990 Brooke had to announce to the Commons that he had not been able to achieve agreement on a formula for talks.

Throughout the Brooke initiative, the basic formula for talks was that put forward persistently by John Hume throughout the 1980s – that there were three dimensions to the conflict in Northern Ireland which needed to be discussed and resolved, viz.:

- that between the two communities in Northern Ireland
- that between North and South in Ireland
- that between Great Britain and Ireland

Unionists went along with this, if at all, with reluctance, some adding that an initial fourth dimension, Great Britain–Northern Ireland, was being ignored. The problem the talks process faced was that the two main groups in

Northern Ireland had agendas that were wider apart than ever. From October 1982, when he led the SDLP into boycotting Prior's Assembly, John Hume had pursued an 'Irish dimension' strategy, and the SDLP was not interested in any local Northern Ireland constitutional developments which sidelined it. The Anglo-Irish Agreement was the key success of this strategy to date. What was notable about the role of Dublin in the post-Agreement period, especially after the departure from office of Garret FitzGerald in March 1987, was the extent to which it not only *endorsed* John Hume's strategy but appeared virtually to have contracted out its Northern policy to him. In contrast, while Unionists *might* have contemplated some form of devolved administration with power-sharing, the Ulster Unionist Party under James Molyneaux was now largely integrationist, as was 60 per cent of the unionist population, according to an opinion poll of July 1991. And as far as unionists were concerned, they would not accept an Irish dimension that had any substance beyond the consultative and symbolic. On the contrary, one of their main objectives in the Brooke process remained that of finding a way of getting rid of the Agreement.

The 1990 phase of the pre-talks process failed to reach the talks start-line. Ostensibly the main problem was the involvement of Dublin in the process, Unionists insisting that Dublin be brought in on the talks only when sub-stantial agreement had been reached on the proposed structure of government for Northern Ireland, whereas the SDLP and Dublin wanted talks on their agenda of 'sharing the island of Ireland' at an early stage. The Unionists moreover insisted that they be included in the talks as part of the British delegation.

The Unionists' critics chose to view them as using procedural points purely as obstructive ploys. This may have been true; but it devalued to mere tactics the political consequences of the deep divide between the two traditions in Ireland, which the Agreement had done nothing to narrow. On the other hand, no party, including both the Unionist ones, was willing to accept the oppro-brium of being held responsible for the failure of the process. The talks process would go on – but not for the time being.

1991 opened to one of the bloodiest and most despair-generating phases in the history of post-Agreement Northern Ireland. The Provisional IRA killed eight Protestant workers at Teebane Cross, County Tyrone, on 17 January 1991, and the inevitable retaliation came at Graham's betting shop on the Lower Ormeau road on 5 February, with five Catholic deaths. (On 29 August 1991 came the 3000th death since 1969.) All these were occasions of public pressure for peace, and calls for the politicians to come to the negotiating table.

Brooke's explorations eventually bore fruit in an agreement to embody the three territorial dimensions in three 'strands' of talks, beginning with the internal Northern Irish dimension. The one concession, a meagre one, won by the Unionists, was that there would be a ten-week gap in the meetings of the Inter-Governmental Conference, within which the discussions could take place; and a start for the strand one talks was due to take place on 30 April 1991.

However the parties did not actually sit down together till 17 June, owing to procedural difficulties which had not been dealt with before 30 April – chiefly the venue for the second strand of talks, when the Irish government would be involved, and the identity of a chairman for these.

The British proposal of Lord Carrington was unacceptable to the Unionists, owing to his association with the Foreign Office, which they believed was out to wind down British commitments everywhere, and which they chiefly blamed for the Anglo-Irish Agreement. There were dark hints that perhaps Carrington's name had emerged as a deliberate attempt to wrong-foot the Unionists – not a difficult task at this time. But by the time this issue was resolved with the appointment, instead, of the Australian Sir Ninian Stephen, 17 June left too little time before the next due meeting of the Inter-Governmental Conference. Unionist pleas for the seven lost weeks to be treated as 'injury time' were unavailing, and, with the next Inter-Governmental Conference due on 16 July, the inter-party talks broke down on 3 July.

What was notable about this episode was the clear evidence that the British government valued its relationship with Dublin, and specifically the Agreement's legacy of the Inter-Governmental Conference, more highly than the sensibilities of their own citizens of the British tradition in Ireland. This might have offered proof, if proof were needed, that the Anglo-Irish Agreement was coming into its own as a permanent feature of the management of Northern Ireland.

In announcing the failure of the talks, Brooke promised to be listening out for 'rustlings in the undergrowth', for signs that they could resume at a later date but, although there was some fencing around the issues that autumn of 1991, they ran into the British election timetable and were not resumed again until Sir Patrick Mayhew, the new Secretary of State, reconvened them on 30 April 1992. On 1 July Mayhew announced the formal launch of strands two and three, though strand one had not been completed. The talks resumed in the autumn of 1992; on this occasion, the Unionists travelled to Dublin, for the first time since the foundation of the two Irish states. Dublin's failure to appreciate the significance of this gesture on the Unionists' part was notable. There was no sign of movement from Dublin on articles two and three of the Irish constitution. The talks came to a stalemated end on 10 November. The participants issued a statement saying that, while unable to find a basis for a settlement, nevertheless they had 'identified and discussed most, if not all, of the elements which would comprise an eventual settlement', had developed a clear understanding of each others' positions, and established 'constructive dialogue on the ways in which an accommodation might be reached on some of the key issues which divide them'. Sir Patrick Mayhew thought the objective of the talks process remained 'valid and achievable' and all participants 'had a duty to build on what had begun' (*Irish Times*: 11 November 1992). Later, on 7 April 1993, John Major, visiting Northern Ireland, said 'I think many people underestimate the progress that has actually been made in the talks' (*Irish Times*: 8 April 1993). This could do little to gloss over the essential fact of deadlock. On 24 January 1993 James Molyneaux said that the inter-party talks were actually *creating* instability.

There was bound to be some truth in this. 1993 opened to the prospect of yet another year of deadlock and instability. Dramatic moves were, in fact, afoot to break the deadlock, in a quite different quarter from the stumbling (and now indefinitely halted) three strands process. The public were not, however, to know of this until most of the year's leaves had fallen from the trees. It is remarkable how well-kept a secret this was, considering how leak-prone the British governmental system in general has shown itself to be. The breakthrough was, of course, the reopening of contact between the government and the Provisionals, with a view to a cessation of the 'armed struggle'.

1992 – A UNIONIST OPPORTUNITY

If this opened up for the British government one possible route out of its long Northern Irish entanglement and for the Provisionals an opportunity to move, with their agenda, closer to the centre stage, the Unionists, for their part, found themselves presented with an unexpected, if temporary, political resource with which to constrain any freedom of the government to move too far in an antiunionist direction. While the 1992 General Election failed to produce the change of government that had seemed, to the last minute, on the cards, it did produce a parliamentary situation in which the Northern Ireland MPs enjoyed a strategic position that had not obtained since the dying years of the Callaghan government. John Major had a parliamentary majority of twenty-one, just above safety level but, given the early re-establishment (as at Newbury in May 1993) of the tendency for governments to lose most, if not all, by-elections, it was highly vulnerable to attrition. Moreover the government faced a fractious Conservative Party. On Europe, in particular, it could not rely on total support. Unionist muscle was first shown in the great pit-closures fracas of October 1992, when the nine 'Official' Ulster Unionist MPs abstained; in November they joined Labour in voting against the government over the Maastricht Treaty. On 22 July 1993 the nine Unionists helped secure the government in the vote on Maastricht, when it otherwise risked defeat. This support, doubling the Conservatives' effective majority, was widely believed to have been part of a broader 'understanding' and there was much speculation as to what might be the *quid pro quo*. Certainly in December 1993, immediately after the Downing Street Declaration, the Unionists got confirmation of the earlier earnest of the government's intention to deliver a Commons Select Committee on Northern Ireland, something of an integrationist symbol for which James Molyneaux had been pressing for a decade. While Labour spokesmen denounced the July 'deal' and deplored its effects on the inter-party talks process, it was simply part of a tradition, going back at least to 1886, that Irish parties of whatever kidney would naturally choose to exploit parliamentary mathematics to their own advantage whenever there arose an opportunity to do so. Moreover, Labour was in a particularly unfavourable position for calling 'foul' since, only a few days before the Maastricht showdown, Kevin McNamara, the shadow Secretary of State, had been associated with a document advocating joint authority, a position that might have been calculated to drive the Ulster Unionists into the Conservatives' arms.

[. . .]

THE PIRA – 'SICKENING THE BRITS'

The Anglo-Irish Agreement had had little evident effect in preventing the PIRA from pursuing its own strategy of 'sickening the Brits'. In their armed campaign the Provisionals could frequently rely on the British themselves to turn even PIRA failure to good PIRA account. They could ensure that for the British, Northern Ireland would continue to embroil them in, as O'Leary and McGarry strikingly termed it, 'the politics of embarrassment' (1993: 171).

If the classic illustration of this was the handling of the 1981 hunger strikes by a British administration which appeared never to have heard of Easter 1916, the post-Agreement years produced a fresh crop of their own. One was the Birmingham Six and the interrelated Guildford Four and Maguire Seven cases, with their blatant evidence of justice denied and the vindication of all republican and left-wing charges against the British police and judicial system. The Six were finally released on 14 March 1991. In the furore and embarrassment the Birmingham Twenty-One, murdered by the PIRA in November 1974, were forgotten. Even the unionist side had their cause for grievance, in the case of 'the UDR Four'.

Another public relations fiasco was the aftermath of Gibraltar shootings of 6 March 1988. The first reports of these to be given by British officials were simply untrue; in particular the first statement from the Ministry of Defence on the afternoon of the shooting spoke about the finding of a suspected bomb, and a later one said it had been dealt with. This remained the official line until the following afternoon, when Sir Geoffrey Howe said in the Commons that no bomb had been found and that the three PIRA members were unarmed. (The bomb was subsequently found, but at Marbella; it had not yet been moved to Gibraltar.) [. . .]

Another case, redolent of British policy made without apparent thinking through of longer-term implications, was the introduction of the broadcasting ban in the autumn of 1988. The immediate precipitating event was the killing, on 20 August 1988, of eight young soldiers in a bus at Aughnacloy. The 'ban' emerged out of an emergency meeting of Ministers held at Downing Street. Introduced by Douglas Hurd in the Commons on 19 October, it gave the impression of being something produced at short notice from a scraping of the bottom of a barrel (though it had been discussed by Ministers earlier in the year). At first the 'ban' appeared quite effective, in that it did keep *Sinn Féin* off the screens, since broadcasters tended to opt to avoid them in cases where circumstances did not *compel* them to cover *Sinn Féin*. *Sinn Féin* regarded the ban's chief effect as preventing them explaining themselves to their own supporters and potential sympathizers. There was a strong civil liberties case against the ban; but its fatal weakness as an instrument of broadcasting policy was also its vagueness. Broadcasters considered this unfair, in that it placed on them the onus for interpretation of the regulation, a task properly belonging to government but which the latter refused to shoulder itself. [. . .]

But undoubtedly the PIRA's biggest success was in their capacity to keep their campaign going regardless of whatever the British did. On 7 February 1991, they brought their war to the British Cabinet directly, for the second time, with their daring and ingeniously conceived mortar bomb attack on 10 Downing Street. But the most ominous development was their pair of bombs in the City of London on 10 April 1992 (the day after the General Election) and just over a year later on 24 April 1993. The first, at the Baltic Exchange, caused damage estimated at first at £750 million or more. Though later much reduced, it was still more than all the criminal damage claims in Northern Ireland since 1969. The second, at Bishopsgate, was even more costly, and extensively damaged the buildings of several prestigious international financial houses. Where bombs on Protestant towns in Northern Ireland, or assassinations of British military or diplomatic personnel on the continent, were part of a long war in which either side could square up for a test of endurance, the two city bombs, like the attack at Heathrow in March 1994, were aimed at a jugular vein of the British state. No government, least of all a Conservative one, could afford to have the PIRA destroy the one economic complex left in Britain which still has a world class role – the financial centre of the City of London. As for British public opinion, at the very least the message conveyed by this campaign was that the Government had failed to keep the conflict within Ireland, and would probably continue so to fail.

The PIRA was fond of using the image that the British were painfully slow learners, but *they* were wondrously patient teachers. The British were, in fact, learning quite a lot – about the need to go as far as possible, and to be as explicit as possible, in explaining to the Provisionals the terms on which they were still in Northern Ireland, and the scope and limits of any putative British negotiating position *vis-à-vis* Irish republicanism.

TOWARDS AN UNARMED STRATEGY

The Provisionals, for their part, had also been engaging in a far-reaching process of reappraisal of their position, their view of Britain, the Republic and the unionist community. This was going on throughout the period from Hillsborough to Downing Street, though it was never quite clear how far it would go, or how far it was the work of an avant-garde who might have much difficulty in bringing the whole movement along with the consequences of their analyses. The first signs of fresh thinking appeared in the 1987 document, *Scenario for Peace*. Subsequently, *Ard Fheis* reports and other *Sinn Féin* documents indicate that an 'unarmed strategy' was under active consideration from at least 1991. Not only had the 'ballot box', when allied to the armalite, reached the apparent limit of its scope in the May 1985 elections (when fifty-one *Sinn Féin* councillors were elected) but, more importantly, the Provisionals' 'Southern strategy' had failed miserably. Demonstrably lacking significant support in the Republic, and with the SDLP now enjoying wind assistance from the Anglo-Irish Agreement and pulling away from *Sinn Féin* in popular support, the movement was increasingly stalemated. *Sinn Féin* as a political party had shown itself as having several pockets of significant support, but it was manifestly ghettoized within those limits. As long as the armed struggle went on, so would it confine the scope for republican political influence.

To some degree, the very success of the ballot box strategy, limited though it was, fed back new viewpoints into the *Sinn Féin* thought process. Many of *Sinn Féin*'s councillors had deeply felt community serving objectives, which they could best pursue by some discreet distancing of themselves from the physical force element in their tradition. Importantly, violence came to be seen less as the 'cutting edge' of the struggle than simply a symptom of the conflict. As Fintan O'Toole put it in November 1993, the community had 'remade *Sinn Féin* in its own image, forcing it to move away from the assumed authority of violence and towards the earned authority of hard graft' (*Irish Times*: 24 November 1993).

As for Britain, John Hume, in the abortive Hume-Adams talks of 1987–8, had tried to persuade *Sinn Féin* that Britain was effectively neutral (following Article 1c of the Anglo-Irish Agreement) on the constitutional future of Northern Ireland, and did not stand in the way of an Irish unity achieved by the persuasion of those who opposed it by those who supported it. From 1990 British official statements and speeches gave support to this view, especially Peter Brooke's November speech. *Sinn Féin*'s *Towards a Lasting Peace in Ireland*, launched at its February 1992 *Ard Fheis* in Ballyfermot, set out how far they had now travelled in developing a new view of Britain's role in the conflict – not just as the original creators of the problem who should simply withdraw, but now as potential *facilitators* of 'a democratic resolution and a lasting peace'. [. . .]

Sinn Féin was thus turning on its head its traditional demand for precipitate British withdrawal leading to a united Ireland. The implication now was that Britain's role was to *remain* 'in' Northern Ireland for the time being in a new role as 'persuader' of the unionists. While the latter were not to be accorded the freedom to withhold consent to unification, since 'the British bestowed unionist veto needs to be removed', the specific arrangements for attaining unity did require a measure of unionist consent (referred to as 'a debate about national reconciliation') and Britain was to facilitate this. *Sinn Féin* writings, of course, continued to accuse Britain of political, economic and military repression, and of having a pro-unionist political agenda. Nonetheless, the roots of a possible 'unarmed strategy' can be seen in the new doctrine that saw Britain as a key member of the 'ranks of the persuaders' for a new, unified Irish dispensation.

In parallel with its reappraisal of the British the republican movement was reappraising its view of the Protestant community. As with its view of Britain, the reappraisal repositioned the Protestants. Hitherto seen as political collaborators in imperialism, of little account in their own right, now the Protestants were appreciated as a group with real fears and insecurities – which were also attributed (with good reason) to the British connection. Unionists, argued Gerry Adams, have rarely had confidence in the British government; they were victims of a history they had not made. Out of unionism's historical identity crisis arose an opportunity for 'national reconciliation'. Adams, and even more, Mitchel McLaughlin, who was emerging as an important contributor to the new approach, argued for an inclusive, broad Irishness, in a language which echoed more the republicanism of the 1790s than the Catholic–nationalist approach of the mid-twentieth century. *Sinn Féin*'s approach to unionism still nonetheless presumed that they had no right not to consent to unification, and that unification remained the inevitable end, predetermined by demography and the certainty of sometime British withdrawal.

THE BRITISH RESPONSE – BROOKE AND MAYHEW

What is striking about *Sinn Féin*'s more advanced language in the early 1990s, and that publicly used by British politicians, is the extent to which they were beginning to converge. While the public politics of solution-seeking was focused upon Brooke's faltering talks process, vital developments were unfolding behind the scenes, namely the reactivation of contact between the British government and the Provisionals. [. . .] A message had been sent to a *bona fide* intermediary, indicating a British wish for a meeting between him, a British Government representative, and Martin McGuinness, the foremost link between political *Sinn Féin* and the PIRA. The meeting took place in October 1990, McGuinness playing the role of silent observer (such was the

Provisionals' scepticism). Within weeks came Peter Brooke's speech of 9 November, one of the most significant speeches on Ireland made by any British politician since 1968 (if not long before). Although Brooke affirmed the majority consent principle once again, he portrayed the British as neutral on the Union, an honest broker between the two Irish aspirations. [... He] then pointed to the prospect of an inclusive political settlement, which would involve reconciliation 'between the communities in Northern Ireland; within Ireland; and between the peoples on both these islands'. He concluded: 'The British Government has no selfish strategic or economic interest in Northern Ireland: our role is to help, enable and encourage.'

This speech went further than any British minister had gone before to spell out that partition, and the British involvement in Ireland, was a product of Irish realities, not British interests or even preferences. [...] Brooke's speech was not, of course, enough to satisfy the Provisionals, but they had received an advance copy of it and, Dillon reports, they debated it with great interest. Meanwhile, their campaign went on in 1991 unabated, including, early on, the mortar attack on the Cabinet in 10 Downing Street on 7 February.

Despite this, contact was maintained, with the PIRA continuing to be highly suspicious of British overtures. These continued after the 10 April 1992 Baltic Exchange bomb, indicating not only that the British were serious in wanting dialogue, but also that the message intended by the bombing was getting home. The British kept the Provisionals informed of the progress of the inter-party talks chaired by Sir Ninian Stephen. In October 1992 the British told the Provisionals of their scepticism about the future of the talks and indicated the possibility of a joint British-Irish 'imposed solution', in the framing of which the Provisionals would have an input.

Britain's next major public move in response to the Provisionals came in Mayhew's Coleraine speech of 16 December 1992, when, returning to Brooke's theme of two years earlier, he was even more explicit in spelling out what the British government now offered to Irish nationalism in general, and, perhaps, the Republicans in particular. He identified four dividing lines in Northern Ireland – those of national identities, major religious groupings, cultural traditions, and that deriving from the economic and social disadvantages experienced by the minority community. Problems required a solution that recognized those divisions. He recognized that the nationalist aspiration to a united Ireland was no less legitimate than the unionist one to maintain the Union. 'Provided it was advocated constitutionally, there can be no proper reason for excluding any political objective from discussion. Certainly not the objective of an Ireland united through broad agreement fairly and freely achieved.' Then came the heart of the speech, the reward awaiting republicans following a cessation of violence:

In the event of a genuine and established cessation of violence, the whole range of responses that we have had to make to that violence could, and would, inevitably be looked at afresh. When terrorism is seen to have genuinely ended, there will indeed be profound consequences for the maintenance of law and order, and for the administration of justice.

[. . .]

There was an element of disingenuousness in Mayhew's disavowal of predeterminacy of British 'steering'. Integration with Britain, the Ulster Unionist preference, was predetermined *out*, just as power-sharing local institutions, with an all-Ireland dimension, were just as surely predetermined *in*. As with Brooke's two years earlier, this speech spelled out to the republicans that Britain recognized the validity of their aspirations and their cultural identity; that Britain had 'no self interest leading to pursue a separate agenda of its own', and held out the carrot of the consequences, on the security forces side, of a cessation of PIRA violence. But, in this, and in subsequent speeches (Belfast, 2 March; Liverpool, 23 April) Mayhew at no time pointed to a scenario of British withdrawal or explicit support for a reunification of Ireland. The Provisionals, if they were to take up Mayhew's offer, would have to settle for less than the goal to which twenty-three years of armed struggle had been aimed. On the other hand, the offer was not inconsiderable. A declaration of neutrality on the future of Northern Ireland, plus full recognition of Irish identities within it, including the pledge to remove as soon as practicable the legislation prohibiting street-names in any language other than English (in practice street-names were in Irish only in republican districts already, and Derry City Council had erected Irish names alongside the English ones, in the City centre); plus the removal of the security force presence from nationalist areas, could be claimed by the Provisionals specifically as an achievement of theirs rather than one won by the SDLP. It was not 'freedom' in the republican sense; but with their sense of Irish history the Provisionals would have been conscious of the possibility that, as Michael Collins said of the 1921 Treaty, it *could* mean the freedom to win freedom, as they would understand (and work for) it.

1993 – TOWARDS DOWNING STREET

The Provisionals' response to Mayhew's Coleraine message came at their *Ard Fheis* in February 1993, when in a speech by Martin McGuinness, *Sinn Féin* appeared to accept the concept of a talks process involving all sides in Ireland. [. . .] A first meeting was held with an intermediary on 22 February. The British account of this meeting, released with yet another flurry of embarrassed confusion in November, had the Provisionals saying that 'The conflict is over, but we need your advice on how to bring it to a close.' The Provisionals themselves repudiated this wording, and certainly this would have been a remarkably grovelling message to have come from a body still to explode its two Warrington bombs and its Bishopsgate one. Dillon attributes the British wording simply to a desire to create the impression in Britain that the exchanges of spring 1993 were entirely due to a PIRA decision to end its campaign (Dillon 1994).

Three days after the second, fatal, Warrington bomb (i.e. on 20 March) dialogue continued at a meeting between McGuinness and the British representative. The *Sinn Féin* internal report of this meeting, released in November 1993 and referred to subsequently in October 1994 by McGuinness, is crucial (if true and correct). It has the British representative saying that Mayhew was determined to have *Sinn Féin* play a part in political negotiations, his Coleraine speech being a significant pointer in this direction. Mayhew, said the British representative:

> wants Sinn Féin to play a part . . . because it cannot work without them. Any settlement not involving all of the people North and South won't work. A North/South settlement that won't frighten the Unionists. The final solution is Union. It is going to happen anyway. The historical train – Europe – determines that. We are committed to Europe. The Unionists will have to change. This island will be as one (Dillon 1994: 238).

Mayhew subsequently denied that any British representative was *authorized* to say that government policy was aimed at unification. He did not, however, deny that the meeting did take place, with approval at the topmost level, or indicate precisely what the British representative *was* authorized to say.

Talks between *Sinn Féin* and John Hume of the SDLP recommenced on 10 April, and from this point on much of the dynamic of the moves towards a Provisional cessation of violence based upon a set of agreed declaratory principles about the parameters of a 'solution' lay in the Hume–Adams talks.

In all, the British and *Sinn Féin* exchanged sixteen written and four oral messages in the spring of 1993. According to Dillon's account, by mid-May 1993 John Major had decided he would talk to the Provisionals. However, he was dissuaded almost at once from this course by Cabinet colleagues who felt that, in the aftermath of Warrington and Bishopsgate, and with the government's parliamentary position weak without Ulster Unionist support, the political risks were too high. Thereafter the government was looking for a way out, or at least of avoiding serious commitment to the Provisionals. At the same time, the government had to head off a risk that the latter would expose its secret exchanges with them. The logic of this pointed to seeking an accord with Dublin. This would override the Hume–Adams talks, drown out any Provisional revelations about the spring series of communications, and engage both governments in the peace-seeking process. It would also put pressure on the Provisionals and test their real commitment to peace – exposing them if they failed it.

Although the Hume–Adams agreed document was never published, to the intense frustration of many, it became Provisional policy to press for talks towards political settlement along its lines; and the two governments, working through the autumn of 1993 towards what became the Downing Street Declaration, clearly had in mind the principle of reflecting in the joint declaration as much of 'Hume–Adams' as possible, while retaining the irreducible minimum of the British (and latterly also Irish) pledges of 1920, 1949, 1973 and 1985 to respect majority wishes in Northern Ireland as to remaining in or leaving the United Kingdom.

The Declaration committed Britain to the role, not of persuader for Irish unification, but of validating the concept of Irish self-determination, and it fitted unionists neatly into this concept by splitting it into two components, North and South, which were to endorse the proposed new settlement concurrently. This, plus the concession of the Commons Select Committee, was enough to keep the UUP though not the DUP, 'on side' for the Declaration. The Declaration, like the Anglo-Irish Agreement eight years and one month earlier, was presented as a balanced package, offering comfort and reassurance to both aspirations and traditions in Northern Ireland.

[. . .]

1994: DOWNING STREET TO THE CEASEFIRES – CONCLUSION

[. . .]

It took the Provisionals another eight months from the Declaration before they declared their ceasefire on 31 August 1994. While an instantaneous response to the Declaration from them was not to be expected (notwithstanding media expectation to the contrary) the length of time was inordinate, punctuated as it was by two occasions on which an answering cessation of operations might have been decided upon, but was not. The Declaration clearly put the Provisional leaders on something of a spot, given that it went some considerable way to meet what Hume and Adams had thrashed out, but fell well short of a full endorsement of the republican position. The two governments did not require the Provisionals, before they came into the negotiating arena, to accept the Declaration, but merely to cease their armed operations permanently. The Provisionals' response was to do neither but to call for 'clarification' of points in the Declaration, though they were often irritatingly vague as to precisely what needed clarifying. The call for clarification served several Provisional purposes. It might have prised open some clear ground between the British and Irish governments; it served as a cover for the leadership while it played for time to convince its followers of the novel 'unarmed struggle' strategy; and it helped to gain their acquiescence in an eventual ceasefire by showing that the leaders had done their best to pull the meaning of the Declaration further over towards the Provisional position. (While a permanent ceasefire would have required a PIRA Army Convention, for which the political ground would have needed much preparation, a provisional one presented much less of a problem, but the above considerations still applied in delaying its arrival.)

The Provisionals made much, at this point, of the need for Britain to go beyond endorsement of Irish unification as a 'valid objective', to 'joining the ranks of the persuaders'. While the Declaration clearly signalled British intention to remain, for the time being, in Northern Ireland, it equally clearly indicated the contingency of this upon majority wishes there. For Britain to join the ranks of the persuaders, therefore, would be tantamount to declaring an intention to withdraw. Even if this would not be until Britain had succeeded in its persuasion of the necessary proportion of unionists to produce 50-per-cent-plus-one for unification, a shrewd assumption would be that Britain 'joining the persuaders' would *in itself* lead to an erosion of the unionist majority, since the obvious next step for at least a section of the unionist population would be to seek terms as an Irish national minority, while for others the indication that Britain wished to leave would be a signal that anyone wishing to stay British should leave for Great Britain. The indications were that many Protestant school leavers were doing that in any case.

Although the incumbent British government would not take the persuasion role, Provisionals could note that a Labour Party committed to Irish unification and which had plans for 'persuading' the unionists by tying them into a series of cross-border arrangements creating unificationist facts, was well ahead in opinion surveys and stood a good chance of forming a British government before too long. The government also resisted the Provisional call for clarification, interpreting it as an attempt at pre-emotion of post-ceasefire negotiation. But this came in time to appear a barren and counterproductive attitude, and one which did open up, to British detriment, a division between London and a more complaisant Dublin. Eventually, on 19 May, Britain did supply a twenty-one page commentary on twenty questions about the Declaration submitted by *Sinn Féin*, and this put an end to the Provisional campaign on this, without their having elicited significant movement from London.

This left the ball back in the Provisional court, but now they stood to lose ground. John Hume came under criticism from within the SDLP. Adams's triumphant trip to the USA from 31 January to 2 February had a bill attached which had not yet been paid in terms of movement by the Provisionals. On 29 June they announced there would shortly be a delegate conference to discuss the Declaration. Comparisons were made with the 1970 conference which crystallized the split between the Official and Provisional IRAs.

Minds may have been concentrated by the continuing evidence of aroused loyalist militancy. On 18 June the UVF killed six Catholics in a bar at

Loughinisland, County Down. In 1991 loyalists had virtually matched republicans in deaths caused; subsequently they outnumbered them. From February 1989 to the ceasefire loyalists shot dead twelve active *Sinn Féin* members and as many again of their close relatives and associates – whereas only seven *Sinn Féin* members had been killed in the previous twenty years. In 1994 alone, to 1 September, loyalists were to kill in all thirty-three Catholics, while twenty-four deaths were attributed to republican paramilitaries. The loyalist attack on the Widow Scallan's pub in Dublin on 21 May, using sixteen kilograms of Powergel, appeared to confirm the security forces' assessment that the loyalists were acquiring sophisticated bomb-making capability.

If *Sinn Féin* did not get much joy from Britain out of their campaign for further clarification (i.e. amendment) of the Downing Street Declaration, the British response on 19 May did hint at a possible acceptance of a trade-off of amendment of the Government of Ireland Act, 1920, for amendment of articles two and three of the Irish constitution. Hardly mentioned in Anglo-Irish discourse before 1994, the 1920 Act emerged during the year as an issue, its amendment being taken up by nationalists as a symbol of significant British movement towards recognition of the process of Irish self-determination. Virtually on the eve of the PIRA ceasefire, the Dublin press confirmed that among several draft documents exchanged between the two governments were proposals by the British side for removing the clause in section seventy-five of the 1920 Act which stated: 'Notwithstanding . . . anything contained in this Act, the supreme authority of the Parliament of the United Kingdom shall remain unaffected and undiminished over all persons, matters and things in Northern Ireland. . .' and inserting the principle, already in the 1985 Agreement and the 1993 Declaration, that there could be a change to a united Ireland if a majority so wished. This was rightly seen as purporting to hand over sovereignty from Westminster to 'the people' of Northern Ireland. Virtually all the rest of the 1920 Act had been repealed by the Northern Ireland Constitution Act of 1973. Since Section 75 reiterated the 'truism' that 'the Westminster Parliament retained its power to trump anything that a regional parliament enacted', its dropping would reverse the situation, for it would *subordinate* the United Kingdom legislature, in matters relating to Northern Ireland, to the wishes of the people of Northern Ireland, as, for example, expressed in an Assembly. A Westminster government would be unlikely to tolerate such a situation for long, except as a transition to a permanent abdication of responsibility for Northern Ireland. In contrast, any modification by Dublin of articles two and three (or possibly only of article three) was pretty insignificant stuff.

The Provisionals' convention to discuss the Declaration was held at Letterkenny, County Donegal, on 24 July. Once again, as at their February *Ard Fheis*, they came out with an equivocal, balanced statement, welcoming the Declaration in some respects as 'a further stage in the peace process', but not accepting it or suggesting the imminence of a ceasefire. This was interpreted by the media and most politicians and commentators as a rejection. [. . .] The *Sinn Féin* leadership was reported as surprised and dismayed by this, and indeed on 3 August Adams confirmed that he *had* discussed the possibility of a ceasefire with PIRA leaders before Letterkenny. On 12 August Danny Morrison, *Sinn Féin* Publicity Director before his imprisonment, said Republicans were discussing the possibility of 'an unarmed strategy'. It became increasingly clear, as the month progressed, that a cessation of PIRA violence was likely within a short time, the once-canvassed possibility of a three-month stoppage having been ruled unacceptable by the two governments, and especially on 22 July by Deputy Premier (and leader of the Irish Labour Party) Dick Spring. By now, the momentum had built up to the point where the PIRA and *Sinn Féin* stood to lose much of what they had been gaining since Downing Street if they failed to call a halt to armed operations.

Clearly the long delay of the Provisionals after Downing Street was testimony to the risk its leaders were taking that a ceasefire would be repudiated by part of their movement, especially in the rural sections of the PIRA, and that the resulting peace process would fail to deliver sufficient to satisfy republican aspirations. But the position was even more critical for unionists. Firstly, deny it though some of its component partners would, the years since Hillsborough had seen the forging of a *de facto* pan-nationalist alliance, with only the Conservative British government and the unionists on the 'other' side. And Britain, for its part, had publicly declared itself no longer unionist, while the Provisionals, at least, believed they had privately gone significantly further. Ultimate Irish unification was, to a greater or less degree, on everyone's agenda except that of the unionists. Maintenance of the Union, on the other hand, was only on theirs. The state of which Northern Ireland was part had, officially, no view at all on the matter. The disavowal of a selfish or strategic interest in the Union meant that, at the high constitutional level, what mattered to Britain was simply that the decision as to whether Northern Ireland should stay in the Union or leave it should be made in a procedurally correct way, i.e. peacefully and subject to periodic local head-counts until a majority for leaving should emerge. What the Declaration appeared to be saying, judging from its content, was that Britain had no particular views on how Northern Ireland might become a valued part of the United Kingdom family but only on under what circumstances it might leave. The Declaration did not say that this was what Britain would prefer, nonetheless, except for a small number of Conservative right wingers, the silences of the majority as well as the spoken views of a minority of British politicians indicated assent to the view that Britain's best interest lay in the dissolution of the Union, provided only that this should not too overtly be seen as a capitulation to terrorism. Hardly a single utterance by a British politician of weight, since the departure of Thatcher, indicated any valuing of or emotional attachment to Northern Ireland as part of the United Kingdom. (Compare, by contrast, the position of the Anglo-Scottish Union.) This was a singular situation, little appreciated in Britain; for it meant that as long as violence continued, the state's agents, the Army and the RUC, as well as others, would continue to put their lives at risk in defence of a state which had proclaimed to the world that it did not care whether the territory remained in its jurisdiction or not. Moreover, even Britain's official neutrality could be expected to last only until the arrival of the next Labour government, unless it turned out to be one which needed to court the Westminster Unionists for reasons of parliamentary mathematics.

Labour's position was, in fact, remarkably similar to that now espoused, after its radical reappraisal, by the Provisionals. On 22 October 1993, for example, Kevin McNamara, the long-standing (since July 1987) Labour spokesman, reiterated in the Commons that no Labour government would 'allow its commitment to consent to be transformed into a veto on political progress towards seeking Irish unification by consent'. Labour would, in essence, become one of the persuaders; and it would do so by creating such all-Ireland institutions as would erode away the issue of 'consent' to the point of meaninglessness.

[. . .]

The change in the British position on Ireland in the years between Hillsborough and Downing Street may be approached simply by contrasting the political thrust of the two documents. The Anglo-Irish Agreement was an attempt to contain and if possible reverse the rise of *Sinn Féin* by addressing the needs of the Catholics of Northern Ireland as interpreted by the SDLP to the Irish Government. In signing it the British 'bought in' to the SDLP's analysis and project, while maintaining its long-standing constitutional commitment to the majority. The unionists would have been wiser to accept the Agreement and then hold the two governments to the letter of it. As it was, their rejection of the Agreement had profound consequences. While it stalled further constitutional development for some years, it did not succeed in wrecking the Agreement, and the main losers from their attitude were the unionists themselves. The language of the next major constitutional document, the Downing Street Declaration, indicated a degree of 'buying in' to the analysis and project of *Sinn Féin*, albeit courtesy of the brokerage skills of John Hume, even while remaining faithful once again, to the bare essential of the seventy-three-year-old majority consent principle. Intriguingly, however, on the eight-year journey from Hillsborough, *Sinn Féin*, for its part, had developed its analysis considerably, moving closer to a position with which the British, given a credible ceasefire, could do some business. At least some of the credit for this could be given to the Anglo-Irish Agreement, its consequences, and to British policy and politicians since 1985.

If Britain would not join the ranks of the persuaders, unionists would be foolish to rely passively upon their 'greater number'. For one thing the pro-union plurality among the electorate was not overwhelmingly large, and it showed every sign of diminishing in future electoral tests. In the European elections of June 1994 the difference between those voting for pro-Union and anti-Union candidates was 105,875. In other words, only 52,998 voters, or 9.5 per cent, needed to be persuaded to change sides for an anti-partition majority to have emerged. Of course, what would determine this matter would be demography, not persuasion; though what matters politically may be more a question of what people believe future trends, and their implications, to be, than of what specialist analysts may make of them. More widely, the politics of solution seeking in Ireland, as it developed in the 1980s and 1990s, put all parties into the position of having to be persuaders. Ulster's Unionist parties were rather bad at this; often they didn't even seem to be trying.

The Economist (3–9 September 1994) greeted the PIRA ceasefire, when it came, with the observation that 'extraordinarily, it does seem to have given up its armed campaign without achieving any of its goals.' Certainly, the PIRA and *Sinn Féin* were obliged to forgo the satisfaction of being seen to have brought about a sudden, eastern European style collapse of the British state in Northern Ireland. Nonetheless, a reasonable view was that, as Martin Dillon put it, British policy was 'moving inexorably towards disengagement. No writer about the conflict, myself included, would deny that PIRA violence, particularly in mainland Britain, has changed the political landscape more than any series of events in the last twenty-five years' (Dillon 1994: 262).

Indeed, and yet the paradox of PIRA military operations was that, deep and genuine though British loathing of the PIRA and its apologists might be, the language of the Downing Street Declaration testified amply to their success in driving home the point that republicans and their campaign were *not* the essence of Britain's Irish problem. Rather, it is the persistence of the majority in Northern Ireland's desire to stay in the United Kingdom which is the basic reason why the British cannot get out of their costly Irish imbroglio. The logic of that was and is ineluctable.

On 31 August 1994 the PIRA announced that at midnight there would be 'a complete cessation of military operations'. They did not accept the Downing Street Declaration, but noted instead that it 'is not a solution, nor was it presented as such by its authors. A solution will only be found as a result of inclusive negotiations.' Gerry Adams chose to mark the occasion by praising the PIRA leadership and 'a generation of men and women who have fought the British for 25 years and are undefeated by the British' (*Irish Times*, September 1994). He did not claim victory. To most in Northern Ireland, relief was genuine, celebration premature. An opinion poll in the *Belfast Telegraph* indicated a majority (comprised of 75 per cent of the Protestants and 25 per cent of the Catholics) disbelieving in the permanence of the ceasefire. Overall, 31 per cent believed *Sinn Féin* had done a 'secret deal' with the government. The word 'permanent' would not be uttered by the Provisionals, pending the calling of an Army Convention which alone could make an authoritative decision to that effect. Nonetheless, by the time the loyalist paramilitaries followed suit with their ceasefire declaration on 13 October, the British government was on the brink of accepting as a 'working assumption' the permanence of a cessation of military operations. So were the people of Northern Ireland: at least provisionally. There was, however, no consensus on what it all meant – except maybe a consensus for caution, whether optimistic or pessimistic. Military writers, referring to the inevitable confusions of the battlefield, have a useful phrase – 'the fog of war'. Northern Ireland now peered into a fog of peace. 'It's over', proclaimed the *Belfast Telegraph* on 31 August. Perhaps.

REFERENCES

O'Leary, B. and J. McGarry (1993), *The Politics of Antagonism*, London: Athlone Press.
Dillon, M. (1994), *The Enemy Within*, London: Doubleday.

Ethnic cleansing in former Yugoslavia
CHRISTOPHER BENNETT

> 'The line separating good and evil passes not through states, nor between political parties – but right through every human heart.'
> Alexander Solzhenitsyn

LIMITED INTERVENTION, HUGE EXPENSE, TOTAL FAILURE

In retrospect, it is difficult to envisage a worse strategy towards the Yugoslav wars than that which the international community has thus far pursued. While Yugoslavs are responsible for creating the conflict, international attempts to halt the fighting have been farcical. Indeed, even had the great powers set out to manufacture a state of permanent turmoil in the Balkans, it is unlikely that they could have created a greater quagmire. Yet the level of failure should not come as a surprise, since at no stage has there been any attempt to deal with the Yugoslav wars on their own merits or to address the causes of conflict. Instead, the running has been made by statesmen who had made up their minds in advance that the order of the day was damage limitation, not conflict resolution.

In its defense the international community cannot plead ignorance. Yugoslavia did not fall apart without due warning, nor have the manner and course of the disintegration been anything but predictable. Many years before Yugoslavia formally broke up, symptoms of the country's malaise were clearly evident and Western intelligence agencies had alerted their governments to the potential danger in good time. Moreover, as a result of saturation media coverage since the outbreak of hostilities, spurred in large part by a sense of shame among Western journalists at the cynicism and inaction of their own governments, anybody wishing to discover more about the conflict has certainly had the opportunity and should have a good idea of what has taken place in the former Yugoslavia.

The international response to the Yugoslav wars is a case study in the way the world is ordered and illustrates, above all, how ethical considerations play no part in the foreign policies of the great powers. The overriding aim has not been to bring about a just settlement, but to manage the conflict and make sure that the violence does not spill over into neighboring countries. Indeed, as far as the great powers were concerned, the ideal solution for Yugoslavia in 1991 was almost certainly a rapid victory for the JNA (Yugoslav National Army). For, had the JNA succeeded in crushing Slovenia, Croatia and Bosnia-Hercegovina, Yugoslavia would never have become a diplomatic headache. No matter how brutal the resulting repression, the international community would have been able to wash its hands of the country with a series of carefully worded condemnations at the United Nations and public expressions of profound concern all round. However, despite an overwhelming superiority in firepower, which was further boosted by the UN-imposed arms embargo against Yugoslavia, the JNA failed first in Slovenia, then in Croatia and then again in Bosnia-Hercegovina.

The refusal of Slovenes, Croats and Bosnians of all nationalities loyal to the Sarajevo government to lie down and die, coupled with heart-rending television images of the war have made events in the former Yugoslavia, and the international community's response to those events, a vital political issue across much of the world, and forced the international community reluctantly to become directly involved in the Yugoslav conflict. However, the sense of outrage among world public opinion at the horror and injustice of what has taken place in the former Yugoslavia has not persuaded those statesmen in positions of influence to alter the essence of their approach to the conflict. The fundamental reason for the international community's failure to halt the fighting is quite simple, namely that the great powers have not considered their national interests sufficiently threatened by the conflict to merit the political risk involved in a more ambitious strategy. Though the Yugoslav wars are undoubtedly an inconvenience, they are an inconvenience which the great powers feel they can live with as long as the conflict is contained within the territory of the former Yugoslavia.

The central plank of the international peace effort has, from the beginning, been mediation, based on the premise that all sides to the conflict shared equal responsibility. Perhaps, had all sides been both equally guilty and well-matched, this policy might conceivably have enabled international mediators to broker some form of compromise settlement. But in the Yugoslav context mediation was fundamentally flawed by the nature of the conflict and was never likely, on its own, to end the bloodshed. The Yugoslav wars were not the consequence of an unfortunate series of events and misunderstandings, but of a calculated attempt to forge a Greater Serbia out of Yugoslavia. Moreover, the principal factor fuelling the fighting was the massive imbalance in firepower between militant Serbs and the JNA, on the one hand, and Yugoslavia's other peoples, on the other, which enabled one side, Serbia, to act with impunity and to pursue all its goals, including the elimination of non-Serb culture from those lands ear-marked for a Greater Serbia, without recourse to arbitration. And until either Serb military superiority was neutralized, or the Serb war effort came unstuck, negotiations would inevitably be meaningless.

Despite the military imbalance, the UN Security Council decided to impose an arms embargo against the whole of Yugoslavia in September 1991, and then to maintain it while Serb forces laid waste and ethnically cleansed great tracts of Bosnia-Hercegovina and Croatia. Whatever the original thinking behind the embargo, its only effect has been to make Serb military superiority a permanent feature of the conflict and to facilitate Serb victories. Yet, having made it as difficult as possible for non-Serbs to organize effective resistance, the great powers refused to protect defenceless communities or even to acknowledge what was taking place in the former Yugoslavia. And it is this indifference to the fate of the innocent victims of the conflict on the part of the UN Security Council, which has bordered on complicity in ethnic cleansing, that has brought shame on the great powers and brought the entire mediation process into disrepute.

Though a series of UN Security Council resolutions have expressed disgust and horror at ethnic cleansing, the great powers have, nevertheless, done their best to play down its true extent. For, in both Croatia and Bosnia-Hercegovina, ethnic cleansing was not simply a by-product of the war, it was, in fact, the principal aim, and, as unpalatable as it may be to international mediators, ethnic cleansing is but a euphemism for genocide. Yet to admit that what has taken place constitutes genocide would carry with it an obligation to intervene against the perpetrator; and, above all, the great powers have sought to avoid military entanglement. Indeed, had it not been for the courage of a handful of journalists and filmed evidence of atrocities, the international community would have continued to turn a blind eye to the many Serb-run detention camps across Bosnia-Hercegovina. Moreover, in the interests of a quick settlement, the proceedings of the War Crimes Tribunal, which was ostensibly founded to prosecute war criminals from the former Yugoslavia, have been repeatedly undermined to ensure that nobody is even brought to trial.

Despite going to ridiculous lengths to avoid any condemnation of Serb aggression, international mediators have failed to come even remotely close to an overall settlement. At the same time, their impact on the broader Yugoslav equation has been highly pernicious. By pandering to extremists in both Belgrade and Zagreb, the mediators have reinforced the nationalists' claims to speak on behalf of all of their respective peoples and, in the process, have legitimized the results of ethnic cleansing. To be fair to the individuals in question, they have not had much choice in the matter. Without the political will among the great powers to reverse Serb territorial gains, there has never been a credible military threat, and, given the imbalance in firepower, the mediators could only aspire to discovering Serbia's minimalist position and then exerting pressure on all other parties to the conflict to accept it.

Media-generated pressure and the threat of a massive influx of refugees into western Europe have forced the international community to take on a more active role in the former Yugoslavia, though damage limitation has remained the order of the day. The provision of humanitarian aid is no less than a cruel deception which has addressed some of the symptoms of the conflict, but not the causes, as if Bosnians were victims of a natural disaster. When UN troops first opened Sarajevo airport to relief flights they were greeted as saviours, but Sarajevans rapidly came to realize that their presence was no more than a sop to Western public opinion. By placing troops on the ground in a humanitarian role, rather than as peacekeepers or peacemakers, the international community could be seen to be doing something, even though that something was not going to have any impact on the war itself. In addition, the provision of humanitarian aid has enabled Britain and France, the principal troop-contributing nations, to control the conflict more effectively and ensure that it does not come to threaten their own national interests. As a result, media coverage has shifted towards the humanitarian operation and away from politics, and, at the same time, the humanitarian operation has even been used as an argument against more concerted military action to halt the war.

The cost of the Yugoslav conflict to the international community is virtually impossible to calculate and, in any case, the bill is rising by the day. In purely financial terms the UN budget for peacekeeping and humanitarian operations has soared to about $2 billion a year. But even this is only a fraction of total costs and the wider implications of the failure to end fighting may yet prove infinitely more expensive. The Yugoslav wars have made a mockery of western European pretensions to a greater role in world politics and severely undermined the credibility and reputation of international institutions and great powers alike. At the same time, the West has wasted a great opportunity to build bridges with the Islamic world and, in the process, has created a reservoir of potential terrorist recruits in Europe. The international community wants only to wash its hands of the entire affair, but the conflict refuses to go away and seems destined to haunt world leaders for the foreseeable future, if not in Bosnia-Hercegovina then almost certainly in the host of remaining trouble spots which are currently on the verge of bloodshed.

MYTH AND REALITY

Despite several years' saturation media coverage of the Yugoslav wars in most of the Western world, understanding of the conflict among the public at large is generally poor. This is partly because Yugoslav affairs are indeed complex and do not translate easily into journalism; partly because, as in any war, matters have been obscured and distorted by the propaganda of the belligerents; and partly because of what can only be described as a deliberate campaign to confuse the issue by Western commentators and statesmen seeking, above all, to justify the policy of inaction and exonerate their own positions, irrespective of what has, or has not, actually taken place in the former Yugoslavia.

From the outset the great powers have appeared to devote more time to developing the case against military intervention than analyzing the conflict, and more energy to finding scapegoats for their own diplomatic failures than attempting to halt the war. Hence persistent attempts to deem all sides to the conflict equally guilty, and even to pin blame for the war on the victims of aggression: Slovenia and Croatia for declaring independence against the wishes of the great powers, and the Bosnian government for rejecting the European Community's plan for the cantonization of Bosnia-Hercegovina. Hence also attempts to attribute the failures of mediation first to German and then to US diplomatic interference, and, at the same time, to bend over backwards, on the one hand, to consider the Serbian point of view and, on the other hand, to exaggerate Serbia's military prowess. Statesmen and diplomats have generally chosen to interpret the war as a peculiarly Balkan phenomenon, the result of ancient and irrational animosities, which cannot be understood, much less resolved, by intervention from the outside and clearly more civilized world. Though superficially compelling, the 'ancient hatreds' thesis does not stand up to serious examination. At best, it conceals great ignorance, at worst, it is downright disingenuous.

While there is clearly a great deal of hatred in the former Yugoslavia, it is hardly ancient or irrational. Indeed, it is only this century and, in particular, since the creation of the Kingdom of Serbs, Croats and Slovenes in 1918, that the south Slavs have had sufficient dealings with each other to fall out and come to blows. The wars fought in the Balkans in past centuries were not fought between the south Slavs, but between and against the multinational empires of the Habsburgs and the Ottomans, which held sway there for the best part of 500 years. Far from being perennial enemies, Serbs from Serbia and Croats from Croatia were, until very recently, essentially strangers. Moreover, Serbs who lived within the Habsburg empire had more in common with their Croat neighbours than they did with Serbs from Serbia, and Serbs, Croats and Muslim Slavs from Bosnia-Hercegovina had far more in common with each other than they did with either Serbs from Serbia or Croats from Croatia.

During the centuries of Habsburg and Ottoman rule, relations between the many peoples living in the two empires were regulated from above and the south Slavs had little say in their own affairs. It was only with the demise of the great multinational empires and the emergence of an independent south Slav state that they began to take control of their own destinies, and only then that they had to come to terms with the ethnic complexity of their lands. Given the separate traditions and identities of the various Yugoslav peoples, south Slav union was bound to be a difficult process, but there was no inherent animosity between Serbs, Croats and Slovenes damning the Kingdom bearing their name from its inception. The hatred which is now so overwhelming is, in fact, a very recent phenomenon and reflects the failure of the south Slavs to develop a durable formula for national co-existence in the course of the twentieth century. It is a hatred bred of fear which is rooted not in history, but in contemporary interpretations of the past and can be dated to the 1980s and the media offensive which accompanied Slobodan Milošević's rise to power in Serbia.

Slovenes, Croats, Muslim Slavs, and even Hungarians and Albanians were no more blood enemies of Serbs than Jews were of Germans in the 1930s and 1940s. Yet, from the moment that Milošević launched his anti-bureaucratic revolution, that is how they were portrayed in the Serbian media, and that is what ordinary Serbs, who were on the receiving end of the media offensive, came to believe. What had, or had not, actually taken place in the distant past, during the Second World War and even during the four decades of communist rule, ceased to matter as the Serbian media dredged up and distorted every conceivable event from Serb history. Yugoslavia's non-Serbs were simply scapegoats for the economic and political failings of communist society in the 1980s and a convenient tool which Milošević was able to exploit to further his own political ambitions. However, the xenophobia cultivated by the Serbian media was very real and, in time, it destroyed Yugoslavia.

When Milošević crushed Kosovo in March 1989, the Titoist vision of Yugoslavia as a country in which every nation could feel at home was already dead and buried. By this time, Milošević had come to control four out of Yugoslavia's eight federal units and his ambitions could no longer be blocked at the federal level by a coalition of the republics which remained beyond his influence. Moreover, he was now able to use his newly acquired federal muscle to turn up the pressure on those republics and generally make life as difficult and unpleasant as possible for the country's non-Serbs. The omens for the future of the Yugoslav state were terrible. In fact, the only reason that a full-scale war had not already broken out was that Kosovo's Albanians did not have the weapons to fight back. Yet, at this stage, Franjo Tudjman and Alija Izetbegović had played no part in the Yugoslav drama whatsoever and were but relatively celebrated dissidents in their respective republics.

To try to equate Tudjman with Milošević or Croatia with Serbia is absurd. Tudjman did not become President of Croatia until 30 May 1990 – that is, four years after Milošević rose to the top of the League of Communists of Serbia and only a little over a year before the outbreak of full-scale hostilities in Yugoslavia. Moreover, he inherited a situation which was already on the verge of bloodshed and over which he had little control. Though Tudjman cannot be considered an especially pleasant character, he arrived on the scene too late to be anything more than a scapegoat in the events leading to Yugoslavia's disintegration. It was actually Milan Kučan, the President of Slovenia, who made much of the running in Yugoslavia's twilight years and, in a calculated attempt to boost his own popularity and look after Slovenia's best interests – though not necessarily those of the rest of Yugoslavia – decided to stand up to Milošević.

Negotiations on Yugoslavia's future never got off the ground because Milošević held all the trump cards and had no need to negotiate. Serbia effectively controlled Yugoslavia's federal institutions and, as communist authority disintegrated throughout eastern Europe and then in Slovenia and Croatia, Milošević was able to forge a close alliance with a disillusioned and increasingly desperate military. Perhaps the most critical single event, as far as the nature of Yugoslavia's disintegration is concerned, was the disarming of the territorial defence forces of Slovenia and Croatia which took place on 17 May 1990, just before the formal transfer of power to the new non-communist authorities. While Slovenia managed to hang on to about 40 per cent of the weapons belonging to its territorial defence force and thus retained the nucleus of a republican army, Croatia found itself completely defenceless. As a result, Milošević and his proxies in Croatia were in a position to wreak havoc throughout the republic, secure in the knowledge that the Croatian authorities could not retaliate. Yet the Serbian media portrayed the growing conflict within Croatia as fundamentally a question of Serb rights, alleging, as earlier in Kosovo, that the republic's Serb minority was subject to genocide.

The tactics which Milošević pursued towards Serb communities outside Serbia during the 1980s and early 1990s were essentially identical to those pursued by Hitler towards the German diaspora across eastern and central Europe in the 1930s. In the same way that Nazi Germany alleged that the German minorities of Czechoslovakia and Poland were being persecuted by their Czech and Polish governments, Serbia alleged that Serbs in Croatia and Bosnia-Hercegovina were victims of Croat and Muslim oppression. However, in both instances the plight of the respective minorities was simply a pretext for intervention. Milošević aimed to destabilize both Croatia and Bosnia-Hercegovina and had no regard for the long-term interests of the Serb communities in the two republics. Had the conflict in Croatia and Bosnia-Hercegovina really been a question of Serb rights, Milošević had ample opportunity to resolve it. Moreover, given the imbalance in firepower between Serbia and the rest of Yugoslavia and the desperation of the Croatian and Bosnian authorities, he could easily have obtained a settlement which was extremely generous to the Serb position. However, the conflict was not a question of Serb rights, and Milošević had no desire to see it resolved.

Another parallel between Yugoslavia in the 1980s and 1990s and central Europe in the 1930s is the international reaction to what was taking place. Far from condemning early Nazi aggression, contemporary Western statesmen and media commentators with a few notable exceptions, including Winston Churchill, generally sought to see the Nazi point of view and justify it. In effect, they were prepared to turn a blind eye to the excesses of Nazism as long as it did not affect them directly, and it was only when Britain saw its own interests as threatened that it changed its tune. Herein lies the great difference between Milošević's Serbia and Hitler's Germany from the point of view of the international community. For the great powers are aware that Serbia can never harm them in the manner that Nazi Germany could. Moreover, since the demise of the Eastern bloc, the West has decided that it no longer has any strategic interests in the former Yugoslavia. While the international community undoubtedly wanted Yugoslavia to remain a single entity, the great powers were not prepared either to invest in democracy there or to intervene to avert tragedy.

When Slovene leaders pressed ahead with an independence declaration, they did so because they felt that they had already exhausted the negotiating process. In the seventeen months of inter-republican talks following the disintegration of the League of Communists of Yugoslavia there had been no progress whatsoever. Moreover, there was no prospect of any breakthrough since, irrespective of what was agreed at the negotiating table, Milošević's proxies had already begun to carve a Greater Serbia out of Croatia and Bosnia-Hercegovina.

In the same way that Chinese intransigence has forced Britain to take unilateral measures in Hong Kong, Slovenia, too, decided that the only option was to act unilaterally and, in retrospect, this would appear to have been the best possible course of action. For Croatia, too, despite the brutality and destruction of the six-month war which followed the independence declaration, it is again difficult to envisage an alternative strategy which would have been less painful. Indeed, the criticism which has been levelled at Tudjman within Croatia is not that he was too belligerent in the run-up to the outbreak of hostilities, but that he was excessively timid and should have sought out weapons more aggressively and, critically, gone to war at the same time as Slovenia.

While the international community could conceivably be forgiven for misinterpreting certain aspects of the war in Croatia, the refusal to protect innocent communities in Bosnia-Hercegovina is unpardonable. In contrast to the governments of Slovenia and Croatia, which defied the international community with their independence declarations, the Bosnian government could not have been more accommodating. Izetbegović and his manifestly multinational government did everything in their power to avoid a war: they attempted to defuse all potential areas of conflict; they refused to arm their people; and they tried to act in accordance with the advice of the European Community. Indeed, as conflicts go, it is virtually impossible to find one which is more black and white than that in Bosnia-Hercegovina. Moreover, the international community had no excuse for not learning in the course of six months of war in Croatia how to distinguish between genuine causes of conflict and pretexts. Nevertheless, the great powers chose to remain on the sidelines and to consider the conflict a purely civil war in which all three belligerents were equally guilty.

The fundamental cause of the war in Bosnia-Hercegovina was not the decision to recognize Slovene and Croatian independence, but the massive imbalance in firepower between Muslims, Croats and Serbs loyal to the Sarajevo government, on the one hand, and militant Serbs, on the other, and the eagerness of those militant Serbs first to threaten and then to use violence. The only way that bloodshed could conceivably have been averted was by massive preventative deployment of UN troops with a mandate to neutralize Serb military superiority. But this was never an option because no country was prepared to commit the necessary troops. Instead, EC mediators aimed to persuade the Bosnian Muslims and Croats to accept the Serb position and worked towards dividing Bosnia-Hercegovina into ethnic territories, even though such entities did not exist at the time and could not come into existence without massive population transfers.

THE YUGOSLAV TRAGEDY

In Bosnia-Hercegovina militant Serbs set out in a *blitzkrieg*-style operation to exterminate the non-Serb population as well as any Serbs who refused to go along with the Greater Serbian vision of the republic's future. Once the killing started there was no way to turn the clock back and no hope of any reconcili-ation. The burning hatred which Croats and Muslims now feel towards Serbs is by no means irrational; rather it is an understandable reaction to the atrocities which have been committed against them in recent years, simply on account of their national origins. And it was this premeditated campaign ethnically to cleanse regions earmarked for a Greater Serbia which, after seventy-three years, finally confined Yugoslavia to the dustbin of history.

The savagery of the Yugoslav wars has made it easy for statesmen and commentators opposed to intervention to write the conflict off as essentially 'tribal' and to attribute the slaughter to the Balkan mentality, as if Balkan peoples were somehow predisposed to committing atrocities. However, this interpretation does a gross injustice to all the peoples of the former Yugoslavia and again does not stand up to serious examination.

The key to an understanding of the inhumanity of the Yugoslav wars is the phenomenon of war itself. The state of mind which is capable of committing atrocities is one which has been disturbed by war, not some mythical Balkan mentality. For war is dehumanizing; it destroys the very fabric of society and leaves psychologically unstable people in its wake, people who have lost contact with reality and are no longer in control of their own actions. After almost half a century of peace in the Western world, in which time many people have grown up without experiencing conflict, the brutality of war, albeit via a television screen, has come as a nasty shock. But war, and especially a protracted civil war, is brutal. Moreover, Westerners who are sucked into wars, such as the US troops who were engaged in Vietnam, are by no means above committing atrocities themselves.

While Yugoslavia's misery is generally measured in terms of the numbers of dead and wounded and the level of destruction, there is, perhaps, an even greater tragedy, namely the demise of the Yugoslav ideal. It is tragic because, when considered rationally, the Yugoslavia envisaged by the country's intellectual and spiritual founding fathers – that is, a state in which all south Slavs should feel that they belonged – was not only the best formula for national co-existence, it was the only arrangement in which it was possible to reconcile the national ambitions of all Yugoslav peoples. Moreover, contrary to the propaganda currently emanating from both Belgrade and Zagreb, the Yugoslav experiment was by no means an unmitigated failure. Indeed, both before and after the Second World War there were periods of great optimism and excitement, and, until the very end, the country continued to produce visionary leaders with a strong ideological commitment to some form, though not necessarily the same form, of Yugoslavism – from Svetozar Pribičević, King Alexander and Vlatko Maček, to Josip Broz Tito, Milovan Djilas and Ante Marković.

The beauty of the Yugoslav state was that, since all the south Slav lands were in the same country, the various Yugoslav peoples could not fall out over rival claims to ethnically mixed territories. Though Yugoslavia could never entirely satisfy the nationalist ambitions of every Yugoslav nation, it was a fair compromise and infinitely preferable to the alternative, which is today's carnage. Yet even though the preservation of a Yugoslav state with a commitment to national equality was patently in the interests of virtually all its citizens, the country broke up. But what makes the disintegration especially tragic is that Yugoslavia did not simply fall apart but was systematically destroyed. Moreover, it was destroyed by at most a handful of people, and to a great extent by a single man, Slobodan Milošević.

Milošević's role in Yugoslavia's disintegration cannot be over-estimated. Indeed, his career is testimony to the impact that an individual can have on the world around him or her, given exceptional circumstances and ruthless ambition, and comparisons with both Stalin and Hitler are not far-fetched. For, like the twentieth century's two most notorious dictators, Milošević is essentially an aberration. Though he has played the Serb national card, he is not, and never has been, a Serb nationalist. Moreover, Milošević is no more typical of Serbian statesmen than Hitler was of German leaders, and there is no precedent in Serbia's past either for the man or for the destruction he has sown in his wake.

That Milošević has had such a huge impact on events in Yugoslavia is, in part, due to the nature of communist societies in general, and, in part, a result of the economic malaise afflicting Yugoslavia in the mid-1980s. The Party apparatus in any communist country was an astonishingly powerful mechanism for control, and, from the moment that he became President of Serbia's League of Communists in 1986, in exactly the same manner as Stalin in the Soviet Union, Milošević put it to work shaping Serbian society in his own image. At the same time, Milošević capitalized on the desperate economic climate prevailing in Serbia in the mid-1980s and the frustrations of ordinary people who had seen their living standards collapse during the previous decade. But instead of attempting to correct the deficiencies of the existing economic system, he offered only simplistic solutions and scapegoats to revamp communist authority with nationalism and further his own career.

The key to Milošević's rule and an understanding of modern Serb nationalism is the Serbian media and their sustained campaign to generate national hysteria. Indeed, the Serbian media have played a very similar role in Milošević's Serbia to that played by the Nazi media in Hitler's Germany, though, on account of technological advances in the intervening half century, their influence has been more pervasive and more insidious. At least three years before the shooting war formally began in Yugoslavia, a war psychosis had already set in in Serbia – though, it should be noted, not in the Serb communities of Croatia and Bosnia–Hercegovina, since, at that time, they had not yet been exposed to the media offensive. Irrespective of whether or not Serbs were facing genocide in much of Yugoslavia, as the Serbian media alleged, Serbian society was already gripped by fear and ordinary people genuinely came to believe that they were under siege and, critically, began behaving as if they were surrounded by blood enemies determined to wipe them out.

To anyone who cared to question the allegations of genocide, the image of Yugoslavia portrayed in the Serbian media was a gross distortion of reality. In fact, much like the Nazi propaganda of the 1930s, the Serbian case has never added up, but then arguments do not have to be especially plausible when backed by the kind of military muscle which both Hitler's Germany and Milošević's Serbia could count on. And, irrespective of the relative merits of the Serbian case, Milošević's military alliance and his control over four federal units all but enabled him to dictate terms to the rest of the country. However, the terms on offer, which amounted, at best, to second-class citizenship, were worse than non-Serbs, and especially the Slovenes, were prepared to stomach.

Slovenia was a very different proposition from the rest of Yugoslavia, since, in the absence of a significant non-Slovene minority, Slovenes were in a position to turn their backs on the rest of the country. While the Yugoslav state had generally been good to Slovenes and had certainly fostered the evolution of a modern Slovene national identity, since the emergence of the new Serb nationalism in Milošević's Serbia, Yugoslavia had become a liability. Ironically, by the late 1980s Slovenia – that is, Slovenia's continued presence in

Yugoslavia – was in many ways more important to Yugoslavia than Yugoslavia was to Slovenia. For Slovenia was an essential counter-weight to Serbia, and, without Slovenia, Serbs would come close to forming an overall majority in Yugoslavia and conditions for non-Serbs were almost certain to deteriorate. However, as war appeared imminent in the rest of the country and Serbia refused to moderate its hard-line position – which included an economic boycott of Slovene products – Slovene leaders decided that their best strategy was to distance themselves as much as possible from the rest of the country.

Although one of the most enduring impressions of the Yugoslav conflict is the degree of hatred on all sides, it actually took many years to erase the Titoist ideal of brotherhood and unity, which had been drummed into all Yugoslavs from an early age, to the point where hostilities could break out. Even then, most Yugoslavs were extremely reluctant to take up arms against their fellow citizens. While Serbia had effectively been at war since 1987, the rest of the country – including the Serb community outside Serbia and out of range of the Serbian media – remained generally tranquil. Where disputes were left in the hands of local people, who were aware how much all sides stood to lose in the event of war, they remained manageable and could be resolved relatively easily. Inter-communal relations proved remarkably durable, to the consternation of nationalist *agents provocateurs*, whose early attempts to tip the country into war failed. And even when war broke out in Slovenia, many in the JNA chose to surrender rather than fight fellow Yugoslavs.

The brutality of the Croatian and Bosnian wars may, in fact, be interpreted as a backhanded tribute to the Titoist vision of Yugoslavia and the genuine bonds which had developed between the country's many peoples since the Second World War. For the atrocities committed by Serb irregulars were necessary to destroy all vestiges of the Yugoslav ideal and formed part of a calculated campaign to shatter, once and for all, relations between Serbs and non-Serbs. What is especially depressing is that, though the impact of the atrocities was enormous, the number of individuals behind the campaign was not great, nor were they representative of the wider Serb community in whose name they claimed to act. The Četniks and *Arkanovci*, who were responsible for the greatest excesses of ethnic cleansing in both Croatia and Bosnia-Hercegovina, were generally outsiders. They were also fanatical nationalists who had been deliberately indoctrinated with a pathological hatred of Albanians, Croats and Muslims.

In the two previous wars which pitted south Slavs against each other this century, the Yugoslav ideal, nevertheless, triumphed on both occasions. This time, however, a Yugoslav state cannot be resurrected in any meaningful form, since the current conflict is very different from its predecessors. Whereas Yugoslavs had little control over events leading to both the First and the Second World Wars and conflict was largely imported from abroad, the present war is a thoroughly home-grown creation. Moreover, in the Second World War in particular, most Slovenes, Croats, Serbs and Muslims actually fought not against each other, but on the same side. For Tito's partisans offered all Yugoslavs an alternative to the parochial nationalism of their respective nations, and, in the aftermath of the Second World War, all opponents – Ustašas, Četniks and anti-communists – were executed without mercy. This time, by contrast, though many Serbs have served in both the Croatian and Bosnian militaries, there has not been a comparable Yugoslav course open to them, allowing them to stand up to Milošević's brand of nationalism, yet retain their Serb identity.

Few Serbs from Croatia and Bosnia-Hercegovina rushed headlong into battle. Despite concerted attempts by nationalist agitators from Serbia to stir up Serb communities in the neighbouring republics from 1988 onwards, the vast majority of Croatian and Bosnian Serbs wished only to steer clear of trouble. Most have been dragged reluctantly into the war and are as much victims as their Croat and Muslim neighbours. Indeed, even those who voted for the nationalist SDS (Serb Democrats) were voting not for the wholesale destruction of their homeland but for security in a period of change. And in most instances their only crime is their backwardness which has made them susceptible to Milošević's propaganda offensive.

Nevertheless, the analogy with Hitler's Germany and the German communities which used to live across eastern Europe is pertinent. In the 1930s, when Nazi propaganda alleged that the German communities of Czechoslovakia and Poland were being mistreated, the allegations were groundless. However, when Nazi Germany was finally defeated in 1945, even though Germans had lived throughout eastern Europe for centuries, they were no longer welcome and their communities disappeared. In the same way, when the Serbian media alleged genocide in the 1980s and early 1990s, the charges were unfounded. But after several years of war the allegations have become self-fulfilling and few Croats or Muslims are still prepared to put up with a Serb neighbour.

Meanwhile, the war goes on and, irrespective of UN involvement, is likely to continue for at least as long as Milošević remains in power. Whereas Serb leaders are now eager for a peace agreement which might cement their gains, their Croatian and Bosnian counterparts are equally determined to prevent them from permanently enjoying the fruits of aggression. Though weapons are coming in more slowly than if the arms embargo were to be lifted, they are, nevertheless, coming in, and the Croatian and Bosnian positions improve by the day. Moreover, Croats, Bosnians and Albanians consider that any agreement requiring Milošević's consent is worthless and are prepared psychologically for the long slog. Given Milošević's record, they all expect him to become embroiled in another conflict and are just waiting for the chance to strike back.

4 Ethnicity and Self-determination

Nations without states: Catalonia, a case study
MONTSERRAT GUIBERNAU

Nationalism is a doctrine of political legitimacy subjected to diverse uses and interpretations, and invoked by people seeking radically different objectives. Nationalism is sometimes associated with xenophobia and racism, sometimes with movements which defend the rights of oppressed peoples. There is no common agreement about how to define nationalism, nor is it likely that one could be reached. However, nationalism stands as one of the most potent ideologies of our century.

The power of nationalism stems from its dual character as a political doctrine and as a source of identity for individuals living in modern societies. The major strengths of nationalism contributing to an understanding of its success are: its flexible nature, its ability to present itself as an ideology of inclusion, and its strong emotional character. Nationalism is based upon a political discourse capable of embracing different political ideologies. Nationalism has been appropriated by ideologies as wide-ranging as Marxism, liberalism, conservatism and fascism. One should conclude that nationalism is insufficient as a programme for political action since the ideology to which nationalism is linked decides how the nation will be constructed, and what social, political and economic policies will be pursued in its name. This paper draws attention to the common platform which emerged out of the main political clandestine parties and organizations opposing Francoism in Catalonia in 1971, and its subsequent dismantlement once democracy was introduced in Spain. At that time the major political parties showed concern about the continuity and development of a threatened Catalan identity and claimed to be nationalist. However, their images of what Catalonia was and should be depended upon the political ideology attached to their nationalism.

As I have argued, the first and foremost strength of nationalism is its flexibility, the second is its capacity to present itself as a collective enterprise appealing to all members of the nation. Nationalism is an ideology of inclusion and exclusion at the same time. It seeks to increase the coherence of the nation, develop a sense of solidarity and strengthen the consciousness of forming a group. All members of the nation, regardless of social class, age or gender, are part of this collective project. One can disagree with this and argue that nationalism is created by the elites or the bourgeoisie in order to legitimize and secure their privileged position. Marx argued that 'the working men have no country' (Marx and Engels 1976: 49). While it is possible to defend this argument intellectually, it does not seem to work when applied to concrete situations. Nationalism is today a potent ideology because it has an enormous capacity to mobilize large sectors of the population cutting across class, age and gender boundaries.

Constructing a group implies setting up the boundaries of this group: nationalism can be termed as an ideology of exclusion when we acknowledge its role in distinguishing between 'insiders' and 'outsiders', 'friends' and 'enemies', 'us' and 'them'. But emphasizing difference does not necessarily mean encouraging hostility towards those who are not members of our group. Difference can be portrayed as a source of value if respect towards the other instead of hatred is fomented. However, in conditions of scarcity and struggle for resources the other is likely to be blamed for one's problems and becomes an easy scapegoat. Solidarity has little chance to develop and violence may emerge.

The present analysis of Catalan nationalism confronts this issue by posing the question of who is considered to be a Catalan. The response depends on establishing who is to be included and excluded in the Catalan nation. The appeal to common descent in the definition of Catalan nationality would have implied that almost 50 per cent of the inhabitants of Barcelona could not be considered Catalans. Furthermore, the high percentage of intermarriages between people with Catalan ancestry and people from other parts of Spain is so high that the number of 'pure' Catalans would still be lower. This would have led to a conflictual situation. The nationalist discourse of Jordi Pujol, main ideologist of the Convergence and Union Party (CiU, or Convergència i Unió) and president of the Catalan government since 1980, seeks skilfully to bridge this tension by defining a Catalan as someone 'who lives and works in Catalonia and wants to be a Catalan' (Pujol 1980: 20). This includes two elements: territory and will. To live and work in a certain territory, Catalonia, opens the possibility of becoming a Catalan; to be a Catalan is an option which requires the individual's engagement with a culture, a territory and a collective project.

The third key feature of nationalism is its emotional character. By strengthening the consciousness of belonging to a group with common objectives, nationalism may arouse deep feelings of love or indeed hatred. Love for the country is stimulated by the identification of individuals with a set of symbols, the internalization of their culture as valuable, and the conviction that the nation is a transcendent entity. To give up one's life for the nation is the highest sacrifice. In extreme situations, the individuals' attachment to their community might lead them to be willing to sacrifice themselves for what they perceive as a contribution to the well-being of their descendants. Internal discrepancies and problems are minimized when there is an external threat to the group. The nation in these cases is sensed as an extended family. Individuals are carried away by an internal *élan* which enhances self-image and eliminates any sense of mediocrity. They perceive themselves as valuable and capable of self-sacrifice. Under such exceptional circumstances the individual might consider his or her death as a contribution to the life of his or her nation. Death is not regarded as an end since the individual continues to live through his or her nation.

A further question concerns the issue of how nations are created. This statement implicitly assumes that nations are not eternal entities; they have limited lives and are constrained by historical events. While it is difficult to cite an exact date to mark the birth of a nation, it is more feasible to explore what Anthony Smith calls 'the ethnic origins of nations' (Smith 1986).

The distinction between 'state nationalism' and that of 'nations without states' contributes to an understanding of nationalism in many parts of the world and is particularly illuminating in relation to Catalonia. The state as a political institution seeks legitimacy as a representative of the people it rules. The state's objective is the creation of a nation. This involves the cultural homogenization of its citizens as a means to establish links of solidarity among them and transcend a mere political relation. The existence of more than one nation within a single state implies potential tension and conflict. When the state, which is usually run by the dominant nation, ignores differences within it and represses the other nations or parts of nations it contains, they either surrender and are made uniform to the rest of the state's population, or promote counter-strategies to oppose the power of the state. In this scenario, nationalist parties are clandestine and usually manage to create a common opposition to the state. The survival of Catalan nationalism under Franco illustrates this point.

During the Francoist regime (1939–75) the state imposed an image of Spain defined by centralism, Conservatism, Catholicism and the pre-eminence of Castilian culture. As we shall see, the 1978 Constitution transformed the nature of Spain. Democracy forced the Spanish state to recognize the differences that existed within it and to confer the status of autonomous community upon Catalonia and the Basque Country in the first instance, thus proceeding to a radical modification of the Spanish model of the state. In the new democratic Spain, the creative role the state plays in relation to nationalism in the interconnection between Catalonia and Spain applies reflexively. The definition of Spain has to be examined and reformed in the light of incoming information about Spain itself; this concerns nations or, in the terms of the 1978 Constitution, the 'nationalities and regions' forming Spain.

The power structure through which the Francoist state was able to impose its own constructed image of Spain, persuading social actors – when necessary by force – to adjust at least their public life to it, has now been eroded. Spanish identity has to be defined in relation to its constituent nations, while these nations are at the same time struggling to recuperate and develop the key elements of their specific identity suppressed under Franco. The very definition of Spain is at stake here: by defining itself as a nation, Catalonia alters the homogeneous image of Spain defended not only by Francoism but also by some Conservative sectors currently complaining about the substantial autonomy acquired by Catalonia and the Basque Country.

THE PATH TO DEMOCRACY

A change in the international political environment, the unstoppable industrialization of Spain, the emergence of a new middle class and the influence of voices pressing for democracy all progressively undermined the Franco regime. Its decomposition was of course accelerated by Franco's physical decline. In Catalonia, clandestine nationalist parties and left-wing forces created the Assembly of Catalonia in 1971; its objective was to turn Catalonia into a free, democratic and autonomous nation. Franco's death in 1975 opened a process of political reform which led to the ratification of the 1978 Spanish Constitution and the 1979 Catalan Statute of Autonomy. Once Catalonia was accorded the right to a certain degree of political autonomy and to cultivate its language and culture, the role of its political parties changed. Unity and cooperation made sense while they had a common goal, but now competing 'images' of what Catalonia was, and should be, emphasized the distance between the content of their political discourses. The national question is an issue that Catalan parties are obliged to come to terms with. However, by showing substantial differences in the ways in which they approach this particular topic, they confirm my argument that nationalism as an ideology is insufficient to inform political action except during periods of harsh repression when their unique and common goal is to avoid the nation's extinction.

The 1978 Spanish Constitution

The 1978 Spanish Constitution was the product of the consensus achieved between the main political parties that emerged from the first democratic election. The need to obtain the support of both Francoist reformists and antiFrancoists generated endless discussions in the writing of the Constitution and even contributed to a lack of precision and coherence in some parts of the text.

The Preamble to the Constitution acknowledges the will of the 'Spanish nation to protect all Spaniards and all the peoples of Spain in the exercise of human rights, their cultures and traditions, languages and institutions' (*Constitución Española* 1979: 19). Article Two, probably the most controversial in the whole text, exemplifies the tension between the unity of Spain and the social pressure to recognize historic nations such as Catalonia, Galicia and the Basque Country: 'The Constitution is founded upon the indissoluble unity of the Spanish nation, the common and indivisible *patria* of all Spaniards, and recognizes and guarantees the right to autonomy of the nationalities and regions integrated in it and the solidarity among them' (*Constitución Española* 1979: 26).

By emphasizing the indissoluble unity of Spain as well as recognizing and guaranteeing the right to autonomy of the nationalities and regions, the Constitution put forward a radically new model of the state that rejected Francoist centralism. The right to autonomy of the nationalities and regions forming Spain materialized into what is called the Autonomous Communities System (*el Sistema Autonómico*), which responded to pressure exerted primarily by the Basque Country and Catalonia. Both Catalans and Basques felt that they had not only the right but also the power to press for a political solution to their claims for self-determination. However, what some saw as a solution was seen by others as a threat to the integrity of the 'Spanish nation'. During Franco's dictatorship the regime employed the term 'Spanish nation' to refer to the whole territory of the Spanish state; Spain was identified with Castile, so that cultural diversity was rejected. The groups hostile to the Autonomous Communities System included large Conservative sectors of the Army, the Administration and former Francoists. For them, it was extremely risky to recognize the existence of 'nationalities' as well as 'regions' within Spain. Even today there is no common agreement about what the term 'nationality' means, especially when some nationalist politicians who belong to these 'nationalities' refer to them as 'nations' and use the term 'Spanish state' while avoiding the expression 'Spanish nation', arguing that there is no such thing.

Since 1978 conflict between some autonomous communities and the central government has reached a point of being deemed a necessary forerunner of negotiations and agreements between both political institutions. This is inevitable when two entities seek the same objective, that is the creation and enhancement of the nation. The Spanish state endeavours to create a nation in order to gain legitimacy and elude reducing its relationship to its citizens to a merely political form of interaction. In many ways the *Generalitat* (government of Catalonia) acts as a state. It has the power to implement socio-cultural policies that pursue the restoration of the Catalan nation.

The 1979 Catalan Statute of Autonomy[1]

Continuity over time and differentiation from others are the defining criteria of identity. Both elements are emphasized in the Catalan Statute of Autonomy. Continuity over time is stressed from the very first line of the Preamble: 'In the process of *regaining* their democratic freedom, the people of Catalonia also *recover* their institutions of self-government' [my italics]. A few lines further on this is emphasized again: 'the *Generalitat* was established by the Catalan Parliament which met in Cervera in 1359 in the reign of Peter III the Ceremonious (1336-1387) as an associated body delegated to by the Catalan Parliament itself'.

But continuity over time is not restricted to looking backwards. It also requires, in the case of Catalonia, filling the gap between the past and the present. Franco's regime was a black spot on the cultural and political life of the community. The 1979 Statute of Autonomy had to acknowledge this and to redress the historical balance by setting in motion a common project for the future that would strengthen the sense of forming a group.

> The collective freedom of Catalonia finds in the institutions of the 'Generalitat' a link with a long history of emphasis on and respect for the fundamental rights and public freedoms of individuals and peoples: a history which the people of Catalonia wish to continue, in order to make possible the creation of a forward-looking democratic society (*The Catalan Statute of Autonomy* 1986: 7).

Continuity over time is the basis for the transcendent character of the nation, a feature to which the individual attributes particular significance by identifying with the group and thereby transcending his or her own lifespan. Yet the rituals and symbols that link the individual to the community are charged with the most intense power: existence beyond one's birth and death.

Differentiation from others, the feeling that the self, or in this case the group, has specific traits that distinguish it from the rest, is crucial to acquire a distinctive identity. Allusion to this appears in the Preamble of the Catalan Statute of Autonomy: 'This Statute is the expression of the *collective identity* of Catalonia'; the text goes on to refer to the *'collective life'* and the *'collective freedom'* of Catalonia. The Statute defines Catalan institutions and their links with the Spanish state 'within a framework of free solidarity with the other nationalities and regions of Spain. Consequently and according to the Statute, Catalans are able to vindicate their specificity and have their collective identity acknowledged within the Spanish state. There is no room for independence, at least without changing the Constitution. This constrains Catalan nationalism by forcing it to be a nationalism that rejects the ideal 'one nation, one state'. It is the source of constant trouble, especially since this situation is not acceptable to all Catalan political parties.

The Preliminary section of the Statute defines Catalonia as a nationality that 'constitutes itself as a self-governing community' (article 1.1) (note that

Catalan sovereignty is implicit in this assertion); the *Generalitat* as the institution around which the self-government of Catalonia is politically organized (article 1.2); and the powers of the *Generalitat* as emanating 'from the Constitution, this Statute and the people' (*The Catalan Statute of Autonomy* 1986: 9). This makes it clear that the empowering agent in the first instance is the Constitution. 'The people' (the Catalans) are given third place. It is only as a result of the sovereignty of the Spanish electorate (including the Catalans) who sanctioned the Constitution that the Catalan Statute could be written and approved by the Congress of Deputies, reaffirmed by the Catalan people and ratified by the Spanish Parliament.

Article Two sets up the territory of Catalonia as limited to the areas which make up the provinces of Barcelona, Girona, Lleida and Tarragona. Two points need to be made concerning territoriality. First, by limiting Catalonia to the four provinces, the Statute rejects the claim of some Catalan nationalists who envisage the creation of an extended Catalonia (*Països Catalans),* including Valencia and the Balearic Islands (both of which turned into different autonomous communities in contemporary Spain). Second, although Article Five of the Statute confers on the *Generalitat* the right to set up larger administrative districts within the Catalan territory, the province's organization and the structure of *diputaciones provinciales* created by Franco continues, even if there is a certain degree of overlap between them and the territorial organization of the Autonomous Communities.

A further and controversial issue considered by the Constitution involves the explicit denial of the possible federation of autonomous communities. This is of great relevance for some Catalan nationalists who vindicate the unity of the *Països Catalans.* According to the Catalan Statute, the collaboration and cultural exchange with other self-governing communities and provinces shall be encouraged, and special attention given to all those with which Catalonia has had particular historical, cultural or commercial links (*The Catalan Statute of Autonomy* 1986: 39). The Statute recognizes 'the Catalan language as the heritage of other territories and communities' and refers to article 145.2 of the Constitution, which states that 'the co-operation agreements between Autonomous Communities will need the permission of the Spanish Parliament for authorization; such treaties or agreements shall make possible the establishment of cultural relations' (note that political relations are not mentioned) 'with states where such territories are located and such communities reside' (article 27.4).

After dealing with territory, the Preliminary section focuses upon language and symbols. Catalan is considered 'the proper language of Catalonia'. Furthermore, 'Catalan is the official language of Catalonia as Castilian is the official language of the whole of the Spanish state' (article 3.2). The path to bilingualism is set when the Statute highlights a task of the *Generalitat* as 'guaranteeing normal and official use of both languages, adopting all measures necessary to ensure they are known, and creating those conditions which shall make possible their full equality with regard to the duties and rights of the citizens of Catalonia' (article 3.3).

It is significant that after determining the territory of Catalonia and the language, both fundamental elements in defining the collective identity of a group, the official text moves on to consider the Catalan flag. Here, once again, there is a call upon continuity over time embodied in tradition.

Territory, history, culture, specific reference to language and symbols, a common project, and awareness of forming a distinctive group are all present in the 1979 Catalan Statute of Autonomy. However, the question of who is to be considered a Catalan remains to be addressed. The relevance of this issue is implicit in the fact that around 1975 nearly half the Barcelona municipality was composed of immigrants from other parts of Spain (Giner 1984: 42). In line with the Statute, 'the political status of Catalans shall be granted to all Spanish citizens who, in accordance with the general laws of the State, are legally resident in any of the municipalities of Catalonia' (article 6). This definition ignores racial or ethnic elements and has to be linked with the Preamble's statement in which the 'Catalan people' is equated with 'all who live and work in Catalonia'.

'IMAGES' OF CATALONIA

In 1977 the *Generalitat* was re-established. Its president, Josep Tarradellas, who had been in exile since 1954, triumphantly returned to Catalonia. In 1978 the PSC (Socialist Party of Catalonia) and the PSOE (the Spanish Socialist Workers Party) merged to form the PSC-PSOE. The PSOE was almost non-existent in Catalonia before 1975, but after its amalgamation with the Catalan Socialists it managed to impose its initials and structure. Although the PSC has always argued that the federal structure of the PSOE allows enough space for them to defend Catalan interests, the PSC-PSOE merger meant that Catalan Socialism was subsumed under the auspices of the PSOE and thus lost part of its nationalist image. The PSUC (the Catalan United Socialist Party) repres-ented Communism and was one of the major opposition forces during the Francoist regime. The left, primarily exemplified by the PSC and the PSUC, achieved an overwhelming majority in the first general election. However, the left did not overemphasize its distinction from right or centre options through-out the writing of the Spanish Constitution and the Catalan Statute of Autonomy. The result was a significant loss of popular support.

In 1974 Jordi Pujol founded the Catalan Democratic Convergence Party (*Convergència Democràtica de Catalunya* or CDC), which sought both to modernize Catalonia and to maintain the bourgeois Catalan tradition. In the first regional election, the CDC, in coalition with the Democratic Union Party (*Unió Democràtica* or UD), formed the Convergence and Union Party

(*Convergència i Unió* or CiU) and obtained 27.7 per cent of the votes. The CiU became the first ruling party of Catalonia within the newly created Spanish democratic state.[2] Once in government, Pujol pursued a policy of a rapid transfer of powers from the central state to the *Generalitat*, a process facilitated by Adolfo Suárez, prime minister and protagonist of the Spanish transition to democracy. Suárez's party needed the support of the CiU to attain a majority in the Spanish parliament. A radical shift took place after the attempted military *coup d'état* in 1981. The new prime minister, Leopoldo Calvo Sotelo, yielded to the pressure of Spanish conservatives and halted the transfer of power to the Autonomous Communities. The new centralist policy reached its climax with the endorsement of the Organic Law for the Harmonization of the Autonomous Process (*Ley Orgánica de Armonización del Proceso Autonómico* or LOAPA), which was sanctioned by the votes of the party in government, the Democratic Centre Union (*Unión del Centro Democrático* or UCD) and the PSOE. This contributed to a deterioration of the image of the PSC-PSOE in Catalonia. Only the CiU stood against the LOAPA in the Spanish Parliament. The PSC representatives did not even present the amendments their party had produced against the LOAPA (Lorés 1985: 186). The tension emanating from the state's recognition of diverse 'nationalities and regions' resulted in a withdrawal of confidence in the new model. The state perceived the endorsement of difference as a threat to its integrity.

In the General Election of 1982 the PSC-PSOE obtained the majority in Catalonia, 36.5 per cent of the votes. However, in the Autonomic Election of 1984, the PSC-PSOE received only 30 per cent and the CiU, which had obtained 22.2 per cent in the General Election, now received 46.6 per cent. This initiated a voting pattern in which Catalans vote 'Socialist' in general elections but support the nationalist CiU in regional elections.

The CiU, the PSC, the PSUC and the ERC (the Catalan Republican Left) are the major political parties in Catalonia. They offer differing interpretations of Catalan nationalism and present distinct 'images' of Catalonia and its relation to Spain, proposing alternative projects for the future.

Socialists and Communists envisage a development of the Autonomous Communities System that would turn Spain into a federal state. There are some differences between the two parties in terms of the degree of autonomy Catalonia should enjoy, and a slightly different emphasis given to Catalan national identity. The PSC and the PSUC (now merged into Initiative for Catalonia: *Iniciativa per Catalunya* or IC) show great concern for the integration of immigrants from other parts of Spain and regard Catalan culture as one in which indigenous and immigrant elements should merge, giving rise to a distinct and new identity.

The Communists' discourse emphasizes Catalonia as a nation integrated within the single state of Spain. Rafael Ribó, the Communist leader, condemns a strong centralist component present in the building-up of the Spanish state, 'a centralism usually accompanied by political authoritarianism' (Ribó

1977: 27). In his view, the unity of the *patria*, the Spanish secular tradition and the anti-separatist movements have continuously been manipulated by different political tendencies that share a strong Spanish nationalism. The Catalan Communists define Spain as a multinational state and point out that the recognition of sovereignty and national trends are the initial condition for a democratic advance towards a federal union. They regard the Autonomous Communities System as a first step in the process leading to federalism (*I.C. Projecte Manifest Programa: Segona Assemblea Nacional* 1990: 104).

In the fifth PSC-PSOE Congress, the Catalan Socialists put forward the idea of creating a federal state. The PSC leader Raimon Obiols stresses the party's defence of federalism, but he also recognizes that within Spanish Socialism there is a tension between federalism and centralism, the latter being strongly influenced by the Jacobin and statist ethics impregnating left-wing French culture. The federalist proposal of the PSC encountered some hostile reactions among the PSOE. Objections to the federalist project stemmed from some sectors which argued that the transformation of Spain into a federation would require the reform of the Constitution. Further opposition to the federalist proposal came from Catalan nationalist parties such as the CiU. In their view, federalism would reduce Catalan influence by making all Spanish Autonomous Communities equal in status.

A contrasting position is developed by the ERC, the only political party which claims independence and seeks to create a new state, the Catalan Republic. The nationalism of the ERC distinguishes itself from the other political options and appears as a major challenge both to the Spanish Constitution and the Catalan Statute of Autonomy. In the regional election of 1995, the ERC increased its number of votes but lost its place as third political force in Catalonia, after the CiU and the PSC, in favour of the Popular Party (*Partido Pupular* or PP). The ERC's message is addressed to the 10 million inhabitants of the *Països Catalans*. Angel Colom, one of the party's main ideologists and among those to abandon the ERC in 1996 to found the Independence Party (*Partit per l'Independència* or PI) with Pilar Rahola, has the conviction that a nation cannot survive without its own state. The Spanish state, he argues, is obsolete, lacks a history and a system of values able to unite the different nationalities it contains. Carod Rovira, the ERC's current leader, stresses that 'the modification of the Spanish institutional framework with the aim of attaining full political sovereignty has so far proved impossible and utopian'; in his view 'the only alternative is to achieve a pro-independence majority in the Catalan elections and then open the path to the creation of a Catalan state' (Argelaguet, Colom *et al.* 1992: 77).

The CiU offers a nationalist discourse which does not require independence for Catalonia. The novelty of its message lies on the insistence on Catalan identity within the framework of the Spanish state. The CiU's nationalism insists on the distinct character of Catalonia when compared with the rest of

Spain and claims further levels of self-government for the Catalan nation (see below).

The differences I have mentioned provide evidence for my assumption that the co-operation and solidarity between nationalist parties representing minorities who suffer from strong repression within the state that includes them soon disintegrates when this same state grants them a certain degree of autonomy. Once political parties are allowed to compete in free elections they stand a chance of achieving political power and implementing their policies. Furthermore, by acknowledging that nationalism is invoked by Socialist, Communist, Christian-Democrat and Republican politicians, among others, I corroborate my assumption that nationalism does not contain a doctrine capable of informing political action. This touches upon one of the complexities of defining nationalism. It is my contention that nationalism is not sufficient to determine the policy of a party, except during periods in which a nation suffers repression and is constantly struggling for survival. Nationalism can adopt many faces depending on the political ideology of the party defending it. Nationalism is the shape; Marxism, social democracy, liberalism or fascism are the colours which can eventually produce opposing pictures of the nationalist message.

THE CONVERGENCE AND UNION PARTY (CiU)

The CiU's ideology is based on the work of its founder Jordi Pujol, president of the Catalan government since 1980; his mandate was renewed for the fifth time in 1995. As the CiU has been playing a unique role in the reconstruction of Catalonia within the new democratic Spain, the study of the party's understanding of Catalan nationalism is particularly significant.

Nationalism

Pujol defines nationalism as the 'will to be' (*voluntat de ser*), 'the will to have a particular way of being' and as 'the possibility to build up one's own country' (Pujol 1980: 22). His definition excludes ethnic or racial factors. In his view, nationalism is the effort of a country to strengthen its identity neither by standing against others nor by attempts at defence through isolation.

During the Franco regime the CiU's ideology stressed the need to build up the country according to three major ideas: national restoration, change in social structures and democratic recovery. Pujol called on people from all ideologies to agree with these very elemental aims and struggle together to bring them about (Pujol 1980: 271). Strongly influenced by Progressive French Catholicism and a member of the Catholic Catalan para-political group, the CC, he puts forward what he calls 'personalist nationalism'. This involves the will to create a new socio-economic agenda for Catalonia, an open and generous attitude towards the acceptance of immigrants, and the need to locate the individual and the nation at a wider level. He writes: 'the nation should provide individuals with the opportunity of projecting themselves towards further horizons. Individuals should have a universal vocation' (Pujol 1980: 282).

Pujol mentions two constant elements in Catalan nationalism: the vindication of an institutional, political and cultural recognition of Catalonia as a different people, and the proposal of a reform of the Spanish state that would imply the creation of a pluralist internal structure and the modernization and Europeanization of Spain (Pujol 1991a: 23).

Identity

Pujol's nationalist discourse is centered on the idea that 'Catalonia possesses a differentiated identity based on language, culture, social cohesion, collective consciousness, common project and country pride, opposing absorption and homogenizing policies' (Pujol 1991a: 18). In his view, it is crucial that Catalonia maintains and develops its particular identity rooted in the Middle Ages. He points to the role of language as a distinctive element and suggests that it should be made compulsory for people living in Catalonia to understand and speak Catalan (Pujol 1991b: 34).[3] But in predicting the possible conflicts that this may engender if Spanish-speaking Catalans were to feel threatened, he asks them to make a greater effort by using Catalan in all situations within the public sphere. Pujol emphasizes the value of good relations between Catalans and stresses that 'it is the task of all those who live in Catalonia to preserve its personality and strengthen its language and culture' (Pujol 1991b: 36).

Identity 'is also linked to the conviction that Catalonia has a role to play both within Spain and Europe' (Pujol 1991b: 32). Pujol regards European integration and the whole process of internationalization as a challenge that can only be faced if people recognize their need for identity: 'the model of country we want and we can offer is linked to our identity [. . .] it is not a matter of sacrificing our Catalan identity to modernity or competition. In fact, I am convinced that if we were to lose our collective personality we would lose in all senses the capacity and the initiative, and therefore, competitiveness' (Pujol 1991b: 32). He establishes a link between identity and success. His nationalist discourse suggests that if the nation can restore itself by regaining and invigorating its own identity, then people will feel more motivated and their actions will increase in initiative and achievement. Pujol promotes an image of a flourishing Catalonia able to combine 'a global life-style and the strengthening of its own cultural identity' (Pujol 1991b: 32). 'The concept of identity', he argues, 'intrinsically implies the projection of Catalonia towards [. . .] the great spiritual and intellectual tendencies of our times' (Pujol 1991b: 41). In Pujol's brand of nationalism, the presence of Catalonia in the world is necessary to obtain a minimum recognition of Catalan culture, to do business and learn from other countries.

History

For Pujol, continuity over time is a key concept of nationalism: 'a people is the work of several generations' (Pujol 1980: 39), a people 'cannot exist if it breaks with tradition' (Pujol 1980: 28). The emphasis on the role of identity takes on a new dimension with his exploration of its sources and conclusion that it owes a great deal to historical developments. 'You must admit', he writes, 'that everybody has the right to see in history not only a point of reference but also an explanation of the present and an understanding of one's own personality' (Pujol 1990: 77).

The CiU's leader examines the historical origins of Catalonia and uses them to legitimize the distinction between Catalans and Spaniards. As a member of the Carolingian empire, Catalonia, he argues, possesses a distinct origin from that of the rest of a Spain which was occupied by the Moors for seven centuries.

Pujol accentuates the difference between Catalonia and the other areas of the Spanish state by alluding to the positive attitude of the Catalans in the late eighteenth century towards European ideas, industrialization, agrarian reforms and mercantilism, in contrast to their Spanish counterparts (Pujol 1990: 37). He also points to the innovation and modernization brought about by Carlos III in the second half of the eighteenth century. In the set of lectures Pujol delivered during the commemoration of the bicentennial of Carlos III, he argued that Spain did not react to the modernizing message of the 'Despotic king', and that after his death, *progress continued only in Catalonia*. Pujol emphasizes the Catalans' positive attitude towards hard work and quotes the Catalan intellectual Josep Aparici, who in 1708 wrote: 'Business is the soul of the state and the republic', thus praising economic and commercial activities. The major factors which prompted a flourishing industrial revolution in Catalonia are identified as the existence of a civil society and a relatively high degree of social cohesion, especially compared with the rest of the Spanish state and the sentiment of being a country, thus implying collective hopes and ideals.[4]

The awakening of the nation

Nationalist discourse always involves the assumption that the nation has to 'wake up' and be made 'aware' of its own possibilities. The religious patriotic mysticism of Pujol's early work projects a certain degree of messianism. He was imprisoned in 1961–2 for his political activities against the dictatorship, and his writings of that time affirm the need for restoration, cohesion and national sentiment: 'We need true virtues, strong individuals [. . .] who will awake hundreds of thousands of sleeping individuals and will make hundreds of distrustful and separated people re-encounter a sense of community [. . .] they will then again transform a group into a country' (quoted in Colomer 1984: 256). Pujol's sense of mission is evident: 'From time to time there is a generation that plays a crucial role [. . .] Our generation shall be one of those' (Pujol 1980: 39). He goes on to say that 'to confer a political form to Catalonia, our youth has to be ready to give a lot, even life' (Pujol 1980: 93).

His call for mobilization in the 1990s, from his post as president of the Catalan government, arises in a different context from that of the 1960s, when he was engaged in the development of counter-strategies to oppose the Francoist regime. 'It will be positive', Pujol argues, 'to initiate a campaign of national awareness. The institutional and political consolidation of Catalonia requires a profound and vast process involving the whole country' (Pujol 1990: 31). He demands 'a collective effort of reflection and definition, and a project to find the right answer to current challenges' (Pujol 1990: 16).

Building a common future

Pujol's project for the future of Catalonia entails taking 'Catalonia and its history as a whole' (Pujol 1990: 24) and focuses on three major issues: the strengthening of Catalan identity; the relation between Catalonia and Spain; and the link between Catalonia and Europe. Yet the reinvigoration of Catalonia should develop in three major areas: nationalist experience, social sensibility and moral demand (Pujol 1991b: 50). In his view Catalonia can only be restored by collective work and effort leading to the construction of a country of quality. He suggests that quality, once achieved, will bring about collective and individual respect, self-esteem and freedom (Pujol 1991b: 82). Identity, competitiveness, a sense of community and cultural projection are the four key ideas that Pujol introduces in the service of building up Catalonia. Identity is indispensable and regarded by him as a *sine qua non* for Catalonia's existence as a country.

Competitiveness is an imperative if Catalonia is to continue benefiting from economic success and to occupy a place among the most dynamic European areas. Yet, Pujol warns competitiveness can lead to a rather inhuman society if more transcendent values are ignored (Pujol 1991b: 38). In his view, a country needs a spiritual definition, not necessarily a religious one, but a spirituality that takes 'generosity, sense of honour, spirit of service, noble ambition, magnanimity and the recognition that oneself is not the supreme value' (Pujol 1980: 43). He insists on the need to create a collective mysticism which extends to the social and economic arenas (Pujol 1980: 51). Stressing the importance of the person within the trilogy of person–society–nation (Pujol 1991b: 38), he also appeals to the 'creative, constructive and serene force of Catalonia' springing from its collective consciousness and for civil society peacefully to defend the rights of the Catalans as a nation (Pujol 1991b: 67).

The sense of forming a community is crucial within any nationalist discourse. Although he claims to understand the great difficulties of immigrants, he recommends 'assimilation', that is, their integration into a Catalan society which neither could nor should change its identity.

Pujol compares the country to a fleet and uses this example to stress the need for a global development of a Catalonia that 'cannot ignore those who cannot follow' (Pujol 1991b: 39–40). In his earlier writings, Pujol demonstrates an explicit social concern, stressing the urgency of human promotion for the working class (Pujol 1980: 113) and the idea that 'a national movement has to embody the longings of the whole country being necessarily popular and social' (Pujol 1980: 115); he asserts that 'Catalonia cannot be fully restored without the contribution of the working class' (Pujol 1980: 137) and even that 'Catalonia will not exist in plenitude until the day when its working class achieves power' (Pujol 1980: 138). These ideas were to be substituted later by a more conservative discourse. The explicit references to the working class, present in the writings of the late 1960s and early 1970s, reflect a strong influence of Marxism; having then turned his emphasis to the need for social cohesion in order to create a prosperous society in the 1980s, Pujol is now concerned to maintain the welfare state. He regards this as a major challenge faced by contemporary Western governments as a central issue in the social content of the CiU's nationalist discourse (Pujol 1996: 20).

Catalonia and Spain

A revealing aspect of the way in which Catalonia projects itself cross-culturally concerns its relation not only to Spain but to Europe as a whole. In terms of the relationship that should exist between Catalonia and Spain, Pujol at first rejected the concept of a unitary state, aiming to confer upon Catalonia a degree of autonomy which would allow it to develop future formal links with the other Catalan-speaking countries (Pujol 1980: 91). In the Middle Ages Valencia and the Balearic Islands were part of the Crown of Aragon, of which Catalonia was the main component. Their inhabitants speak Catalan dialects – Mallorquí and Valencià – and their culture is closely connected to that of Catalonia. However, the 'Catalan-ness' of these areas is an extremely controversial issue, particularly in Valencia: some nationalist groups defend their Catalan roots, while others defend Valencian culture and regard Valencià as a proper language (not as a Catalan's dialect). The Constitution and the Catalan Statute of Autonomy clearly deny the possibility of a political association between autonomous communities and the nationalist discourse of Pujol is limited to the encouragement of cultural relations with Valencia and the Balearic Islands.

Pujol condemns lack of trust, knowledge and understanding between Catalonia and the rest of Spain (Pujol 1991a: 11). The origin of such a situation highlights the different historical processes pursued by Catalonia and the other parts of Spain. In particular Pujol refers to the qualities that favoured an industrial revolution in Catalonia, transforming it into the first industrialized area of a backward, closed Spain which was opposed to the Catalan cultivation of a more European outlook (Pujol 1991a: 25).

A certain ambivalence cuts across Pujol's evaluation of the Autonomous Communities System and the current status of Catalonia within the new democratic Spain. He recognizes that Catalonia had never enjoyed such a degree of autonomy. At the same time he points out that during the initial stages of the Spanish transition to democracy the Catalan problem was not posed with sufficient conviction due to the fragility of the new political scene and the Catalans' sense of historical responsibility. He complains that the degree of autonomy achieved so far does not reach the expectations that he, his party and the Catalan people had held (Pujol 1991b: 73).

This implies that it continues to make sense to vote for a nationalist party such as the CiU to defend the rights of Catalonia. According to Pujol, however, Catalan autonomy has been watered down by the generalization of an Autonomous Communities System which equalizes historically distinct parts of Spain possessing different languages, cultures and a strong sense of identity, with Autonomous Communities that have been newly created. But the conflict between Catalonia and Spain is not simply about tensions due to the transference of power from the state to the *Generalitat*. Rather, it has an important economic dimension concerning the *Generalitat*'s budget. Pujol accepts that Catalonia has to contribute more than other Spanish areas to the maintenance of the Spanish state and show solidarity with poorer regions, but he also condemns an insufficient allocation of resources to Catalonia (Pujol 1991a: 33).

Pujol's nationalism does not contemplate the creation of an independent Catalan state. In other words, Catalonia has to collaborate with Spain. Furthermore: 'Spain cannot be built without conferring upon Catalonia the place, role, possibilities, right to hope, status and respect it deserves, unless we accept a handicapped and insufficient Spain, a Spain rejecting one of the best possibilities it has in the current historical situation' (Pujol 1991b: 93). The tension between the acceptance of Catalonia as part of Spain and the desire to extend its degree of autonomy thus emphasizing its distinctive character lies at the core of Pujol's nationalist discourse. He defines Catalonia as a nation, but he does not question the unity of what he regards as a multinational Spain (*La Vanguardia*, 7 January 1990). The CiU supported the PSOE between 1993 and 1995, when it lost the majority in the Spanish parliament, and it is currently backing the PP, which did not obtain enough votes to enjoy the majority in the 1996 General Election. This illustrates Pujol's idea that it is actually feasible to be a Catalan nationalist and at the same time to contribute to the governance of Spain. Pujol granted support to the PSOE in a climate fraught with constant political corruption scandals affecting socialist leaders. During this period he managed to attain a substantial development of the Catalan Statute of Autonomy. The right to retain 15 per cent of the taxes collected in Catalonia without having to wait for them to go to Madrid and then get distributed is probably his greatest achievement. A considerable increase in the percentage of taxes directly collected by the *Generalitat* (30 per cent) is currently under consideration by the PP.

Catalonia and Europe

Pujol insists on the European character of Catalonia, a feature that allows the CiU to combine tradition and the cultivation of Catalan identity with a desire to overcome parochialism and appear as a modern European option. As early as 1964 Pujol wrote that 'Catalan nationalism has to be a form of European nationalism' (Pujol 1980: 121). The contemporary discourse of Pujol stresses the need of Catalonia to raise itself to the level of other EU countries (Pujol 1990: 36). He regards the European integration of Catalonia as a major challenge that requires constant modernization (Pujol 1990: 80). 'Catalonia's contribution to Europe', Pujol argues, 'stems from its capacity to offer a new concept of the European nation based upon culture, a good standard of living, strong identity and the ability to live within a larger political unity' (Pujol 1991b: 74). According to Pujol, 'the development of this new concept of a nation capable of strengthening itself and confident enough at the same time, to accept a role as being a part of a larger political organization, constitutes one of the most urgent challenges facing Europe' (Pujol 1991b: 32).

The nationalist discourse of Pujol can be summarized in six points. First, the rejection of ethnic or racial factors in defining who is to be considered a Catalan and the emphasis on the 'will to be' as a decisive element in the construction of national identity. Second, the sentiment of belonging to a national community is primarily based on common language and history. Third, the distinction between 'us' (Catalans) and 'them' (Spaniards) is a result of different historical pasts. Fourth, the need to waken the members of the nation and engage them in a collective project. Fifth, there is a sense of a 'chosen people' with a special mission. In the case of Catalonia this involves the creation of a modern European nation able to enhance its identity by combining tradition and modernity. Pujol defends a Europe of the Regions in which nations without states such as Catalonia would play a key part. His strong pro-European attitude responds to a long-term Catalan tradition which takes European ideas as a point of reference. A further element concerns Catalan nationalism as capable of developing within a larger state containing other national minorities while maintaining peace. Finally, there is a conviction that the Catalan situation remains unsolved within the Spanish Autonomous Communities System. Consequently, it makes sense to support a nationalist party such as the CiU since it discourages violence, it respects the current Spanish political framework and yet still demands a higher degree of autonomy for Catalonia.

CONCLUSION

Spain has been radically transformed in socio-political terms during the last twenty years. The Autonomous Communities System was established to deal with the nationalist demands of Catalans and Basques. Although controversy and tension have proved to be a constant feature in the relation between Madrid and the regional governments, the Autonomous System deserves a positive evaluation. It has been able to defend and promote diversity within a single state, avoiding a process that could have led to endless fragmentation and violence. Its major weakness stems from the absence of precise and clear-cut rules determining the degree of autonomy that can be enjoyed by the communities. The central government maintains enough power either to push the System and make it work in a quasi-federal way, or reduce it to an administrative device.

Jordi Pujol's ideology represents a major attempt to articulate a nationalism that presents a particular image of Catalonia, but this does not imply a single and homogeneous Catalan society faithful to Pujol's ideas. As I have shown, there are other political parties which put forward substantially different images of what Catalonia is, how immigrants from other parts of Spain should be dealt with, and what should be the status of Catalonia in relation to Spain. It can be argued that Catalan society is certainly plural, but in this context, Pujol's discourse gains significance from the fact that he has managed to win in five consecutive regional elections from 1980, when the first post-Franco Catalan parliament was elected; during this period, he has been the president of Catalonia and this has enabled him to implement his ideas, thereby contributing to the shape of Catalan society.

A close link between modernity and tradition pervades the nationalism of the CiU. Nationalism focuses on a common past and culture and employs them to legitimize a discourse based on the value of the specific identity of the nation. Tradition entails repetition and transcendence. Civic symbols and rituals obtain legitimacy from their status as old components in the life of the community. The appeal to tradition in Catalan nationalism attempts to restore a glorious past, a legendary and pristine time idealized by nationalism. But tradition shall not be understood as a synonym for immobility; rather, it must be transformed and reinvented to avoid loss of meaning. Pujol's view of Catalan nationalism is an attempt to reconcile tradition and modernity by accepting the former as a basis for the distinctiveness of the group, and the latter as a necessary challenge to be faced by the nation. A nationalism unable to modernize the nation is condemned to fade away. This explains Pujol's insistence on the need to convert Catalonia into an advanced society enjoying a relatively good standard of living: a modern nation within a progressive Europe.

The most significant contribution of Pujol is the idea that it is possible to be a nationalist without seeking the independence of one's own nation, that nations such as Catalonia may live and develop within the framework of larger political institutions. But, how coherent is this assumption from a nationalist viewpoint? If, as Gellner argues, the nationalist claim can be reduced to the idea 'One nation, one state' (or 'each nation should have its own state'), can we still refer to Pujol's ideas as nationalism or should we be employing the term 'regionalism'? The answer is far from straightforward.

It is impossible to understand Pujol's discourse without examining the recent history of Spain. After forty years of dictatorship, Catalan intellectuals saw the annihilation of the Catalan language and culture as a real threat. The large number of immigrants from other parts of Spain contributed to the homogenization processes implemented by the Spanish state. Pujol, who was politically active in the Francoist opposition, had a clear picture of the precarious chances for survival of Catalonia as a nation and was aware of the extremely delicate process leading to the democratization of Spain. The formulation of a nationalism seeking the independence of Catalonia would have been a suicidal move in an environment of suspicion against the people defending the creation and development of the Autonomous Communities System. Spain was not a country with a long-term democratic tradition in which federalism would be possible. In the twentieth century the people of Catalonia had seen their specificity recognized during two brief periods of some autonomy (*Mancomunitat* 1913-23, *Generalitat* 1931-8); on both occasions the rights conferred upon them were almost immediately abolished. In 1975 there was no space for speculation or gambling. Spain had a powerful state that would not allow Catalonia, its richest part together with the Basque Country, to secede.

In this context, the political discourse of Pujol had to be carefully designed to fulfil two crucial conditions: to avoid the accusation of separatism, something that would immediately disqualify it and ignite the old flames of Francoism in the hearts of those still envisaging a unified, free and great Spain ('España: Una, Grande y Libre'), and to define Catalonia as a *nation* defending its language and culture.

Pujol's nationalism aims at obtaining the best possible deal for Catalonia within the current framework – this is not to say that he would not seek independence. Rather, what makes feasible his original discourse is the compromise achieved in 1978: after years of backwardness and isolation, all Spanish political forces initiated a process of democratization and modernization which included becoming a member of the European Union and NATO. A democratic Spain had to acknowledge the cultural and political aspirations of the Catalans. The relevance of Pujol's nationalism stems from the assumption that it is possible for a nation to live and develop within a multinational state if this state is genuinely democratic and allows enough space for its nations to feel represented and cultivate their difference. This is an innovative concept which could contribute to the resolution of nationalism in some areas particularly since it seems politically unviable suddenly to multiply the number of states covering the world.

However there are at least three questions to be considered when analysing Pujol's alternative. First, how far can a state such as Spain go on recognizing and financing difference within itself without threatening its own integrity? If states seek the creation of a single culture and language and the emergence of feelings of solidarity among their members, i.e. if states seek the creation of a nation to legitimize their power, is it coherent for a state to contribute to the development of more than one nation within itself? Second, does Pujol's discourse fully respond to the nationalist aspirations of the Catalans and other nations without a state, or should it be regarded as a transitional nationalism which will eventually seek independence? Belgium and Canada – two federal democratic states – have granted substantial autonomy to Flanders and Quebec, however this does not seem to halt the nationalist demands of the Flemish and the Québécois. Does it mean that nationalist claims can only be satisfied by achieving independence? Once the Catalan Statute of Autonomy is fully developed, will he and the Catalans who vote for his party feel satisfied or will they regard autonomy within Spain as a step towards independence?

Third, the claim that the state is an 'independent authority' or a 'circumscribed impartial power' accountable to its citizens, a notion that, as Held argues, lies at the centre of the self-image or ideology of the modern state, is today fundamentally flawed (Held 1991: 200). The nation state is caught up in profound processes of transformation prompted by alterations in the conditions of its existence *vis-à-vis* a changing world economy and international order. Nation states have lost aspects of their sovereignty and are forced to face patterns of increasing global interconnections. The nationalism of nations without a state and the proliferation of supranational organizations such as the EU are transforming the nature of the state. In this new political scenario, Pujol's brand of nationalism represents a useful device since not only nations without a state but also nation states should learn to maintain their identity while living and evolving within larger political institutions, such as the EU, which are being currently created.

The future shape of the European Union has not yet been decided, and the prospective role of nations without states, such as Catalonia, will be influenced by it. Llobera distinguishes between three possible frames for the new Europe: centralized federalism (all powers exerted by the centre), confederalism (general government subordinated to constituent states) and federalism (general and regional governments to be each autonomous within a clearly defined sphere) (Llobera 1993). Only a federalism understood as the agreement of equal independent members where the principle of subsidiarity is applied could generate a 'Europe of the regions'. This is a construction cherished by many who oppose the emergence of a European supernation state. A decentralized federal democratic Europe would not only respond to sound economic arguments, but it would also offer the adequate framework within which nations without states could preserve and develop their cultures. At present, the degree of autonomy, co-operation and subsidiarity that will constitute the European Union remains uncertain. It is important to consider that nation states are the agents designing the shape and limits of the EU, and that in doing so they are inevitably recasting their own nature.

NOTES

I would like to thank Anthony Giddens, Ernest Gellner and Martin Albrow for their comments on an earlier version of this paper.

1 The Statute of Autonomy was submitted to referendum and approved by the Catalan people on 25 October 1979. It was ratified by the Congress of Deputies on 29 November and by the Senate on 12 December; on 18 December King Juan Carlos I gave his sanction to the Catalan Statute of Autonomy as an Organic Law of the State and it was published in the *Diari Oficial de la Generalitat de Catalunya* on 31 December 1979.

2 The PSC was second with 22.3 per cent of the votes; the PSUC obtained 18.7 per cent.

3 According to statistics of 1991, while 90.3 per cent of the population of Catalonia understands Catalan, only 64 per cent is able to speak in Catalan (Colomines 1992: 170).

4 In the mid-nineteenth century, 40 per cent of the industrialization of Spain was concentrated in Catalonia (Fontana 1988: 386).

REFERENCES

Argelaguet, J., Colom, A. *et al.* (1992), *Republica Catalana*, Llibres de l'índex, S.A.: Barcelona.

Colomer, J. M. (1984), *Espanyolisme i catalanisme: La idea de nació en el pensament polític català (1939–1979)*, L'Avenç: Barcelona.

Colomines, A. (1993), *El Catalanisme i l'estat*, Publicacions de l'Abadia de Montserrat.

Colomines, J. (1992), *La llengua nacional de Catalunya*, Generalitat de Catalunya: Barcelona.

Constitución Española: Edición comentada (1979), Centro de estudios constitucionales: Madrid.

Fontana, J. (1988), *La fi de l'antic régim i la industrialització*, vol. V of *Història de Catalunya*, ed. P. Vilar, Edicions 62: Barcelona.

Giner, S. (1984), *The Social Structure of Catalonia*, The Anglo-Catalan Society: Sheffield.

Held, D., ed. (1991), *Political Theory Today*, Polity Press: Cambridge.

I.C. Projecte Manifest Programa: Segona Assemblea Nacional 30 November–1 December 1990.

Llobera, J. (1993), 'Els canvis a Europa i la crisi dels models clàssics: El futur de les etnonacions dins d'una Europa unida', in *Sisenes Jornades. El nacionalisme Català a la fi del segle XX. Reus 1992*, Edicions de la Revista de Catalunya: Barcelona.

Lorés, J. (1985), *La transició a Catalunya (1977–1984): El Pujolisme i els altres*, Empúries: Barcelona.

Marx, K. and Engels, F. ([1959], 1976), *Basic Writings on Politics and Philosophy*, ed. L. S. Feuer, Collins, Fontana Library: Glasgow.

Ponència V Congrés PSC-PSOE, 11–13 December 1987.

Pujol, J. ([1979], 1980), 'Fer poble, fer Catalunya', *Construir Catalunya*, Pórtic: Barcelona.

Pujol, J. (1990), *Quatre conferències: Analitzar el passat per renovar el projecte*, Edicions 62: Barcelona.

Pujol, J. (1991a), *La forca serena i constructiva de Catalunya*, Generalitat de Catalunya: Barcelona.

Pujol, J. (1991b), *La personalitat diferenciada de Catalunya*, Generalitat de Catalunya: Barcelona.

Pujol, J. (1996), 'Convergència Democràtica de Catalunya: Què ha estat, què és, què volem que sigui', Teatre Tívoli, 17 June: Secrataria d'organització CDC, 1996.

Ribó, R. (1977), *Sobre el fet nacional, Catalunya, Països Catalans, Estat Espanyol*, L'Avenç: Barcelona.

Smith, A. D. (1986), *The Ethnic Origins of Nations*, Basil Blackwell: Oxford.

The Catalan Statute of Autonomy, ([1982], 1986) Generalitat de Catalunya: Barcelona.

Scotland: towards devolution
JAMES McCORMICK AND WENDY ALEXANDER

[. . .] The prospect is of a vibrant Scottish Parliament demonstrating the potential of constitutional change to the rest of the UK; a strengthened civic life; improvements in individual life-chances; and a democratic forum rooted in pluralism, helping to realize Scottish aspirations. [. . .] The significance of the legislative task should not be underestimated. The Scotland Bill will face, as earlier Bills have, the UK's unwritten constitution. It will have to overcome the tensions between the Scottish Constitutional Convention's declaration that sovereignty rests with the Scottish people and the English Parliamentary tradition that sovereignty is indivisible and rooted in the Westminster Parliament. These distinct philosophical starting-points, proceeding from very different understandings of where legitimacy can be located in the British state, will complicate the reform process.

The climate surrounding the passage of the legislation will be crucially influenced by the priority that the government gives to the constitutional agenda. If the Scotland Bill is not firmly located in a project to modernize the British state, and comes to be regarded as a 'special deal for the Scots', the degree of hostility will intensify. Discomfort in other parts of the UK can be assuaged by addressing head-on the appropriate future role of a national legislature and sub-UK tiers in a member state of the European Union. Encouragingly, the parties of the Convention seem increasingly willing to place constitutional reform centre-stage in their projects for modernization.

BOX 1: Powers of the Scottish Parliament (as proposed in Scotland's Parliament, Scotland's Right)

The Scottish Constitutional Convention's final report (1995) states that the Parliament's powers will include all areas of policy currently within the remit of the Scottish Office; and that the primary matters to be retained to Westminster will be defence, foreign affairs, immigration, nationality, social security policy and central economic and fiscal responsibilities. Devolved powers will thus include:

Economy and business
The responsibilities of industrial development (including Scottish Enterprise); tourism development (the Scottish Tourist Board); energy (including regulation of electricity generation and supply); agriculture (including land tenure and crofting), fisheries and forestry.

Infrastructure
Transportation (public passenger and freight services, roads); planning and land use; water and sewerage; environment (including pollution control and flood protection).

Health and social welfare
The National Health Service (organization and administration); community care; housing (including regulation of rents and rebates); welfare of children and elderly people.

Education and leisure
Education (from nursery to higher education provision); youth and adult training provision; broadcasting; arts and culture; recreation (including sports and parks provision).

Law and regulation
Local government (including revenues and expenditure); charities; licensing; the police and prison services; the fire service; the courts and legal system; civil law; legal aid; equal opportunities.

Many factors combine to create a more favourable climate for devolution than twenty years ago. The evolution of the European Union has dealt a number of fatal blows to the notion of undivided Parliamentary sovereignty and should alter the debate on the legitimacy of a division of legislative powers between different tiers of government. It is only a small step in theory from Westminster's endorsement of the principle of subsidiarity for relations between itself and European institutions to acceptance that such a relationship should also govern the division of powers between Westminster and sub-UK tiers. Secondly, the essential adaptability of the British constitution has again been highlighted by the Government's 1995 proposals for a Belfast Assembly. These go at least as far as the earlier Stormont Parliament (1921–72), reiterating that the British constitution can cope with the notion of transferred legislative power. Thirdly, the building of a widespread consensus around the blueprint of the Constitutional Convention will undermine the charge of partisanship which bedevilled earlier efforts.

The work of the Scottish Constitutional Convention (1995) is in many ways a remarkable achievement. It has proposed defined powers and responsibilities for a Scottish Parliament (see box 1); reached agreement on a proportional system of election and balanced representation of the sexes; made significant progress since its report in 1990 on the fiscal relationship with Westminster and the Parliament's economic remit; and set out a clearer vision of future relations with local government and the European Union.

The result is a more coherent and impressive case for a Scottish Parliament than either the Convention's 1990 proposals or the Scotland Act of 1978. It anticipates many more of the difficult questions than past attempts, but it has also left others for resolution during and beyond the legislative period. Despite the good reasons for optimism, unhappy memories of earlier attempts at major constitutional reform may be revived. As with other areas of policy, the ramifications of campaign commitments will be more wide-ranging in government than can be anticipated in advance. It is vital that those committed to Home Rule are alert to the outstanding issues, are clear about which may be left for resolution in government, and are prepared for the likely tactics of opponents. This essay highlights a number of these issues. The urgency surrounding a first session Bill will diminish opportunities for later discussion. Our aim is to demonstrate that such issues need not become weapons against the devolution settlement. It is not so much that Convention proposals are inappropriate, rather that a full engagement with some of the more contentious issues lay outside its remit. It will fall to a new government to make the devolution legislation water-tight. The Convention was not charged with looking much beyond the passage of the legislation.

[. . .]

THE WEST LOTHIAN QUESTION AND SCOTTISH REPRESENTATION AT WESTMINSTER

Devolution raises the question of the continuing role of MPs sitting for devolved areas at Westminster. In the 1970s in the case of Scotland and Wales, Labour argued that there should be no change in arrangements at Westminster. The issue came to public prominence when Tam Dalyell posed the 'West Lothian Question' in the House of Commons.[1] More recently, the Convention has generally avoided the issue, presumably because the operation of Westminster lay beyond its remit. Yet this is precisely why it will be so visible during the passage of the Bill. Those committed to making devolution work will be justified in turning Conservative criticism back on itself: if constitutional anomalies are on the agenda, the House of Lords is surely the most prominent of all. Yet, winning the argument is not necessarily the same as achieving a legislative objective.

Answers to the Question?

The starting-point for this debate is that the UK's unwritten constitution offers no ready-made answers. The West Lothian Question is essentially a political matter, and so are the potential answers. How should Westminster respond to the anomalies thrown up by carving a federal part (Scotland) out of a state which is culturally multinational but constitutionally unitary? In the period since 1979, none of the responses has managed to win a broad consensus. Below we review the four main responses offered since it was first raised. We conclude by highlighting the dynamic nature of the Question, offering two possible ways forward for a future government and suggesting how the appropriate answer might change as the role of Parliament itself evolves and the prospect of electoral reform emerges.

Federalism

Like independence, federalism offers constitutional clarity. There are two federal options within the UK. The first is built on four federal units – England, Wales, Northern Ireland and Scotland – each with the ability to claim equal legislative and fiscal powers. Federalism seems technically attractive since it offers clearly defined powers at defined levels, irrespective of the size of the federal units. This has superficial appeal in the UK where future constitutional arrangements must accommodate one much larger constituent relative to the other three. In practice, however, no federal system has had to sustain that kind of constitutional arithmetic (Munro 1994).

This model of federalism fails on the grounds of political plausibility – it is simply not desired in the UK. [. . .] Most English citizens view Westminster as wholly adequate as their national Parliament. For the foreseeable future the constitutional questions that will dominate English politics are British ones, such as the relationship with the European Union.

A second quasi-federal solution based on Parliaments in Wales, Scotland, Northern Ireland and the English regions may be more plausible but would fail the test of constitutional balance, since it is not envisaged that English regional assemblies would gain legislative powers, at least not in the medium term. Although the success of devolution in Scotland is likely to fuel demands for more devolved responsibilities in England, as long as Scotland aspires to greater transferred powers than the English regions, some variation on the West Lothian Question will remain.

The apparent constitutional convenience of a fully federal UK founders on the lack of popular support. In contrast, devolution can avoid imposing change that lacks public support, without delaying devolution for those parts of the UK that demand it while others make up their minds on the questions of whether, when and how far (Tindale 1995). In the midst of confused British, national and regional identities, this by definition leads to a variable constitutional geometry, as has emerged in other European countries. There is no convenient route to by-pass different aspirations. Consequently the problem of imbalance in Westminster responsibilities imposed by an asymmetric constitutional form is rooted in popular demand.

Await future developments

A second approach is effectively to ignore the West Lothian Question while awaiting further developments in the UK constitution towards a variable geometry. The Constitutional Convention has taken this line. Although the Convention failed to mention the issue in its final report, an interim report by its Constitutional Commission argued against an immediate reduction in the number of Scottish MPs and in favour of deferral on the grounds that Scotland is likely to be the first in a series of devolutionary steps towards an entirely new constitutional settlement in the UK.

The Convention's 'wait and see' response was appropriate to its remit. Labour has argued that it sees no need to address the issue of Westminster representation concurrent with devolution: 'It is ironic that those who are preoccupied with this appear unconcerned by the converse Westminster Question. Why is it that 560 non-Scottish MPs decide legislation which will be implemented only in Scotland?' (Scottish Labour Party 1995, p. 6).

The anomaly created by a Scottish Parliament is considered less significant than many which already exist, and the devolutionary package offers a huge democratic advance. The British constitution is seen as an 'imperfect creature' with the ability to accommodate new anomalies thrown up by the resolution of old ones.

Underlying Labour's case is the belief that Scotland's over-representation has historically been (and will continue to be) justified on the basis of sensitivity to policy-making in a unitary state that must accommodate significant internal diversity. Since Westminster will retain responsibility for the reserved powers, it is argued that the historic bargain should therefore continue. The need for Scotland's distinct status to be recognized within the UK is all the more vital in the absence of a second chamber that adequately reflects national and regional diversity. A parallel can be drawn with the USA, where the Senate represents all states, irrespective of their population. The UK has no comparable safeguard in the shape of its Upper House. By implication, altering

Scotland's House of Commons representation should only be on the agenda when other reforms occur – such as a reformed Second Chamber which reflects Scotland's status in the Union.

Labour's difficulty in convincing impartial observers that the new anomaly can be ignored arises partly because many English observers view its devolution proposals as a deal that confers extra benefits in addition to the existing advantages of a separate Cabinet position, public spending advantages and over-representation at Westminster. The irony is that many of these advantages were conferred over the years to reflect, or simply buy off, Scotland's legitimate aspirations for genuine democratic control of its own affairs. Yet whatever the origins of such arrangements, there is a case for their reassessment when democratic aspirations are finally being met through a directly elected Scottish Parliament. Faced with the question of whether over-representation should continue when no separate Scottish legislation will be considered by the House of Commons, Labour cites two precedents from Northern Ireland. One is the apparent failure of a parallel West Belfast Question to emerge when Northern Ireland's legislation was dealt with by Stormont and its MPs continued to vote on all Westminster issues. The other concerns the British Government's 1995 Framework Document, in which no proposals are made for a reduction in the number of MPs from Northern Ireland. However these precedents, like much else in the British constitutional debate, are contradictory. Bogdanor (1996) notes that a West Belfast dilemma was indeed posed by Labour, in government with a small majority in 1965, although no steps were taken in response. Moreover, Northern Ireland does not today have more MPs than its per elector or parity entitlement.

The danger for a new government arises not so much from the repetition of charges of partisanship or gerrymandering in the heat of a general election campaign but the potential of such charges to later undermine the legitimacy of the Scottish constitutional settlement in the eyes of English voters. Furthermore, that risk might not materialize until well after the Parliament is established. It is therefore possible for a Scottish Parliament to be established without responding directly to the West Lothian dilemma; but the future Parliamentary debate will nevertheless range over all the options for Scotland's representation at Westminster.

In and out

A third response is the so-called 'in and out' approach, the formal restriction of the voting rights of Scottish MPs preventing them from voting on any specifically English, Welsh or Northern Irish legislation concerning matters which had been devolved in the case of Scotland. There has occasionally been the informal practice in the Commons, observed by both Labour and Conservative governments, that MPs representing England, Wales or Northern Ireland do not override the wishes of Scottish MPs on issues such as Scottish divorce law reform. On mainstream political matters, however, governments have generally insisted on deploying their full voting powers to get their way, for example in the early introduction of the poll tax in Scotland. Yet, however abhorrent the poll tax was to Scotland, there was at least a mutual ability for Scottish and non-Scottish MPs to vote on each other's legislation, even if the relationship is clearly an unbalanced one. After devolution there will be no such mutual voting power. Should Scottish MPs then be able to vote on anything other than powers retained at Westminster?

Despite the simplicity of 'in and out' as a response, it has never found favour with any major party, principally because the creation of two classes of MP at Westminster is highly controversial and a departure from all UK constitutional practice. It was not imposed on Northern Ireland while the Stormont Parliament sat. However it attracts considerable support among Conservative backbenchers and there has also been recent interest in Scotland among those proponents of Home Rule who believe 'in and out' would help to morally entrench a Scottish Parliament by defusing English opposition.

[. . .]

Reduced Scottish representation – or a devolution discount?

Reducing Scotland's representation at Westminster has been proposed as a fourth partial answer to West Lothian. On a strict per elector basis, Scotland is currently over-represented in the House of Commons by around 20 per cent compared with England and Northern Ireland (McLean 1995). Although Conservative backbenchers have occasionally sought to reduce Scottish representation in the context of the constitutional *status quo*, there is a general recognition that a degree of over-representation is justified on the grounds of Scottish and Welsh geography. [. . .] Whether over-representation continues or not, it can hardly be justified post-devolution simply by the argument that Westminster is considering distinctively Scottish legislation.

A reduction of fourteen from the current seventy-two Scottish Westminster seats would be required to match the prevailing electoral quotas used in England and Northern Ireland. However a cut of twelve seats would effectively eliminate the bias towards Scotland while accommodating smaller electorates in the most rural and remote constituencies. Cutting Scotland's number of MPs while allowing those who remain to have full voting powers is a quintessentially political response to West Lothian. It acknowledges that Scotland should accept a paring back of some of the benefits granted in the absence of a Scottish legislature when such an institution is created. A cut to give parity with England and Northern Ireland in the number of MPs would avoid the shortcomings of 'in and out', namely two classes of MP and potentially two administrations. It is essentially for these reasons that a reduction to parity was favoured by the Kilbrandon Commission in 1973.

There are a number of objections, however. One is simply that it would not address the West Lothian Question. Fewer Scottish MPs would not mean no Scottish MPs voting on English legislation. A second objection is that it would undermine the territorial settlement within the UK which, it could be argued, devolution does not fundamentally alter. A third objection, and a reason why Conservatives might support it, is that its political impact would disproportionately hit Labour's important Scottish base. A number of exaggerated claims have been made on this point. Although a reduction of fourteen MPs might mean a net Labour loss of six seats compared with all other parties, that would leave Labour needing to gain three seats to maintain its position in the rest of Britain. That kind of disadvantage could of course prove crucial in a tight election, as the Conservative Government's precarious majority in 1995–6 demonstrates. However, the overall impact would not be much greater than the effect of the recent Boundary Commission review and can hardly be seen as a clinching argument against a reduction.

A variant on the cut to parity following devolution is the steeper 'devolution discount' imposed on Northern Ireland at the establishment of the Stormont Parliament in 1920. Northern Ireland's quota of MPs was deliberately reduced from an entitlement of seventeen (parity level) to twelve, and returned to seventeen by the Callaghan government after Stormont's abolition. There was no neat constitutional rulebook to consult, pointing to such a 'devolution discount' of five MPs. But cutting the number of MPs appears to be only a selectively applied principle. As already noted, the 1995 Framework Document for Northern Ireland proposing a ninety-member Assembly in Belfast did not propose cutting the number of MPs back again, even though the new Assembly could include 'legislative and executive responsibility over as wide a range of subjects as in 1973' with the possibility of a further transfer of power later.

[. . .]

DEVOLUTION: THE POOR COUSIN OF INDEPENDENCE?

The overriding task, in advance of the Parliament's establishment and in its early work, will be to make it relevant to the millions of people who remain ambivalent, sceptical or simply uninformed of its potential. An equally important, but trickier, task is to maintain a sense of its limits. Home Rule will highlight some home truths. The new Parliamentarians will be held responsible for their decisions in a way that most Scottish politicians have not been for twenty years. The rhetoric of the 'Thatcher blame hypothesis' will be put in perspective: the Tory-voting south-east of England cannot be held entirely responsible for the trends that are facing every developed economy. Devolution will not cure all of Scotland's economic and social ills. It cannot shield people from the quickening pace of change any more than the UK Parliament can. It can, however, assist people to cope with change, above all through its education and training powers.

In all the excitement surrounding early hopes fulfilled and expectations dashed, the SNP will constantly seek to contrast devolution unfavourably with the independence option. Supporters of the Home Rule settlement will have to become highly familiar with the terms of this argument. When a Scottish Parliament is established, the so-called 'third option' of no change will disappear. It seems likely that the Conservatives will then accept the Parliament's existence and propose modification in its powers. In these circumstances, the economic debates will focus more directly on the relative benefits of devolution and independence.

For supporters of devolution, the critical case will be that a devolved Scotland is the constitutional arrangement that will most advance the development of a modern, globally competitive economy. They will have to become wholly familiar with the gamut of arguments against independence. The economic ones stand out: the overnight contraction of Scotland's domestic market by 90 per cent, the costs imposed by different currencies, transactions across a national frontier and exchange rate uncertainty (pre-Monetary Union), the disruption to transport infrastructures, the impact of dislocated relationships with English-based financial institutions, suppliers and customers, and an inherited structural budget deficit following the end of equalization. The proponents of independence repeatedly return to oil revenues, but even with an overwhelming share of the royalties these would be insufficient to close the structural deficit. Post-Monetary Union, the core of the economic case against separatism will rest on a judgement about whether the scope available to an independent Scotland to formulate distinctive economic policies could possibly justify the permanent economic damage involved in leaving the United Kingdom. Any benefits that might accrue from additional discretionary powers for a small open economy would in no way compensate for the costs in terms of disruption, upheaval and economic uncertainty. A devolutionary settlement will offer unique opportunities to enhance Scotland's competitiveness while avoiding a collapse in confidence, depressed living standards, and years of uncertainty as the price of independence.

Of course independence is and will remain a political choice, but its romantic appeal is likely to fade in light of the real world implications. For those who fear that devolution represents a slippery slope, they might recall that there is not one European parallel of a part of a modern state using devolution as a stepping stone to independence. The Spanish experience highlights the ability of variable constitutional geometry to accommodate the aspirations of historical nations within the wider state. If anything it is the denial of self-determination which is more likely to provoke demands for separation.

In conclusion, the establishment of a Scottish Parliament will create a very different climate for debate. The economic dimensions will encompass both the earning and spending priorities as well as the alternative constitutional options. We move now from this broader survey of the economic debate to anticipate some of the practical political scenarios that may emerge following the establishment of the Parliament and the ways in which they will shape the Scottish political agenda.

[. . .]

We begin with the possible dividing lines in the first Scottish Parliament: electoral scenarios; the adjustment to coalition politics; winning popular support; the impact of a new voting system and revised Parliamentary procedures. We then look at how political debate within parties will evolve. More speculatively, we lay out some of the issues that may define a second term. We are assuming that the Parliament will be elected in the manner outlined by the Convention: an Additional Member System (AMS) with voters casting two votes, one for constituency MPs by First Past The Post (FPTP) and a second for a preferred party, with top-up MPs elected by a list system. Seventy-three MSPs (Members of the Scottish Parliament) would be elected in the first section and fifty-six (seven in each of the eight European Parliamentary constituencies) in the second section, giving a total of 129 members. Within each Euro-constituency, top-up seats will be allocated to give each party a share of the total number of seats as close to its share of the vote as possible. This element, correcting for the distortions of the FPTP allocation, will ensure that the overall result comes very close to proportionality.

Labour and the Liberal Democrats have also signed an Electoral Agreement as part of the Convention's work, pledging that they would aim for the representatives in the inaugural Parliament to be 50 per cent women and 50 per cent men. They have left open the question of the appropriate response if the other parties do not match this commitment. It is not yet clear how the ruling against Labour's women-only shortlists policy for Britain will affect this commitment.

THE FIRST SCOTTISH PARLIAMENT

The earliest date for the first Scottish Parliament elections might be spring 1999, assuming a spring 1997 general election, Royal Assent for a devolution bill by the end of 1998 and Scottish Parliament elections the following April. Spring 1999 is likely to coincide with the mid-point in the UK Parliament electoral cycle, and the probable trough in the popularity of a Labour government. The timing is therefore unlikely to be helpful for Labour and there is a strong likelihood that, as with mid-term elections in the past, the electorate will view these elections partly as a referendum on the government of the day. It may be that the historical significance of the inaugural Scottish Parliament elections will reduce the protest element and that the Convention parties will benefit from an electoral dividend from having delivered a Scottish Parliament. A Labour government would be wise not to expect gratitude from the voters but well advised to avoid delaying elections until their fortunes were revived. When the initial elections for regional councils in France were delayed for that reason, the Socialist Government was punished for its delaying tactics.

[. . .] The proportional electoral system will mean that the share of seats in the Parliament is unlikely to be more than 3 per cent away from the actual share of votes polled. It is therefore reasonable to assume that at least 47 per cent will be required for any party to gain an outright majority. Scottish election results in the past suggest that this is unlikely. Here we make two working assumptions: Labour polls at least 30 per cent of the popular vote and the SNP exceeds 20 per cent in the first two SP elections (possibly 1999 and 2003). This means that any stable administration will require one of these two parties to be part of the governing coalition. Furthermore we assume that Labour receives more seats than any other party in the first elections. In such circumstances, we envisage them aiming to form an administration with the Liberal Democrats. Having created the Scottish Parliament, the Convention partners are likely to want to form the first administration.

We suggest two scenarios for the first term. The first is a Labour/Liberal Democrat administration based on projections from the 1992 general election result. We call this the Majority Scenario (and one which has generally been assumed the most likely). The second possibility, the Minority Scenario, assumes a weaker Labour/Liberal Democrat administration based on a result similar to the 1992 district elections. The Majority Scenario assumes that Labour derives an electoral benefit from delivering Home Rule which a government in mid-term would not normally receive. Sixty-five seats will be required for an absolute majority in a Scottish Parliament. As the Majority Scenario demonstrates, a repeat of the 1992 general election results (where the distribution of second votes is assumed to be the same as for first votes) translates into a majority for the Convention parties of thirteen over other parties (six seats above the threshold for a majority). This scenario underlines the importance of the top-up seats. In at least three of the Euro-seats, the final top-up seat is likely to be very closely contested.

A new voting system will result in outcomes which cannot be predicted at this stage, not least in the campaigning strategies adopted by the parties. The parties will have to adjust to a new electoral system if they aim to attract the second votes of electors who backed a different party for their constituency MP (i.e. electors who may be prepared to 'split their ticket').

For example, the Liberal Democrats already win a significantly higher share of seats than their votes justify in the Highlands and Islands constituencies. If they managed to repeat that performance in Scottish Parliament elections, but not do significantly better in the second party list section, they would be unlikely to win top-up seats. One could then argue that second votes for the Liberal Democrats would be unlikely to benefit the party through extra seats. Labour and the other parties will presumably be aiming to attract voters in order to deliver them top-up seats which could prove vital in determining who is able to govern. Similarly, Labour would be unlikely to win any top-up seats in four of the eight European Constituencies if its share of second votes matched its share of first votes.

Will the parties encourage 'split ticket' voting? We cannot predict how such an effect will develop as the parties adjust to an Additional Member System (AMS), but we can conclude that transfers between parties cannot be ignored. Indeed they could prove crucial in deciding who can command a majority in the Scottish Parliament (or indeed whether one can be formed at all).

On the Minority Scenario, we assume Labour slips to around 35 per cent (as in the 1992 district elections and 1983 general election) and that the Liberal Democrats are also squeezed. Here the Convention Parties would be unable to form a majority administration. In these circumstances the nature of the first administration is not clear. There appears no politically feasible majority coalition. A key factor will be the strength of the SNP. If they benefit at Labour's expense, gaining the protest vote against a mid-term government as in the 1977 local elections, or if devolution has had a long and fraught passage with the obstruction of even a few English Labour MPs, they might take a quarter of the votes compared with around one-third for Labour. This would translate into a difference of a dozen seats between Labour and the SNP in a Parliament of 129 members.

If the Minority Scenario occurred, the Tories and the SNP could not be expected to form a joint administration, but they would together be in a strong position to deprive the Minority Labour/Liberal Democrat coalition of an overall majority through *ad hoc* alliances. We regard it as politically impossible for the SNP and Tories to co-operate in a formal way in the course of the first administration, although it cannot be ruled out thereafter.

ADJUSTING TO PLURALISM

How will the Convention parties work together? Their relationship must be expected to change substantially. Cross-party differences may be delayed until after the first Scottish Parliament elections, although this would crucially depend on the degree of co-operation during the Parliamentary passage. After the first Scottish Parliament elections, the Liberal Democrats in particular will wish to assess the impact of their relative closeness to Labour on their electoral standing. Under both scenarios we also anticipate discomfort as the Scottish Labour Party adapts to negotiating in a coalition, and some opposition to the new voting system. The Convention parties were right to adopt the AMS system. FPTP would send entirely the wrong signal, that there was no need to reflect many strands of political opinion in Scotland. Labour supporters of FPTP should recall that one of the central flaws of the 1978 Act was its power to confer a majority of seats on a party gaining a minority of votes. An SNP majority of seats is unlikely, but less unlikely under a distortionary voting system such as FPTP.

The electoral arithmetic will have a strong bearing on the debate about the use of the revenue variation powers and on policy priorities. Will Labour's commitment to tackling social exclusion be compromised by the need to co-operate with the Liberal Democrats, for example by having to modify its policies on social rented housing to reflect the Liberal Democrats' predominantly rural constituency? Or will it have to be more responsive to those within its own ranks pushing for further and faster reforms? A comparatively poor Labour performance, forcing it back into its urban and central belt heartlands, might make for a more traditionalist grouping among the Labour ranks, less predisposed to cross-party co-operation.

WINNING POPULAR SUPPORT

If Scotland's voters were asked today what they hoped the first administration would achieve, few would mention a fairer voting system, a less adversarial political culture or even more women MPs. These issues have exercised the minds of the Convention with good reason, but they will not be high on the list of 'most important issues' when the inaugural Parliament is being elected. All parties, including those which remained outside the Convention's work, will have to prepare their programmes for the first Parliament.

If a Scottish Parliament is to help build a more inclusive democracy, it must aim to be geographically sensitive to the whole of Scotland. The more remote communities returned the highest negative verdict in the 1979 Scottish Assembly referendum. They will need to be convinced that government from Edinburgh will be more sensitive to their needs than government from Westminster or Brussels. What can be said with some optimism is that the Convention's proposed electoral system will provide every party with new incentives to devise a national policy platform and maximize its support, even in their least promising territory.

Devolution will be extending representative democracy at a time when the narrower managerial elements of governance appear triumphant and public cynicism is high. Sceptics dismiss democratic innovation as a distraction from the 'real issues', and indeed if these were developed instead of a clear policy programme, the charge would have credibility. Scotland is not immune to the decline in public confidence in the integrity of politicians. The answer lies not simply in enabling the new parliamentarians to be effective representatives, but in ensuring that there are routes to more direct participation for the public. For example, the Scottish Parliament will provide an opportunity to consider further innovations in the process of democratic consultation, including regional public hearings in the work of parliamentary inquiries on areas as diverse as housing policy in rural communities and crime reduction in urban estates. Such initiatives could help build the foundations of public confidence. We turn now to how the structure of the Scottish Parliament may influence political debate and the issues that are likely to shape each party's approach to the politics of devolution.

THE IMPACT OF CHANGE: PROPORTIONAL REPRESENTATION AND PARLIAMENTARY PROCEDURE

One of the most intriguing elements of the Scottish Parliament will be how far it differs from Westminster both in how it works and what it achieves. We discuss two key differences: the impact of proportional representation; and the new structure for Parliamentary business.

How far will a new voting system transform Scottish political culture? The Additional Member System will go some way to breaking down the regional heartlands which exaggerate differences in voting preferences: Conservative and SNP candidates will be elected in Glasgow, Liberal Democrats in Lothian and Labour candidates in the Highlands. This is likely to have a greater impact on those parties, particularly the SNP, who are under-represented in the FPTP section. A clear majority of SNP and Conservative MSPs will be elected to list seats. Those MSPs will be disproportionately selected on a regional rather than a constituency basis. How far this will influence the standing of the parties will depend on how far the list MSPs have a different approach from constituency members. The list MSPs may be more policy-oriented in their concerns than constituency members, for example. The proportional system will also give each party a renewed incentive to devise a national platform and avoid being too closely identified with one part of Scotland.

The Convention parties have placed great stress on the Electoral Agreement which sets out their objective of an equal number of women and men elected to the first Scottish Parliament. The potential legal difficulties have been noted, but if it stands the Agreement will be a historic one. More women representatives would redress the long-term gender imbalance in British politics. The extent to which it changes the nature of politics will depend upon how far the women elected seek to ensure that this is so. Although we do not explore the technical details of the Agreement here, it is clearly a matter that deserves the attention of the architects of devolution.

One further issue is the impact of new Parliamentary procedures. If, as was proposed by the Convention, the Parliament's committees have the right to initiate legislation, the opportunities for *ad hoc* cross-party alliances will be considerably enhanced. The proposed diminution of executive power is likely to alter the political tone. The extent to which the very tight rules on party discipline that characterize Westminster will be reflected in Edinburgh is open to conjecture. Most will agree that the new Parliament should not aim to be simply a 'Westminster of the North' (Crick and Millar 1995). But nor should committed devolutionists underestimate the implications of proposals such as removing control of parliamentary business from the executive. Further consideration must be given to the appropriate balance for Scotland between the executive and the legislature.

RELATIONS WITHIN THE PARTIES

The first Scottish administration will pose challenges for each of the political parties represented in Edinburgh. A Labour-led government in Edinburgh is almost certain to wish to move in a different direction in some areas from a majority Labour government at Westminster. Indeed that government should legislate for a Scottish Parliament with this expectation. The drivers of such diversity will be various: geographic; cultural; institutional; and historical. The UK's political culture, and more importantly each party's internal culture, will have to learn to accept and accommodate such differences. The transition will not be easy, but it is likely to affect all major parties. The SNP may appear to have the luxury of being able to avoid taking a position on UK issues as it wishes, but it will also encounter the problems of liaising between its Edinburgh and Westminster MPs. Today, intra-party differences are invariably seen as splits. But this characterization of genuine diversity in approach need not dominate in the future, if a high level of discipline is exercised with regard to separate spheres of influence and competence. It will involve the recognition of the sovereignty of the Scottish parties in all areas of devolved responsibility. Negotiated goodwill on all sides will be vital to handle these sensitive issues.

On the politics of education, for example, the Scottish debate will be very different from that in England. Many will consider English education policy to be of little relevance to the programme of a Scottish Parliament. Although the number of Scottish schools opting for grant-maintained status can be counted on one hand, the issue retains a strong symbolic importance. Labour in Scotland might lead an anti-Conservative majority in favour of removing the option of schools leaving local authority management. There are also likely to be differences on teaching standards and the development of the profession.

Relations between the Scottish and the UK party will loom largest for the party or parties in government at Westminster. In the first term, most attention will probably therefore focus on relations between the Scottish Labour Party, its MPs and MSPs and the UK Party.

[. . .]

Whatever scenario unfolds, the future of Scottish politics seems certain to be more complex and intriguing than in recent years. Pessimists and opponents of devolution will characterize these scenarios as a recipe for crisis. Yet, one of the goals of constitutional reform is to establish a system of checks and balances by ensuring power is held at a number of levels and shared between different political groupings. The unhappy relationship between local and central government since the mid-1970s has reflected the growing centralization of power. Legitimate policy differences, reflecting party control and geography, were denied expression. Devolution will certainly be a recipe for diversity, but it is not beyond the capacity of British government to devise more appropriate means of managing disagreement.

CONCLUSION

We have explored how a Scottish Parliament can be established on firm political foundations, secure into the future and rooted in its relevance to Scotland. Institutional reform can significantly improve the governance of Scotland. The establishment of that Parliament will indeed be a historic achievement, but it will not of itself conclude the 'unfinished business' of devolution.

The passage of the legislation and wider constitutional settlement will set the tone for what follows. The arguments for supporting devolution are rooted in the demand for democratic expression. The political dividend from devolution cannot be expected to belong to only one party. The establishment of the Parliament will provide a new impetus to multi-party politics and Scottish civic life. Each party will face difficulties in adjusting to the new climate. In the period before the general election, and up to the establishment of the Parliament, the task for the advocates of devolution is to align the wide public sympathy that undoubtedly exists with a sense of the practical policies that might then follow. Giving Scotland's voters a sense of the difference that devolution will make is essential to avoid opponents turning sympathy into anxiety and scepticism.

Scottish commentators often make much of Scotland's differences with England: the much smaller level of Conservative support and the rejection of Thatcherism; the greater commitment to public services like comprehensive education; and the greater willingness to finance social and economic improvements. While the degree of diversity can be exaggerated, devolution represents the appropriate opportunity to draw upon those resources of social capital.

Scotland will also have the chance to pioneer the new politics of pluralism. That will place devolution in its true context – as the means to a more cohesive and better governed society, not as an end in itself. A process which is truly relevant to Scotland's needs will make demands on its citizens, not just its politicians. A process which is seen to work will have attractions for the rest of Britain as well, in terms of both policy and constitutional change. The twentieth century's failed attempts at devolution might thus be consigned to history by the start of the twenty-first.

NOTE

1 The anomaly whereby Scottish MPs would retain the right to vote on matters affecting only England and Wales but no Westminster MP would have such a voting entitlement on the same issues for Scotland (having been transferred to the Edinburgh Parliament). This issue was acknowledged earlier by the Kilbrandon Commission, who favoured a reduction in Scottish representation at Westminster to parity levels (but rejected the case for a further 'discount').

REFERENCES

Bogdanor, V. (1996) 'Devolution', in *Options for Britain*, ed. D. Halpern *et al.*, Dartmouth Publishing: Aldershot.

Crick, B. and Millar, D. (1995) *To Make the Parliament of Scotland a Model for Democracy*, John Wheatley Centre: Edinburgh.

McLean, I. (1995) 'The Representation of Scotland and Wales in the House of Commons', *Political Quarterly*, Vol. 66.4, pp. 250–68.

Munro, C. R. (1994) 'The Union of 1707 and the British Constitution', *Scotland and the Union, Hume Papers on Public Policy*, Vol. 2.2.

Tindale, S. (1995) *Devolution on Demand: Options for the English Regions and London*, Institute for Public Policy Research: London.

Canada and Quebec: two nationalisms in the global age
MICHAEL KEATING

BACK TO THE CONSTITUTION (AGAIN)

In September 1994 the Parti Québécois (PQ) came back to power in the Quebec provincial elections, promising a referendum on 'sovereignty' within

Table 1 *Quebec election 12 September 1994*

	%	*seats*	*candidates*
Parti Québécois	44.7	77	125
Liberals	44.3	47	125
Parti Action Démocratique du Québec	6.5	1	80

a year. This followed the breakthrough of October 1993 when the Bloc Québécois swept the province in the federal elections and, with the collapse of the governing Conservatives, became the official opposition in Ottawa. Canada's constitutional saga, temporarily put to rest after the failure of the 1992 referendum on the Charlottetown Accord, began anew. Many Canadians see this as an irritating distraction from the pressing issues of the economy and government budget deficits. Others welcome the opportunity to settle the issue clearly once and for all, with Quebec either in or out. The latter group is likely to be disappointed. Quebec's relationship with its Anglophone neighbours has been an issue for over two hundred years and, whatever the outcome of the referendum, will be subject to constant negotiation over a wide range of matters. Sovereignty, a difficult concept at any time, has become almost impossible to define in the modern world, with its interdependence and permeable borders and in which the state is giving up powers to the market, to civil society and to supranational and subnational actors. Furthermore, the people have not given a clear verdict at the polls. While the PQ gained a large parliamentary majority in 1994, they were virtually tied in the popular vote with the provincial Liberals. The balance in the popular vote was held by the fledgling Parti Action Démocratique du Québec, whose policy was to seek a third way between the existing federal system and independence (table 1). Opinion polls showed that, even while voting for the PQ, most Québécois rejected independence. They merely wanted a change of government, after nine years of Liberal rule. The referendum of October 1995 gave an equally unclear result, with another tied vote.

Ambivalence is not a new feature in Quebec politics. It runs through the entire history of Quebec's position within Canada, as a distinct people within a larger federation. In the last twenty years, however, the issue has taken a new form as a movement has developed for Quebec independence, and the old mechanisms for managing the relationship have broken down. Quebec and the rest of Canada are both seeking a formula for asserting their national identity in a changing and interdependent world. These nation-building projects are increasingly in conflict.

THE TWO FOUNDING PEOPLES

Canada traditionally sustained a doctrine of 'two founding peoples', the French and the Anglophone community, the latter rooted culturally in the British Isles (English, Scots, Welsh and Irish are, for Canadian census and other purposes, treated as a single ethnic group). There were brief attempts at assimilation after the conquest of Quebec in 1763 and again in the mid-nineteenth century, but for most of Canada's history the Quebec issue was managed by a combination of devolution and consociational accommodation. Under confederation from 1867 Quebec had its own government with extensive powers in cultural and social matters. It retained its educational system, its religious settlement, its language and its own civil code. At federal level, Quebec politicians occupied prominent positions in the main Canadian parties.

The two founding peoples in practice were anything but equal. Anglophones soon outnumbered Francophones and as the Canadian nation was built from sea to sea during the late nineteenth century the west came to be largely an Anglophone preserve. Francophone rights were infringed in the Manitoba school legislation of 1890 and in Ontario, the Orange Order gained influence with a militantly anti-French and anti-Catholic stance. Within Quebec, there was a cultural division of labour. The main sectors of the economy and the financial centre in Montreal were controlled by an Anglophone bourgeoisie; Francophones, although in the majority, were concentrated in lower status occupations. Politics, the small provincial bureaucracy and the legal profession, were Francophone domains. From the mid-nineteenth century, immense power was wielded by the ultramontane wing of the Catholic Church, which resisted modernization, industrialization and urbanization as a threat to traditional values and Francophone culture. The Church controlled the education system and social services, focusing on the need for the Francophone minority to survive by drawing in on itself and resisting outside influence. This was a form of ethnic particularism but cannot be called nationalism, since it did not make demands for constitutional change. Under the regime of Maurice Duplessis and his Union Nationale (1936–9, 1944–60), this strategy was carried into the modern era. Closely allied to the Church, Duplessis resisted social modernization and liberalization and suppressed trade unions, while making deals on favourable terms with Anglophone and US corporations to invest in Quebec. Intrusions of the federal government into Quebec's affairs were resisted, even to the point of refusing federal funds tied to new programmes.

The system broke down in the 1960s with the Quiet Revolution, a programme of economic, social and political modernization associated with the Liberal government of Jean Lesage (1960-6), and with the reforms of successive Liberal and PQ governments in the 1970s. Modernization did not, despite the fears of the traditionalists and the theories of the diffusionist school of social science, entail a loss of Quebec's Francophone identity. Rather, this identity was itself updated and recast, and used as an instrument of modernization. The slogan of the Quiet Revolution, *maîtres chez nous* (masters in our own house), signalled the desire of the repressed ethnic group to improve its socio-economic status. The main instrument for this was an expanded, revitalized and secularized Quebec state. A Ministry of Education was set up to [reduce the Church's] control of instruction. A Ministry of Culture was established. Selective nationalization was used to take control of key enterprises and to open up opportunities for Francophones. Quebec established its own pension scheme, separate from the rest of Canada, and used it to fund the Caisse de Dépôt et de Placement, an investment agency with a brief to develop Quebec-owned industry. With this and other instruments, a Francophone business class was brought into being and the balance of control in the economy shifted markedly. A series of language laws in the 1970s sought to promote French and to offer opportunities for Francophones in the business world. The main provisions were: a requirement for firms to use French in their business activities; a restriction on the ability of parents to send their children to English schools, with a view to ensuring the assimilation of immigrants into the French culture; a restriction on the use of languages other than French in commercial advertising.

This all brought into being a new type of nationalism in Quebec (Langlois 1991a; Gagnon and Rocher 1992; Latouche 1993), based less on ethnic particularism than on the territory of Quebec and the society which it sustains. It is outward-looking and self-confident, open to change rather than resistant. It is concerned with the promotion of Quebec rather than Francophones in the Canadian context. *Canadiens*, who in the nineteenth century came to identify themselves as French-Canadians, now see themselves as *Québécois*. Surveys have shown that the percentage of Francophones identifying themselves as Québécois increased between 1970 and 1990 from 21 to 59, while the proportion identifying themselves as Canadians fell from 34 per cent to 9 per cent (Pinard 1992). The meaning of this shift can be gauged from comparing the definitions given by the traditionalist Tremblay Commission of 1954 with that of the National Assembly Commission on sovereignty in 1992. According to Tremblay:

> The French Canadians are almost all of the Catholic faith. [...] The French Canadians are of French origin and culture [...] the French Canadians are the only group whose religious and cultural particularism almost exactly coincide. Only French Canada, as a homogeneous group, presents the double differentiating factor of religion and culture (Tremblay 1973: 6).

By contrast, the 1992 commission defined Quebec as:

> a modern, multi-ethnic community, founded on shared common values, a normal language of communication, and participation in collective life.

Rather than seeing itself in ethnic terms, Quebec is becoming a 'global society', a complete nation containing a diversity of interests and identities (Langlois 1991a). Many Quebec intellectuals see this as the only way in which Quebec can integrate itself as a society while projecting itself in the world (Gagnon and Rocher 1992; Balthazar 1993; Latouche 1993).

Some claim that Quebec has made the transition from ethnic particularism to civic nationalism; others, noting that nationalism is still almost entirely confined to the Francophone community, merely hope that this may become the case. A narrowly based ethnic nationalism would risk depriving the nation-building project of both internal and external legitimacy. Civic nationalism, while continuing to promote a French-speaking Quebec, could welcome other ethnic groups into the community and allow cultural pluralism. While such a comprehensive notion of national identity might reduce ethnic conflict within Quebec, it might also make the accommodation of Quebec within Canada more difficult; this is because it makes Quebec the primary unit of identity and legitimizes the government of Quebec's claim to general powers of social and economic regulation, not reducible to pre-defined constitutional competences.

Quebec nationalism has made only part of the transition from ethnic to civic. Political parties in Quebec now include non-Francophones within their conception of the society and the Parti Québécois parades candidates of non-French origin. Yet the PQ programme of 1991 defines Québécois as Francophones and in 1993 the PQ leader Jacques Parizeau declared that independence is possible merely with the support of the old-stock Québécois (*Québécois de souche*) (*La Presse*, 24 January 1993). Similar declarations are regularly made by prominent nationalists and equally regularly denounced by the nationalist mainstream elite. The collective rights which are invoked by nationalists are in practice those of the Francophone community. Support for Quebec nationalism of any sort is almost entirely confined to Francophones. There is a sharp antagonism between Quebec nationalists and native peoples, particularly the Cree in the north and the Mohawks in the south. Native leaders have made it clear that they will not recognize the authority of an independent Quebec. The PQ, while supporting native self-government, denies the aboriginal peoples the right of sovereignty or the right to secede from Quebec.

Another doctrinal shift was from a closed, inward-looking and protectionist nationalism to a continental and global outlook. From the time of the Quiet Revolution, Quebec governments had sought an opening to the world and a counterbalance to Ottawa (Québec 1991). In the 1980s both main Quebec parties became ardent supporters of free trade with the United States and later Mexico (Martin 1996). This was a strategy both political and economic, intended to weaken the influence of the Canadian federal government while promoting the modernization and restructuring of the Quebec economy on liberal market lines. The nationalist agenda no longer focuses merely on Quebec's relationship with the rest of Canada. It is concerned with how Quebec, as a collectivity and society, fits into the new international trading and political order. Particular emphasis is placed on Quebec's position as a small, French-speaking society within North America. English Canadian nationalists, especially on the left, are vehemently opposed to free trade with the United States, which they see as a threat to Canada's independence, its welfare state and its distinct model of society. Left-wing nationalists in English Canada, who had previously sympathized with Quebec's aspirations, broke with them on this issue (Resnick 1990; Latouche 1990).

Modern Quebec nationalism, having broken with the Catholic traditionalism of the Duplessis era, has contained both a liberal, modernizing strand and a social democratic one. During the 1960s and 1970s the two strands shared an interest in using the government for social and economic modernization. By the early 1980s the gap between the social democratic and liberal concepts of Quebec nationalism was more in evidence as the PQ government adopted much of the agenda of the new right, with fiscal austerity, public sector wage cuts, cutbacks in social services and privatization. By the early 1990s both main parties in Quebec were committed to getting Quebec into the mainstream of North American advanced capitalism. This too, however, took a distinctively Québécois form, geared to the interests of the local business class (Balthazar 1991) and the PQ retained a social democratic wing. In the aftermath of the 1995 referendum, as the PQ government turned its attention to deficit reduction, a split reopened between the pro-business and social democratic wings of the movement.

Also during the 1960s and 1970s a rival and very different nation-building process was taking place in Canada as a whole. In 1966 Canada acquired its own flag, with its maple leaf design. Under Pierre Trudeau, a vision was developed of a united Canadian nation, which could accommodate Francophone–Anglophone differences, immigrant cultures and individual rights. The national policy of bilingualism enshrined in the Official Languages Act of 1969 was intended to make Francophones feel at home anywhere in Canada, rather than cleaving to Quebec nationalism. The policy of multiculturalism was intended to forge a Canadian identity which, unlike the US melting pot, could recognize and cultivate cultural identities. The Charter of Rights finally incorporated in the Constitution Act of 1982 was intended to provide protection of individual rights from coast to coast, as a badge of civic equality and citizenship. These visions clashed with the emerging national self-image of Quebec. Canadian bilingualism was seen as a way of weakening French predominance in Quebec and the consequential protection of Francophones elsewhere in Canada was now of little concern. Multiculturalism was seen as a way of reducing Francophones to just one of a multiplicity of ethnic groups rather than a co-founding people. Quebec's own territorial nationalism, like that of France itself, emphasizes the need to integrate immigrants linguistically and culturally in order to incorporate them into the national society. The Charter of Rights was seen as emphasizing individualist rights, in the fashion of the USA, rather than collectivist values which are more important in Quebec (as in European) society. This conflict became very intense when provisions of Quebec's language laws were struck down in the 1980s as conflicting with the Charter.

Quebec nationalist intellectuals insist that these nation-building projects are incompatible (Langlois 1991a, 1991b; Gagnon and Rocher 1992; Laforest 1992). While the rest of North America supports an individualist liberalism in which the role of government is confined to regulation of relations among individuals and corporations, Quebec retains a larger view of the public domain in which society as a whole may adopt goals and promote its version of the desirable life (Taylor 1993). This produces a form of debate more familiar in continental Europe than in the Anglo-Saxon tradition, one in which entire rival projects for society are counterposed and the agenda of politics is extended. Nationalists of all stripes in Quebec insist that this emphasis on collective goals and rights is a defining feature of their society. The Bélanger-Campeau commission (1991) insisted that Quebec could not accept the 1982 Canadian constitution and charter of rights because it entrenched the equality of all Canadians on the same basis, thus denying Quebec's distinct society; its provisions for multiculturalism reduced the Québécois to one ethnic group among many; and the equality of provinces deprived Quebec of the means for promoting its distinct society. In this vision, Quebec is not defined as an ethnic group, but nor is it a society of atomized individuals, brought together for mere convenience. Rather it is a territorial collectivity bound together by common values, with a dominant language, but containing a variety of minority ethnic communities.

There is a certain irony here in that it is precisely these characteristics which are invoked in slightly different terms by Anglophone Canadians to distinguish their society from the United States. The irony is compounded by the conflicting views on close relationships with the United States held by English Canadian and Quebec nationalists. Canadian nationalists, especially on the left, have resisted the US-Canada Free Trade Agreement and NAFTA as a threat to national sovereignty. Quebec nationalists (except for the trade unions) support it as an opportunity to gain national independence. There is a further paradox that, as Quebec has become economically and socially more like the rest of Canada (and North America generally) its identity has been strengthened. This is more of a paradox to observers outside Quebec, who tend to judge modernization from their own standpoint, than to those within, to whom it seems perfectly natural. One could make a very similar argument about Scotland, Catalonia and a number of other stateless nations (Keating 1996).

We are confronted, then, with a clash of two 'global societies' (Langlois, 1991a, 1991b). Both Quebec and Canada claim to be the basic frame of reference for identity, and for political decision-making and legitimacy. Nationalists insist that the only way out of this is national independence. Yet at the same time there is a keen awareness of mutual dependence and the need for co-operation. Most Québécois are fearful of the costs and disruption of independence and would like to resolve the question without risking these.

THE MEANING OF NATIONALISM IN QUEBEC

The meaning of nationalism and independence in Quebec has always been ambiguous. The first important separatist party, the Parti Québécois (PQ), was formed in 1968 under René Lévesque, a former Liberal minister. Lévesque won the 1976 provincial elections on 'sovereignty association', proposing a referendum to obtain a mandate to negotiate a new relationship with Canada. This would leave the economic union intact, while making Quebec into a sovereign state. The referendum was lost by a substantial margin in 1980 but the PQ government was easily re-elected the following year. In its second mandate, it split on the constitutional question. Lévesque and the majority virtually abandoned independence and took the *beau risque* of negotiating with the Conservative federal government of Brian Mulroney, elected in 1984 with the support of some prominent Quebec nationalists. A quarter of the Quebec cabinet, including Jacques Parizeau, resigned in protest and, following the defeat of the PQ government in 1985, seized control of the party and turned it in a more radical direction. In 1988 Parizeau was elected leader and the party committed itself to a policy of outright independence. The hard line did not survive the PQ's defeat at the provincial elections of 1989. By the early 1990s it was once again following a very ambivalent line. The cumbersome phrase 'sovereignty association' was discredited by the referendum of 1980 and replaced by the simple idea of 'sovereignty'. This, however, is equally open to interpretation, which makes the outcome little different. The PQ's official policy is to win a referendum on sovereignty, after which Quebec will become an independent state. Yet at the same time, the party wishes to retain the economic union with Canada, use the Canadian currency, maintain dual citizenship and allow free movement of labour. There would be joint commissions to handle matters of common interest (Parti Québécois 1993). Lucien Bouchard, then leader of the Bloc Québécois in the federal parliament, advocated joint institutions on the lines of the European Parliament. This might look very much like sovereignty association all over again but there is an important difference in procedure. In 1980 Lévesque asked for a mandate to negotiate a new deal with Canada. In 1995 Parizeau proposed to ask for a mandate for sovereignty and then, as a sovereign state, to negotiate with Canada. Even this was fudged for a while in late 1994 when Parizeau, aware that many Québécois would not take the risk, started to argue that even non-separatists could vote YES and then press for a confederal rather than independent arrangement in the aftermath.

The policy of limited sovereignty is given more credibility this time by the

external context. The most important factor is the North American Free Trade
Agreement (NAFTA), which would ensure the maintenance of economic links
with the rest of Canada and beyond. NAFTA is invoked frequently as a new
framework for a sovereign Quebec and one which will ensure that Canadian
influence is balanced by that of the United States. More widely, the PQ also
promises to adhere to all Canada's existing international institutions, including
the Francophonie, the Organization of American States, NATO, GATT, the
Organization for Security and Cooperation in Europe and even the (British)
Commonwealth (Parti Québécois 1993). Defence issues are not widely discussed but there is a general understanding that American pressure will ensure
that these are little changed and that, in any case, the United States would have
a strong interest in keeping intruders out of Quebec (Jockel 1992). The PQ has
thus transformed the meaning of national independence but in a manner which
arguably is in tune with the modern world of limited sovereignty.

If the PQ has proposed retaining much of the infrastructure of Canadian
federalism, the non-separatist parties have insisted on radical transfers of
powers and have been prepared to flirt with sovereignty. Daniel Johnson,
leader of the Union Nationale in the late 1960s, demanded 'equality or
independence'. Provincial Liberal governments in the early 1960s pressed for
additional powers and contemplated independence. Robert Bourassa, Liberal
leader before and after the PQ governments of 1976-85, was a master of
ambiguity. Starting and ending his long career as a committed federalist, he
talked of 'profitable federalism' and refused to sign on to the Canadian
constitution without additional powers for Quebec. When the Meech Lake
Accord collapsed in 1988, he unleashed the nationalist wing of his party. The
Allaire report, which was briefly party policy, proposed such a radical transfer
of powers to Quebec as to rival the PQ programme. He set up a parliamentary
committee of inquiry to examine the practicalities of sovereignty and promised
a referendum on sovereignty if a suitable offer were not received from the rest
of Canada within a specific time frame. Bourassa even mused that, given the
consensus on Quebec's right to self-determination, it was really 'sovereign'
already.

THE SUPPORT BASE OF NATIONALISM

Gauging popular support for Quebec nationalism is made difficult by the
variations and ambiguities in the nationalist project. Public opinion has been
highly unstable, with support for nationalism increasing at times of constitutional crisis such as the aftermath of the 1988 Supreme Court ruling on the
language laws and the crisis over the ratification of the Meech Lake Accord in
1990-1. Support for the status quo also tends to rise in periods of economic
recession. There is more support for 'softer' nationalist options, allowing for

continued association with Canada, than for 'harder' ones which suggest complete separation. Polls in the 1970s and 1980s showed more support for sovereignty association than for unqualified sovereignty but by the 1990s the difference had largely disappeared (Cloutier *et al.* 1992), probably because the PQ had ceased to use the phrase sovereignty association while incorporating much of its meaning into the new sovereignty formula. Support for the strongest status quo position, which is that Quebec should have the same status as other provinces, stood at 72 per cent in 1975; it then declined, but rose again to over 50 per cent in 1983–5, following the economic recession and the backtracking of the PQ on the independence issue (Cloutier *et al.* 1992). Support for the various sovereignty options shows considerable fluctuations but support has never fallen below 30 per cent and, at times of particular excitement, has risen above 50 per cent. This appears to be the range of support for serious nationalist positions in Quebec.

Most Québécois believe that the softer question about sovereignty does mean something substantively different from independence, more akin to the sovereignty association formula of the 1970s. A poll taken in March 1994 indicated that 58 per cent thought that sovereignty and separation were not the same thing (Léger and Léger, *Globe and Mail*, 10 March 1994). One in June 1994 showed 49 per cent believing that sovereignty implied a formal economic association with Canada (*Reid Report*, 9.6, June 1994). Of those inclined to vote for independence, only 40 per cent envisaged complete independence ('like France or Britain') while 57 per cent interpreted it as including an economic association with Canada. The assumption that sovereignty means something less than separatism is clearly reflected in the fact that it scores more highly in public opinion.

There is some evidence about what Québécois mean by sovereignty and more powers (Blais and Nadeau 1992). Most want Quebec to have full powers in the area of culture and language, including education. Few want it to be responsible for defence and foreign affairs. A majority favour Quebec having sole responsibility in social policy, but want joint arrangements in economic matters. So they are concerned to protect their cultural and national identity and believe that they can maintain the social balance, but recognize the interdependence of economic policy and have little interest in the classic state functions of defence and diplomacy. A poll of 1991 showed that 75 per cent of Québécois believed that an independent Quebec should have an economic association with Canada, over 33 per cent supported dual citizenship and over 50 per cent favoured a joint department of defence (*Reid Report*, 7.2, 1992).

One might reasonably conclude that most Québécois want a system in which the government of Quebec is the primary focus of their national allegiance but in which powers are shared with the rest of Canada where appropriate. They are fearful of the risks of separatism and want to retain existing economic relationships. This might be characterized as a confederal arrangement, or as something on the lines of the European Union. The problem is that this sort of arrangement is not on offer, either from Quebec elites or from the rest of Canada.

NEGOTIATING A SOLUTION

There have been many attempts over the years to accommodate Quebec within the Canadian confederation. The focus of these efforts was the patriation of the Canadian constitution which, until 1982, consisted of the British North America Act, amendable only by the British Parliament. In the 1960s the Fulton and Favreau formulas were rejected by Quebec as not giving the province enough power. Under Trudeau the federal government sought to build a Canadian identity in which the provinces would all be equal, there would be identical rights throughout the country, bilingualism would accommodate the needs of Francophones, and multiculturalism would satisfy the aspirations of minority populations. There would be an amending formula which would not allow any one province to block constitutional changes. The federal government could extend the welfare state by spending in areas of provincial jurisdiction. This collided with the view of both major parties in Quebec. They insisted that Quebec's distinct status should be recognized, especially in cultural and linguistic matters, that Quebec should have a veto on future constitutional changes, and that the federal spending power in matters of provincial jurisdiction be limited. In 1971 Bourassa, Liberal leader of Quebec, accepted the Victoria formula for constitutional repatriation but had to reject it following pressure at home. After the failure of the Quebec referendum in 1980, the Lévesque government re-entered talks with Ottawa and the other provinces but failed to agree. The constitution was patriated without Quebec's consent, including a Charter of Rights and Freedoms. At the insistence of leaders of the western provinces, the latter included a 'notwithstanding clause' allowing a federal or provincial government to override court decisions to strike down laws in certain instances. The notwithstanding clause was then used extensively by the PQ government of Quebec in effect to opt out of the charter.

In 1985 the Conservative government of Brian Mulroney reopened the dossier. Mulroney had assembled a rather precarious coalition of Quebec nationalists and disaffected westerners. His vision of Canada was very different from Trudeau's and his style of government relied heavily on the making of deals rather than the pursuit of general principles. Three measures were of particular importance in breaking from the Trudeau form of Canadian nationalism. The National Energy Policy, which had forced the western provinces to sell their oil cheaply to the industrialized east, was repealed. A free trade agreement was negotiated with the United States, though opposed by Canadian nationalists who feared that economic integration would entail the loss of political independence. To accommodate Quebec, Mulroney negotiated the Meech Lake Accord of 1987, agreed by all ten provinces and the federal government. This provided for the recognition of Quebec as a 'distinct society', for a Quebec veto on constitutional change, for the appointment of Quebec judges to the Supreme Court of Canada, and gave Quebec a role in selecting immigrants to the province. Although agreed by all the provinces, Meech Lake was unpopular in English Canada, where it was seen as giving too much to Quebec.

Interminable debates took place on the meaning of the 'distinct society' clause, presented in Quebec as a substantial concession to the identity of the Québécois, and in English Canada as a mere form of words. Three years were given for all provinces to ratify Meech Lake, by which time several had changed their governing majorities so that, when the deadline approached, Manitoba had failed to ratify and Newfoundland had rescinded its ratification resolution. One of the key factors in destroying support for Meech Lake outside Quebec was the reaction of the Bourassa government to the Supreme Court decision in 1988 to strike down the provision of the Quebec language law that all commercial signs should be in French. Bourassa invoked the notwithstanding clause to protect a characteristic compromise in which bilingual signs would be allowed indoors but French only outdoors. Another element was the rising demands from other groups that, if Quebec were to be accommodated in the constitution, then their demands must also be recognized. The most important were the western provinces, demanding an elected Senate with equal representation from all provinces, a demand known as the Triple E Senate (equal, elected and effective); and native peoples who sought constitutional guarantees for their status.

Reaction in Quebec to the failure of Meech Lake was a rise in nationalist feeling. Bourassa withdrew from intergovernmental talks and put a resolution through the national assembly providing for a referendum on sovereignty in 1992 if new offers were not received from the rest of Canada. The Bélanger-Campeau commission was set up to examine the constitutional future of Quebec and two parliamentary committees established, one to consider the mechanics of the transition to sovereignty, and the other to consider offers from the rest of Canada. During 1992 the temperature cooled sufficiently for Bourassa to return to the negotiating table for another marathon session, which produced the Charlottetown Accord. This was intended to give Quebec the substance of Meech Lake, while also satisfying the demands of the west and the native peoples and pan-Canadian nationalists. It started with a general declaration of principles, the Canada clause, into which was inserted the Quebec 'distinct society' clause, together with clauses about aboriginal peoples, racial and gender equality and the rights of the provinces and the government of Canada. The 'inherent right' of aboriginal self-government was recognized. There was provision for a new Senate with equal representation from the provinces, with the mode of election left to provincial laws. The Senate would have equal legislative powers with the House of Commons, except for money bills; conflicts would be resolved in joint sittings. Provinces were given a role in nominating justices of the Supreme Court, with reserved positions for Quebec. There was a clarification of exclusive provincial jurisdiction in several fields and a provision for provinces to opt out of federally funded programmes, as long as they were pursuing programmes compatible with the objectives of these. There was a complicated clause on responsibility for labour market development and training. The federal government had tried to insist on a commitment to a Canadian common market, with the dismantling of the extensive trade barriers between the provinces. Social advocates had sought guarantees for a nationwide health care system, education and social services. All that was achieved was a vague clause of economic and social union, which explicitly did not alter the powers of any level of government.

The Charlottetown Accord had fifty-one pages of legal draft, representing the apogee of efforts to constitutionalize the problems of Canadian diversity and resolve them with forms of words. The referendum campaign was marked by minute exegeses of the meaning of the various clauses and their compatibility. Quebec nationalists objected to their concerns being put on a plane with those of the west and the aboriginal peoples and to the distinct society clause being incorporated in the Canada clause. Some Anglophone feminist groups (though not those in Quebec) continued to argue that the distinct society clause was a threat to gender equality. The western-based Reform Party complained that the Triple E Senate had not been achieved. Left-wing and labour groups complained about the internal free trade clause, weak though this was. Anglophones complained that the deal gave too much to Quebec; Quebec nationalists that it gave too little. Supported by all three federal parties, the governments of all the provinces and territories and the leadership of the Assembly of First Nations, Charlottetown could still be attacked as an elite accord, done over the heads of the people. It was also brought home that the accord contained so many loose ends that it did not provide a final solution to the constitutional conundrum. The battle would merely move to the courts where the accord would be interpreted; and further rounds of negotiation would be needed to fill in the details. As the campaign progressed, support unravelled and the accord went down to defeat both in Quebec and in English Canada. There matters rested until the election of the PQ government in Quebec in 1996.

Jacques Parizeau, the new leader, had promised a referendum on sovereignty within a year of winning power. His allies Lucien Bouchard, then leader of the Bloc Québécois and Mario Dumont, leader of the Parti Action Démocratique, a 'soft sovereigntist' breakaway party from the Quebec Liberals, pressed for postponement if the polls were adverse, and for a softer question. By the summer of 1995 they had forced Parizeau to concede and a joint statement on 12 June promised sovereignty with a partnership. This would include a common market and the use of the Canadian currency, together with a joint executive for Quebec and Canada to decide on common issues, with representation according to population, and an advisory parliamentary assembly, with parity of representation. This was modelled on the European Union and represented an effective return to the old sovereignty association formula. The referendum question was a hybrid, committing Quebec to sovereignty in the event of victory but keeping the association element in the forefront. It read:

> Do you agree that Quebec should become sovereign, after having made a formal offer to Canada for a new economic and political partnership, within the scope of the Bill Respecting the Future of Quebec, and of the agreement signed on June, 12, 1995?

This is clearly in the sovereignty association tradition, but the difference with 1980 is that the accession to sovereignty is not conditional upon Canada accepting the offer of association. If Canada were to say No, Quebec would still become independent. The interpretation of this dominated the early stages of the campaign. Bouchard put a strong sovereignty association spin on it, promising that Canada would have to agree and that there was minimal risk. He spoke of a Yes vote as a 'lever' to force Canada to give Quebec a better deal. Parizeau, and occasionally Bouchard himself, at the same time insisted that a Yes vote would mean that Quebec was sovereign. Polls showed that up to a third of Yes voters believed that a sovereign Quebec on these terms would still be a province of Canada sending MPs to Ottawa, and that they would keep their Canadian passports.

The campaign started with a small No lead and most observers expected this to consolidate as voters contemplated the risks of independence. This did not happen and instead the two sides settled to a dead heat. The federalist campaign, led by Daniel Johnson, leader of the Quebec Liberals, focused almost exclusively on the economic risks and warnings of doom. The No campaign, initially led by the dull Parizeau, was taken over in late September by Bouchard, who gave it a new and emotive edge. Dismissing the studies of the costs of independence, including those commissioned by the PQ government itself, Bouchard spoke to the Québécois sense of pride and reminded them of Canada's persistent refusal to recognize their distinct national status. Minimizing the risks, he insisted that financial markets would force Canada to come to terms with Quebec after a Yes victory. On the day there were few undecideds left, and the turnout was a massive 93 per cent. 49.4 per cent voted Yes and 50.6 per cent voted No. The Yes side won a majority of Quebec constituencies and all the regions except for the Montreal region, the Anglophone Eastern Townships and the Outtawais region, home to many federal civil servants. Francophones voted about 60-40 for Yes, and Anglophones and Allophones (those whose native language is neither French nor English) voted 90-10 No.

CONCLUSION

The demise of Meech Lake and of the elaborate Charlottetown Accord indicate that a comprehensive, constitutionalized solution incorporating the Quebec issue is simply not possible. Quebec will not be satisfied with the mere status of a province like the others. Anglophone Canada will not concede it more. The 'distinct society' clause was an effort to paper over the cracks, presented in Quebec as a substantive power and in the rest of Canada as a mere declaratory statement. To be acceptable in Quebec, any solution requires a recognition of Quebec's national identity and the implications which this has for its government as the primary reference point for Québécois. Such a recognition is not in prospect. A solution acceptable in Quebec would also require an asymmetry in powers, with Quebec enjoying powers and a status which the other provinces do not want. This too is unacceptable. Canada has its own version of the West Lothian Question and the other provinces would not tolerate a Quebec with substantially greater powers having the same representation in the House of Commons. On the other hand, it could be argued in Canada as in the UK that there is already considerable asymmetry. Each province came into confederation on different terms. Representation in the House of Commons is biased heavily to the smaller provinces, and the government of Quebec has a domestic and international status which is rather different from those of the other provinces. Meech Lake and Charlottetown also showed that a constitutional settlement for Quebec alone is not acceptable to other groups who have entered the constitutional game. Yet an overall settlement involves too many actors, too many decision points and too many veto options to be viable.

Canadian and Quebec nationalism face very similar problems in the new global age. Nationalism has traditionally been sustained by ethnic identity, the state, and the institutions, traditions and practices of civil society. As it shifted from its basis in ethnic particularism, the state became more important as the expression of identity. Yet as the state retreats in the face of neo-liberal ideology and continental integration, it is less able to sustain this role. More of a burden then falls on civil society to maintain national identity in the face of weakened ethnic identity and a retreating state. This is true of Canada as much as for Quebec.

An asymmetrical federalism which recognizes the ambiguity of sovereignty, divided loyalty and multiple identity, is the preferred solution of most Québécois, to judge from the opinion polls. They would like to negotiate with the rest of Canada on a bilateral basis rather than being one of ten provinces. This is not on offer. Instead Québécois are to be asked about their second choice, between status quo federalism, or independence, categories which are of ever less relevance in the contemporary world. Francophones in Quebec see independence as their second choice, after special status within Canada.

Canadians outside Quebec tend to give symmetrical federalism as their first choice and Quebec independence as their second. The prospect is that both sides will end up getting their second choice, as an unplanned outcome. Anglophone Canadians and Québécois did not believe that the Charlottetown accord would settle the matter once and for all, and this explained much of the No vote then. The relationship between Quebec and the rest of Canada will continue to evolve and will always be the subject of negotiation. It is just part of normal politics.

REFERENCES

Assemblé Nationale (1992a), Commission d'étude des questions afférentes à l'accession du Québec à la souveraineté, *Projet de Rapport.* Québec: Assemblé Nationale.

Balthazar, L. (1990), *Bilan du nationalisme au Québec.* Montreal: l'Hexagone.

Balthazar, L. (1991), 'Conscience nationale et contexte internationale', in L. Balthazar, G. Laforest and V. Lemieux, *Le Québec et la restructuration du Canada, 1980–1992.* Saint-Laurent: Septentrion.

Balthazar, L. (1992), 'L'émancipation internationale d'un Etat fédéré (1960–1990)', in Rocher, F. (ed.), *Bilan québécois du fédéralisme canadien.* Montreal: vlb.

Balthazar, L. (1993), L'évolution du nationalisme québécois', in G. Daigle and G. Rocher, *Le Québec en jeu. Comprendre les grands défis.* Montreal: Presses de l'Université de Montréal.

Bélanger-Campeau (1991), *Rapport de la commission sur l'avenir politique et constitutionnel du Québec.* Co-chairs, M. Bélanger and J. Campeau, Quebec.

Blais, A. and Nadeau, R. (1992), 'To Be or Not to Be Sovereignist: Quebeckers' Perennial Dilemma', *Canadian Public Policy,* XVIII:1, pp. 89–103.

Cloutier, E., Guay, J. H. and Latouche, D. (1992), *Le virage. L'évolution de l'opinion publique au Québec depuis 1960, ou comment le Québec est devenu souverainiste.* Montreal: Québec/Amérique.

Dion, L. (1975), *Nationalismes et politique au Québec.* Montreal: Hurtubise.

Gagnon, A-G. and Rocher, F. (1992), 'Faire l'histoire au lieu de la subir', in A-G. Gagnon and F. Rocher, *Réplique aux détracteurs de la souveraineté du Québec.* Montreal: vlb.

Gagnon, A-G. and Montcalm, M.B. (1992), *Québec: au delà de la Révolution tranquille.* Montreal: vlb.

Jockel, J. T. (1992), 'Armée, securité du territoire et souveraineté', in A-G. Gagnon and F. Rocher, *Réplique aux détracteurs de la souveraineté du Québec.* Montreal: vlb.

Keating, M. (1996), *Nations against the State. The New Politics of Nationalism in Quebec, Catalonia and Scotland.* London: Macmillan.

Laforest, G. (1992), 'La Charte canadienne des droits et libertés au Québec: Nationalist, injuste et illégitime', in Rocher, F. (ed.), *Bilan québécois du fédéralisme canadien.* Montreal: vlb.

Langlois, S. (1991a), 'Le choc des deux sociétés globales', in L. Balthazar, G. Laforest and V. Lemieux, *Le Québec et la restructuration du Canada, 1980–1992.* Saint-Laurent: Septentrion.

Langlois, S. (1991b), 'Une société distincte à reconnaître et une identité collective à consolider', Commission sur l'avenir politique et constitutionel du Québec (Bélanger-Campeau Commission), *Document de travail,* 4, pp. 569–95. Québec: Commission.

Latouche, D. (1990), in Resnick, P., *Letters to a Québécois Friend, with a Reply by*

Daniel Latouche. Montreal: McGill-Queen's University Press.

Latouche, D. (1993), '"Québec, See Canada": Québec Nationalism in the New Global Age', in A-G. Gagnon (ed.), *Québec. State and Society*, 2nd edition. Scarborough, Ontario: Nelson.

Martin, P. (1996), 'When Nationalism Meets Continentalism. The Politics of Free Trade in Quebec', *Regional and Federal Studies*, 5.1, pp. 1–27.

Parti Québécois (1993), *Le Québec dans un monde nouveau*. Montreal: vlb.

Pinard, M. (1992), 'The Quebec Independence Movement. A Dramatic Reemergence', *McGill Working Papers in Social Behaviour*, 92–106. Montreal: Department of Sociology, McGill University.

Québec (1991), *Le Québec et l'interdépendance. Le monde pour l'horizon*. Québec: Gouvernement du Québec, Ministère des Affaires internationales.

Québec (1993), *Ministère des Affaires internationales. Rapport annuel 1992–3*. Quebec.

Reid Report, 1992–4, monthly, Toronto: Angus Reid.

Resnick, P. (1990), *Letters to a Québécois Friend, with a Reply by Daniel Latouche*. Montreal: McGill-Queen's University Press.

Taylor, C. (1993), 'The Deep Challenge of Dualism', in A-G. Gagnon (ed.), *Québec. State and Society*, 2nd edition. Scarborough, Ontario: Nelson.

Tremblay, A. (1973), *Report of the Royal Commission of Inquiry on Constitutional Problems*, ed. David Kwavnick. Toronto: McClelland and Stewart.

First nations in the USA
FRANKE WILMER

THE MORAL DILEMMA – SAVAGE PEOPLES AND CIVILIZED NATIONS

By the late sixteenth century several European states had made contact with the indigenous peoples of the Americas. The Spanish invasion in the southern hemisphere opened up a debate among theologian advisers to the Spanish crown regarding the existence and extent to which the European doctrine of natural rights extended to the indigenous peoples of the region. Further north, the Dutch, English and French were dealing with the native peoples on the basis of international treaty relationships. Agreements between the European states and Indian nations addressed issues of peace, trade, territory and free passage. International norms compelled the Europeans to approach the indigenous political communities as international equals. During the colonial era, individuals were appointed (Benjamin Franklin, among others) to serve in an official capacity as diplomatic envoys to certain Indian societies. The British joined with the Iroquois in a security alliance known as the Covenant Chain (Jennings 1975).

Although treaties, diplomatic ties and security alliances attest to the international character of the relationship as between equals, there was also an element of moral arrogance in the attitude of the Europeans towards the 'savage natives' (Sheehan 1973). Therefore, although from the international level relations were conducted more or less on a basis of mutuality, on a cultural level the moral boundaries, from the viewpoint of the Europeans, were clearly marked. It should also be kept in mind that war as an instrument of foreign policy, and one by which territory could be acquired and dominance over the local population by the victorious conqueror could be established, was quite acceptable and unregulated in the eighteenth century.

[. . .]

International law, much weaker then than now, compelled the European powers and their colonial offspring to take into consideration the international legal norms that might pertain to the settler-native relationship. However, international law, as designed by the Europeans primarily to regulate relations among themselves, was understood as a system governing relations between 'civilized nations' (Lindley [1926] 1969). The natives, in the judgement of the European mind, did not belong to the class of 'civilized nations'. Still, they often functioned as politically distinct communities in a manner recognizable to the Europeans as organized and orderly (Lindley [1926] 1969). So, was extending the civilities of international law to the indigenous population a gratuitous act on the part of the Europeans? Could it be rescinded unilaterally? This was the first moral dilemma of the colonizers.

In part, favouring a civil approach to relations with the indigenous population was probably as much a function of economic and political expedience as a sense of moral obligation. Initially, the Europeans did not know the extent of the indigenous population nor their capacity to organize in resistance. Competition among several European powers and their tendency to involve the indigenous population in their alliances further complicated matters. Finally, the Europeans had established trade relations, and the indigenous communities simply had the appropriate knowledge and skills needed by the Europeans in order to exploit local resources. It was in the material interest of the colonizing Europeans to attempt to maintain good relations with the indigenous population as long as these factors remained influential.

Does the idea of an ambiguous but evolving moral boundary explain contradictions that were already developing in the colonial policy towards the Indians? I think it is significant at this point to note that the moral necessities flowing from international relations indicated a respect on the basis of sovereign equality among political communities more or less recognizable as states. Now understandable, at the time the Europeans may not have been certain about whether or not, or to what extent in each case, the indigenous nations they encountered resembled the European image of a state as a political community. Coupled with unknown variables – the size, ability to mobilize, and effectiveness of combat technologies on the part of the native population – there were good reasons to approach the indigenous nations on the basis of international equality.

But there are other indications that the moral community might help to explain the growing conflict between the equality required by international norms and the exclusion that would follow from marking off moral boundaries as the new European immigrant political community solidified.

[. . .]

Dissimilarity was clearly the dominant influence and became the basis for labelling the indigenous peoples as subhuman or savage – a strong antecedent for rationalizing moral exclusion. In fact, although there were numerous cultural differences among Indian tribes as well as among the Europeans, the metacultural distinction between European and indigenous peoples can be traced to this period. That is, the Europeans did not, for the most part, see many different cultures but rather only Indians; and the indigenous peoples as well saw only Europeans. Pan-European and pan-Indian selfconsciousness have since become important sources of identity in the larger global context. And in light of the association of moral superiority with the concept of civilization relative to the inferior status of the so-called savage, these also served as markers circumscribing the boundaries of a moral community dominated by Europeans and their descendants.

Conflict between the settler and native population progressively worsened, creating even more pressure on policy-makers to articulate moral justification for either public or private violence, or both, against the Indians. Perhaps the Indians' superior knowledge of the terrain and resources, along with the fact that during this time the Europeans were unsure of the extent of the indigenous population, only served to delay the process of moral exclusion. The following passages from official policy documents between 1785 and 1789 illustrate the growing tension between the moral imperatives of justice and the pressure to expand, giving rise to increased conflict:

> That the Indians may have full confidence in the justice of the United States, respecting their interests, they shall have the right to send a deputy of their choice, whenever they think fit, to Congress (Article 13, Treaty of Hopewell with the Cherokees, 28 November 1788; see Prucha 1975: 6).

> The utmost good faith shall always be observed toward the Indians, their lands and property shall never be taken from them without their consent; and in their property, rights and liberty, they never shall be invaded or disturbed, unless in just and lawful wars authorised by Congress (Northwest Ordinance, 13 July 1787; see Prucha 1975: 9).

> An avaricious disposition in some of our people to acquire large tracts of land and often by unfair means, appears to be the principal source of difficulties with the

Indians. There can be no doubt that settlements are made by our people on the lands secured by the Cherokees, by the late treaty between them and the United States (Committee Report on the Southern Department, 3 August 1787; see Prucha 1975: 10).

[. . .]

RELOCATION

The practice of relocating whole communities of indigenous peoples so that industrializing societies might gain access to certain resources began during the early colonial era, and continues into the present time.

[. . .]

First of all, it is perhaps not entirely accurate to characterize the post-colonial white society as dominant in every respect to the Indian population. In terms of numbers, and the extent of occupied territory, it clearly was not. But the white society was deliberately expanding, especially during the era of manifest destiny between 1850 and 1860 (Trennert 1975). The frontier of expansion changed rapidly and dramatically, and with it the front line of private violence and encroachment into Indian territory also moved.

Second, the American government during the 1820s and 1830s developed a policy of separation between the Indians and whites primarily as a means of controlling the conflict, evincing Washington's view that 'the country is big enough for us all'. This policy was embodied in the Indian Trade and Intercourse Acts of 1789, 1819 and 1834 and in the creation of an Indian Affairs Bureau administered by the War Department. The acts placed restrictions on whites, not Indians, reflecting the fact that the government did not consider the Indians to be proper subjects of US law. Accordingly, American citizens were required to obtain a licence from the American government before trading with the Indians, prohibited from trapping and hunting in Indian territory, and prohibited from settling or inhabiting any land that had been guaranteed to the Indians. Furthermore, the government promised to forcibly remove anyone (non-Indians) violating the settlement prohibition.

In 1819 a second policy track also emerged that would ultimately combine with removal during the reservation era beginning roughly around 1851. The second track emphasized the civilization of the Indians and was initiated by the Civilization Fund Act of 1819. Civilizing the Indian was believed to be both a humanitarian act and a peaceful, least-cost solution to the so-called Indian problem. The fund was created 'for the purpose of providing against the further decline and final extinction of the Indian tribes, adjoining the frontier settlements of the United States' (Prucha 1975: 33).

Another factor complicating relations between whites and Indians during the first few decades of the nineteenth century was the growing conflict between the federal and state governments over their respective reserved and shared powers. This became particularly evident in the court cases involving conflicts between Indian, state and federal sovereignty, for example, *Fletcher* v. *Peck* (1819), *Johnson* v. *MacIntosh* (1823), *Cherokee* v. *Georgia* (1831) and *Worcester* v. *Georgia* (1832). Talk of a removal policy began in earnest in 1825, and, although initially conceived of as voluntary, the so-called removal treaties with the south-eastern tribes thinly disguised the coercive nature of the policy, as evidenced by the use of the military to implement its terms (Trennert 1975). The Mississippi River would provide an Indian barrier, necessary to their protection against the press of white expansion until such time as they could be readied for assimilation. It was believed, however naively, that

> the land to the west was so vast that white encroachment would not be significant for a long time. By then it was hoped, the Indians would be ready to integrate into American society without disturbance (Trennert 1975: 10).

There are two reasons for questioning the sincerity of the desire to reculturize the Indians satisfactorily as a prerequisite to their enjoyment of peaceful co-existence with the whites. First, the very tribes first subjected to the harsh reality of removal were precisely those which had already demonstrated a remarkable ability to adapt by forming a European-style government, passing 'fixed laws' and a constitution in 1827. They were then and are now called the Five Civilized Tribes for this reason. The government took the following initial position on the morality of removal:

> [Removal] should be voluntary, for it would be as cruel as unjust to compel the aborigines to abandon the graves of their fathers and seek a home in a distant land (President Jackson, 8 December 1829; see Prucha 1975: 47).

These were a settled people, living peacefully in the Smokey Mountain region until the discovery of gold in their territory led to the rapid infiltration of miners and an ensuing perpetual conflict with the Cherokee. Suddenly, efforts to civilize them were pronounced a failure and removal was espoused as the only hope for their survival. Six years after renouncing the immorality of forced removal, President Jackson, known as Sharp Knife to the Cherokee, had altered his view:

> The plan of removing the aboriginal people who yet remain within the settled portions of the United States to the country west of the Mississippi River approaches its consummation. . . . All preceding experiments for the improve-ment of the Indians have failed. It seems now to be an established fact that they cannot live in contact with a civilized community and prosper.
> . . . Such are the arrangements for the physical comfort and for the moral improvement of the Indians. The necessary measures for their political advance-ment and for their separation from our citizens have not been neglected. The

pledge of the United States has been given by Congress that the country destined for the residence of this people shall be forever secured and guaranteed to them (President Jackson, 7 December 1835; see Prucha 1975: 71–2).

Anyone who doubts the cruelty of implementing this policy might consider this confession of a white American soldier in his diary on his eightieth birthday. It is a powerful testament to the moral dilemma of Indian-white ethnohistory in the United States. For this reason, it is worth quoting at length. Private John G. Burnett wrote:

> The removal of the Cherokee Indians from their life long homes in the year of 1838 found me a young man in the prime of life and a Private soldier in the American Army. Being acquainted with many of the Indians and able to fluently speak their language, I was sent as interpreter into the Smokey Mountain Country in May, 1838, and witnessed the execution of the most brutal order in the History of American Warfare. I saw the helpless Cherokees arrested and dragged from their homes, and driven at bayonet point into the stockades. And in the chill of a drizzling rain on an October morning I saw them loaded like cattle or sheep in six hundred and forty-five wagons and started toward the west.
> . . . The trail of the exiles was a trail of death. They had to sleep in the wagons and on the ground without fire. And I have known as many as twenty-two of them to die in one night of pneumonia due to ill treatment, cold and exposure.
> . . . The long painful journey to the west ended March 26th, 1839, with four-thousand silent graves reaching from the foothills of the Smokey Mountains to what is known as Indian territory in the West. And covetousness on the part of the white race was the cause of all that the Cherokees had to suffer.
> Future generations will read and condemn the act and I do hope posterity will remember soldiers like myself, and like the four Cherokees who were forced by General Scott, to shoot an Indian chief and his children had to execute the orders of our superiors.
> . . . However murder is murder, whether committed by the villain skulking in the dark or by uniformed men stepping to the strains of martial music.
> Murder is murder and somebody must answer, somebody must explain the streams of blood that flowed in the Indian country in the summer of 1838. Somebody must explain the four thousand silent graves that mark the trail of the Cherokees to their exile. I wish I could forget it all, but the picture of six-hundred and forty-five wagons lumbering over the frozen ground with their Cargo of suffering humanity still lingers in my memory, (Burnett [1890] 1956: 21–7).

One young volunteer from Georgia summed up his feelings this way: 'I fought through the Civil War, and have seen men shot to pieces and slaughtered by thousands, but the Cherokee removal was the cruellest work I ever knew' (quoted in Price 1950: 16).

INTERNMENT AND GUARDIANSHIP

[. . .]

Geographic separation as the final solution to the Indian problem was hopelessly unrealistic. Expansion fuelled by manifest destiny and the discovery of gold in California in 1848 brought Mormons, miners, lumberjacks, farmers and cattle ranchers into the territory of Indian country from the Mississippi along the Oregon Trail to the Pacific Northwest. Reporting on a study completed in 1939, one author writes that

> owing largely to the gold discoveries the whites disrupted the Indians of the Pacific areas before they descended on those of the plains. In Oregon and California from the eighteen forties to the eighteen seventies miners and settlers displayed a brutality, and the United States Government a neglect, which were all the more scandalous because they extended into allegedly civilised times. In Oregon, the legislature, politicians, subordinate Indian agents and even Methodist clergy participated in massacres which were embellished but not disguised by the title of Indian wars. In California the whites killed Indians as 'a sport to enliven Sundays and holidays'. In 1871 the kindly Kingsley wrote that he had to use his 38 calibre revolver to shoot children as his 56 calibre rifle 'tore them up so bad.'
> . . . Those who escaped slaughter or enslavement were ruthlessly pushed up and down the country. Women were raped and enslaved in a sudden and brutal race-miscegenation that created many mixed bloods (Price 1950: 16–17).

[. . .]

Viewed as a 'contest of civilization with barbarism' that had been going on 'since the commencement of time' (Prucha 1975: 77), the Indians were blamed for their own demise, marked for extinction by a Christian God or by nature in the form of evolution. In this way, the policy of colonizing the Indians – which would be rapidly transformed into an official reservation policy – came to be thought of as an act of ultimate benevolence in light of the Indians' otherwise inevitable fate: extinction (Trennert 1975).

Thus began a new era in the white society's Indian policy. The whites could not be restrained because, as a superior race, they believed themselves to be ordained to take command of the territory and resources of North America. If the Indians continued to roam freely while the whites advanced and settled west of the Mississippi, the Indians would all surely die. To save them, they had to be segregated and civilized, by force if necessary, for their own good. Ironically, the legal justification for such a policy can be traced to the same majority decision written by Chief Justice Marshall in 1831, *Cherokee* v. *Georgia*, that has for over 150 years attested to the existence of Indian nationhood and land rights extinguishable only by voluntary cession, to their sovereign status before European contact, and their residual sovereignty after contact (Wilkinson 1987; Price and Clinton 1983). Drawing specifically on international law, Marshall wrote that the Indians 'are in a state of pupilage. Their relation to the United States resembles that of a ward to his guardian' (Prucha 1975: 59).

In this spirit, the 'great work of regenerating the Indian race' (Trennert 1975: 56) began by 'forcing the Indians to cease their wandering ways' (Prucha 1975: 92). Responsibility for Indian affairs was transferred from the War Department to the newly created Department of Interior in 1849. The 'limited efforts to domesticate and civilize' the Indians by 1858 was attributed to

> three serious, and, to the Indians, fatal errors. . . . [T]heir removal from place to place as our [white] population advanced; the assignment to them of too great an extent of country, to be held in common; and the allowance of large sums of money, as annuities, for the lands ceded by them (Prucha 1975: 92).

A reservation policy was also proposed as the solution to the constant 'threat' of intertribal wars (Prucha 1975: 92). The trust relationship, in combination with the creation of reservations, was outlined in 1856 by Commissioner Manypenny.

[. . .]

Understandably, white as well as Indian writers recalling this period have concluded that the so-called Indian wars of the second half of the nineteenth century were caused by the US government policy by the military, and the use of the military to prevent them from leaving the reservations (Brown 1971; Price and Clinton 1983). These wars were never declared, and, in fact, responsibility for Indian affairs remained within the Interior Department. Until 1871 the government continued to deal with the Indian tribes in treaties and referred to many of them as nations. However, by 1868 it had also become the official policy of the United States to consider any Indian violation of treaties – in particular, breaches of the peace between Indians and whites – as grounds for extinguishing such recognition. A tribe failing to maintain good faith would 'no longer be regarded as a nation with which to treat, but as a dependent uncivilized people, to be cared for, fed when necessary, and governed' (Prucha 1975: 117).

[. . .]

AMERICANIZING THE INDIAN

Although the Civilization Fund had first been established in 1819, and the involvement of various private missionary and reform groups in efforts to civilize the Indians had long been encouraged by official policy, it was not until the 1870s that the focus shifted entirely to the goal of assimilation. Such a policy, of course, presumed that the individual may be separated from his or her culture with no net loss to the individual. In fact, in the case of the 'uncivilized' Indians, they would be better off without it. The Indian culture was perceived to be the only prohibition to the progress of the Indian, awaiting the reculturized individual at the moment of enlightenment upon achieving the so-called civilized state (Sheehan 1973).

Assimilation policy proceeded in several stages. These included replacing the traditional communal economic base with a system of private property; intensified education, primarily through boarding schools; the regulation of every aspect of Indian social life, including marriage, dispute settlement and religious practice; the granting of citizenship, thus further eroding any claim of a relationship between tribal membership and political affiliation; and finally, allowing the Indian tribes to become self-governing by adopting constitutions ultimately subject to the approval of the US government. The transition from communal to private property was accomplished through the passage of the Dawes Allotment Act in 1887, which not only allotted lands to individual Indians but opened up 'surplus' lands to white homesteaders. By all estimates, the net loss of land held by Indians as a result of this policy was staggering, somewhere around 86 million acres (Wilkinson 1987). The law required that land allotted be held in trust for twenty-five years, and that before achieving sole ownership an Indian title holder must be proven to be competent. Much of the loss was due to scheming land-grabbers who swindled the very old, very young or descendants of original title holders. Yet the allotment policy was supported by both friends and enemies of the Indians. Friends saw it was the only means of Indian adaptation to white economic and political institutions, which in turn was the only way to prevent their complete extermination, 'as many people in the West and certain officers of the army desired' (Deloria and Cadwalader 1984: 5).

The practice of issuing certificates of competency continued until the early years of the twentieth century. Exemptions were allowed for 'able-bodied adult Indians of less than one-half Indian blood' (Prucha 1975: 212). The allotment programme also left Indian country in what is widely characterized today as a checkerboard pattern of 'tribal land, allotted trust land held by individual Indians, fee land held by non-Indians, federal public land, state and county land' (Wilkinson 1987: 9).

Boarding schools not only instructed students in the English language, and punished them for using their native tongue, but were also used to inculcate patriotism. By 1901 some sixteen thousand pupils, five to twenty-one years old, were attending 113 boarding schools. Here, students were prepared for citizenship and self-support:

It is freely admitted that education is essential. But it must be remembered that there is a vital difference between white and Indian education. When a white youth goes away to school or college his moral character and habits are already formed and well defined.

... With the Indian youth it is quite different. Born a savage and raised in an atmosphere of superstition and ignorance, he lacks at the outset those advantages which are inherited by his white brother and enjoyed from the cradle. His moral character has yet to be formed. If he is to rise from his low estate the germs of a nobler existence must be implanted in him and cultivated. He must be taught to lay aside his savage customs like a garment and take upon himself the habits of civilized life.

... In a word, the primary object of a white school is to educate the mind; the primary essential of Indian education is to enlighten the soul.

... That being done, he should be thrown entirely upon his own resources to become a useful member of the community in which he lives. ... He must be made to realize that in the sweat of his face he shall eat his bread.

... In pursuance of the policy of the Department to cut off rations from all Indians except those who are incapacitated in some way ... and to inaugurate, wherever it is possible, the policy of giving rations only in return for labour performed (Prucha 1975: 201–2).

Through a series of congressional actions, executive orders and favourable decisions in the Supreme Court upholding the plenary powers of the US government in Indian affairs, few areas of Indian life remained untouched by the 'civilization' programme. At the end of the twenty-five year trust, an allottee could apply for a certificate of competency and, if granted, would be issued a patent in fee to the allotted land as well as citizenship in the United States. Because the allotment act had originally excluded the Five Civilized Tribes in the Indian territory, these were dealt with in separate legislation and granted citizenship in 1901. Two more acts of Congress in 1919 and 1924 granted citizenship to veterans of the First World War and all other Indians not yet citizens, respectively.

REFORM AND REPARATION

The period from 1933 to 1945 is often called the era of reform in federal Indian policy, or the 'Indian New Deal'. It was strongly supported by President Roosevelt. It was embodied in the Indian Reorganization or Wheeler-Howard Act, or IRA, of 1934. It was brought on by the combination of three forces: the political activism of social reformer and Indian Commissioner John Collier, who held that position for this entire period; the legal advocacy of Felix Cohen during the 1930s and 1940s; and the publication of the Meriam report for Congress in 1928.

For many, the most significant feature of the IRA, as the act is known, was that it would bring an end to the allotment and assimilation programmes and even make it possible to begin a process of land recovery by the tribes and their members. It was widely believed that without radical reform, the Indians' days were numbered. The Indian population had declined by 82 per cent from the time of contact in the sixteenth century until the 1930s. In 1917 one Bureau of Indian Affairs staff member conveyed to Congress the opinion that 'since the Indians were by policy being liquidated' there was no need for a continued concern for the conservation of their resources which were being held by the US government in 'trust' for the tribes. The transcontinental railroad and successful white home steading had resulted in a secure annexation of the western lands; allotment destroyed reservations, now a checkerboard of titles held by individual whites, individual Indians, the tribes and the US government. The destruction of reservations meant the destruction of tribal life. In 1890 the last battle in the war on Indian culture was won by the US government when troops left an estimated three hundred Sioux men, women and children dead after attempting to hold a ghost dance ceremony in celebration of the Indian Messiah ghost dance religion. From a pre-European contact population of between 10 and 20 million native people in the area now occupied by the United States, there were only about 290,000 Indians left by 1890 (Prucha 1984).

In 1928 the Meriam report concluded that neither the reservation nor the allotment and citizenship policies had benefited the Indians and were failures in accomplishing any official policy objectives as well. In fact, the report suggested, the net effect had been to serve only the interest of white land-grabbers who swindled the Indians both directly as well as by applying political pressure to Congress and the Bureau of Indian Affairs. [. . .]

In addition to ending the allotment of Indian land and authorizing the Secretary of Interior to purchase land for tribes and individual Indians, the IRA had two other objectives: to strengthen tribal self-government and to promote economic development by helping tribes incorporate for business purposes and to make available 10 million dollars for development loans. The act also provided funds for tuition at colleges and vocation schools as well as funds to help tribes establish constitutions and draw up by-laws and charters for incorporation (Philp 1986).

The act was, and still is, very controversial because it was supposed to give tribes self-government; many of them never believed that they had lost it. The tribal elections held to approve of the act were surrounded by charges of fraud and misrepresentation. Tribal governments would derive legitimacy from the American government, whose approval of their constitutions was required; the government derived its legitimacy in the matter from the fact that the act was accepted by the tribes through referenda. After a century of undeclared war, forced relocation and assimilation, and reservation internment, it was an attempt to re-establish a consent relationship between the US government and the Indian tribes.

[. . .] In August 1946, a year after Collier left office, the Indian Claims Commission Act was approved (Philp 1986). The act allowed suit for monetary compensation for lands taken by Congress by executive order or by treaty when taken without compensation, as a result of 'unconscionable dealings' or with inadequate compensation due to the inclusion of 'gratuitous offsets' (Prucha 1975: 341). All claims were to be filed between 1946 and 1951. Attorneys' fees were limited to a maximum of 10 per cent; many settlements have been between 10 and 12 million dollars. Approximately 800 million dollars have been awarded under the act. The five-judge commission was disbanded in 1978 and its cases transferred to the Court of Claims. Long delays are said to be common.

TERMINATION – ENDING FEDERAL RESPONSIBILITY FOR AND OBLIGATION TO THE INDIANS

The establishment of the Claims Commission was supported by many in Congress as a necessary step towards reparation between the federal government and the aboriginal inhabitants of the country. It was necessary, they said, as a prerequisite for terminating the special status of the tribes. By providing monetary compensation, although not allowing recovery of actual land, the settlement of claims would quiet aboriginal title while at the same time provide funds for economic development and eventually, therefore, self-sufficiency. It was viewed as a part of the termination process. Termination would also encourage Indians to leave the reservations and 'join the rest of American society' (Fixico 1986). The policy of termination was rife with the paternalistic rhetoric that had always characterized federal Indian policy. By ending the trust relationship, unsupervised Indians would be free and self-supporting; the government would solve the 'Indian problem' for once and for all (Fixico 1986). The policy consisted of four parts: wiping the slate of Indian-white relations clean through the payment of reparative compensation through the Claims Commission; a determination of readiness for termination, made by the Bureau of Indian Affairs on a tribe-by-tribe basis; a unilateral declaration to terminate the historic relationship with tribes determined to be ready; and a relocation programme to assist Indians in making a new life in the American mainstream, mostly in cities.

[. . .]

THE MODERN ERA – RED POWER, ACTIVISM, AND FIGHTING BACK

Termination was not only not the end of the story but in some ways, along with the creation of the Claims Commission and earlier developments related to the IRA, it fostered the kind of mobilization on the part of Indians leading to the present national and international activism. Even though many Indian lawyers were preoccupied with suits brought before the Claims Commission when, their critics say, they should have been working to prevent termination actions, Indians nevertheless fought and won hard legal and political battles against the termination policy (Wilkinson 1987; Philp 1986).

Ironically, the first signs of modern Indian activism surfaced even as the new termination policy was being outlined in Washington and the post-war world order was being negotiated by the European states. A group of intellectual Indian youth in 1944 organized the first meeting of the National Congress of American Indians, representing approximately one hundred Indian groups and called informally the United Nations of Tribes. This historic meeting provided the first step towards the development of intertribal consensus and pan-Indian political dialogue.

A second important meeting during the termination era took place in Santa Fe in 1954. This time the concern was over the direction and impact of Indian education, particularly at university level. The conferees sought strategies to bridge the cultural gap between reservation and traditional Indians, on the one hand, and the growing number of college-educated off-reservation youths who had no desire to abandon their traditional identity. The most important outcome of the meeting was the formation of the Southwestern Regional Youth Conference, which, meeting in the early spring of 1960, brought together representatives from fifty-seven tribes. Here they began to discuss the idea of Indian nationalism as a goal of Indian activism.

A third historic conference took place in Chicago in 1960 and was organized by anthropologist Sol Tax in order to engage Indian leaders in developing policy guidelines for the new administration. The conference produced a final 'declaration of Indian purpose' which affirmed Indian

> self government, sovereignty, and nationalism, [and] made it clear that Indian people wanted complete autonomy to protect their land base from expropriation and to make their own plans and decisions in building an economic system to rid themselves of poverty while reasserting traditional cultural values (Day 1972: 512).

Also as a result of this conference a new organization was formed by a group of young Indian college students who, impatient with the 'routine rhetoric of the official Indian leaders', had created their own 'Youth Caucus' at the Chicago meeting (Day 1972). Some had chaired groups at the Chicago meeting. They later formed the National Indian Youth Council (NIYC) and were the first to articulate the Indian viewpoint on a policy of self-determination and self-help. They have gained widespread support among reservation elders and traditionalists as well as many of the more mainstream Indian leaders. The NIYC was probably the first contemporary pan-Indian organization to emphasize Indian sovereignty, and it now has the status of an official and non-governmental organization with the United Nations. The council has expanded its communications and monitoring role to include Indians in other countries.

During the 1960s activism became increasingly apparent in the courts, largely due to the fact that Congress acted in 1966 to strengthen the statutory footing of 'any Indian tribe or land with a governing body duly recognized by the Secretary of Interior' (Price and Clinton 1983) by allowing them to bring suit in federal district court regarding controversies arising under the US Constitution, laws of Congress and treaties. Tribes expanded their land rights in the north-east, hunting and fishing rights in the Pacific Northwest and Great Lakes region, and water rights in the west as a result of cases filed following the 1966 action. By 1968, the year Congress passed the Indian Civil Rights Act, President Johnson announced 'a new goal for our Indian programs: A goal that ends the old debate about "termination" of Indian programs and stresses self-determination; a goal that erases old attitudes of paternalism and promotes partnership and self-help' (Prucha 1975: 248).

A report on the state of Indian education, begun under the chairmanship of Robert Kennedy and completed by his brother Ted, said:

> We are shocked at what we discovered.
> Others before us were shocked. They recommended and made changes. Others after us will likely be shocked, too – despite our recommendations and efforts at reform. For there is much to do – wrongs to right, omissions to fill, untruths to correct – that our own recommendations, concerned as they are with education alone, need supplementation across the whole board of Indian life. We have developed page after page of statistics. These cold figures mark a stain on our national conscience, a stain which has spread slowly for hundreds of years.
> . . . One theme running through all our recommendations is increased Indian participation and control of their own education programs. For far too long, the Nation has paid only token heed to the notion that Indians should have a strong voice in their own destiny. We have made a number of recommendations to correct this historic, anomalous paternalism (Prucha 1975: 254–5).

In 1970 President Nixon called for an Indian policy of 'Self-Determination without Termination'. In the opening statement of his Special Message on Indian Affairs, he said:

> The first Americans – the Indians – are the most deprived and most isolated minority group in our nation. On virtually every scale of measurement – employment, income, education, health – the conditions of the Indian people rank at the bottom.
> This condition is the heritage of centuries of injustice. From the time of their first contact with European settlers, the American Indians have been oppressed and brutalized, deprived of their ancestral lands and denied the opportunity to control their own destiny (quoted in Prucha 1975: 256).

In 1970, after sixty-four years of struggling to regain lands sacred to the Pueblo Indians' religious ceremonies that had been taken by President Roosevelt for a national park, President Nixon signed a bill returning the lands to the Indians

(Prucha 1975: 258). President Nixon also proclaimed the termination policy both immoral and illegal in light of the reciprocal nature of treaties between the US government and Indian tribes. The federal obligation to Indians, President Nixon suggested, was not based on a paternalistic trust relationship with its implicit assignment of Indian moral incompetence. Rather the obligation flowed from the agreement of the US government through treaties to guarantee the well-being of the tribes in consideration of their having ceded large tracts of territory. The obligation of the US government towards the Indian tribes was contractual. In 1973 the restoration of terminated tribes began.

In 1974, in the aftermath of the scathing report on Indian education, the Indian Self-Determination and Educational Assistance Act was passed by Congress. The Indian Child Welfare Act was passed in 1978 in order to maximize tribal jurisdiction in child custody and adoption cases. Before 1978, in states with larger Indian populations, as many as 25 to 35 per cent of the Indian children were placed in foster care homes – a rate which is 660 to 2240 per cent higher than for non-Indian children (McShane 1987).

The Indian activists of the 1960s formed an alliance, for a while, with the broader movement for the civil rights of American minorities but never abandoned their claim to a special status based on aboriginal identity. The IRA had provided support for the development of business savvy. Many tribal councils now retained legal counsel. A number of Indians attended colleges and law schools by using funds provided through educational assistance initiated by the IRA. They had gained experience in suits brought before the Claims Commission, not to mention recognition of their legal standing to sue, which had previously been denied. Ironically, the urbanization of American Indians, deliberately promoted by relocation programmes, was also an important factor in the emergence of a new pan-Indian activism.

In asserting a right to cultural integrity, they were and are supported by the resurgence of ethnic minorities throughout the modernized Western world. They had become survivors of a colonial experience. Thus they are also linked to indigenous peoples worldwide as well as, less directly, to the populations in the Third World struggling to retain, rediscover, or redesign their own identities in a system of world order brought on largely by developments arising out of the Western experience.

[. . .]

REFERENCES

Brown, Dee (1971) *Bury my heart at Wounded Knee: An Indian history of the American West*. New York: Holt, Rinehart & Winston.

Burnett, John (1890) 'Removal of the Cherokees 1838–39', in *Cherokee legends and the trail of tears*, ed. Thomas Bryan Underwood, 1956, pp. 21–7. Knoxville, TN: McLemore Printing Co.

Day, Robert C. (1972) 'The emergence of activism as a social Movement', in *Native Americans today*, ed. Howard M. Bahr, Bruce A. Chadwick and Robert C. Day, pp. 506–31. New York: Harper & Row.

Deloria, Vine, Jr., and Sandra Cadwalader (1984) *The aggressions of civilization: American Indian policy since the 1880s*. Philadelphia: Temple University Press.

Fixico, Donald Lee (1986) *Termination and relocation: Federal Indian policy, 1945–1960*. Albuquerque: University of New Mexico Press.

Jennings, Francis (1975) *The invasion of the Americas*. Chapel Hill: University of North Carolina Press.

Lindley, M. F. ([1926] 1969) *The acquisition and government of backward territory in international law: Being a treatise on the law and practice relating to colonial expansion*. Reprint. New York: Negro Universities Press.

McShane, Damian (1987) 'Mental health and North American Indian/native communities: Cultural transactions, education and recognition'. *American Journal of Community Psychology* 15(1): 95–116.

Philp, Kenneth R. (1986) *Indian self-rule: First hand accounts of Indian-White relations from Roosevelt to Reagan*. Salt Lake City, UT: Howe Brothers.

Price, Grenfell (1950) *White settlers and native peoples*. Cambridge: Cambridge University Press.

Price, Monroe E., and Robert N. Clinton (1983) *Law and the American Indian: Readings, notes and cases*. Charlottesville, VA: Michie.

Prucha, Francis Paul (1975) *Documents of United States Indian policy*. Lincoln: University of Nebraska Press.

Prucha, Francis Paul (1984) *The great father: The United States government and the American Indian*. Lincoln: University of Nebraska Press.

Sheehan, Bernard W. (1973) *Seeds of extinction: Jeffersonian philanthropy and the American Indian*. Chapel Hill: University of North Carolina Press.

Trennert, Robert A., Jr. (1975) *Alternative to extinction: federal Indian policy and the beginnings of the reservation system*. Philadelphia: Temple University Press.

Wilkinson, Charles F. (1987) *American Indians, time and the law: Native societies in a modern constitutional democracy*. New Haven, CT: Yale University Press.

Part II
Multiculturalism, Migration and Racism

5 Multicultural and Plural Societies

The concept of a multicultural society
JOHN REX

Most researchers in the field of ethnic relations feel that they should perform more than a technical role, gathering facts which might be useful to government in the pursuit of undisclosed policy objectives. If the *ends* of such policies are subject to criticism, however, some way has to be found of distinguishing the value standards used by researchers from those of political partisans.

VALUE ORIENTATIONS IN SOCIAL SCIENCE

These problems were discussed in 1939 by the great Swedish social scientist Gunnar Myrdal when he was invited to make a definitive study of race relations in the United States (Myrdal 1944). The fundamental principles governing his research were as follows:

1 Social science always involves something more than the mere description of facts.

2 It claims not merely that such-and-such is the case but that it is necessarily the case. That is to say, it not merely describes but explains.

3 The concept of something being necessarily the case, however, has a special meaning in sociology. What is necessary from the point of view of one value standpoint is not necessary from another. What is necessary from the point of view of one interest is not necessary from the point of view of another.

4 Sociology cannot of itself declare one value standpoint to be morally

preferable to another. All it can do and what it certainly should do is to make its value standpoint or the state of affairs which it is taking as desirable, clear and explicit.

In studying American race relations, Myrdal chose to ask the question, 'what structures, institutions and policies are necessary to achieve the ends set out in the American constitution, as interpreted?'

The key to any honest approach to policy-oriented research is to be found in Myrdal's fourth principle. If asked what conditions are necessary for the successful implementation of policy, the researcher should ask for a clear and explicit declaration of policy goals. Unfortunately, all too often, when policy questions are posed there is no such explicitness or clarity. The honest researcher must therefore begin with a critical review of policy goals, focusing on what states of affairs are being held to be desirable and claiming 'necessity' for any policy, institution or structure only relative to the stated goals.

What I am going to suggest in this essay is that a new goal has become widely accepted in British race relations, namely that of the multicultural society, but that the meaning of this term remains remarkably obscure. One of the first and central tasks of a Centre for Research in Ethnic Relations must be to clarify its meaning, because it is in relation to the meaning given to the concept that our various specific researches fall into place.

Multiculturalism is a new goal for British race relations. It was not discussed much before 1968 and even today much research is directed by another and quite different value standpoint, namely that which emphasizes equality of individual opportunity. In theory, if not in practice, this other ideal is shared across a wide political spectrum and is certainly the basis of much discourse in the social service departments about social policy.

Much ethnic relations research in Britain has concentrated very largely on the study of inequality and racial discrimination in the spheres of housing, employment, education and urban planning. Most of this work has served to confirm in special institutional contexts the conclusion reached in successive analyses of national samples carried out by the Policy Studies Institute: that in all these spheres immigrant minorities from Asia, Africa and the West Indies have suffered disadvantage due to racial discrimination (Daniel 1968; D. Smith 1977).

There is, of course, a need to continue such studies and to locate and publicize the origins of and responsibility for discrimination. But more and more of the problems posed to us are not about equality and how it can be promoted, but about the multicultural society, which *prima facie* at least, must mean a society in which people are not equally but differently treated. If in fact we pretend that multiculturalism and equality are the same goal under different names we are creating precisely that kind of fuzziness which Myrdalian principles would suggest we should avoid.

The issues which arise here originally crystallized for me when I participated in the UNESCO experts meeting on the nature of racism and race prejudice in 1967 (Montague 1972). The main theme of the statement which we drew up was about racial discrimination and inequality and how they could be overcome. Some black Americans on the committee then argued that the statement should begin with an affirmation of 'the right to be different'. We eventually decided to exclude such a reference because, as one member of the Steering Committee put it, 'every racially oppressive and segregationist government would seize on the statement as a justification of inequality'.

It was surprising perhaps that the desire to include a reference to difference came from black Americans. After all, the whole history of the civil rights movement had turned upon a rejection of the Plessey versus Ferguson decision of 1896 that facilities which were separate and segregated could nonetheless be equal. What was evident now, however, was that black politics included another theme. Assimilation was rejected as a sign of equality. The goal of the black movement was to attain *equality of respect* for a separate black culture.

In Britain today there are many egalitarians who take a similar view. They believe that anti-racism and the goal of equality requires that all minority cultures should enjoy equal respect. The unfortunate thing, however, is that because of the fuzziness of the ideal of multiculturalism, they gain apparent support from those who aim to ensure that minorities should receive something different and inferior, the very reverse of equality. This is particularly true in the sphere of education.

PLURAL AND MULTICULTURAL SOCIETIES

One good way of clarifying these issues is to look at the theories which sociologists and anthropologists have developed in studying plural multicultural and multiracial societies. It can be seen from these studies that [the definition of an ideal varies widely], and it must therefore be in some very special sense that we speak of such an ideal in contemporary conditions.

Most sociological theory had dealt with unitary societies or with conflict within society. Furnivall broke new ground, however, with his study of the plural society in Indonesia (Furnivall 1939). There he found different ethnic groups living side by side but interacting with each other only in the market place. The result of this was that, while the separate ethnic communities were governed by the morality and the religion and the kinship order, the market place was subject to no kind of moral control. While European capitalism had grown slowly out of the past and was constrained by some kind of common will, capitalism in Indonesia involved a market place in which one group simply oppressed or resisted another. The plural society was plural in two senses. One was that each ethnic community existed separately and had its own communal morality. The other was that the private and communal world was separated from that of the market place. The question which this raises for us is whether a multicultural society will encourage tight-knit communal morality within groups or a world of total exploitation between groups.

M. G. Smith argues along similar lines (M. G. Smith 1965 and 1974). As he sees it, unitary social systems have a single and complete set of institutions covering the spheres of domestic life, religion, law, politics, economics, education and so on, whereas plural societies in the British West Indies characteristically have no such overall institutional set but a number of ethnic segments each of which has its own nearly complete institutional set. These segments would in fact be separate societies were they not bound together by the political institution, i.e. the State. In other words, such societies are held together only because one group dominates the others. The various groups are differentially incorporated, if not *de jure*, at least *de facto*. Here again it would seem the plural society model is a model of racial domination.

If we are to maintain the model of the multicultural society it must clearly be distinguished from that suggested by Furnivall and Smith. This can best be done by drawing a distinction between the public and the private domain. There appear then to be four possibilities:

1 One might envisage a society which is unitary in the public domain but which encourages diversity in what are thought of as private or communal matters.
2 A society might be unitary in the public domain and also enforce or at least encourage unity of cultural practice in private or communal matters.
3 A society might allow diversity and differential rights for groups in the public domain and also encourage or insist upon diversity of cultural practice by different groups.
4 A society might have diversity and differential rights in the public domain even though there is considerable unity of cultural practice between groups.

The ideal of multiculturalism, in which multiculturalism is held to be compatible with equality of opportunity is represented by the first possibility. The second might be represented by the French ideal of assimilation of minority groups. The third is common under all forms of colonialism and was represented above all by the South African apartheid system, while the fourth is the state of affairs which existed in the Deep South of the United States before the civil rights programme took effect. The crucial point about our multicultural ideal is that it should not be confused with (3). All too often it is, and those who support that possibility are likely to accept the slogan of multiculturalism and bend it in that direction.

Let us now be more precise about what we mean by the public and private domain.

The notion of the two domains seems at first to be at odds with mainstream sociological theory, as most sociologists see all institutions as being interconnected with one another in a single system. This seems to me to be equally true of the functionalist paradigm as developed by Malinowski (1962) and Radcliffe Brown (1952), of the structural functionalism of Talcott Parsons (Parsons 1952; Parsons, Shils and Bales 1953) and the structuralism of French Marxism (Althusser 1969). In all of these the private domain is not an optional extra but plays a part in socializing individuals for participation in the public sphere. On the other hand the public domain is seen as shaped by the morality which is inculcated in the family and through religious institutions.

The actual history of European social institutions, however, belies functionalist theory. The polity, the economy and the legal system have been liberated from control by traditional values and have been based upon new values of an abstract kind. Yet it has seemed possible to permit the continuance of folk values and folk religions as long as these do not interfere with the functioning of the main political, economic and legal institutions of society.

A great deal of classical sociological theory deals principally with the evolution of the new abstract value systems which a large-scale society requires. Ferdinand Tönnies ([1887] 1963) saw that folk community must give way historically to association and society, the first being based upon the natural or real will, the second upon the deliberate artificial and rational will. Durkheim wrote about 'organic solidarity' based upon the division of labour, which would replace the 'mechanical solidarity' of small-scale community based upon kinship ([18..] 1933), and, even more radically of an 'egoistic society'([1897] 1952) in which values were located in the minds of separate individuals. Finally Weber saw in Calvinist religion and the Protestant ethic the end-point of an increasingly rationalistic trend in religion and, together with that, the development of political leadership based upon rational legal authority (Weber [1965] 1930).

Moral and legal systems of an abstract character thus were seen by all these authors as governing the social evolution of the modern state and of a formally rational capitalist economy. This is how what Parsons calls the Hobbesian problem of order (i.e. of how to avoid a war of all against all) was solved. This too is the significance of Furnivall's observation that the common will which characterized European capitalism was absent in Indonesia. It is under colonialism that we find what Marx called 'the callous cash nexus'. Economic and political institutions in Europe were embodied in what one might call 'the civic culture'.

The development of this 'civic culture' (e.g. the abstract public morality, law and religion) by no means implied the disappearance of folk morality, folk culture and folk religion. These now came to fulfil new functions. On the one hand they bound men together into separate communities into which individuals were socialized and within which they achieved their social identities. On the other they provided for what Parsons called 'pattern maintenance and tension management'. Living in a larger world with abstract moral principles was, so Parsons believed, psychologically possible only if individuals could retreat somewhere conducive to intimate relations and letting their hair down.

The ideal of the multicultural society which I have outlined above really presupposes the evolution of the modern type of society, of which Weber and Durkheim especially wrote. In simple societies morality and kinship structures had to govern the whole range of human activity. In an abstract and impersonal society a new more abstract form of law and morality had to be developed to govern large-scale political and economic organizations, while the old folk culture and morality helped the individual to retain some sort of psychological stability through more immediate social interdependence. Thus multiculturalism in the modern world involves on the one hand the acceptance of a single culture and a single set of individual rights governing the public domain and a variety of folk cultures in the private domestic and communal domains.

How does the above discussion relate to Marxist sociology and political thought? I think that the latter contains a certain duality. On the one hand the liberation of the market from traditional restraints represents for Marx the creation of precisely that type of society without a common will to which Furnivall refers. On the other Marx may be seen as envisaging the emergence through class struggle of a new rational socialist economic order. To the extent that he does one may see Marx too as envisaging the possibility of a new civic culture.

THE INSTITUTIONS OF THE PUBLIC DOMAIN

We must now consider more closely the institution of the public and the private domain and in each case look more closely at the ways in which they are likely to intrude on one another. As we shall see education intrudes into both spheres and the communal ideologies which bind people together in the private sphere may have implications for their integration or non-integration into public life.

The main institutions which constitute the public domain are those of law, politics and the economy.

Law determines the rights of any individual and the way in which he or she is incorporated into society. The very mark of the plural society is that different groups and categories of people are differentially incorporated. In our ideal multicultural society, however, we are positing that all individuals are equally incorporated and that they have equality before the law. The ideals of the multicultural society and of its civic culture are not realized insofar as any individual or category of individuals is harassed or under-protected by the police or are denied access to the protection of the courts.

In the sphere of politics again, in the plural society different groups have differing degrees of political power. In the ideal multicultural society each individual and group is deemed to have the same right to exercise political power through the vote or by other means. This by no means excludes the notion of conflict but no individual or group should find the rules governing such conflict disadvantageous. Participation in such a political system is a part of the multicultural ideal.

The economy refers in the first place to the institution of the market. This involves the processes of bargaining and competition and the sole sanction which an individual may use against the other is the threat to go to another supplier. The market should exclude the use of force and fraud. But while it is a rule-governed institution it excludes by definition the concept of 'charity', a concept which belongs to the world of community and folk morality. What is involved in market behaviour is the more abstract morality of sticking to the rules of peaceful market bargaining. The maintenance of such a system is another and quite central part of the civic culture and the multicultural ideal.

This is not to say that a market economy cannot be replaced by another type or allocation system or what is sometimes called the command economy. Here certain abstract goals are made explicit and organizations are set up to advance them. But the best that such a system can achieve is formal justice. Here as in the market economy there is no principle of charity, which is again assigned to the folk community.

To say that these are the macro-institutions which are required in the civic culture of a multicultural society is not to say that such a society will always be totally harmonious and peaceful. The pursuit of directly political goals involves conflict and markets too break down and give way to collective bargaining and political conflict. All that I wish to claim is that it is to be assumed in a multicultural society that no individual has more or less rights than another or a greater or lesser capacity to operate in this world of conflict because of his or her ethnic category.

Any suggestion that individuals or groups should receive differential treatment in the public domain is a move away from the multicultural ideal towards the plural society of colonialism. It would mean that groups were differentially incorporated *de facto* if not *de jure*. And this is true even in an atmosphere of paternalism. This would be the case, for example, if, while other groups had their needs provided by separate functional departments, all the needs of the minority were provided by a single Department of Minority affairs.

It may perhaps be suggested here that the efflorescence of race relations programmes at local level reflects not a genuine multiculturalism but this trend towards different and separate provision. It is moreover a process which it is very difficult to stop once it is in train because a considerable number of individuals from minority groups may be rewarded for staffing it.

THE BOUNDARIES OF THE PUBLIC DOMAIN

So far I have discussed the institutions of law, politics and the economy as institutions of the public domain, and I have suggested that matters relating to the family, to morality and religion belong in the private sphere. It is now necessary to note, however, that the public domain is often extended through bureaucratic state activity in matters of the family and morality, particularly in the welfare state.

Two kinds of barrier are breached in the modern state: the state may intervene in the economic sphere through ownership, through control and through subsidies to ensure efficient production; but it also intervenes in what are essentially family and community matters. It directs the economy towards full employment so that all bread-winners may have jobs. It permits as well as directs trade union activity to ensure job security. It makes provision through social insurance to ensure that individuals without employment have an income. It may build homes for letting or subsidize the building of houses for private ownership. It may provide education for children and for adults and it may provide social work services to help in resolving personal and family problems. All of these activities involve breaches in the barrier between public and private domains. When the state provides, moreover, its provision is universally oriented. It cannot easily make its provision multicultural; if it does, it may provide unequally and unfairly for different groups.

T. Marshall (1950) has suggested that it is the mark of the modern state that it provides, in addition to legal and political rights, a substantial body of social rights and that this has led workers to feel a greater sense of loyalty to the state and nation than they do to class. In terms of my argument, however, there is an even more fundamental point: much of the feeling of identification which individuals once had with the private domain and the local community is transferred to the state.

Undoubtedly functions have been lost by the family and community to the state, although there is an argument that state intervention actually supports the family and enables it to perform its primary tasks of consumption and primary socialization more effectively (Fletcher 1966). What seems to be the case is that there is inevitably a degree of state socialist provision for family welfare in the modern world and that this is an area of collaboration between public and private domains. When the state intervenes in education, however, more difficult problems arise.

EDUCATION AND THE PUBLIC AND PRIVATE DOMAINS

A modern educational system has three clear functions. *It selects individuals* on the basis of their achievement for training for various occupational roles. *It transmits important skills* necessary for survival and for work in industry. And *it also transmits moral values.* It is this third function which brings it into conflict with the private domain, for clearly one part of the socialization process consists precisely in the transmission of moral values.

Clearly no ethnic minority will object to the selection mechanism being part of the public domain. What is important is simply that this mechanism should give equal opportunity to all. Again, if the minority is committed to living by employment in the industrial system, it will itself wish to take advantage of any skill training which is available. Moral training, however, involves other issues. Insofar as such training at school level is concerned simply with the transmission of what we might call civic morality and culture, the problems arising will be small. True, there will be doubts about the desirability of encouraging competitive and individualist values, because, taken out of context, these conflict with the principles of charity and mutual aid underlying local communities and the private domain. But this is an inherent tension in industrial society and one with which industrial man has learned to live. Moreover there are parts of civic morality which are of value and importance to minorities, especially in relation to the notion of equality of opportunity. Much more important than any objection to this aspect of the school's moral role is the objection to its interference in matters considered to be private or to involve individual choice. This is true of all matters relating to sex, marriage, the family and religion.

It is arguable that schools ought not to intervene in these matters at all or to do so only on the most general and basic level. Such an argument hinges on showing that these practices do not prevent the proper functioning of the state and may positively assist it. The counter-argument is that it is of concern to the state how family matters are arranged, both because the state is concerned with the law of inheritance, and because it has to uphold individual rights even against the family.

On family matters, however, there are considerable tensions between minority communities and the school in contemporary Britain. Among Asians, for example, there is a great emphasis upon arranged marriage and the relative exclusion and modesty of females. Neither the official curriculum of British schools nor the peer group culture in which minority children inevitably participate fosters the relevant values. Sometimes schools may be unnecessarily provocative, for example when girls are required to take part in mixed swimming classes, but more generally the whole ethos of the school, based as it is on the encouragement of individual choice and free competition, strikes at the root of any tight-knit marriage and family system.

There is often a fundamental clash of values on these matters in any modern society. The notion of equality of opportunity appears to point to the rights not merely of families but to those of individuals, male and female, against the constraints imposed by families. Feminism has made the issues here especially sharp. It is unacceptable in terms of feminist values that a woman should be forced into a marriage or that girls should be denied the maximum degree of education because of some preconceived notion of the female role.

Such emphases in the argument are, however, quite misleading from the point of view of Asian parents. They fail to acknowledge the fact that an arranged marriage reflects the care which the family shows towards its daughters: the guaranteed dowry is likely to be far more substantial than anything a European girl might get from her parents to initiate married life. Indeed it can be said that the whole system gives the bride more rights than does the notion of marriage based upon random selection and romantic love. Furthermore, the assertion of freedom in the sexual sphere is bound up with a whole set of values about the marketability of sex as reflected in the media and in sex shops. The feminist demand for greater freedom is therefore seen as part of this larger package which offends against all Asian concepts of modesty and love.

This clash of values cannot be examined here. It is simply important to note that it exists and that in a society which seeks to achieve *both* equality of opportunity *and* the toleration of cultural diversity, institutional arrangements will evolve to deal with this tension. Parents may seek to limit the role of equality of opportunity offered at certain schools by withdrawing their children from certain kinds of activity; they may also seek to provide supplementary moral education outside the school.

Another potential source of discord is religion. Here, however, the way has been prepared in a Christian society for dealing with potential conflicts. Because the various Christian sects and denominations have engaged in conflicts, even in international and civil wars, which have threatened the unity of the state, most nominally Christian societies have already downgraded religion to a matter of minor importance towards which there was no danger in exercising toleration. Once Roman Catholics had been given the right to teach their own religion in schools, there was no barrier in principle to allowing Islam or Sikhism or Hinduism to be taught in a similar way. Difficulties seemed to arise only with quasi-religious movements, for example Rastafarianism, because of their strong political associations.

Wider than the religious question was that of instruction in minority cultures, thought by many to be the key issue in any programme of multicultural education. Such innovations, however, are often far from popular with minority communities, who see them as diverting energies from subjects more important to examination success, and, in any case as caricatures of their culture. The strong preference of minority people is that, unless such teaching can be carried out by minority teachers in schools, it is best done outside school hours. What may perhaps be important is that while minority children learn about majority culture, provision should also be made for majority children to learn about minority culture, since this will foster equality by encouraging equal respect for other cultures.

The question of language creates greater dilemmas. Teaching *in* mother tongues and teaching *of* mother tongues have both been seen to be important in a wide variety of minority communities. Teaching *in* mother tongue is important at the outset for those who do not speak the main school language. If children are simply confronted by another language on entering school, their education is likely to be seriously retarded. What is required therefore is initial teaching in the mother tongue with the main language of the school gradually introduced until it replaces the mother tongue as a medium of instruction. Paradoxically, the importance of using mother tongue as an initial medium of instruction is that it can facilitate assimilation. Much more important, however, is the fact that it promotes equality of opportunity.

The teaching *of* mother tongue is of separate importance. Systematic provision for such teaching is beyond the means of most minority communities, and, if it were literally left to mother, the mother tongue would simply become a restricted ghetto language. What minority people want is to have financial support so that it can be used to enlarge the cultural experiences of the group. In the kind of society under consideration here it cannot ever attain anything like equality with the main language in some sort of bilingual state. But there is no reason why minority people should not be able to express themselves and communicate with each other about their experiences in their own language.

What I am suggesting here is that, once the inherent tensions of the educational system are recognized, it is possible to envisage a balance of control because education belongs to both the public and private domains. The school should be concerned as the agent of the public domain with selection, with the transmission of skills and with civic morality. The community should control education in all matters concerning language, religion and family affairs, for which the state should provide financial support in a multicultural society.

The other alternative is to take education out of the public domain and make it an intra-communal matter. This is what has been done in England in the case of Roman Catholic schools and, in principle, no new ground is opened up if, say, Muslim or Hindu schools receive similar recognition. Obviously there would be a danger in such schools that the task fulfilled by the mainstream schools would be subordinated to the inculcation of communal values, but it is also possible that a balance could be struck here in which the controllers of minority schools themselves recognized the instrumental value of education in a modern society along with education in its own culture. If this were recognized it might be more possible to achieve the right balance in a school controlled by the minority than in normal majority schools which find themselves in tension with minority cultures.

THE PROBLEM OF ETHNIC SOCIAL WORK

Clearly education is a sphere in which the distinction between that which is necessary from the point of view of maintaining the culture of minorities and that which is necessary from the point of view of a large-scale society is difficult to draw. Another even more difficult area is that which arises in connection with social welfare and social work. Social workers have sometimes claimed that what is necessary in dealing with minorities is a special kind of multicultural social work. If, however, the problems of minority people are so different would it not be possible for the community to be subsidized so that it could take care of its own? Alternatively, is the problem not that of *combining* professional standards with sensitivity to community values? In that case would not the answer be to train social workers from the minority communities so that they could add professionalism to their existing sensitivity? The problem of trying to train majority social workers in sensitivity is much more difficult than that of training already sensitive minority people in professional standards.

THE STRUCTURES OF THE PRIVATE DOMAIN

The nature of the sociological problem with which we have to deal is this. For a member of the majority as a society, the world of the family and the primary community is an integrated structural part of the whole network of social relations which constitutes his or her society. It is also a functional subsystem of the whole and its culture is continuous with that of the main society. Among ethnic minorities the situation is wholly different. For such minorities the family and community are part of another social system and another culture. Quite possibly in that society the extended kinship group carried much more weight than it does in industrial society and in some cases provided the whole of the social structure.

The most important function of the immigrant minority kinship group is, of course, primary socialization. In the case of the majority this function is performed by the family, which exists in relative isolation from any larger community or network. In the case of the minority communities, however, the family is part of a wider network of communal and associational ties, the socializing community is larger and more people are involved in the child's socialization. The extended family is not solely a socializing agency but also provides a unit for economic mobilization; this function may even be performed when members are separated from one another by migration. The family and kin group has an estate to which members may be expected to contribute either in terms of property or in terms of skills and qualifications.

An event like marriage is not, therefore, and cannot be solely a matter of individual choice. It involves the transfer of capital from one group to another and, as a result, the linking of two groups. At the same time the new family constituted by marriage starts with a carefully husbanded inheritance of material and social capital.

Because extended kinship is seriously damaged by the fact of migration, the networks within which family life occurs come to depend more on artificial structures which are thought of as associations, but which are actually structures through which the wider community life is expressed. In my study of Sparkbrook (Rex 1973) I suggested that these associations had four functions. They helped individuals to overcome social isolation; they did pastoral work among their members and helped them to deal with moral and social problems; they served as a kind of trade union defending the interests of the group; and it was through them that values and beliefs were affirmed and religious and political ideologies perpetuated.

Of particular importance is the role of the association in the affirmation of values and beliefs. Included in this is that individuals can be offered beliefs about themselves, that is to say identity options or ideas about who he or she is. Naturally it is not the case that individuals automatically accept these options, but the associations are flexible instruments through which new identities appropriate to the new situation are suggested as possible.

Values and beliefs, however, cohere around the more systematic teachings of minority religions. Such religions have belief systems which go far beyond the present situation in explaining mankind's relation to nature and to our fellows. As such they can never be simply functional in a modern society. Nevertheless, whatever their particular content, these religions provide a metaphysical underpinning for beliefs of all kinds and therefore help to provide the psychological security which the whole community structure gives.

To a very large extent the kinship structures, the associations and the religions of the minorities may be seen as acting together to perform a function for the larger society. It is the function of what Parsons calls 'pattern maintenance and tension management' (Parsons 1952). We may say that they provide individuals with a concept of who they are as they embark on action in the outside world and also give them moral and material support in coping with that world. To the extent that they perform these functions, communal structures and belief systems become a functioning part of the larger society, whatever the particular form of the social structure and whatever the content of its culture.

Minority communities and minority cultures do not threaten the unity of society. Nor do they imply inequality between groups. They can have their place within a society which is committed in its main structures to equality of opportunity. What I have tried to suggest is that a multicultural society must find a place for both diversity and equality of opportunity. Emphasis upon the first without allowing for the second could lead to segregationism, inequality and differential incorporation. Emphasis upon the second at the expense of the first could lead to an authoritarian form of assimilationism. Both of these are at odds with the ideal of the multicultural society.

CONFLICT AND COMPROMISE IN THE MULTICULTURAL SOCIETY

Finally, to qualify what l have said about the functionality of minority structures, I believe that we would do an injustice to the religious, cultural and political ideas of minority groups if we saw them as fitting easily and snugly into the social status quo. Sometimes their ideas and their institutions may be revolutionary or secessionist. Sometimes they are not addressed to the problems of the society of settlement at all, but to those of the original homeland. Should this mean that they are dangerous and should be repressed?

I think not. After all, British culture is by no means unitary. It can be and I think should be interpreted in terms of class struggle. The working classes nationally and regionally have developed definite forms of organization and revolutionary notions of social solidarity which challenges the social order and the culture of the ruling classes. The result of all this, however, is that what I have called civic culture includes the notion of conflict. The social order which we have is the resultant of social conflict. I see no reason why there should not be a similar process as that between majority and minority groups. Ours is a society which has produced institutions to deal with the injustices of capitalism. Surely it is not impossible to envisage a similar outcome to the struggle initiated by Rastafarianism which seeks to set right the injustices of the past 400 years. The only belief system which must be outlawed in the multicultural society is that which seeks to impose inequality of opportunity on individuals or groups. That is why the multicultural society must be an anti-racist society.

SUMMARY: THE ESSENTIALS OF A MULTICULTURAL SOCIETY

1 The multicultural ideal is to be distinguished from the notion of a plural society.

2 In a multicultural society we should distinguish between the public domain in which there is a single culture based upon the notion of equality between individuals and the private domain, which permits diversity between groups.

3 The public domain includes the world of law, politics and economics. It also includes education insofar as this is concerned with selection, the

transmission of skills and the perpetuation of civic culture.

4 Moral education, primary socialization and the inculcation of religious belief belong to the private domain.

5 The structure of the private domain among immigrant minority communities includes kinship that extends back into a homeland, a network of associations and a system of religious organization and belief. This structure provides a valuable means in an impersonal society of providing a home and a source of identity for individuals.

6 Nonetheless minority communities at any one time may conflict with and challenge the existing order as have communities based upon social class in the past. The new social order of the multicultural society is an emergent one which will result from the dialogue and the conflict between cultures.

Is a society of this kind likely to come into being in Britain? I think not. The concept of a multicultural society which is now in vogue is too confused for that. It might lead much more readily to 'differential incorporation'. Moreover there are still many to whom the very idea of multiculturalism is anathema and they would oppose the emphasis upon diversity which I have advocated. But it never was the task of a sociologist to provide happy endings. All I can do is to clarify my value standpoint and indicate what institutional arrangements are necessary for its realization.

REFERENCES

Althusser, L. (1969) *For Marx*, Allen Lane: London.
Daniel, W. (1968) *Racial Discrimination in Britain*, Penguin: Harmondsworth.
Durkheim, E. (1933) *The Division of Labor in Society*, Free Press: Glencoe, Illinois.
Durkheim, E. ([1897] 1952) *Suicide*, Routledge and Kegan Paul: London.
Fletcher, R. (1966) *The Family and Marriage in Britain*, Penguin: Harmondsworth.
Furnivall, J. S. (1939) *Netherlands India*, Cambridge University Press: Cambridge.
Malinowski, B. (1962) *A Scientific Theory of Culture*, University of North Carolina Press: Chapel Hill.
Marshall, T. (1950) *Citizenship and Social Class*, Cambridge University Press: Cambridge.
Montague, A. (1972) *Statements on Race*, Oxford University Press: London.
Myrdal, G. (1944) *The American Dilemma: The Negro Problem and Modern Democracy*, Harper and Row: New York.
Parsons, T. (1952) *The Social System*, Tavistock: London.
Parsons, T., Shils, E. and Bales, R. (1953) *Working Papers in the Theory of Actions*, Free Press: New York.
Radcliffe-Brown, A. (1952) *Structure and Function in Primitive Society*, Cohen and West: London.
Rex, J. (1973) *Race, Colonialism and the City*, Routledge and Kegan Paul: London.
Smith, D. (1977) *Racial Disadvantage in Britain*, Penguin: Harmondsworth.
Smith, M. G. (1965) *The Plural Society in the British West Indies*, University of California Press: Berkeley and Los Angeles.

Smith, M. G. (1974) *Corporations and Society*, Duckworth: London.

Tönnies, F. ([1887] 1963) *Community and Association*, translated by C. P. Loomis, Routledge and Kegan Paul: London.

Weber, M. ([1905] 1930) *The Protestant Ethic and the Spirit of Capitalism*, Allen and Unwin: London.

Weber, M. ([1922] 1968) *Economy and Society*, Vol. l, Bedminster Press: New York.

Plural societies
LEO KUPER

[. . .] There are two quite antithetical traditions in regard to the nature of societies characterized by pluralism. The first tradition, which I am following, is relatively recent. It is expressed in the theory of the plural society. In this tradition, the stability of plural societies is seen as precarious and threatened by sharp cleavages between different plural sections, whose relations to each other are generally characterized by inequality. The second tradition is much older, and offers a conception (or ideal type) of the pluralistic society, in which the pluralism of the varied constituent groups and interests is integrated in a balanced adjustment, which provides conditions favourable to stable democratic government. The second tradition is well established in the United States, and I refer below to some contemporary examples of this tradition. The adoption of, or affinity for, one tradition or the other is no doubt shaped by different experiences of social life, in the colonies or in the United States, but it seems also to derive from the opposition between two basic social philosophies expressed in the antithesis between equilibrium models of society (particularly consensual) and conflict models of society. The difficulties that arise in the attempted synthesis of these models also affect attempts to relate the different conceptions of the plural society and the pluralistic society in a broader framework.

'EQUILIBRIUM' MODEL OF PLURALISM

The 'equilibrium' model tends to associate democracy with pluralism (Kornhauser 1960; Shils 1956; Aron 1950). Shils indeed emphasizes his view that pluralism is consistent with diverse political positions – conservatism and liberalism, *laissez-faire* and socialism, traditionalism and rationalism, hierarchy and egalitarianism. But he does not regard these differences in political position as crucial; he argues instead that the really crucial dividing line in politics lies between pluralistic moderation and monomaniac extremism (Shils 1956); and much of his discussion of pluralistic society concerns liberal democracy, which presumably exemplifies for him the ideal realization of the principles of pluralism. Kornhauser also finds in pluralism a basis for liberal democracy. He writes that a pluralist society supports liberal democracy; that liberty and democracy tend to be strong where social pluralism is strong; and that where the introduction of democracy is not based on a pluralist society, democracy may readily lose out to new forms of autocracy (Kornhauser 1960).

The political structure of the society, in the 'equilibrium' model, is itself plural. A system of constitutional checks and balances is designed to effect a separation of powers among the legislature, the executive, the administrative sector, and the judiciary, and in this way to ensure pluralism in the structure of authority. The struggle for power by political parties and leaders is seen as the plural political counterpart of the social pluralism of competing interest groups, and as the basis for democratic rule (in the sense of popular choice among competing candidates). If analysis of political process is directed to the role of elites, then political pluralism is represented by a divided elite.

As the preceding references indicate, the social basis for political pluralism is to be found in social pluralism. This may be conceived as a balance, and a relative autonomy, between institutional spheres. Shils, in his discussion of the pluralistic society, describes this aspect:

> Every society is constructed of a set of spheres and systems: the domestic and kinship system, the political system, the economic system, the religious sphere, the cultural sphere, and the like. Different types of societies are characterized by the preponderance of one of the systems or spheres over the others. ... The system of individualistic democracy or liberalism is characterized by an approximate balance among the spheres. Liberalism is a system of pluralism (Shils 1956: 153–4).

In addition to the separation of spheres, Kornhauser emphasizes the presence of a strong structure of stable and independent groups, intermediate between the individual and the state. This provides the basis for a system of social checks and balances, a dispersion of power contributing to the maintenance of political pluralism.

Integration is seen as effected in part by a system of crosscutting loyalties or multiple affiliations. Thus Kornhauser argues that a multiplicity of associations is not in itself a sufficient basis for the pluralist society. The different associations, such as ethnic associations, may be highly inclusive, encompassing many aspects of their members' lives, and thus encouraging social cleavage, divisive loyalties, and submission to authoritarian control. Hence Kornhauser insists on multiple affiliation as a further condition of pluralism. This extends the concept of pluralism to the level of individual pluralism, in the sense of individual participation in a variety of plural structures. The pluralist dispersion of the individual's different roles is expected to foster diversity of interests, to restrain exclusive loyalties, and to link the plural structures together by innumerable ties of personal relationship. It may also be expected to contribute to integration by promoting the diffusion of common values.

The commitment to common values is, of course, the main basis for integration in the consensual form of the 'equilibrium' model. Shils, in his discussion of pluralistic societies, refers to some of these common values – sentiments of communal affinity among the elites, respect for the rule of law and belief in its sanctity, moderation in political involvement, commitment to gradual change, and recognition of the dignity of other values and activities within the society. But the 'equilibrium' model of the pluralistic society does not necessarily postulate consensus. Kornhauser describes it as exhibiting a fluidity and diversity of value standards which make difficult the achievement of consensus; and he finds the basis for integration in the competitive balance of independent groups and in the multiple affiliation of their members.

The model of the society is thus one of political pluralism, with a corresponding social pluralism in which the units are bound together by crosscutting loyalties and by common values or a competitive balance of power. It is a model that appeals to an optimistic view of society and of the relationships between social groups. The wide acceptance in the United States of models of this type as fairly descriptive of the society is encouraged by the experience in the acculturation and absorption of white immigrants from many different nations (Simpson and Yinger 1953; Berry 1951). From this point of view, optimism is easy to understand. It is more difficult to understand in the context of the relationship between American whites and American Negroes. Here there is much that recalls the more pessimistic view of the plural society of conflict theory.

'CONFLICT' MODEL OF PLURAL SOCIETIES

The 'conflict' model of the plural society derives from Furnivall, who applied the concept to tropical societies. For Furnivall, the political form of the plural society is one of colonial domination, which imposes a Western superstructure of business and administration on the native world, and a forced union on the different sections of the population (Furnivall 1939 and 1945).

The social basis is a medley of peoples living side by side, but separately, within the same political unit. It is in the strictest sense a medley of peoples, 'for they mix but do not combine. Each group holds by its own religion, its own culture and language, its own ideas and ways. As individuals they meet, but only in the market place, in buying and selling' (Furnivall 1945: 304–7). Economic symbiosis and mutual avoidance, cultural diversity and social cleavage, characterize the social basis of the plural society.

In the functioning of the society, there is a primacy of economic forces, relatively freed from social restraint. Furnivall argues that the plural society, arising where economic forces are exempt from control by social will, is a specifically modern invention, because only in modern times have economic forces been set free to remould the social order; and he quotes with approval, as applicable to plural societies, the following description of colonial Java by Dr Boeke:

> There is materialism, rationalism, individualism, and a concentration on economic ends far more complete and absolute than in homogeneous western lands; a total absorption in the exchange and market; a capitalist structure with the business concern as subject, far more typical of capitalism than one can imagine in the so-called 'capitalist' countries, which have grown up slowly out of the past and are still bound to it by a hundred roots (Furnivall 1945: 312).

The economic forces act as determinants, creating and maintaining the plural society in situations of cultural and social diversity under colonial domination.

Integration is not voluntary, but imposed by the colonial power and the force of economic circumstances. Furnivall emphasizes the prevalence of dissensus: there is a failure of the common or social will not only in the plural society as a whole, but also within each of the plural sections, which are atomized from communities with corporate life to crowds of aggregated individuals. Lacking a common social life, men in a plural society become decivilized, and share in common only those wants that they share with animal creation. Even the worship of Mammon, the sole common deity, does not create consensus, for the typical plural society is a business partnership in which bankruptcy signifies, for many partners, release rather than disaster. At many points, economic forces tend to create friction, 'and the plural society is in fact held together only by pressure exerted from outside by the colonial power; it has no common will' (Hinden 1945: 168). The failure of the common will is a crucial element in Furnivall's discussion of the plural society; and the institutions he discusses under the heading 'Resolutions of Plural Economy', namely, caste, the rule of law, nationalism and federalism (Furnivall 1939; Rex, 1959), may each be viewed as a possible mechanism for attaining some measure of consensus.

The most extensive analysis of the 'conflict' model of the plural society is given by M. G. Smith (1960). In the tradition of Furnivall, he sees plural societies as characterized by cultural diversity, social cleavage and dissensus, but he organizes these characteristics within a different theoretical framework.

The political form of the plural society, in Smith's concept, is domination by one of the units, or more precisely, domination by a unit that is a cultural minority. This is in part a matter of definition. Smith argues that if the different units of the plural society were to carry on their different institutional practices, including the political, they would constitute separate societies. Since they are bound together within a single polity, however, it must follow that the formal political institutions of subordinate sections have been repressed as a condition of the political unity of the total society under control of the dominant group: 'plurality of form in political institutions cannot obtain.' The further specification of the form of government as domination by a cultural minority is again a matter of definition, suggested perhaps by the observation that in these circumstances pluralism attains its most characteristic expression. Smith writes that when the dominant section is also a minority, the structural implications of cultural pluralism have their most extreme expression, and the dependence on regulation by force is greatest. Pluralism under a dominant minority corresponds to an extreme type.

The specification of domination by one section as characteristic of plural societies is not, however, simply a matter of definition. The necessity for it arises also from theoretical consideration of the nature and consequences of cultural pluralism. Smith defines cultural pluralism as the practice of different forms of compulsory institutions, such as kinship, education, religion and economy, these different forms being incompatible in the sense that roles are not interchangeable. Since institutions combine social and cultural aspects, the culturally differentiated sections will also differ in their internal social organization. There is therefore a social pluralism corresponding to the cultural pluralism, but the boundaries of the culturally differentiated units and the structurally differentiated units may not fully coincide, since there may be a marginal association between adherents of different cultural traditions, and conversely there may be social division between adherents of the same cultural tradition.

Cultural pluralism is the major determinant of the structure of the plural society. It plays much the same role of primacy as economic forces in Furnivall's analysis. It is cultural pluralism that imposes the necessity for domination by a cultural section. Smith writes that 'where culturally divergent groups together form a common society, the structural imperative for maintenance of this inclusive unit involves a type of political order in which one of these cultural sections is subordinated to the other. Such a condition derives from the structural requisites of society on the one hand, and the condition of wide cultural differences within some populations on the other' (1965a: p. 62). Elsewhere, he describes the monopoly of power by one cultural section as the essential precondition for maintenance of the total society in its current form (1965a: p. 86).

Other factors are secondary to cultural pluralism. Thus racial differences derive social significance from cultural diversity. They are stressed in contexts of social and cultural pluralism. Culturally distinct groups of the same racial stock may even express their cultural differences in racial terms. In culturally homogeneous units, on the other hand, racial differences lack social significance (1965a: p. 84). Hierarchic race relations in a society reflect conditions of cultural heterogeneity and tend to lapse or lose their hierarchic character as cultural uniformity increases.

Plural societies are held together by regulation and not by integration. Smith appears to restrict the term 'integration' to a social cohesion which derives from consensus. He writes that 'social quiescence and cohesion differ sharply, and so do regulation and integration' (1965a: p. 90). There is no predominance of common values and of common motivations in the plural society, and in consequence the society must be held together by regulation. This regulation consists in the rigid and hierarchical ordering of the relations between the different sections. Since the various sections are culturally differentiated, consensus is a remote possibility. Further, the subordinate sections are unlikely to accord equal value and legitimacy to the preservation of the hierarchic pattern. Thus authority, power and regulation are of crucial significance in maintaining, controlling and co-ordinating the plural society. Changes in the social structure presuppose political changes, and these usually take a violent form (1965a: p. 91).

Comparing the approaches of Furnivall and Smith, there is basic agreement on domination by a cultural minority as characteristic of the plural society. This is a matter of historical fact for Furnivall, and a matter of definition and theoretical necessity for Smith. Again, both writers emphasize social cleavage and cultural diversity as qualities of the plural society. For Furnivall, this cultural diversity is again historical fact, tropical colonial societies having brought into contact two contrary principles of social life: a tropical system resting on religion, personal custom, and duties, and a Western system resting on reason, impersonal law, and rights (Hinden 1945: 162). For Smith, cultural diversity is implicit, as a theoretical necessity, in the concept of the plural society: it is the necessary and sufficient condition of pluralism.

Major differences between the two models are first in the range of societies conceived as plural. Furnivall is primarily concerned with colonial tropical societies under the impact of Western economic expansion. Smith includes societies other than colonial pluralities, whether originating in conquest and consolidation or by migration, and whether attributable to Western economic activity or to other forces. They differ also in the approach to causal factors. Furnivall stresses the role of colonial capitalism in the formation of the plural society; cultural diversity is the context within which the primacy of economic forces disintegrates the common will and transforms groups into mass aggregates. Smith, on the other hand, imputes causal significance to cultural incompatibility or wide cultural differences, regardless of the specific content of the cultural differences.

The model proposed by Smith has the advantage of extending the perceptions of Furnivall within a general theoretical framework. But it has serious social implications and a number of critical questions must be raised. Smith distinguishes two basic mechanisms, one of integration and the other of regulation, by which groups may be held together within the same society. Integration rests on common values and common motivations at the individual level, and on the functional relations of common institutions at the societal level. It presupposes cultural homogeneity (or cultural heterogeneity, but only in the form of variations around a common basic institutional system). Cultural diversity or pluralism automatically imposes the structural necessity for domination by one of the cultural sections. It excludes the possibility of consensus, or of institutional integration, or of structural balance between the different sections, and necessitates non-democratic regulation of group relationships.

This implies a distinction between two basic types of society, integrated societies characterized by consensus and cultural homogeneity (or cultural heterogeneity, as described above), and regulated societies characterized by dissensus and cultural pluralism. It implies that cultural homogeneity (or heterogeneity) is a requisite for democratic forms of government; and it suggests the prediction, in concrete terms, that many of the newly independent states may either dissolve into separate cultural sections, or maintain their identity, but only under conditions of domination and subordination in the relationships between groups.

Since cultural diversity is assigned a crucial role in political structure, it becomes necessary to define the nature and extent of the diversity, which necessitates political domination. Smith recognizes that there are differences in the degree of cultural pluralism, and presumably also in the degree of incompatibility between institutions. While it is no doubt true, as he remarks, that these differences do not affect the analytical status of the social phenomena as expressions of cultural pluralism, they may be highly relevant for the political consequences. This relevance seems also to be accepted by Smith in his reference to 'wide cultural differences' as imposing the need for domination. No doubt a certain measure of cultural pluralism may be entirely consistent with democratic participation in government by the different sections.

There are also distinctions to be made in the texture or patterns of cultural pluralism. Thus cultural pluralism between sections may be expected to vary in different institutional contexts. There may be a greater incompatibility in familial institutions, for example, than in religious ones; and presumably some institutions have greater salience for the political constitution of a society. Thus in many plural societies which seek to unify their peoples through a uniform system of law, institutional diversity in family law is nevertheless often given explicit recognition, the customary regulation of family relationships in the different sections being accorded legal status. This cultural pluralism in family institutions may have little relevance for political structure; or it may have political significance under certain social conditions, but not others. In order to assess the political consequences of cultural pluralism, it is therefore necessary to distinguish different patterns of cultural pluralism and to relate them to the varied social conditions under which they appear.

The problem is further complicated by the inevitable co-existence of common institutions and plural institutions. The model of cultural pluralism represents an extreme type which would be most nearly approximated immediately after the establishment of a plural society by conquest. Even then, certain shared activities are likely to have preceded conquest. Once the plural society is constituted, some growth of common institutions, in addition to common governmental institutions, and some association between members of different cultural groups, are inevitable. Intersectional association and common institutions may be expected to modify the political consequences of cultural pluralism, and the relationship between what is common and shared and what is divisive and incompatible must therefore be analysed as part of the social context of cultural pluralism, affecting its political expression.

Social conditions may also influence the perception of cultural pluralism. To some extent, objective measures of cultural pluralism can be devised without regard to particular social contexts or the perceptions of members of the society. Thus it is possible to make paired comparisons between different family institutions, and to assert that one set of differences exceeds the other. But there is also a relative and subjective element in the measurement of cultural pluralism. Cultural differences may be magnified or minimized. Members of the society may seek out and emphasize elements of cultural similarity as a basis of association, or they may stress cultural differences as absolute impediments to association. The political significance of pluralism is likely to fluctuate with the changing conditions of domination. Rather than accord primacy to cultural pluralism, it may contribute to understanding to analyse its significance in a plural society as in part a derivative of domination. Smith sees racist ideology as derivative, as symbolizing and legitimizing intersectional relations (1965a: p. 90). In much the same way it may be argued that cultural pluralism is, in some measure, an ideology of domination or of conflict in a struggle for power between different groups, the significance that the parties attach to cultural difference varying with changes in the structure of their relationships, and more particularly, with changes in relative power.

Cultural pluralism may also be seen as relative to the systems of government in the plural societies and to their dominant legal and political philosophies. Some systems of government may be more tolerant of cultural differences than others. Political philosophies influence the extent to which cultural sections are the basis of administration, as in systems of indirect rule, or are denied recognition and replaced by other categories of administration. In a paper dealing with 'The Sociological Framework of Law (Smith 1965b; Kuper and Kuper 1965), Smith assigns a significant role to the theory of law of the dominant power. He argues that the common law tradition in the British system and the acceptance of the ruler's discretion as a legitimate source of law in Islam contributed to a flexible recognition of African traditional systems of authority and law, whereas the French emphasis on the imperium of the French state as the source of law impeded the administrative and legal acceptance of African cultural pluralism. If there is validity to these comments, then cultural pluralism may be seen not only as a cause but also as a consequence of political domination.

[...]

REFERENCES

Aron, R. (1950), 'Social Structure and the Ruling Class', *British Journal of Sociology*, Vol. I (March 1950), London.
Berry, B. (1951), *Race Relations*, Houghton Mifflin, New York.
Furnivall, J. S. (1939), *Netherlands India*, Cambridge University Press, Cambridge.
Furnivall, J. S. (1945), 'Some Problems of Tropical Economy', in *Fabian Colonial Essays*, ed. R. Hinden, Allen and Unwin, London.
Furnivall, J. S. (1948), *Colonial Policy and Practice*, Cambridge University Press, Cambridge.
Hinden, R., ed. (1945), *Fabian Colonial Essays*, Allen and Unwin, London.
Kornhauser, W. (1960), *The Politics of Mass Society*, Routledge and Kegan Paul, London.
Kuper, L. and Kuper, H., eds (1965), *African Law: Adaptation and Development*, University of California Press, Berkeley and Los Angeles.
Rex, J. (1959), 'The Plural Society in Sociological Theory', *British Journal of Sociology*, Vol. 10 (June 1959), London.
Shils, E. (1956), *The Torment of Secrecy*, Heinemann, London.
Simpson, G. E. and Yinger, M. (1953), *Racial and Cultural Minorities*, Harper, New York.
Smith, M. G. (1960), 'Social and Cultural Pluralism', *Annals of the New York Academy of Sciences* (January 1960), pp. 761–916.
Smith, M. G. (1965a), *The Plural Society in the British West Indies*, University of California Press, Berkeley and Los Angeles.
Smith, M. G. (1965b), 'The Sociological Framework of Law', in *African Law: Adaptation and Development*, University of California Press, Berkeley and Los Angeles, pp. 24–48.

6 Citizenship in Multicultural Societies

Ethnicity in the USA
WILL KYMLICKA

RETHINKING THE LIBERAL TRADITION

[. . .] Few contemporary theorists have explicitly discussed the rights of ethnic and national minorities, or developed any principles for evaluating claims to language rights, for example, or federal autonomy. It was not always this way. For most of the nineteenth century and the first half of the twentieth, the rights of national minorities were continually discussed and debated by the great liberal statesmen and theorists of the age. As I will show, they disagreed about how best to respond to multinational states, but they all took it for granted that liberalism needed some or other theory of the status of national minorities.

Contemporary liberals, by contrast, have been surprisingly silent about these issues. There are very few discussions of the differences between nation states and polyethnic or multinational states, or of the demands associated with each form of ethnic or national diversity. And when contemporary liberals have addressed these issues – often in brief pronouncements or parenthetical asides – they have tended to recite simplistic formulas about 'non-discrimination' or 'benign neglect', formulas that cannot do justice to the complexities involved.

In this [essay], I will trace the origin of contemporary liberal attitudes towards minority rights. I will first explore some of the historical debates about national minorities, then consider some of the reasons why this issue virtually disappeared from view after the Second World War [. . .].

In the process, I hope to correct some common mistakes about the liberal tradition. It is widely believed that liberals have always opposed the political recognition and support of ethnicity and nationality, and that demands for group-differentiated rights for cultural groups are a recent and illiberal deviation from long-established liberal practice (Kymlicka 1989).

This is simply not true. Minority rights were an important part of liberal theory and practice in the nineteenth century and between the world wars. If anything, it is the idea of 'benign neglect' which is a recent arrival in the liberal tradition. Moreover, its emergence can be traced to a series of contingent factors, including ethnocentric denigration of non-European cultures, fears about international peace and security, and the influence of racial desegregation decisions in the United States. These factors have had a profound but often distorting effect on liberal thinking. Issues and arguments that were relevant in one set of circumstances have been mistakenly generalized to other cases where they do not apply. Once we sort out these confusions, it should become clear that minority rights are a legitimate component of the liberal tradition.

THE HISTORY OF LIBERAL VIEWS ON NATIONAL MINORITIES

The liberal tradition contains a striking diversity of views on the rights of minority cultures. At one end of the spectrum, there have been strong proponents of minority rights. Indeed, there have been times in the last two centuries when endorsement of minority rights was considered a clear sign of one's liberal credentials.

For example, it was a common tenet of nineteenth-century liberalism that national minorities were treated unjustly by the multinational empires of Europe, such as the Habsburg, Ottoman and Tsarist empires. The injustice was not simply the fact that the minorities were denied individual civil and political liberties, since that was true of the members of the dominant nation in each empire as well. The injustice was rather the denial of their national rights to self-government, which were seen as an essential complement to individual rights, since 'the cause of liberty finds its basis, and secures its roots, in the autonomy of a national group' (Barker 1948: 248; cf. Mazzini 1907: 51–2, 176–7; Humboldt [1836] 1988: 21, 41–3, 153). The promotion of national autonomy 'offers a realization of the ideal of an "area of liberty", or in other words, of a free society for free men' (Hoernlé 1939: 181).

The precise connection between individual freedom and nationality is not always clear in these theorists. In some cases, it was simply the assumption that multinational states were inherently unstable, and so liable to authoritarianism (I discuss this claim below). But in other theorists, such as Wilhelm von Humboldt and Giuseppe Mazzini, the claim is that the promotion of individuality and the development of human personality is intimately tied up with membership in one's national group, in part because of the role of language and culture in enabling choice.

This liberal commitment to some form of national self-government was so common that George Bernard Shaw once quipped that 'A Liberal is a man who has three duties: a duty to Ireland, a duty to Finland, and a duty to Macedonia' (Zimmern 1918). (All three nations were incorporated into multinational empires at the time.) Notice that the liberal aim was not to grant individual rights to all citizens of these multinational empires, but rather to grant political powers to the constituent nations within each empire. Liberals predicted (accurately) that these empires would fall apart because of their reluctance to grant 'any system of autonomy under which the various nations could have enjoyed the position of quasi-States' (Barker 1948: 254).

It may seem odd that a liberal could ever have been defined (even in jest) by a commitment to national rights rather than individual rights. But we find the same linkage between liberalism and support for the rights of national minorities between the world wars. Leonard Hobhouse, for example, said that 'the more liberal statesmanship' of his day had recognized the necessity of minority rights to ensure 'cultural equality' (Hobhouse 1966: 297, 299). There is more than one way to meet the legitimate demands of national minorities, he thought, but 'clearly it is not achieved by equality of franchise. The smaller nationality does not merely want equal rights with others. It stands out for a certain life of its own' (Hobhouse 1928: 146–7). One manifestation of this liberal commitment was the minority protection scheme set up under the League of Nations for various European national minorities, which provided both universal individual rights and certain group-specific rights regarding education, local autonomy, and language.

Again, the precise connection between equality and minority rights was rarely spelled out. But the general idea was clear enough. A multinational state which accords universal individual rights to all its citizens, regardless of group membership, may appear to be 'neutral' between the various national groups. But in fact it can (and often does) systematically privilege the majority nation in certain fundamental ways – for example, the drawing of internal boundaries; the language of schools, courts and government services; the choice of public holidays; and the division of legislative power between central and local governments. All of these decisions can dramatically reduce the political power and cultural viability of a national minority, while enhancing that of the majority culture. Group-specific rights regarding education, local autonomy and language help ensure that national minorities are not disadvantaged in these decisions, thereby enabling the minority, like the majority, to sustain 'a life of its own'.

We have here the two major claims which, I believe, underlie a liberal defence of minority rights: that individual freedom is tied in some important way to membership in one's national group; and that group-specific rights can promote equality between the minority and majority. [. . .]

These two claims were widely accepted by many nineteenth- and early twentieth-century liberals. To be sure, some liberals opposed various demands for minority rights. But not because of a commitment to the principle of 'benign neglect'. Rather, they believed, with John Stuart Mill, that free institutions are 'next to impossible' in a multination state:

> Among a people without fellow-feelings, especially if they read and speak different languages, the united public opinion necessary to the workings of representative institutions cannot exist . . . [It] is in general a necessary condition of free institutions that the boundaries of governments should coincide in the main with those of nationalities (Mill 1972: 230, 233).

For liberals like Mill, democracy is government 'by the people', but self-rule is only possible if 'the people' are 'a people' – a nation. The members of a democracy must share a sense of political allegiance, and common nationality was said to be a precondition of that allegiance. Thus T. H. Green argued that liberal democracy is possible only if people feel bound to the state by 'ties derived from a common dwelling place with its associations, from common memories, traditions and customs, and from the common ways of feeling and thinking which a common language and still more a common literature embodies' (Green 1941: 130–1; cf. Rich 1987: 155). According to this stream of liberal thought, since a free state must be a nation state, national minorities must be dealt with by coercive assimilation or the redrawing of boundaries, not by minority rights.

The alleged need for a common national identity is an important issue which, as we will see, has been raised again and again throughout the liberal tradition. Some liberals support the need for a common national identity, others deny its necessity. Moreover, some liberals deny that a multinational state even has the capacity to promote a common national identity which will displace or take precedence over the existing identity of a national minority. [. . .]

However, in the nineteenth century, the call for a common national identity was often tied to an ethnocentric denigration of smaller national groups. It was commonplace in nineteenth-century thought to distinguish the 'great nations', such as France, Italy, Poland, Germany, Hungary, Spain, England and Russia, from smaller 'nationalities', such as the Czechs, Slovaks, Croats, Basques, Welsh, Scots, Serbians, Bulgarians, Romanians and Slovenes. The great nations were seen as civilized, and as the carriers of historical development. The smaller nationalities were primitive and stagnant, and incapable of social or cultural development. So some nineteenth-century liberals endorsed national independence for great nations, but coercive assimilation for smaller nationalities.

Thus Mill insisted that it was undeniably better for a Scottish Highlander to be part of Great Britain, or for a Basque to be part of France, 'than to sulk on his own rocks, the half-savage relic of past times, revolving in his own little mental orbit, without participation or interest in the general movement of the world' (Mill 1972: 363–4). Mill was hardly alone in this view. As I discuss later in this chapter, nineteenth-century socialists shared this ethnocentric view, which was also invoked to justify the coerced assimilation of indigenous peoples throughout the British Empire.

Other liberals argued the opposite position, that true liberty was possible only in a multinational state. For example, Lord Acton argued, against Mill, that the divisions between national groups and their desire for an internal life of their own serves as a check against the aggrandisement and abuse of state power (Acton 1922: 285–90). This debate was revisited by British liberals during and after the First World War. For example, Alfred Zimmern defended Acton's claim that a multinational state checks the abuse of state power (Zimmern 1918), while Ernest Barker defended Mill's belief that a nation state can best sustain free institutions (Barker 1948). Here again very different views about the status of national minorities were defended, yet each side claimed that it represented the truly liberal view.

So there is a considerable range of views on minority rights within the liberal tradition. Notice also that none of these earlier positions endorses the idea – championed by many contemporary liberals – that the state should treat cultural membership as a purely private matter. On the contrary, liberals either endorsed the legal recognition of minority cultures, or rejected minority rights not because they rejected the idea of an official culture, but precisely because they believed there should only be *one* official culture.

This is just a quick sketch of the way many earlier liberals viewed nationality. A fuller account would probably reveal an even greater range of views, since it was a prominent theme in most major liberal writings of the era. What explains this remarkable level of interest and debate in one era, and its subsequent virtual disappearance in post-war liberal thought? It is partly related to the rise and fall of the British Empire. From the early 1800s to the beginning of decolonization after the Second World War, English liberals were constantly confronted with the issue of how to export liberal institutions to their colonies. The desire to transplant liberal institutions was fuelled by a somewhat contradictory combination of old-fashioned imperialism (expanding England's domain by setting up little Englands overseas), and a universalistic liberal faith in the 'rights of man', which viewed liberal institutions in the colonies as the first step towards their freedom and independence from English power.

But whatever the motives, English liberals were constantly confronted with the fact that liberal institutions which worked in England did not work in multinational states. It quickly became clear that many English liberal institutions were as much English as liberal – that is, they were appropriate for only a (relatively) ethnically and racially homogeneous society such as England. As Lord Balfour put it, while 'constitutions are easily copied', the successful working of English institutions 'may be difficult or impossible' if national divisions in the colonies are 'either too numerous or too profound'. English institutions presupposed 'a people so fundamentally at one that they can afford to bicker' (Hancock 1937: 429).

According to Hancock, who studied national conflicts within the Empire, British colonial policy was at first shaped by 'abstract universalizers of liberal doctrine' who possessed 'an irresistible propensity to generalize the Englishman's "principles" at large, without realizing that in so doing they [were] taking for granted the whole rich and stable background of English history'. They tried to 'assert their "principles" in the Empire without realizing that what they [were] really seeking [was] to impose their own national forms, regardless of the historic life and culture and needs of some quite different community'. In short, they 'thought it sufficient to transplant, where the need was to translate' (Hancock 1937: 496).

As a result, liberals who went to administer or study British colonies found that the liberalism they learned in England simply did not address some of the issues of cultural diversity they faced. An early example of this was Lord Durham, one of John Stuart Mill's circle, who was sent to Canada to head an inquiry into the causes of the Rebellions of 1837. On the surface, the rebellions in English and French Canada were about demands for more responsible and democratic government (like the American Revolution), and this was how British liberals initially interpreted them. But, as Durham put it in his report, 'I expected to find a contest between a government and a people: I found two nations warring in the bosom of a single state.' He also found that existing liberal theory was not much help in resolving this sort of dispute. His solution, endorsed by J. S. Mill and adopted by the British government, was the more or less forcible assimilation of the French, so as to create a homogeneous English nation state. He had no sympathy for the 'vain endeavour' of the French Canadians to maintain their 'backward' culture (Craig 1963: 146–50).

However, Durham's policy was a complete failure, as French-Canadian resistance to assimilation led to a paralysis in colonial government. Most subsequent liberals, therefore, proposed accommodating national divisions in the colonies. Indeed, many liberals believed that developing a theory of national rights was the greatest challenge facing English liberalism if its appeal was to move beyond the boundaries of its (culturally homogeneous) homeland (e.g. Hoernlé 1939: 123–5, 136–8; Hobhouse 1928: 146; Hancock 1937: 429–31, 495–6; Clarke 1934: 7–8).

My guess is that the same story was repeated a hundred times throughout the British Empire, from the early 1800s to the beginning of decolonization. There must have been generations of English thinkers who learned the essentials of liberal theory at universities in England, and who went overseas with the hope of transplanting those principles, but who were then faced with a set of issues regarding minority rights that they were unprepared to deal with. It would be interesting to have a proper study of the ways English liberals adapted their principles to deal with the existence of minority cultures in their various colonies. Problems of nationality arose throughout the Commonwealth – from Canada and the Caribbean to Africa, Palestine and India – and the colonial experience led to a wealth of experimentation regarding communal representation, language rights, treaties and other historical agreements between national groups, federalism, land rights and immigration policy. With the decline of the Empire, however, liberals stopped thinking about these issues, and little of this experience was fed back into British liberal theory.

The issue of minority rights was raised not only in the colonies, but also by events on the Continent. Nationalist conflicts in Europe were a constant threat to international peace before the Second World War, and this too encouraged liberals to attend to the rights of national`minorities. Yet this factor also disappeared after the Second World War, as nationalist conflicts in Europe were replaced by Cold War conflicts over ideology.

So the ushering in of the post-war era relieved British liberals of the two major reasons for thinking about national minorities – governing overseas colonies, and responding to nationalist conflicts on the Continent. Perhaps as a result, many theorists have reverted to being 'abstract liberal universalizers' who cannot distinguish the core principles of liberalism from its particular institutional manifestations in uninational states like England.

American liberals during the nineteenth and early twentieth centuries were less involved in this debate. They did not have to deal with the existence of colonies, and they were some distance from Europe. As a result, they were not forced to develop a more generalized or comparative view about the application of liberal principles to multinational states. Two American liberals who did talk about minority rights were Randolph Bourne and Horace Kallen (Bourne 1964; Kallen 1924). But they were almost exclusively concerned with the status of white immigrant groups in the USA, and ignored the claims of territorially concentrated and historically settled national minorities, of the sort we find in Europe, Quebec and the Third World.

Post-war American liberalism exhibits the same neglect of national minorities. As I discuss later, virtually all American political theorists treat the United States as a polyethnic nation state, rather than a truly multinational state. Perhaps this is because national minorities in the United States are relatively small and isolated (e.g. Puerto Ricans, American Indians, native Hawaiians, Alaskan Eskimos). These groups are virtually invisible in American political theory. If they are mentioned at all, it is usually as an afterthought. This has had a profound effect on liberal thought around the world, since American theorists have become the dominant interpreters of liberal principles since the Second World War.

These factors – the fall of the British Empire, the rise of Cold War conflict and the prominence of American theorists within post-war liberalism – help explain why the heated debate about national minorities amongst pre-war liberals has given way to a virtual silence. But these factors do not explain why contemporary liberals in practice have become so hostile to minority rights. Why, even in the absence of theoretical discussions, have liberals not intuitively supported minority rights – as many did before the war – and seen them as promoting liberal values of individual freedom and social equality? Why have they instead adopted the idea of 'benign neglect'?

I believe this is the result of the convergence of a number of post-war political changes. Three features of the post-war world have conspired to lead liberals to adopt a misplaced antagonism towards the recognition of national rights: (1) disillusionment with the minority rights scheme of the League of Nations; (2) the American racial desegregation movement; and (3) the 'ethnic revival' among immigrant groups in the United States. I will discuss each of these in turn, to see how they have helped shape the new liberal distrust of minority rights.

THE FAILURE OF THE MINORITY TREATIES

The first important change in liberal views came with the failure of the League of Nations's minority protection scheme, and its role in the outbreak of the Second World War. The scheme gave international recognition to the German-speaking minorities in Czechoslovakia and Poland, and the Nazis encouraged them to make demands and lodge complaints against their governments. When the Polish and Czech governments were unwilling or unable to meet the escalating demands of their German minorities, the Nazis used this as a pretext for aggression. This Nazi manipulation of the League scheme, and the co-operation of the German minorities in it, created 'a strong reaction against the concept of international protection of [national minorities] . . . the hard fact was that statesmen, generally backed by a public opinion which was deeply impressed by the perfidy of irredentist and disloyal minorities, were disposed to curtail, rather than to expand, the rights of minorities' (Claude 1955: 57, 69). This curtailing of minority rights was done, not in the interest of justice, but by people 'within whose frame of reference the interests of the national state ranked as supreme values . . . [The majority nationality] has an interest in making the national state secure, and its institutions stable, even at the cost of obliterating minority cultures and imposing enforced homogeneity upon the population' (Claude 1955: 80–1).

This 'frame of reference' is similar to the earlier liberal view that freedom requires cultural homogeneity, although it differs in emphasis. Whereas Mill and Green were concerned with domestic stability, post-war statesmen were primarily concerned with international peace. But the effect was the same – questions about the fairness of minority rights were subordinated to the higher demands of stability. There was an explicit desire to leave the issue of minority rights off the United Nations agenda, and the UN has only recently agreed to reconsider the legitimacy of minority rights claims (Sohn 1981; Thornberry 1980; 1991). The fear that national minorities will be disloyal (or simply apathetic) continues to inhibit discussion of the justice of these claims, both internationally and in the domestic politics of many countries.

Recent events in the former Yugoslavia show that the threat to international peace from irredentist minorities is still a very real one. The likelihood of violence is dramatically increased when a minority is seen (or sees itself) as belonging to an adjacent 'mother country' which proclaims itself as the legitimate protector of the minority. The government of Hungary has declared itself the protector of ethnic Hungarians in Slovakia and Romania; leaders in Russia and Serbia have made similar declarations about ethnic Russians in the Baltics and ethnic Serbs in Bosnia and Croatia. Protecting the rights of a national minority in these circumstances can become a pretext for territorial aggression by the self-proclaimed protector state. This shows the necessity of developing truly international mechanisms for protecting national minorities that do not rely on the destabilizing threat of intervention by kin states.

The problem of irredentism is much greater in Europe than in North America. Indigenous peoples in North America have no protector state to appeal to, and it has been over 100 years since anyone has viewed France as the protector of the Québécois in Canada. It has been almost as long since anyone viewed Spain as the protector of the Puerto Ricans. In these contexts, while minority rights may affect domestic stability, they pose little threat to international peace.

RACIAL DESEGREGATION IN THE UNITED STATES

The modern liberal rejection of minority rights began with worries about political stability, but it acquired the mantle of justice when it was linked to racial desegregation. In *Brown* v. *Board of Education*, the American Supreme Court struck down the system of segregated educational facilities for black and white children in the South. This decision, and the civil rights movement generally, had an enormous influence on American views of racial equality. The new model of racial justice was 'colour-blind laws', replacing 'separate but equal treatment', which was now seen as the paradigm of racial injustice.

But the influence of *Brown* was soon felt in areas other than race relations, for it seemed to lay down a principle which was equally applicable to relations between ethnic and national groups. According to this principle, injustice is a matter of arbitrary exclusion from the dominant institutions of society, and equality is a matter of non-discrimination and equal opportunity to participate. Viewed in this light, legislation providing separate institutions for national minorities seems no different from the segregation of blacks. The natural extension of *Brown*, therefore, was to remove the separate status of minority cultures, and encourage their equal participation in mainstream society.

This reasoning underlay the Canadian government's 1969 proposal to remove the special constitutional status of Indians. Drawing on the language of *Brown*, the government said that 'separate but equal services do not provide truly equal treatment', and that 'the ultimate aim of removing the specific references to Indians from the constitution ... is a goal to be kept constantly in view' (Bowles *et al.* 1972). Similarly, the Canadian Supreme

Court invoked *Brown* when striking down a law which gave group-specific status to Indians.

Brown's formula for racial justice has also been invoked against the rights of American Indians, native Hawaiians, and the rights of national minorities in international law. Under the influence of *Brown*, these national groups have been treated as a 'racial minority', and their autonomous institutions have been struck down as forms of 'racial segregation' or 'racial discrimination'.

But the actual judgement in *Brown* does not support this application of the colour-blind formula to the rights of national minorities. The Court was simply not addressing the issue of national rights, like the right of a culture to the autonomous institutions needed to be able to develop itself freely within a multinational state. Segregationists were not claiming that whites and blacks formed different cultures, with different languages and literatures. On the contrary, the whole burden of their case was that the education received by blacks in their segregated facilities was *identical* with that of whites. The question was whether racial groups could be given separate facilities, so long as the facilities were identical. And the Court ruled that, *in those circumstances*, segregation was inherently unequal, since it would be seen as a 'badge of inferiority', as a sign of racism.

Nothing in the judgement warrants the claim that national rights are incompatible with liberal equality. Indeed, the judgement, examined more closely, may argue *for* the recognition of national rights. Consider the situation of American Indians, whose separate institutions came under attack after *Brown*. As Michael Gross notes:

> Where blacks have been forcibly *excluded* (segregated) from white society by law, Indians – aboriginal peoples with their own cultures, languages, religions and territories – have been forcibly *included* (integrated) into that society by law. That is what [is] meant by coercive assimilation – the practice of compelling, through submersion, an ethnic, cultural and linguistic minority to shed its uniqueness and identity and mingle with the rest of society (Gross 1973: 244).

Integrated education for the Indians, like segregated education for the blacks, is a 'badge of inferiority' for it fails 'to recognize the importance and validity of the Indian community'. In fact, the integration of Indian children in white-dominated schools had the same negative educational and emotional effects which segregation was held to have in *Brown*. Hence the 'underlying principle' which struck down the segregation of blacks – namely, that racial classifications harmful to a minority are prohibited – should also strike down legislated integration of Indians (Gross 1973: 242–8).

The point is not that Indians do not need protection against racism. But whereas racism against blacks comes from the denial by whites that blacks are full members of the community, racism against Indians comes primarily from the denial by whites that Indians are distinct peoples with their own cultures and communities. Unfortunately, the centrality of the civil rights movement for African-Americans has prevented people from seeing the distinctive issues raised by the existence of national minorities.

In one sense, it is paradoxical that *Brown* has been taken as a model for all ethnic and national groups. [. . .] The historical situation and present circumstances of African-Americans are virtually unique in the world, and there is no reason to think that policies which are appropriate for them would be appropriate for either national minorities or voluntary immigrants (or vice versa). But in another sense, this extension of *Brown* is understandable. The history of slavery and segregation represents one of the greatest evils of modern times, and its legacy is a society with very deep racial divisions. It is not surprising that the American government and courts, and public opinion generally, should wish to eliminate anything which even remotely resembles racial segregation. While separate and self-governing institutions for Indians or native Hawaiians have only a superficial resemblance to racial segregation, this has been enough to expose them to legal assault. While understandable, this over-generalization of *Brown* is unfortunate, and unjust. There is no reason why justice for African-Americans should come at the price of injustice for indigenous peoples and other national minorities.

POLYETHNICITY AND THE AMERICAN ETHNIC REVIVAL

The belief that minority rights are unfair and divisive was confirmed, for many liberals, by the ethnic revival which rocked the United States and elsewhere in the 1960s and 1970s. [. . .] This revival began with the claim that it was legitimate (not 'unamerican') for ethnic groups to express their distinctive characteristics (as opposed to the 'Anglo-conformity' model of immigration). But it soon moved on to new demands. For example, one result of the more open expression of ethnic identity was that ethnic groups became more conscious of their status as a group. It became common to measure the distribution of income or occupations among ethnic groups, and some of those groups which were faring less well demanded group-based ameliorative action, such as quotas in education and employment. They also wanted their heritage recognized in the school curriculum and government symbols.

American liberals have had an ambiguous relationship to this ethnic revival. Most liberals accepted the initial demand by ethnic groups for the abandonment of the Anglo-conformity model. But as demands escalated, liberal support diminished. In fact, the increasing politicization of immigrant groups profoundly unsettled American liberals, for it affected the most basic assumptions and self-conceptions of American political culture. And this anxiety has had important repercussions for their attitude towards national minorities.

As I noted earlier, most American political theorists think of the United

States as an immigrant country. Indeed, it is the original immigrant country. The idea of building a country through polyethnic immigration was quite unique in history, and many people thought it untenable. There were no historical precedents to show that an ethnically mixed country of immigrants would be stable. What would bind people together when they came from such different backgrounds, including every conceivable race, religion, language group, sharing virtually nothing in common?

The answer, of course, was that immigrants would have to integrate into the existing Anglophone society, rather than forming separate and distinct nations with their own homelands inside the United States. There was no hope for the long-term survival of the country if the Germans, Swedes, Dutch, Greeks, Italians, Poles and so on each viewed themselves as separate and self-governing peoples, rather than as members of a single (polyethnic) American people. As John Higham put it, the English settlers conceived of themselves as 'the formative population' of the American colonies/states, and 'theirs was the polity, the language, the pattern of work and settlements, and many of the mental habits to which the immigrants would have to adjust' (Higham 1976: 6; cf. Steinberg 1981: 7).

Immigrants would not only have the right to integrate into the mainstream Anglophone society (and so would be protected against discrimination and prejudice); they also had the obligation to integrate (and so would be required to learn English in schools, and English would be the language of public life). The commitment to integrating immigrants was not just evidence of intolerance or ethnocentrism on the part of WASPs (although it was that in part), it was also an understandable response to the uncertainty about whether a country built through polyethnic immigration would be viable.

It was fundamental, then, that immigrants view themselves as ethnic groups, not as national minorities. For a long time, immigrants seemed content with this arrangement. But the ethnic revival challenged this traditional model. As the ethnic revival escalated, some immigrant associations in the United States adopted the language and attitudes of colonized 'nations' or 'peoples' (Glazer 1983: 110–11). They labelled social pressures for integration as 'oppression', and demanded their right to 'self-determination', including state recognition of their mother tongue, and state support for separate ethnic institutions.

As I discuss below, these sorts of demands represented only a minor element among American immigrant groups. However, they caused serious anxiety among liberals. Most liberals viewed the adoption of nationalist rhetoric by immigrant groups not only as a threat to social unity, but also as morally unjustified. Liberals argued that immigrants had no legitimate basis to claim such national rights. After all, they had come voluntarily, knowing that integration was expected of them. When they chose to leave their culture and come to America, they voluntarily relinquished their national membership, and the national rights which go with it.

This attitude towards the ethnic revival is clearly expressed in the writings of Michael Walzer, a leading American political theorist (and editor of the left-liberal journal *Dissent*), and Nathan Glazer, a leading American sociologist (and editor of the right-liberal journal *Public Interest*). According to Glazer, immigrants

> had come to this country not to maintain a foreign language and culture but with the intention . . . to become Americanized as fast as possible, and this meant English language and American culture. They sought the induction to a new language and culture that the public schools provided – as do many present-day immigrants, too – and while they often found, as time went on, that they regretted what they and their children had lost, this was *their* choice, rather than an imposed choice (Glazer 1983: 149).

Similarly, Walzer argues that because the immigrants 'had come voluntarily', the 'call for self-determination' had no basis here. Nor was there any basis or reason for rejecting English as the public language (Walzer 1982: 6–7, 10; 1983b: 224).

Both Glazer and Walzer emphasize how the process of integrating voluntary immigrants differs from the assimilation of conquered or colonized national minorities in the multinational states of Europe. In the latter case, it is wrong to deprive 'intact and rooted communities' that 'were established on lands they had occupied for many centuries' of mother-tongue education or local autonomy. Under these conditions, integration is an 'imposed choice' which national minorities typically (and justifiably) have resisted. The integration of immigrants, by contrast, 'was aimed at peoples far more susceptible to cultural change, for they were not only uprooted; they had uprooted themselves. Whatever the pressures that had driven them to the New World, they had chosen to come, while others like themselves, in their own families, had chosen to remain' (Walzer 1982: 9; cf. Glazer 1983: 227, 283). Demands for national rights by immigrant groups are not only unjustified. They are also divisive, since each group will resent any special rights given to other groups, and impracticable, since American ethnic groups are too 'dispersed, mixed, assimilated and integrated' to exercise collective autonomy. Indeed, any attempt to turn ethnic groups into the 'compact, self-conscious, culture-maintaining entities' necessary for collective autonomy would require coercion, since many immigrants prefer to integrate into the mainstream society, both culturally and geographically. Implementing the extensive new demands of the ethnic revival would, therefore, be unjust, impracticable, divisive and coercive (Glazer 1983: 124, 227).

I think that Glazer and Walzer are right to emphasize the difference between immigrants and national minorities, and to focus on the fact that (in most cases) the decision to emigrate was voluntary. This fact does, I believe, affect the legitimacy of their claims [. . .]; while voluntary immigrants can legitimately assert certain polyethnic rights, they have no claim of justice to national self-government.

Given the centrality of immigration to American society, it is not surprising that liberals have been so hostile to any signs of latent nationalism among immigrant groups. In a country built primarily on immigration, with immigrants from virtually every linguistic and cultural group around the world, any serious attempt to redefine ethnic groups as national minorities would undermine the very fabric of society.

What is perhaps more surprising is that liberals have been so hostile to self-government claims by the few national minorities which do exist in the United States. Having emphasized the difference between immigrants and national minorities, one might have expected Walzer and Glazer to endorse the self-government demands of American Indians, Puerto Ricans, native Hawaiians, etc. These groups, after all, really are conquered and colonized peoples, like the national minorities in Europe.

Glazer recognizes that these groups 'possess much more in the way of national characteristics' (1983: 283–4), and that they are demanding national rights on just the grounds that he emphasizes are inapplicable to immigrant groups:

> Both blacks and the Spanish-speaking point to a distinctive political situation: the blacks were brought as slaves, and the Mexicans and Puerto Ricans were conquered. The American Indians were also conquered. The white ethnic groups, however, came as free immigrants. Thus the blacks, the Spanish-speaking groups, the American Indians, and perhaps some other groups can make stronger claims for public support of their distinctive cultures than can European groups (Glazer 1983: 118).

Glazer accepts that 'there is a good deal of weight' in their demands for national rights (Glazer 1983: 119). Similarly, the logic of Walzer's argument suggests these national minorities should not be forced to accept an approach which is 'not primarily the product of their experience', but rather is 'adapted to the needs of immigrant communities' (Walzer 1982: 6, 27).

Yet liberals in the United States have not endorsed the rights of national minorities. Some liberals simply ignore the existence of such groups. While Glazer and Walzer recognize their existence, they none the less insist that 'benign neglect' is appropriate for them as well as immigrants. Thus Glazer expresses his hope that 'these groups, with proper public policies to stamp out discrimination and inferior status and to encourage acculturation and assimilation, will become not very different from the European and Asian ethnic groups, the ghost nations, bound by nostalgia and sentiment and only occasionally coalescing around distinct interests' (Glazer 1983: 284). Similarly, Walzer hopes that the policies which have worked for immigrants can 'successfully be extended to the racial minorities now asserting their own group claims' (Walzer 1982: 27; cf. Ogbu 1988: 164–5).

Why do Glazer and Walzer reject the implications of their own argument? At one point, Walzer suggests that Indians do not really want national rights:

'Racism is the great barrier to a fully developed pluralism and as long as it exists American Indians and blacks, and perhaps Mexican Americans as well, will be tempted' by national rights. These national rights claims would not be tempting if national minorities had the 'same opportunities for group organization and cultural expression' available to immigrant groups (Walzer 1982: 27).

But there is no evidence that Indians, for example, desire national rights only because they have been prevented from becoming an ethnic group. Indeed, this is completely at odds with the history of Indian tribes in America or Canada. Indians have often been pressured to become 'just another ethnic group', but they have resisted that pressure and fought to protect their distinct status. As I noted earlier, Indians are indeed subject to racism, but the racism they are most concerned with is the racist denial that they are distinct peoples with their own cultures and communities.

In the end, the main reason why Glazer and Walzer reject self-government claims for national minorities is that these claims are, in effect, 'un-american'. According to Glazer, there

> is such a thing as a state ideology, a national consensus, that shapes and determines what attitude immigrant and minority groups will take toward the alternative possibilities of group maintenance and group rights on the one hand, or individual integration and individual rights on the other ... The United States, whatever the realities of discrimination and segregation, had as a national ideal a unitary and new ethnic identity, that of American (Glazer 1978: 100).

Although minority rights are not inherently unfair, they are none the less incompatible with America's 'national consensus' and 'state ideology'.

Similarly, Walzer says that the question of national rights within a multi-national state 'must itself be worked out politically, and its precise character will depend upon understandings shared among the citizens about the value of cultural diversity, local autonomy, and so on. It is to these understandings that we must appeal when we make our arguments' (Walzer 1983a: 29). And in America, the larger political community sees national rights as 'inconsistent with our historical traditions and shared understandings – inconsistent, too, with contemporary living patterns, deeply and bitterly divisive' (Walzer 1983a: 151).

This appeal to a 'state ideology' or 'shared understandings' is puzzling. For one thing, their description of the alleged consensus is biased. Walzer and Glazer say the state must either give political recognition to both ethnic and national groups, or deny political recognition to both sorts of group. But why can the national consensus not emphasize what they themselves emphasize – the difference between the coerced assimilation of minority nations and the voluntary assimilation of immigrants? Why can the national consensus not recognize that national minorities have legitimate claims which voluntary immigrants do not?

Indeed, this is the actual practice in both the USA and Canada. Indians, Inuit,

French Canadians, native Hawaiians and Puerto Ricans all have a special political status that ethnic groups do not have. This has been a long-standing arrangement, and it is not clear why both countries could not continue to support self-government for national minorities but not for ethnic groups.

Walzer and Glazer apparently think that this arrangement is unstable. After asserting that the 'proper' policy is to assimilate national minorities, Glazer goes on to note 'a final complication':

> If the public policy gets turned around to the point where, rather than trying to suppress or ignore the existence of the ethnic group as a distinctive element in American society and polity, it acknowledges a distinctive status for some groups and begins to attach rights in public law to membership in them, will that not react on the others, halfway toward assimilation, and will they not begin to reassert themselves so that they will not be placed at a disadvantage? (1983: 284).

Here is the crux of the matter for Glazer. National minorities who desire recognition of their national rights may have both justice and established practice on their side, but

> Our problem is that we are not a federation of peoples (like Canada or the Soviet Union) but of states, and our ethnic groups are already too dispersed, mixed, assimilated, integrated to permit without confusion a policy that separates out some for special treatment. But if we try, then many other groups will join the queue, or try to, and the hope of a larger fraternity of all Americans will have to be abandoned . . . In a multiethnic society, such a policy can only encourage one group after another to raise claims to special treatment for its protection . . . The demand for special treatment will lead to animus against other groups that already have it, by those who think they should have it and don't (Glazer 1983: 227–9).

In other words, recognizing the legitimate demands of Indians or Puerto Ricans would make European and Asian ethnic groups demand illegitimate and divisive benefits, and thereby jeopardize the 'larger fraternity of all Americans'.

This is yet another version of Mill's argument about the need for a common identity to ensure stability in a democracy. But it adds a new twist to that argument. Unlike Mill, Glazer is not concerned about the destabilizing impact of the national minorities themselves on domestic stability. In the United States, these groups are too small and geographically isolated to jeopardize the overall stability of the country. And, unlike post-war statesmen, Glazer is not concerned about the potential for national minorities to create international conflict. National minorities in the United States are not irredentist.

Instead, Glazer is concerned about the ripple effect of national minorities on immigrant groups. He is worried that according self-government rights to national minorities will encourage immigrant groups to make similar claims. Is this a realistic fear? I think not. The idea that immigrant groups are looking to establish themselves as national minorities is, I believe, based on a misreading of the 'ethnic revival'. The ethnic revival is not a repudiation of integration into the mainstream society. Even the most politicized ethnic groups are not interested in reconstituting themselves as distinct societies or self-governing nations alongside the mainstream society.

On the contrary, the ethnic revival is essentially a matter of self-identity and self-expression, disconnected from claims for the revival or creation of a separate institutional life. People want to identify themselves in public as members of an ethnic group, and to see others with the same identity in prominent positions of respect or authority (e.g. in politics and the media, or in textbooks and government documents). They are demanding increased recognition and visibility within the mainstream society. The ethnic revival, in other words involves a revision in the terms of integration, not a rejection of integration [. . .].

Where then did Walzer and Glazer get the idea that ethnic groups were demanding national rights? In retrospect, it may simply be the fact that the ethnic revival among American immigrants arose at the same time as nationalist movements resurfaced in Europe and Quebec. But as John Stone notes, this 'coincidence in time' does not mean that the two developments 'were part of the same political process' (Stone 1985: 101).

Some commentators point to demands for affirmative action programmes as evidence of a desire to be treated as a national minority. But that is a mistake. Demands for affirmative action within the mainstream economy are evidence of a desire to integrate into the institutions of the larger society, not a desire for separate and self-governing institutions. And there is no reason to think that accommodating the legitimate demands of national minorities will change this aspiration of immigrants.

In any event, it is worth pointing out how, here again, justice is being sacrificed to stability. Neither Glazer nor Walzer suggests there is anything unfair or illiberal about self-government for national minorities. On the contrary, both give good arguments why national minorities should, in principle, have special political status. Moreover, they admit that the 'national consensus' which rejects such rights was defined by settler groups to suit their own distinctive circumstances, and that national minorities do not share its aims. Like Mill and post-war statesmen, however, they feel that rights for national minorities are inconsistent with political unity, and that the latter takes precedence over the former.

This concludes my overview of the history of minority rights within the liberal tradition. I have noted the striking diversity of views about such rights within the tradition, from strong support to deep anxiety. But what is equally striking is that few if any liberals, until very recently, have supposed that such rights are inherently illiberal. Even those liberals who objected to minority rights did so on grounds of stability, not freedom or justice, and indeed they have often conceded that they are purchasing stability at the price of injustice.

Yet somehow many contemporary liberals have acquired the belief that minority rights are inherently in conflict with liberal principles. Liberals today insist that the liberal commitment to individual liberty precludes the acceptance of collective rights, and that the liberal commitment to universal (colour-blind) rights precludes the acceptance of group-specific rights. But these bald statements are no part of the liberal tradition. Few if any liberals, until very recently, supposed that liberal principles allowed only universal individual rights. What contemporary liberals take to be well-established liberal principles are in fact novel additions to the liberal canon.

Moreover, these new 'principles' are primarily the result of confusions and over-generalizations. I have looked at three factors in the development of the post-war liberal consensus against group-differentiated rights for ethnic and national groups: a *realpolitik* fear about international peace, a commitment to racial equality, and a worry about the escalating demands of immigrant groups. Underlying each is legitimate concern. But each has also been over-generalized. Certain arguments against the demands of particular groups, based on localized factors (irredentism, racial segregation, voluntary immigration), have been mistakenly generalized to all cases of cultural pluralism. And the combined effect of all three has been a distortion of liberal thinking on minority rights. Out of this mixture has arisen the belief that minority rights are inherently unjust, a betrayal of liberal equality. But these influences, examined more closely, argue the opposite – the first concedes the fairness of minority rights, and the second and third argue against separate political institutions for racial and immigrant groups on grounds that are consistent with, and indeed support, the legitimacy of national rights.

In fact, none of these factors challenges the two basic claims which, I suggested earlier, underlie a liberal defence of minority rights: namely, that individual freedom is tied to membership in one's national group; and that group-specific rights can promote equality between the minority and majority.

[. . .]

REFERENCES

Acton, Lord (1922), 'Nationalism', in *The History of Freedom and Other Essays*, ed. J. Figgis and R. Laurence, Macmillan, London.

Barker, E. (1948), *National Character and Factors in its Formation*, Methuen, London.

Bourne, R. S. (1964), 'Transnational America', in *War and the Intellectual: Essays by Randolph S. Bourne 1915–1919*, ed. C. Resek, Harper and Row, New York.

Bowles, S. *et al.*, eds (1972), *The Indian: Assimilation, Integration or Separation?*, Prentice Hall, Scarborough.

Clarke, F. (1934), *Quebec and South Africa: A Study in Cultural Adjustment*, Oxford University Press, London.

Claude, I. (1955), *National Minorities: An International Problem*, Harvard University Press, Cambridge, Mass.

Craig, G. (1963), *Lord Durham's Report: An Abridgement of Report on the Affairs of British North America*, McLelland and Stewart, Toronto.

Glazer, N. (1975), *Affirmative Discrimination: Ethnic Inequality and Public Policy*, Basic Books, New York.

Glazer, N. (1978), 'Individual Rights against Group Rights', in *Human Rights*, ed. A. Tay and E. Kamenka, Edward Arnold, London.

Glazer, N. (1983), *Ethnic Dilemmas: 1964–1982*, Harvard University Press, Cambridge, Mass.

Green, T. (1941), *Lectures on the Principles of Political Obligation*, Longman, Green and Co., London.

Gross, M. (1973), 'Indian Control for Quality Indian Education', *North Dakota Law Review*, 49/2.

Hancock, W. (1937), *Survey of British Commonwealth Affairs, 1: Problems of Nationality 1900–1936*, Oxford University Press, London.

Higham, J. (1976), *Send These to Me*, Atheneum, New York.

Hobhouse, L. T. (1928), *Social Evolution and Political Theory*, Columbia University Press, New York.

Hobhouse, L. T. (1966), *Social Development: Its Nature and Conditions*, George Allen & Unwin, London.

Hobsbawm, E. (1990), *Nations and Nationalism since 1780: Programme, Myth and Reality*, University of California Press, Berkeley.

Hoernlé, R. (1939), *South African Native Policy and the Liberal Spirit*, Lovedae Press, Cape Town.

Humboldt, W. von. ([1836], 1988), *On Language: The Diversity of Human Language-Structure and its Influence on the Mental Development of Mankind*, translated by Peter Heath, Cambridge University Press, Cambridge.

Kallen, H. (1924), *Culture and Diversity in the United States*, Boni and Liveright, New York.

Kymlicka, W. (1989), *Liberalism, Community and Culture*, Oxford University Press, Oxford.

Mazzini, J. (1907), *The Duties of Man and Other Essays*, J. M. Dent, London.

Mill, J. (1972), *Considerations on Representative Government*, in *Utilitarianism, Liberty and Representative Government*, ed. H. Acton, J. M. Dent, London.

Ogbu, J. (1988), 'Diversity and Equality in Public Education: Community, Forces and Minority School Adjustment and Performance', in *Policies for America's Public Schools: Teachers, Equity and Indicators*, ed. R. Haskins and D. MacRae, Ablex Publishers, Norwood, New Jersey.

Rich, P. (1987), 'T. H. Green, Lord Scarman and the Issue of Ethnic Minority Rights in English Liberal Thought', *Ethnic and Racial Studies*, 10, pp. 149–68.

Sohn, L. (1981), 'The Rights of Minorities', in *The International Bill of Rights: The Covenant on Civil and Political Rights*, Columbia University Press, New York.

Steinberg, S. (1981), *The Ethnic Myth: Race, Ethnicity and Class in America*, Atheneum, New York.

Stone, J. (1976), 'Black Nationalism and Apartheid: Two Variations on a Separatist Theme', *Social Dynamics*, 2/1, pp. 19–30.

Stone, J. (1985), *Racial Conflict in Contemporary Society*, Harvard University Press, Cambridge, Mass.

Thornberry, P. (1980), 'Is there a Phoenix in the Ashes? International Law and Minority Rights', *Texas International Law Journal*, 15, pp. 421–58.

Thornberry, P. (1991), *International Law and the Rights of Minorities*, Oxford University Press, Oxford.

Walzer, M. (1982), *The Politics of Ethnicity*, Harvard University Press, Cambridge, Mass.

Walzer, M. (1983a), *Spheres of Justice: A Defence of Pluralism and Equality*, Blackwell, Oxford.

Walzer, M. (1983b), 'States and Minorites', in *Minorities: Community and Identity*, ed. C. Fried, Springer-Verlag, Berlin, pp. 219–27.

Zimmern, A. (1918), *Nationality and Government*, Chatto and Windus, London.

Multiculturalism in welfare states: the case of Germany
FRANK-OLAF RADTKE

The process of ethnic formation of migrant workers and their families in Germany must be discussed in the framework of the concept of political pluralism on the one hand and, on the other, the specific condition of the social democratic type of welfare state both of which seem to reflect conflicting principles. [This essay sets out to discuss]: (1) that migrants did not arrive in Germany as 'ethnic minorities' but were created as such as a result of the historic condition of the German nation state; (2) that there is in Germany unlike in other immigration countries no ethnic mobilization in terms of an ethnic bottom up movement which could efficiently claim group interests; (3) that multiculturalism has an unintended effect by transforming social conflicts into ethnic ones and has made them irreconcilable.

A precondition of the functioning of the liberal model of political pluralism is the chance for individuals to articulate and give voice to certain kinds of interest by forming interest-groups. The ability and power to organize one's interest depends, in the market model, on the equality of individual opportunities and rights. Only those interests which can be organized and confronted efficiently with conflicting interests will have the chance to become part of the social compromise in which the distribution of the social wealth is regulated. Common interest in the pluralistic concept cannot in advance be defined in political programmes but appears *a posteriori* as a result of the free game of social powers.

Within the normative model of liberal democracy the task of the state is endowed with the monopoly of force, to make sure a minimum of rules and norms which form the constitution are voluntarily maintained. Liberalism is based on the idea of a division of powers which is more exactly a division of social spheres: the public sphere and the private sphere. Both spheres are composed of different systems, each of them dominated by different principles.

In the public sphere is situated the political system where political participation is organized and state decisions are made and administered within bureaucratic organizations. The governing principle is the equality of universal human and political rights summed up as citizenship, symbolized in the right to vote and to be elected. The system of science, arts and the media also belongs to the public sphere but is strictly separated from the political system. It is governed by the freedom of opinion and the privilege of error. The core of the public sphere is formed by the economic system of the markets of goods, labour and services; this most dynamic system is ruled by the maxim of competition, rivalry and advantage. The youngest but nowadays one of the biggest systems in modern societies has become the educational system which has made socialization and education a public task. It is ruled by the principles of achievement and meritocracy and by the principle of homogeneity which strives to build a national identity by means of language and culture.

The religious community of ethics is situated in the private sphere. During the modernization process in the nineteenth and twentieth centuries in Europe it has more or less been expelled from the public sphere and is now based on the individual freedom of faith. The core of the private sphere is formed around the family which is historically the oldest part of society and one organized on the archaic principles of kinship and descent. Around the family there is the wider community of friendship and neighbourhood which is held together by the principle of exclusiveness (Rex 1986; Walzer 1992).

Political pluralism will work only if the different spheres are separated and their ruling maxims are not confused. But there is no pure realization of the concept of strictly separated spheres anywhere in the world. All existing societies that devote themselves to political pluralism have difficulties in keeping principles, institutions and practices distinct. Conflicts arise especially at those lines where institutions have only recently differentiated themselves or have (been) moved from one sphere to the other. That is the case, for example, with religion which was only recently moved to the private sphere but which frequently intervenes with moral standards into the political ('abortion') or educational system ('school prayer'). Other examples are when the private community claims particular ('cultural') rights ('mother tongue') in public education; when market principles undermine or political restrictions repress science, art, religion or education; when the state intervenes with regard to the principle of equality ('gender') into the labour market or into the privacy of the family etc.

Conflicts of this type are constitutive in plural societies and are part of the process of social change and modernization. The way they are solved gives every society a specific historic appearance. The decision over, for example, whether there should be more morality in the economic system or more commercialization in the science and art systems or more equality in the labour market or more cultural particularity in the education system is subject to political debate and is the outcome of conflicting interests. The existing pluralist societies can be differentiated along these lines.

The programme of the social democratic type of welfare state intentionally crosses the distinctions between the spheres and systems under the title of prevention and intervention. In this concept the task of the state is not only to guarantee certain formal rules and equal rights in the political process of conflict solving but also to create social justice by balancing individual disadvantages. The idea is that the principle of equality (of rights and chances) should not only be valid in the political system but has to be extended to an equality (of outcomes) in the other systems, too. Not satisfied with the mechanisms of self-control and -regulation by non-regulation in the market system, the state establishes a superstructure to manage and control the social process and to define the common welfare in advance. Starting with interventions into the economic system, the state occupies more and more of those tasks which in the liberal model are related to the market, to non-governmental organizations and self-organized interest groups. The importance of the civil society of organized interests (unions, federations, companies, professions, parties, movements) is reduced and transformed if the state claims an overall competence of problem solving.

An outstanding characteristic of the social democratic type of welfare state is the legal regulation of all social relations and the emergence of a client system. This tends to overthrow the old class relations (as group conflicts in the economic system based on solidarity) as well as the functioning of civil society (based on self-organization of social and cultural interests). This also establishes a direct relation between the individual and the state by splitting up interest groups such that their members are isolated against each other and become competing receivers of benefits and substitute payments. The civil society vanishes or is ousted to the private sphere. Freedom is seen to be 'time free of work' and public affairs become the domain of professional politicians and party managers. The process of individualization opens up an empty space between the bureaucratic state and the individual. The necessity of self-organization is superseded in as much as the individual has contentions and claims to make which result from premiums or social rights. Social and political participation is reduced to periodical voting in general elections; political parties are changed from interest groups to 'people-parties' working as clearing organizations to transmit state interest.

A stepped clientelism may emerge if existing organizations of the civil society which organize interests or provide services or care for the socially disadvantaged become dependent upon state money to fulfil their tasks. This is the case where the state follows the subsidiarity principle delegating its duties to private institutions, e.g. private companies or the churches or church-run welfare organizations. The clientele of the state are organizations which have a clientele of individuals themselves. In both cases the dependency is reciprocal: the institutional or individual client will try to present himself as fitting into the programme of the patron; the patron will continue to exist only if he has the lasting support and trust of his clientele. To compensate its notorious deficit the welfare state may not withstand the temptation to use civil institutions as instruments of policy implementation. At this point, civil society is transformed into a corporatistic system where individual rights and claims are only recognized as group rights depending on membership to certain categories. The liberal model of competing interests ends up in patronage, lobbyism and paternalism.

The German model of the 'social market economy' follows the concept of the social democratic type of welfare state even if it was initiated after the Second World War by neo-conservative Christian Democrats. There is a high amount of state interventionism into the economic, the cultural and the educational systems, even into the religious and family spheres. A debate on the limits of the welfare state has only recently begun, and a policy of deregulation, i.e. withdrawal of the state from several fields of activity, is now taking place.

The condition of the German welfare state together with an ethnic nation state tradition has shaped and sustained the way the state acted towards migrant workers. Until recently [West] Germany never considered itself an immigrant country, although more then 20 million people from eastern and southern Europe immigrated into the territory of the [former] Federal Republic between 1945 and 1989, among them 5 million 'guestworkers' and their families. West German capitalism, confronted with a second socialist German state, presented itself as a system of social security. Unlike other immigration countries such as the US, Canada, Australia, but also the UK and France, immigrants in Germany are granted most of the social benefits provided to citizens but enjoy no political rights which would enable them to assert their interests effectively. Nobody can legally enter [West Germany] without immediately being endowed with nearly the full range of social rights. From the beginning of the recruitment of guestworkers in the 1950s until 1973, when a recruitment-stop was declared, the migrant workers were formally granted working conditions and social benefits equal to the German workforce (which could not prevent them from getting the badly paid and dirty jobs). None of the trade unions was interested in having a situation of competition between a German workforce and the legally weakened immigrants who would have to accept any payment and any working conditions – a strategy that eventually brought about illegal work.

Immigrant workers are on the one hand integrated into the social security system but on the other hand not admitted to the political arena. This is due to the ruling interpretation of the German constitution of 1949 which is in essential parts built on the concept of the 'jus sanguinis', reserving citizenship to ethnic Germans based on blood. As non-citizens, foreigners do not have the right to political rights. They can not themselves struggle for their interests in the political system and have to find deputizing majority speakers. These conditions have made them prototypical clients. Private welfare organizations offered their services.

In the [former] Federal Republic of Germany social welfare under the subsidiarity principle is partly the task of private social welfare organizations which are nearly completely subsidized by state money. They are linked to the churches and the trade unions and thus are ideologically fixed. The care for the 'Ausländer' opened a new field of social work but also new spheres of interest: there was a pastoral-missionary interest not to let the uprooted migrants fall into moral disorientation or the influence of communist propaganda but there was also an interest to get state money to run the organization. To that purpose welfare organizations first created a 'guestworker problem'. As there are competing welfare organizations the growing number of migrants in the 1960s was distributed among them. To split up the clientele between the organizations it became necessary to find criteria for the sharing out. The differences of language and religion were emphasized: (1) the Catholic CARITAS got the (Catholic) migrants from Italy, Spain, Portugal and Croatia; (2) the Protestant DIAKONIE got the non-Catholic but Christian migrants from Greece; and (3) the ARBEITERWOHLFAHRT, a non-denominational organization close to the trade unions, got the non-Christian (i.e. Muslim) immigrants from Turkey and the Maghreb.

From a professional point of view it was a pragmatic decision to homogenize the client groups along the lines of language to make communication easier by way of specializing the translating capacities. The decisive factor here – one especially important for the process of ethnicization – was the emphasis on religion – a marker migrants themselves would not have used. The combination of language and religion for professional and administrative purposes created 'cultures', and subsequently 'ethnic groups', whose special needs the welfare organizations had to meet through particular measures.

In Germany today the language of the 'guestworkers' and the denomination or non-denominational orientation of the welfare organizations, turns out to be the hidden scheme of what, since the 1980s, is also in Germany called the 'multicultural society'. Language differences were charged with religious ones and then reintroduced into the society, re-emphasizing a difference that during the process of modernization and secularization had already lost its social importance. Migrants were turned into representatives of their national culture.

The organizations had created the cultures which they were to look after in the coming years by the installation of a system of counselling centres, support systems, learning courses etc. Migrants were no longer dealt with in their social roles as workers or family members, workless and/or homeless, pregnant, school failures, alcoholics, drug addicts etc. but seen from an ethnological viewpoint as representatives of their national culture of descent. Regional studies were conducted to get an idea of the difficulties and conflicts of a life between cultures. This approach opened a new field of operation for social advisers, and often resulted in an endless stereotyping of, especially, Turkish youth and Turkish women (who became the preferred object of social research). Detailed reports of the way of living in a village in Anatolia, in comparison with the living conditions in the German inner city, were used to draw conclusions and make prognoses about the migrants' ability or competence for integration. The differentiation of cultural, instead of social, characteristics offered the chance to constitute groups whose members' behaviour is deterministic. In this way pre- and intervention strategies need not be individualized, but instead can be applied to whole national groups.

When a public discourse on the limits of the welfare system arose, the situation of divided social and political rights allowed the state, after 1975, to start a policy of chicanery and nasty administrative tricks to expel those migrants who were now seen as illegitimate freeloaders. In reaction to the politics of social cutbacks and the restriction of living conditions, migrants themselves had no political means to oppose discrimination; hence they were only to avoid it as best they could. Legal action was taken whereby a group was created within the population whose members were the object of discrimination and paternalization at the same time. Without any power or right to political action, migrants needed deputy speakers and therefore became a permanent topic of the discourse of the majority. In the media migrants were presented as being illegitimate participants in the social welfare system or as victims of discrimination. All participants in the debate following their own aims and interests established a discourse about the migrants and not a dialogue with them.

The terms of the debate among the majority population began to focus attention on the immigrants' abilities and willingness to integrate into the majority culture. In the course of this assimilationist debate, migrants were no longer dealt with in terms of their legal status ('Ausländer') but turned into 'strangers'. The difference of passport was changed into a difference of 'culture'. 'Ethnicity' as an important issue and a category to draw differences was once again in German history, wilfully introduced into the society to discriminate against a social group.

The response of the benevolent part of the society, especially that of the Protestant churches and the welfare organizations, was to adopt the concept of 'multiculturalism' imported from the US and the UK. Multiculturalism was the only way to keep on dealing with cultural and ethnic differences in a positive way. The welfare organizations which, for organizational and professional purposes had once described society in terms of religious and language differences, now tried to get rid of the ghosts they had called up by turning unwanted immigration into a programme of cultural enrichment.

Parallel to the discussion in the social welfare organizations, welfare and labour market politicians who saw themselves confronted with demographic problems in the indigenous population also changed their viewpoint. To stabilize the social security system and to release future labour markets, they welcomed immigration. Looking for a fitting ideology to reconcile those who were afraid of the strangers, they picked up the idea of multiculturalism and painted a colourful picture of a society of cultural plurality in an integrating Europe.

To find an explanation for extremely high quotas of school failures among migrant children, last but not least educationalists in school referred to cultural differences and cultural conflicts. They adopted multiculturalism and transformed it into a concept of intercultural education. It is very rarely implemented in the daily school life, but has the advantage of allowing teachers and headmasters to talk and conform with the benevolent part of the majority by way of offering excuses for the unacceptable outcomes of their schooling practices.

The ascription of ethnic distinctions included a revitalization of the notion of 'Germanness' which after the Second World War had been totally tabooed. If the minorities had a national identity, why should the indigenous people not – definitely after the 'reunification' – feel German? The ethnic formation of the minorities 'from above' opened the floor for a new nationalism in the majority – a defensive nationalism of resentment induced by the political parties in the course of election campaigns to legitimate social cuts and economic disturbances following the national euphoria.

Having no political rights and being the discriminated and/or paternalized object of the discourse of the majority, the minorities in Germany can not take advantage of the programme of multiculturalism to organize and to struggle for their own affairs; instead they had to accept help – individually in the client role.

One small exception where migrants as group representatives have a chance to articulate their interests is found in the 'Committees of Foreigners'. Their task was to inform the decision-makers (at the municipal level) about migrants' interests and claims. Only half the seats were reserved for migrants while the rest were given to representatives of social welfare organizations who felt themselves in charge of migrants and again acted as deputy speakers. During the 1980s, however, the members of these committees in several cities were elected by the migrant communities themselves. Although migrants now have the right to be heard in some city parliaments, they are far from being part of the majority representation with equal participating rights (Bommes 1991). The number of participants in these migrant 'elections' is very low not only because of the symbolic meaning of the vote but also because social and political differences within migrant populations can hardly be represented within a quota system.

The modus of these para-elections together with the discourse of multi-culturalism for migrants made it advisable to present themselves as ethnics emphasizing their cultural heritage. Having no space in the public sphere except as the subject of exploitation, paternalism, advice and help, migrants in the German context were ousted to the private sphere and forced to follow the 'communal option' intensifying their ethnic links. They formed ethnic homogeneous communities around religious and traditional symbols not only to protect a cultural identity in an unfriendly and sometimes racist environment but also to present themselves in the way that the majority wanted to see them. There is a strong interaction between the policy of multiculturalism and the cultural acting out of minorities and their representatives. When the city of Frankfurt, for example, establishes an 'Office for Multi-Cultural Affairs', people who want to get help, advice or money from the office have to present their problems with reference to their ethnic origin. If there is, for example, a conflict between a tenant and a landlord, let's say about noise and smell in a fast-food shop, then the office will surely intervene if one of the conflicting parties plays the ethnic card. The noise and smell must be identified as ethnic noise and smell. The shopkeeper therefore has to be labelled as or to present himself as 'Turkish' to turn a social conflict which would be the responsibility of the

'Office of Public Order' in to an ethnic conflict between representatives of two national cultures.

The effect of multiculturalism in connection with clientelism is not ethnic mobilization but self-ethnicization of the minorities. As long as they do not have any political rights and as long as there is no policy of equal opportunity or affirmative action – and this is an important difference from the situation in the USA and the UK – multiculturalism inevitably ends up in folklorism. Minorities in Germany are kept away from the public sphere and invited by the legal system to form apolitical communities ('Gemeinschaften') in the private sphere instead of interest groups. The communal option in the German context will not favour ethnic corporatism as a means to struggle for one's rights. It is regressive and of doubtful value for coping with the problems of a modern society which follows the social democratic type of welfare state. It is regressive in the psychoanalytic sense of going back to former states of the psychogenetic development where the basic triad of 'individual', 'patria' and 'mother tongue' is reconstructed. Here, 'fundamentalism' finds fertile soil. And it is regressive in a historic sense as it prolongs differentiation patterns once invented in the nineteenth century which have no solving capacity for the global problems of the twenty-first century. Ethnicization and self-ethnicization bring about the danger that the division of the public and the private spheres which is a condition of modern functional differentiated societies is replaced by secret undeclared segregation.

Societies which are subjected to clientelism are characterized by a process of dissocialization, individualization and singularization. Privatism, egocentrism and the decay of universalistic orientations enforce particularistic thinking and acting. Political philosophers and increasingly politicians recommend a recollection of the idea of 'community' (cf. Taylor 1989) for the majority, too. Multiculturalism appears as a form of 'communitarism' promising the solution for the post-modern decay of the society. This might be a serious fallacy. The functioning of pluralism depends on bargaining processes concerning conflicting interests with common rules and shared values. Organized interest groups, in the concept of pluralism, are thought of as 'pouvoir intermediaire' (in the Montesquieu sense) which guarantee the rules of the game in their own interest. Particularistic communities based on ethnic self-definition or external labelling are not able to guarantee the minimum consensus that is essential for pluralism because the principle of their organization is exclusiveness. When it comes to the questions of cultural identity, religious norms etc. differences become irreconcilable and compromises are reduced.

Multiculturalism translates the concept of a plurality of interests into a concept of a plurality of descents. Thus it offers, in the empty space between state and the individual, not an autonomous group but the believed community of those who have in common certain quasi-natural characteristics as religion and language. Multiculturalism is only a reversal of ethnocentrism. When ever more theoretical arguments are turned up side down, the categories used to draw differences remain the same. As long as ethnic differentiation is exclusively an issue for minorities, the German society is not really affected. But if the pattern of ethnic differentiation overcomes the majority as a national backlash – for example in the case of refugees and asylum seekers or in relation to the former 'brothers and sisters' in the connected territories in East Germany – then the fundamental principles of the republic are touched. Multiculturalism encourages such a development where ethnic differences are reified, revitalized and scientifically subsidized instead of deconstructed, reduced and demystified.

REFERENCES

Bommes, M. (1991), *Interessenvertretung durch Einfluss*, University of Osnabrück, Osnabrück.

Rex, J. (1986), *The Concept of a Multi-Cultural Society*, Centre for Research in Ethnic Relations, Occasional Papers, University of Warwick, Coventry.

Taylor, C. (1989), 'Cross-Purposes: The Liberal-Communitarian Debate', in N. Rosenblum, *Liberalism and the Moral Life*, Harvard University Press, Cambridge, Mass.

Walzer, M. (1992), *Zivile Gesellschaft und Amerikanische Demokratie*, Rotbuch Verlag, Berlin.

7 Migration Theory, Ethnic Mobilization and Globalization

Causes of migration

DOUGLAS S. MASSEY, JOAQUIN ARANGO,
GRAEME HUGO, ALI KOUAOUCI, ADELA PELLEGRINO
AND J. EDWARD TAYLOR

[Since the 1960s], 30 years immigration has emerged as a major force throughout the world. In traditional immigrant-receiving societies such as Australia, Canada and the United States, the volume of immigration has grown and its composition has shifted decisively away from Europe, the historically dominant source, towards Asia, Africa and Latin America. In Europe, meanwhile, countries that for centuries had been sending out migrants were suddenly transformed into immigrant-receiving societies. After 1945, virtually all countries in western Europe began to attract significant numbers of workers from abroad. Although the migrants were initially drawn mainly from southern Europe, by the late 1960s they mostly came from developing countries in Africa, Asia, the Caribbean and the Middle East.

By the 1980s even countries in southern Europe – Italy, Spain and Portugal – which only a decade before had been sending migrants to wealthier countries in the north, began to import workers from Africa, Asia and the Middle East. At the same time, Japan – with it slow and still declining birth rate, its ageing population and its high standard of living – found itself turning increasingly to migrants from poorer countries in Asia and even South America to satisfy its labour needs.

Most of the world's developed countries have become diverse, multi-ethnic societies, and those that have not reached this state are moving decisively in that direction. The emergence of international migration as a basic structural feature of nearly all industrialized countries testifies to the strength and coherence of the underlying forces. Yet the theoretical base for understanding these forces remains weak. The recent boom in immigration has therefore taken citizens, officials and demographers by surprise, and when it comes to international migration, popular thinking remains mired in nineteenth-century concepts, models and assumptions.

At present, there is no single, coherent theory of international migration, only a fragmented set of theories that have developed largely in isolation from one another, sometimes but not always segmented by disciplinary boundaries. Current patterns and trends in immigration, however, suggest that a full understanding of contemporary migratory processes will not be achieved by relying on the tools of one discipline alone, or by focusing on a single level of analysis. Rather, their complex, multi-faceted nature requires a sophisticated theory that incorporates a variety of viewpoints, levels and assumptions.

[. . .]

THE INITIATION OF INTERNATIONAL MIGRATION

A variety of theoretical models has been proposed to explain why international migration begins, and although each ultimately seeks to explain the same thing, they employ radically different concepts, assumptions and frames of reference. Neo-classical economics focuses on differentials in wages and employment conditions between countries, and on migration costs; it generally conceives of movement as an individual decision for income maximization. The 'new economics of migration', in contrast, considers conditions in a variety of markets, not just labour markets. It views migration as a household decision taken to minimize risks to family income or to overcome capital constraints on family production activities. Dual labour market theory and world systems theory generally ignore such micro-level decision processes, focusing instead on forces operating at much higher levels of aggregation. The former links immigration to the structural requirements of modern industrial economies, while the latter sees immigration as a natural consequence of economic globalization and market penetration across national boundaries.

Given the fact that theories conceptualize causal processes at such different levels of analysis – the individual, the household, the national and the international – they cannot be assumed, *a priori*, to be inherently incompatible. It is quite possible, for example, that individuals act to maximize income while families minimize risk, and that the context within which both decisions are made is shaped by structural forces operating at the national and international levels. Nonetheless, the various models reflect different research objectives, focuses, interests and ways of decomposing an enormously complex subject into analytically manageable parts; and a firm basis for judging their consistency requires that the inner logical propositions, assumptions and hypotheses of each theory be clearly specified and well understood.

Neo-classical economics: macro theory

[. . .]

The simple and compelling explanation of international migration offered by neo-classical macro-economics has strongly shaped public thinking and has provided the intellectual basis for much immigration policy. The view contains several implicit propositions and assumptions:

1 The international migration of workers is caused by differences in wage rates between countries.
2 The elimination of wage differentials will end the movement of labour, and migration will not occur in the absence of such differentials.
3 International flows of human capital – that is, highly skilled workers – respond to differences in the rate of return to human capital, which may be different from the overall wage rate, yielding a distinct pattern of migration that may be opposite that of unskilled workers.
4 Labour markets are the primary mechanisms by which international flows of labour are induced; other kinds of market do not have important effects on international migration.
5 The way for governments to control migration flows is to regulate or influence labour markets in sending and/or receiving countries.

Neo-classical economics: micro theory

Corresponding to the macro-economic model is a micro-economic model of individual choice (Sjaastad 1962; Todaro 1969, 1976, 1989; Todaro and Maruszki 1987). [. . .] In theory, a potential migrant goes to where the expected net returns to migration are greatest, leading to several important conclusions that differ slightly from the earlier macro-economic formulations:

1 International movement stems from international differentials in both earnings and employment rates, whose product determines expected earnings (the prior model, in contrast, assumed full employment).
2 Individual human capital characteristics that increase the likely rate of remuneration or the probability of employment in the destination relative to the sending country (e.g. education, experience, training, language skills) will increase the likelihood of international movement, other things being equal.
3 Individual characteristics, social conditions, or technologies that lower migration costs increase the net returns to migration and, hence, raise the probability of international movement.

4 Because of 2 and 3, individuals within the same country can display very different proclivities to migration.

5 Aggregate migration flows between countries are simple sums of individual moves undertaken on the basis of individual cost-benefit calculations.

6 International movement does not occur in the absence of differences in earnings and/or employment rates between countries. Migration occurs until expected earnings (the product of earnings and employment rates) have been equalized internationally (net of the costs of movement), and movement does not stop until this product has been equalized.

7 The size of the differential in expected returns determines the size of the international flow of migrants between countries.

8 Migration decisions stem from disequilibria or discontinuities between labour markets: other markets do not directly influence the decision to migrate.

9 If conditions in receiving countries are psychologically attractive to prospective migrants, migration costs may be negative. In this case, a negative earnings differential may be necessary to halt migration between countries.

10 Governments control immigration primarily through policies that affect expected earnings in sending and/or receiving countries – for example, those that attempt to lower the likelihood of employment or raise the risk of underemployment in the destination area (through employer sanctions), those that seek to raise incomes at the origin (through long-term development programmes), or those that aim to increase the costs (both psychological and material) of migration.

The new economics of migration

In recent years, a 'new economics of migration' has arisen to challenge many of the assumptions and conclusions of neo-classical theory (Stark and Bloom 1985). A key insight of this new approach is that migration decisions are not made by isolated individual actors, but by larger units of related people – typically families or households – in which people act collectively not only to maximize expected income, but also to minimize risks and to loosen constraints associated with a variety of market failures, apart from those in the labour market (Stark and Levhari 1982; Stark 1984; Katz and Stark 1986; Lauby and Stark 1988; Taylor 1986; Stark 1991).

[. . .]

The theoretical models growing out of the 'new economics' of migration yield a set of propositions and hypotheses that are quite different from those emanating from neo-classical theory, and they lead to a very different set of policy prescriptions:

1 Families, households or other culturally defined units of production and consumption are the appropriate units of analysis for migration research, not the autonomous individual.

2 A wage differential is not a necessary condition for international migration to occur; households may have strong incentives to diversify risks through transnational movement even in the absence of wage differentials.

3 International migration and local employment or local production are not mutually exclusive possibilities. Indeed, there are strong incentives for households to engage in both migration and local activities. In fact, an increase in the returns to local economic activities may heighten the attractiveness of migration as a means of overcoming capital and risk constraints on investing in those activities. Thus, economic development within sending regions needs to reduce the pressures for international migration.

4 International movement does not necessarily stop when wage differentials have been eliminated across national boundaries. Incentives for migration may continue to exist if other markets within sending countries are absent, imperfect or in disequilibria.

5 The same expected gain in income will not have the same effect on the probability of migration for households located at different points in the income distribution, or among those located in communities with different income distributions.

6 Governments can influence migration rates not only through policies that influence labour markets, but also through those that shape insurance markets, capital markets and future markets. Government insurance programmes, particularly unemployment insurance, can significantly affect the incentives for international movement.

7 Government policies and economic changes that shape income distributions will change the relative deprivation of some households and thus alter their incentives to migrate.

8 Government policies and economic changes that affect the distribution of income will influence international migration independent of their effects on mean income. In fact, government policies that produce a higher mean income in migrant-sending areas may *increase* migration if relatively poor households do not share in the income gain. Conversely, policies may reduce migration if relatively rich households do not share in the income gain.

Dual labour market theory

Although neo-classical human capital theory and the new economics of migration lead to divergent conclusions about the origins and nature of international migration, both are essentially micro-level decision models. Standing distinctly apart from these models of rational choice, however, is dual labour market theory, which sets its sights away from decisions made by individuals and argues that international migration stems from the intrinsic labour demands of modern industrial societies.

[. . .]

Although not in inherent conflict with neo-classical economics, dual labour market theory does carry implications and corollaries that are quite different from those emanating from micro-level decision models:

1 International labour migration is largely demand-based and is initiated by recruitment on the part of employers in developed societies, or by governments acting on their behalf.

2 Since the demand for immigrant workers grows out of the structural needs of the economy and is expressed through recruitment practices rather than wage offers, international wage differentials are neither a necessary nor a sufficient condition for labour migration to occur. Indeed, employers have incentives to recruit workers while holding wages constant.

3 Low-level wages in immigrant-receiving societies do not rise in response to a decrease in the supply of immigrant workers; they are held down by social and institutional mechanisms and are not free to respond to shifts in supply and demand.

4 Low-level wages may fall, however, as a result of an increase in the supply of immigrant workers, since the social and institutional checks that keep low-level wages from rising do not prevent them from falling.

5 Governments are unlikely to influence international migration through policies that produce small changes in wages or employment rates; immigrants fill a demand for labour that is structurally built into modern, post-industrial economies, and influencing this demand requires major changes in economic organization.

World systems theory

Building on the work of Wallerstein (1974), a variety of sociological theorists has linked the origins of international migration not to the bifurcation of the labour market within particular national economies, but to the structure of the world market that has developed and expanded since the sixteenth century (Portes and Walton 1981; Petras 1981; Castells 1989; Sassen 1988, 1991; Morawska 1990). In this scheme, the penetration of capitalist economic relations into peripheral, non-capitalist societies creates a mobile population that is prone to migrate abroad.

[. . .]

World systems theory thus argues that international migration follows the political and economic organization of an expanding global market, a view that yields six distinct hypotheses:

1 International migration is a natural consequence of capitalist market formation in the developing world; the penetration of the global economy into peripheral regions is the catalyst for international movement.

2 The international flow of labour follows the international flow of goods and capital, but in the opposite direction. Capitalist investment foments changes that create an uprooted, mobile population in peripheral countries while simultaneously forging strong material and cultural links with core countries leading to transnational movement.

3 International migration is especially likely between past colonial powers and their former colonies, because cultural, linguistic, administrative, investment, transportation and communication links were established early and were allowed to develop free from outside competition during the colonial era, leading to the formation of specific transnational markets and cultural systems.

4 Since international migration stems from the globalization of the market economy, the way for governments to influence immigration rates is by regulating the overseas investment activities of corporations and controlling international flows of capital and goods. Such policies, however, are unlikely to be implemented because they are difficult to enforce, tend to incite international trade disputes, risk world economic recession, and antagonize multinational firms with substantial political resources that can be mobilized to block them.

5 Political and military interventions by governments of capitalist countries to protect investments abroad and to support foreign governments sympathetic to the expansion of the global market, when they fail, produce refugee movements directed to particular core countries, constituting another form of international migration.

6 International migration ultimately has little to do with wage rates or employment differentials between countries; it follows from the dynamics of market creation and the structure of the global economy.

THE PERPETUATION OF INTERNATIONAL MOVEMENT

Immigration may begin for a variety of reasons – a desire for individual income gain, an attempt to diversify risks to household income, a programme of recruitment to satisfy employer demands for low-wage workers, an international displacement of peasants by market penetration within peripheral regions, or some combination thereof. But the conditions that initiate international movement may be quite different from those that perpetuate it across time and space. Although wage differentials, relative risks, recruitment efforts and market penetration may continue to cause people to move, new conditions that arise in the course of migration come to function as independent causes themselves: migrant networks spread, institutions supporting transnational movement develop, and the social meaning of work changes in receiving societies. The general thrust of these transformations is to make additional movement more likely, a process known as cumulative causation.

Network theory

Migrant networks are sets of interpersonal ties that connect migrants, former migrants, and non-migrants in origin and destination areas through ties of kinship, friendship and shared community origin. They increase the likelihood of international movement because they lower the costs and risks of movement and increase the expected net returns to migration. Network connections constitute a form of social capital that people can draw upon to gain access to foreign employment. Once the number of migrants reaches a critical threshold, the expansion of networks reduces the costs and risks of movement, which causes the probability of migration to rise, which causes additional movement, which further expands the networks, and so on. Over time migratory behaviour spreads outward to encompass broader segments of the sending society (Hugo 1981; Taylor 1986; Massey and Garcia España 1987; Massey 1990a, 1990b; Gurak and Caces 1992).

[. . .]

This dynamic theory accepts the view of international migration as an individual or household decision process, but argues that acts of migration at one point in time systematically alter the context within which future migration decisions are made, greatly increasing the likelihood that later decision-makers will choose to migrate. The conceptualization of migration as a self-sustaining diffusion process has implications and corollaries that are quite different from those derived from the general equilibrium analyses typically employed to study migration:

1 Once begun, international migration tends to expand over time until network connections have diffused so widely in a sending region that all people who wish to migrate can do so without difficulty; then migration begins to decelerate.
2 The size of the migratory flow between two countries is not strongly correlated to wage differentials or employment rates, because whatever effects these variables have in promoting or inhibiting migration are progressively overshadowed by the falling costs and risks of movement stemming from the growth of migrant networks over time.
3 As international migration becomes institutionalized through the formation and elaboration of networks, it becomes progressively independent of the factors that originally caused it, be they structural or individual.
4 As networks expand and the costs and risks of migration fall, the flow becomes less selective in socio-economic terms and more representative of the sending community or society.

5 Governments can expect to have great difficulty controlling flows once they have begun, because the process of network formation lies largely outside their control and occurs no matter what policy regime is pursued.
6 Certain immigration policies, however, such as those intended to promote reunification between immigrants and their families abroad, work at cross-purposes with the control of immigration flows, since they reinforce migrant networks by giving members of kin networks special rights of entry.

Institutional theory

Once international migration has begun, private institutions and voluntary organizations arise to satisfy the demand created by an imbalance between the large number of people who seek entry into capital-rich countries and the limited number of immigrant visas these countries typically offer. This imbalance, and the barriers that core countries erect to keep people out, create a lucrative economic niche for entrepreneurs and institutions dedicated to promoting international movement for profit, yielding a black market in migration. As this underground market creates conditions conducive to exploitation and victimization, voluntary humanitarian organizations also arise in developed countries to enforce the rights and improve the treatment of legal and undocumented migrants.

For profit organizations and private entrepreneurs provide a range of services to migrants in exchange for fees set on the underground market: surreptitious smuggling across borders; clandestine transport to internal destinations; labour contracting between employers and migrants; counterfeit documents and visas; arranged marriages between migrants and legal residents or citizens of the destination country; and lodging, credit and other assistance in countries of destination. Humanitarian groups help migrants by providing counselling, social services, shelter, legal advice about how to obtain legitimate papers and even insulation from immigration law enforcement authorities. Over time, individuals, firms and organizations become well known to immigrants and institutionally stable, constituting another form of social capital that migrants can draw upon to gain access to foreign labour markets.

The recognition of a gradual build-up of institutions, organizations and entrepreneurs dedicated to arranging immigrant entry, legal or illegal, again yields hypotheses that are also quite distinct from those emanating from micro-level decision models:

1 As organizations develop to support, sustain and promote international movement, the international flow of migrants becomes more and more institutionalized and independent of the factors that originally caused it.
2 Governments have difficulty controlling migration flows once they have begun because the process of institutionalization is difficult to regulate. Given the profits to be made by meeting the demand for immigrant entry,

police efforts only serve to create a black market in international movement, and stricter immigration policies are met with resistance from humanitarian groups.

Cumulative causation

In addition to the growth of networks and the development of migrant-supporting institutions, international migration sustains itself in other ways that make additional movement progressively more likely over time, a process Myrdal (1957) called cumulative causation (Massey 1990b). Causation is cumulative in that each act of migration alters the social context within which subsequent migration decisions are made, typically in ways that make additional movement more likely. So far, social scientists have discussed six socio-economic factors that are potentially affected by migration in this cumulative fashion: the distribution of income, the distribution of land, the organization of agriculture, culture, the regional distribution of human capital and the social meaning of work. Feedbacks through other variables are also possible, but have not been systematically treated (Stark, Taylor and Yitzhaki 1986; Taylor 1992).

[. . .]

Viewing international migration in dynamic terms as a cumulative social process yields a set of propositions broadly consistent with those derived from network theory:

1 Social, economic and cultural changes brought about in sending and receiving countries by international migration give the movement of people a powerful internal momentum resistant to easy control or regulation, since the feedback mechanisms of cumulative causation largely lie outside the reach of government.
2 During times of domestic unemployment and joblessness, governments find it difficult to curtail labour migration and to recruit natives back into jobs formerly held by immigrants. A value shift has occurred among native workers, who refuse the 'immigrant' jobs, making it necessary to retain or recruit more immigrants.
3 The social labelling of a job as 'immigrant' follows from the concentration of immigrants within it; once immigrants have entered a job in significant numbers, whatever its characteristics, it will be difficult to recruit native workers back into that occupational category.

Migration systems theory

The various propositions of world systems theory, network theory, institutional theory and the theory of cumulative causation all suggest that migration flows acquire a measure of stability and structure over space and time, allowing for the identification of stable international migration systems. These systems are characterized by relatively intense exchanges of goods, capital and people between certain countries and less intense exchanges between others. An international migration system generally includes a core receiving region, which may be a country or group of countries, and a set of specific sending countries linked to it by unusually large flows of immigrants (Fawcett 1989; Zlotnik 1992).

Although not a separate theory so much as a generalization following from the foregoing theories, a migration systems perspective yields several interesting hypotheses and propositions.

1 Countries within a system need not be geographically close since flows reflect political and economic relationships rather than physical ones. Although proximity obviously facilitates the formation of exchange relationships, it does not guarantee them nor does distance preclude them.
2 Multi-polar systems are possible, whereby a set of dispersed core countries receive immigrants from a set of overlapping sending nations.
3 Nations may belong to more than one migration system, but multiple membership is more common among sending than receiving nations.
4 As political and economic conditions change, systems evolve, so that stability does not imply a fixed structure. Countries may join or drop out of a system in response to social change, economic fluctuations or political upheaval.

[. . .]

REFERENCES

Castells, Manuel (1989) *The Informational City: Information Technology, Economic Restructuring and the Urban-Regional Process*. Oxford: Basil Blackwell.
Fawcett, James T. (1989) 'Networks, linkages, and migration systems', *International Migration Review* 23: 671–80.
Gurak, Douglas T. and Fe Caces (1992) 'Migration networks and the shaping of migration systems', in Mary Kritz, Lin Lean Lim and Hania Zlotnik (eds), *International Migration Systems: A Global Approach*. Oxford: Clarendon Press, pp. 150–76.
Hugo, Graeme J. (1981) 'Village-community ties, village norms, and ethnic and social networks: A review of *evidence from the Third World*', in Gordon F. DeJong and Robert W. Gardner (eds), *Migration Decision Making: Multidisciplinary Approaches to Microlevel Studies in Developed and Developing Countries*. New York: Pergamon Press, pp. 186–225.
Katz, E. and Oded Stark (1986) 'Labour migration and risk aversion in less developed countries', *Journal of Labour Economics* 4: 131–49.
Lauby, Jennifer and Oded Stark (1988) 'Individual migration as a family strategy: Young women in the Philippines', *Population Studies* 42: 473–86.
Massey, Douglas S. (1986) 'The settlement process among Mexican migrants to the United States', *American Sociological Review* 52: 670–85.
——(1989) 'International migration and economic development in comparative perspective', *Population and Development Review* 14: 383–414.

——(1990a) 'The social and economic origins of immigration', *Annals of the American Academy of Political and Social Science* 510: 60–72.

——(1990b) 'Social structure, household strategies, and the cumulative causation of migration', *Population Index* 56: 3–26.

——, Rafael Alarcón, Humberto González and Jorge Durand (1987) *Return to Azilan: The Social Process of International Migration from Western Mexico*. Berkeley and Los Angeles: University of California Press.

——, and Felipe Garcia España (1987) 'The social process of international migration', *Science* 237: 733–8.

——, and Zai Liang (1989) 'The long-term consequences of a temporary worker program: The U. S. Bracero experience', *Population Research and Policy Review* 8: 199–226.

Morawska, Ewa (1990) 'The sociology and historiography of immigration', in Virginia Yans-McLaughlin (ed.), *Immigration Reconsidered: History, Sociology and Politics*. New York: Oxford University Press, pp. 187–240.

Myrdal, Gunnar (1957) *Rich Lands and Poor*. New York: Harper and Row.

Petras, Elizabeth M. (1981) 'The global labour market in the modern world-economy', in Mary M. Kritz, Charles B. Keely and Silvano M. Tomasi (eds) *Global Trends in Migration: Theory and Research on International Population Movements*. Staten Island, NY: Centre for Migration Studies, pp. 44–63.

Piore, Michael J. (1979) *Birds of Passage: Migrant Labour in Industrial Societies*. Cambridge: Cambridge University Press.

Portes, Alejandro and John Walton (1981) *Labour, Class and the International System*. New York: Academic Press.

Sassen, Saskia (1988) *The Mobility of Labour and Capital: A Study in International Investment and Labour Flow*. Cambridge: Cambridge University Press.

——(1991) *The Global City: New York, London, Tokyo*. Princeton: Princeton University Press.

Sjaastad, Larry A. (1962) 'The costs and returns of human migration', *Journal of Political Economy* 705: 80–93.

Stark, Oded (1984) 'Migration decision making: A review article', *Journal of Development Economics* 14: 251–9.

——(1991) *The Migration of Labour*. Oxford: Basil Blackwell.

——and D. Levhari (1982) 'On migration and risk in LDCs.' *Economic Development and Cultural Change* 31: 191–6.

——and David E. Bloom (1985) 'The new economics of labour migration', *American Economic Review* 75: 173–8.

——, J. Edward Taylor and Shlomo Yitzhaki (1986) 'Remittances and inequality', *The Economic Journal* 96: 722–40.

——, J. Edward Taylor and Shlomo Yitzhaki (1988) 'Migration, remittances and inequality: A sensitivity analysis using the extended Gini Index', *Journal of Development Economics* 28: 309–22.

——and Shlomo Yitzhaki (1988) 'Labour migration as a response to relative deprivation', *Journal of Population Economics* 1: 57–70.

——and J. Edward Taylor (1989) 'Relative deprivation and international migration', *Demography* 26: 1–14.

——and J. Edward Taylor (1991) 'Migration incentives, migration types: The role of relative deprivation', *The Economic Journal* 101: 1163–78.

Taylor, J. Edward (1986) 'Differential migration, networks, information and risk', in Oded Stark (ed.), *Research in Human Capital and Development*, Vol. 4, *Migration, Human Capital and Development*, Greenwich, Conn.: JAI Press, pp. 147–71.

——(1987) 'Undocumented Mexico-U.S. migration and the returns to households in rural Mexico', *American Journal of Agricultural Economics* 69: 616–38.

——(1992) 'Remittances and inequality reconsidered: Direct, indirect and intertemporal effects', *Journal of Policy Modelling* 14: 187–208.
Todaro, Michael P. (1969) 'A model of labour migration and urban unemployment in less-developed countries', *The American Economic Review* 59: 138–48.
——(1976) *Internal Migration in Developing Countries*, Geneva: International Labour Office.
——(1980) 'Internal migration in developing countries: A survey', in Richard A. Easterlin (ed.), *Population and Economic Change in Developing Countries*. Chicago: University of Chicago Press, pp. 361–401.
——(1989) *Economic Development in the Third World*. New York: Longman.
——and Lydia Maruszko (1987) 'Illegal migration and US immigration reform: A conceptual framework', *Population and Development Review* 13: 101–14.
Wallerstein, Immanuel (1974) *The Modern World System, Capitalist Agriculture and the Origins of the European World Economy in the Sixteenth Century*. New York: Academic Press.
Zlotnik, Hania (1992) 'Empirical identification of international migration systems', in Mary Kritz, Lin Lean Lim and Hania Zlotnik (eds), *International Migration Systems: A Global Approach*. Oxford: Clarendon Press, pp. 19–40.

The nature of ethnicity in the project of migration
JOHN REX

THE FEAR OF ETHNICITY

Ethnicity today is in ill repute. With the collapse of the bi-polar world system after 1989 the various groups, nations and communities which had been held together by the quasi-imperial systems of the superpowers were left to fight for themselves and among themselves. In the name of ethnicity, nationalism or ethnic nationalism they fought brutally for territory, and the Serbian notion of 'ethnic cleansing' came to provoke something of the horror felt towards the Nazi Holocaust fifty years earlier. Meanwhile, even though they were not engaged in nationalist projects, migrant ethnic minorities became the focus of suspicion and hostility in their countries of settlement.

In these circumstances it has not been easy to argue for the political ideal of multiculturalism in western European societies. It is an ideal which is regarded with grave suspicion in the media, among politicians and social scientists and in public opinion generally, as well as among educated members of the migrant communities themselves who fear that their labelling as 'ethnic' necessarily involves their assignment to inferiority.

Although the unitary nature of western European nations and their cultures can be exaggerated, since, historically they themselves have been ethnically diverse, and divided in terms of class and status, it is nonetheless true that, allowing for this diversity, the range of permissible cultural and political variation has been limited and the culture of new immigrant groups, coming often from long distances and having distinct languages, religions and customs, is seen as 'alien'.

Those members of migrant communities who have been successful in adapting to the demands of their host societies understandably fear that, if they represent themselves as culturally different, they will be treated as inferior and denied equal rights, and they are often supported by democrats who see the setting up of separate multicultural arrangements as something which will undermine established and familiar democratic political procedures.

There are a number of ways in which this democratic and universalistic response of democrats affects the thinking of social scientists. From a simple Marxist point of view, ethnic consciousness is seen as false consciousness and a diversion from the class struggle and class politics which are taken to be normal. Liberals and republicans also see any deviation from the notion of universal and equal citizenship as politically dangerous, while social democrats, with their notion of the reconciliation of conflicting class interests under the welfare state compromise, find it difficult to accept the setting up of special and separate institutions for dealing with minorities. More widely, those who see existing societies as based upon a delicate balance between the cultures of status groups, rather than simply on a class compromise, are inclined to see the coming of more distant and alien cultures as upsetting this balance (Rex and Drury 1995).

These fears are understandable and it is to be expected that European social scientists and politicians will wish to defend institutions which have been slowly and painfully established via political struggles of the past two centuries. Nonetheless such attitudes are literally prejudiced in that they prejudge the nature of ethnic minority cultures and the goals which ethnic minority communities set themselves. What is necessary for a serious sociology of multicultural societies is an empirical as well as a theoretical study of the nature of migrant ethnic minority groups, based, not on the way in which these groups are categorized and classified by the state, but on the way in which they see themselves. This is the object of this [essay]. What I shall do is, first to look at the nature of ethnicity in general, secondly to look at the way in which the two major projects of ethnicity and nationalism branch from this general ethnic stem, and thirdly to look in more detail at the actual structure of migrant ethnic minority communities and their relationship to modern nation states.

THE SIMPLEST FORMS OF ETHNICITY

In the literature on ethnicity and nationalism the first major division is that between 'primordial' and 'situational' or 'instrumental' theory. According to the former, ethnic bonds are quite unlike all others; they are recurrent, largely inexplicable, and have an overpowering emotional and non-rational quality (Geertz 1963). According to the latter, they are, if not wholly invented by political leaders and intellectuals for purposes of social manipulation, at least related to specific social and political projects (Barth 1959, 1969; Roosens 1989).

It is important to understand why the primordialist view can be maintained at all, even if ultimately we reject it as an adequate account of ethnicity and nationalism. What we need to do is to consider the difference between two types of group affiliation, namely that which involves a strong sense of emotional belonging, and even of sacredness, and another in which such affiliation is related in some way to ulterior and rationally formulable purposes. To do this we must consider, first, the very simplest form of ethnicity into which children are born, and secondly, the formation of more extensive groups, now commonly referred to as *ethnies*.

Our human condition is necessarily a social one. Apart from the so-called feral children, brought up by animals, any human infant finds himself or herself caught up at birth in what I have called 'the infantile ethnic trap' (Rex 1995): it is brought up within a kin network in which named and categorized individuals play specific roles, and in relation to whom it has clearly defined rights and duties. He or she will also belong to a neighbourhood group which may coincide with the kin group, but often simply intersects with it. Such groups as these will also share a language as well as religious beliefs and customs.

On a social psychological level these simple groups will be seen as generating positive warm emotions and as possessing some supernatural qualities. The dead as well as the living are thought of as belonging to the group and its origins and history are explained in terms of some kind of myth or narrative which is taught to the young as truth.

It should be noted here that language and religion present special problems in that they are often shared with a wider range of people who are not members of the group. Nonetheless, within these larger linguistic and religious communities, smaller groups are differentiated in terms of kin, neighbourhood, customs and history. Language may be modified by dialect and religious beliefs may be reinterpreted and appropriated to reflect the more specific beliefs of the smaller group.

From this initial base members go on to enter a wider world in two ways. Firstly, through the socialization process (as described in different ways by Freud, Mead, Durkheim and others) the external role players 'enter the head' of the individual whose very personal identity is then a social creation so that he or she acts not simply as a Hobbesian individual but as an ethnic individual. Such an individual may then go on to enter into relations with other individuals of different ethnicity just as his or her ethnic group enters into relations with other groups. Secondly, however, it is possible that the individual will find that there are larger groups than his original one which can give him or her some of the same feeling of belonging and sacredness. It is these larger groups that we refer to as *ethnies*.

The *ethnie* is differentiated from the simpler type of kin- and neighbour-hood-based group by the fact that there is no precise definition of the roles of one member *vis-à-vis* another. Rather the group is constituted, as Smith has suggested (Smith 1986), by the fact that it has a name, shared symbols and a myth of origin. These elements, however, do mean that the *ethnie* claims something of the strong sense of emotional belonging and sacredness which is to be found in the smaller group.

This is not to say, however, that the *ethnie* does not have its own structure of social relations. Usually there is some sort of status and economic differentiation and complementarity among its members, and there will be some type of role differentiation of those who exercise authority of a political and religious sort. What differentiates the *ethnie* from a modern political nation, however, is that these economic and political structures are subordinated to the community structure. Characteristically, a priesthood exercises more authority than it would in the nation state.

Smith also tells us that the *ethnie* normally has some sort of attachment to a territory, even though it does not set up the administrative structures to be found in the modern state which claim authority throughout that territory.

Ethnies will, of course, vary in their size and complexity and the term should probably be extended to cover a range of possibilities, including, at one extreme, a group which has little more than a name, a myth of origin and a shared culture, and, at the other, one which has some of the features of the nation state.

The *ethnie*'s own self-definition may not be the same as that used in referring to it by other *ethnies*. Generally its self-definition involves the notion of moral worthiness, while other groups might describe it in quite derogatory terms. On the other hand it should not be thought that *ethnies* are of their very nature forced into conflict with one another. This may be the case, if control of a territory or other resources is disputed, but it is perfectly possible for different *ethnies* to live at peace with each other.

The primordialist view of the *ethnie* would be that it exists largely for its own sake. The alternative 'situationist' view deriving from the work of Barth would suggest that the boundaries of such an *ethnie* depend upon the situation or on the project in which the group is engaged. There is truth in both these positions, particularly when control of a territory is involved. In this case we should say that the boundaries of the group are at least partly determined by a political project, even though it may call on the solidarity of the pre-existing *ethnie* as a resource. Immediately we will deal with the case in which the project is the creation of a nation. In the latter part of the paper we will deal with groups whose project is almost the opposite of laying claim to a territory in the business of migration.

THE NATION STATE, NATIONALISM AND ETHNIC NATIONALISM

The sort of discourse with which we have been concerned above derives largely from social anthropology, social psychology and history. A quite different discourse, however, has dominated thinking about nationalism and the nation state. In this discourse the nation state is thought of as coming into being almost *ab initio* as part of a modernizing project.

Gellner's account (Gellner 1983) of this modernizing project, of nationalism and the nation state, is probably too narrow. According to him, the nation depends upon a political and intellectual elite imposing a shared culture on the whole population in a territory particularly through a national education system which ensures that all members of the nation have a minimum of competence and a degree of flexibility so that they can fulfil a variety of roles. Such a culture and such an education system is, in Gellner's view, essential to the operation of an industrial society.

There is, however, more to be said about modernization than this. Most important is the fact that the polity and the economy are released from their subordination to the communal institutions and the culture of the *ethnie*. Instead they come to dominate it or to erode the very basis of its existence.

In fact, however, in this conception of the nation, it is the polity which is dominant. It rules and administers the whole of a given territory and, in so doing, faces a problem in that the economy, language and religion have to be brought under its control. The natural tendency of the modern nation state so far as the economy is concerned is towards economic autarchy. On the linguistic front, it has to ensure that, however much minority languages are tolerated for communal purposes, there is a shared official national language. Finally, so far as religion is concerned, the priesthood must in some way come to terms with the state and cannot be allowed to encourage loyalty to some wider community of co-religionists.

Such a nation state is also bound to encounter resistance from *ethnies* within its borders. It may deal with this either by destroying the *ethnies* and their culture or granting them a degree of subordinate autonomy. If it fails to do either of these the *ethnies* themselves may develop in the direction of ethnic nationalism, seeking to establish their own states, whether of a modernizing or traditional sort. Thus the nation state is likely to foster other nationalisms apart from its own.

The modern nation also rarely rests content with the bonding of its own members simply as individual citizens. It needs to create a national sentiment and a sense of belonging to the nation. To some extent it can do this by converting its population to the ideology of nationalism, but this will probably be possible only among an elite. It also therefore has to create its own symbols, mythology and sense of sacredness and belonging. In doing this it will be using many of the techniques used by pre-modern *ethnies*. This is what is happening when the national leaders speak of the mother country or the fatherland.

What the theory of nationalism has to do therefore is to describe a complex process of interaction between modernizing nation states, *ethnies* and ethnic nationalism. The business of creating the modern nation state is therefore always incomplete and what is loosely called nationalism covers a variety of interacting types.

Finally, we have to consider under the heading of nationalism, the fact of imperialism and the creation of multinational states. Nations conquer nations and when they do new imperial structures extending beyond the boundaries of the conquering nation come into being. An imperial bureaucracy is created, metropolitan entrepreneurs gain access to the productive system and the markets of subordinate nations, and settlers from the conquering metropolis go to live and work in the subordinated territories.

Just as the creation of the individual nation provokes resistance from *ethnies* and ethnic nationalism, however, so imperial conquest provokes resistance from subordinate nations. If then the metropolitan power becomes weaker for any reason, or if its rule is overthrown, old nationalisms will be released and will flourish in the formerly subordinate territories. In fact they will be stronger than ever in national sentiment as they add to their myths the story of their resistance and their successful national revolutions. At the same time they may still have their own internal problems of dealing with the resistance of their own *ethnies* and ethnic nationalisms. All of these problems are evident in the wake of the break-up of the Soviet Empire and the USSR.

THE SECOND PROJECT OF ETHNICITY: MIGRATION

Although much of the theoretical writing about ethnicity has been concerned with the attachment of an ethnic group to a territory, in fact ethnic communities are often concerned precisely with their *detachment* from a territory, that is to say with the business of international migration.

In attempting to relate such groups to the theory of nationalism, a commonly used notion is that of diaspora. A diaspora is said to exist when an *ethnie* or nation suffers some kind of traumatic event which leads to the dispersal of its members, who, nonetheless, continue to aspire to return to the homeland. Diasporic nationalism is thus seen as one kind of nationalism. It is exemplified by Jews seeking a return to Zion, black Americans seeking to return to Africa and Armenians seeking a return to Armenia.

The term diaspora has also been loosely used, however, to refer to any national or ethnic group dispersed across several countries and this may be misleading, since many such groups have not suffered a clear traumatic experience, and are not primarily concerned with a return to some kind of Zion.

They are not in fact nationalist at all, even though they have some kind of transnational community as a point of reference. There are three cases to be distinguished.

Firstly there are groups of migrants from economically backward to economically successful countries. Individuals from the former migrate to the latter in order to seek work. Some may have no strong desire to return to their country of origin and simply seek assimilation in the country of settlement. Quite commonly, however, they may send remittances home and plan to return there, and even those who are destined *de facto* to remain in the country of settlement and bring up their children there, may retain some kind of myth of return.

Secondly, there are those who are part of more extensive migration movements, who migrate to a number of countries and who intend to go on living abroad and exploiting whatever opportunities are available within the several countries. For them there is an international community distinct both from the community of the homeland and that of the nations in whose territories they are temporarily or permanently settled. Often such communities consist of secondary colonialists for whom opportunities open up within another country's former empire. Such is the position of Indians from the Punjab settled in countries ranging from South-east Asia, through Europe, to North America.

Thirdly, there are communities of refugees whose situations vary enormously. They may constitute diasporas of a kind, seeing their immediate situation as temporary and envisaging a return to the homeland when political circumstances change; given that they are often fleeing from their fellow nationals, they are not necessarily nationalistic in outlook. There will, moreover, be many, who cannot envisage such a change in political circumstances at home and are committed to finding a new life in the countries of refuge.

Separately from these cases is a case which is more closely related to nationalism, namely that which occurs following the break-up of empires: in this case there are often settlers in the colonized territories who now look for protection to the former metropolis, while in that metropolis there will be those who feel the need to protect or gather in the former settlers. What occurs in this case is best described as irredentist nationalism, hence the case of the white settlers from the former European empires in Africa and Asia or, more recently, of the Russians living in the former territories of the USSR. It is misleading in these cases to speak of diasporas.

In understanding the second project of nationalism, the most important case is the second of those mentioned above. In order to understand its structure, it may be helpful to consider the case of Punjabi migration and, particularly, of the Punjabi Sikh migration by way of illustration.

Looking first at the country of origin, we have to note that the territory of the Punjab, within which the principle language is Punjabi, is divided between India and Pakistan. Huge population transfers occurred there at the time of the partition of the sub-continent and it is, therefore, possible to distinguish

Pakistani and Indian Punjabi migrants, primarily in terms of their religion. Even if we concentrate on the Indian Punjab, however, the population is divided in religious terms between Sikhs and Hindus and there are separate migrant networks deriving from the two communities. Punjabi Sikhs also support a nationalist movement, the most extreme version of which seeks to establish a separate state of Khalistan. This movement has led to violence and terrorism both in Indian itself and abroad.

There are further divisions among the Punjabi Sikhs based upon caste and class. The most important of the caste divisions, at least among migrants, is that between the Jats, who hold (or seek to hold) land, and the Ramgarias, who were originally carpenters. So far as class is concerned, there is a division between those for whom the nationalist movement is most important and those who support either one of the Indian Communist parties or the Indian Congress Party.

Clearly, even if one confines one's attention to Punjabi Sikhs, it is clear that Punjabi Sikhism is not a unitary phenomenon. Nonetheless there is a shared culture based on religion which is a point of reference for all Punjabi Sikhs, even including the Marxists.

The political position of the Punjabi Sikhs was profoundly affected by the fact that they did not support the Mutiny within British India in 1857. They therefore enjoyed a somewhat privileged position within India and also had the necessary skills to enable them to play a role within the wider British Empire, particularly in the development of East Africa, but later in Britain itself. From these bases they were able to seek still further opportunities in other parts of the Empire and in other countries in North America and Europe. It is against this background that the ethnic community of Punjabi Sikhs can be understood.

The basic unit within the international Punjabi Sikh community is probably the extended family. The latter often tries to increase its family estate, a fact which may involve remittances and saving with a view to obtaining land or starting a business in the Punjab itself. This, however, is only one possibility; a Punjabi family in Britain might well envisage further migration to North America and it might have relatives there as well as in the Punjab.

Beyond the family there are, however, other social and cultural links. Even those who are not particularly religious may participate in the life of the temples or *gurdwara* at least with regard to significant life events like birth, marriage and death: in addition, many men still display the five symbols of Sikhism and wear turbans. Thus Sikhism remains an important point of reference within the transnational community. Such wider cultural links help to produce a degree of solidarity even among families who would otherwise be simply competitors; consequently, in planning their affairs, the separate extended families are able to rely on the networks which these cultural links provide.

Notwithstanding this, the Sikh community has still to develop relationships with the various modernizing nation states within which its members settle. It has, however, the experience and skills to do this. The development of class-based industrial and political organizations is not something new to the Sikhs, who are thus quite capable of exploiting the opportunities available to them within the politics of the nation state of settlement. Part of the total political culture of the community is concerned precisely with ensuring that its members have maximum rights in their country of settlement. We are not dealing with a simple traditional *ethnie* facing a modernizing nation. Rather what we have is a community with a changing and developing political culture, characterized by a strong modernizing element.

One may argue that the Punjabi Sikhs represent a special case. In fact most transnational migrant communities are specific in one sense or another. Yet there are always some generalizable elements. In the case of the Punjabi Sikhs, these would be: first, that despite the internal complexity of the community, even prior to migration, the latter has still some basic reference points, particularly those based on religion, which give it an overall unity; second, this community is now located across the world and intends to go on living across the world and exploiting whatever economic opportunities the world provides; third, the existence of this community does not mean that there is no scope for individual family enterprise; fourth, insofar as it is incorporated into the political culture of a modern nation state, it produces its own ways of dealing with this while, at the same time, maintaining contact with the homeland (taking the economic form of remittances and investment in the homeland and the political form of support for the various nationalist and class-based factions and parties in the homeland into account).

Of course the business of dealing with various nation states and their social and political institutions involves some cost to the community. Success in the land of settlement may well mean that some of those who succeed within this system may leave the community altogether and there is strong evidence in the case of Punjabi Sikhs in Britain that some of their successful young members are doing just this. Having achieved educational, business or professional success they find that they can hold their own in British society and become, to all intents and purposes, British. But, even though this may be the case, this very success depends at the outset on the maintenance of communal solidarity and that same communal solidarity projected across the world also provides wider opportunities. There may still be advantages, even for an acculturated British Sikh, in using his or her networks to participate in a wider transnational system. Thus, for example, many professionals and businessmen in Britain may still use their ethnic networks to improve their position still further in North America. It is quite possible in fact to take advantage of membership in two societies and communities, one that of the nation in the country of settlement, the other that of the transnational ethnic community.

Looking more widely at the other minorities in Britain and western Europe, one can, of course, see that there are a number of possible variations from the type suggested for the Punjabi Sikhs, although most of the Asian minorities in Britain reproduce the structural and cultural features mentioned (e.g. Punjabi Hindus, Gujaratis, Kashmiris, Pakistanis and Bangladeshis). In the case of migrants to the Caribbean there is a diasporic element or at least a diasporic myth of return to Africa, although for many the possibilities presented by migration to Britain, Canada or the United States are more important than any such return, and the homeland to which they refer is more likely to be a West Indian island than Africa. In the case of the Turks in Germany mobility to other countries as well as citizenship in Germany is restricted by guestworker status and the main points of reference are simply Turkey and Germany. Algerians find themselves in a dependent post-colonial relationship with France. The Moroccan situation is more like that of the Punjabis though the migrants are more likely to be in poorer occupations. Finally, there are the southern Europeans, who on the one hand can fairly readily assimilate culturally to their countries of settlement, yet are close enough to their sending societies to maintain social and cultural links with them. In all cases much will depend upon the range of occupations which are open to migrants and the skills which they have to exploit them.

Despite all this variation it is clear that in all cases we are dealing with transnational communities which are not primarily nationalist in their orientation (except in relation to surviving homeland issues) and in which an element of diasporic yearning for return is not the overwhelming uniting political factor.

THE RESPONSE OF NATION STATES TO IMMIGRANT ETHNIC MINORITIES

The other party to the relationship in which these immigrant communities are involved is, of course, the nation state and it is to its reaction to immigrant settlement that we must now turn. It is here that we have to deal with the problems of nationalism, particularly nationalism of the modernizing sort.

There are two aspects to the nationalism of European states. On the one hand, they define their own national identity in relation to each other and to their empires and colonial territories, such notions of identity having been reinforced by wars, economic competition and resistance to colonial liberation. On the other, they have created a national cultural and political consensus out of conflicting class and status cultures. In Britain Marshall (1950) suggested that with the acquisition of social rights in addition to legal and political rights, British workers now had reason to identify more strongly with their national citizenship than with social class, as Marx had predicted. Williams also suggested interestingly in his book *The Long Revolution* (1961) that these workers were now also beginning to win their cultural rights.

The notions of legal and social citizenship are central to the modern nation state. In the French Republican tradition it is the legal equality of citizenship which is crucial. Two hundred years after the French Revolution, however, social rights have become more central and most European societies see themselves as having achieved some kind of political compromise between contending classes through the establishment of the welfare state. In any case the central theme of the political culture of these societies involves the recognition of equality of opportunity and, up to a minimum level, equality of outcome. There are, of course, those in most countries who would prefer to define the national culture and identity in terms of upper class culture, but it is the notion of equality which is the central ideological element in the modernizing nation state.

Given an ideological consensus of this kind these societies also tend to recognize the possibility of separate cultures, thought of as private matters in which the state does not interfere. Religious tolerance is therefore the norm. This is achieved in France through the secularization of politics and education, while in the Netherlands the policy of 'pillarization' recognized the right of the separate faiths to control considerable institutional areas. It is less completely achieved in Britain and in northern European countries where there is an established church with special duties and privileges.

The social structure of the nation state is not, however, determined simply by the creation of social equality. There has to be a national language for the conduct of official business; there is a national economy over which the government seeks to retain control even in the face of international markets and multinational business corporations; there is a civil and a criminal legal system to which all are required to conform, even if, through the political process and through the courts themselves, laws which are thought to be unjust can be changed; there is a national educational system concerned with developing the skills of the population as well as imparting shared national values; finally, there is also a developing national literary and aesthetic culture.

The question with which we are concerned is that of how a nation which defines itself in these terms reacts to the presence of immigrant communities and their cultures and how these communities themselves fit into the national system.

Two reactions which are to be expected in the receiving society are those of xenophobia and racism on the one hand and of assimilationism on the other. The terms xenophobia and racism are most frequently too loosely used; as used here they refer to reactions to immigrant communities which involve demands for their expulsion, physical attacks, racial and cultural abuse and racial and ethnic discrimination which gives the immigrants fewer rights than those of full citizens. All of these elements have been involved in the political reactions of European societies to post-war immigrants. Sometimes they occur simply in the propaganda and activities of anti-democratic parties but they have also influenced the policies of governments. Of particular importance here is that, in the German-speaking countries, while measures may be taken to ensure the legal and social rights of immigrants, the latter are not accorded political rights.

The assimilationist alternative has been more prominent in France. There, there is a widespread belief that minority cultures and minority identities threaten French national culture and identity and that while minority members should have equal rights as citizens they should be discouraged from maintaining their own cultures. Politically they should be expected to work through the mainstream parties and there should be no intrusion of minority culture and values into the secular national schools.

The third possible route for the policies of racial and ethnic exclusion on the one hand and assimilationism on the other is multiculturalism. Multiculturalism, professed in Britain, the Netherlands and in Sweden, even if imperfectly practised, involves both the attempt to ensure the full rights of citizens to minorities and the recognition of their right to maintain their separate cultures.

Our next question is that of how migrant ethnic minorities are likely to react to these various regimes. Obviously, so far as the first is concerned, they will organize to fight against 'racism' in all its forms, but in doing this they are likely to have the support of many indigenous democrats. So far as the second is concerned there will be some who are prepared to accept the hard bargain which is offered if it brings sufficient rewards to individual minority members, but generally the attempt simply to destroy minority culture is likely to provoke resistance, both because of the psychological cost in terms of the threat to the identity of minority members, and because of the destruction of helpful community networks which the latter involves.

Clearly it is the third possibility, namely that of multiculturalism which provides most scope for the immigrant minority to attain its own goals. The question is whether it can do this without threatening the society as a whole.

Usually multiculturalism recognizes that there is a private and communal sphere in which there is no need for the government to interfere. This is thought to include the speaking of minority languages within the community, the practice of minority religions and the maintenance of minority customs in matters relating to the family and marriage. There are, however, problems even about this restrictive definition of the private and communal sphere. Whatever minority customs there may be in relation to family matters there are no cases in which such customs are backed by the law, despite an occasionally expressed demand by Muslims that their family affairs are regulated by the *sharia* law. Often these customs are criticized by human rights activists and feminists who believe that they should be a matter of public concern. There is also often an unwillingness to admit that the propagation of minority cultures should have any place within the educational systems or even be subsidized by the state independently. Minority religions might also be denied facilities through such means as planning regulations.

Usually, however, ethnic minority cultures and social organization can be preserved in these circumstances though minority organizations will usually have to work to maximize their area of independence. They will do this in order to maintain their community structure nationally and internationally, but if they enjoy a reasonable measure of tolerance, it is likely that their main concern will be to fight against racism and racial discrimination and for social equality.

Ethnic minorities will, however, also have to accept more than this as part of the implied contract into which they enter with the host nation. They will have to accept that there is an official language and that they will have to use it in their dealings with the public authorities; they will have to recognize the criminal and civil law; they will have to recognize that existing national values will be taught within the educational system; and, they may have to accept that there is an established religion which has special privileges.

Most ethnic minority members do accept some sort of contract of this kind. They see it as part of the cost of living in a particular society of settlement which has to be set against the real gains which migration brings. What is likely, however, is that there will be some members of their communities who are more committed to their cultures than this. These cannot be called nationalists. What they are concerned with is achieving what they think of as adequate recognition and respect for their cultures. They may organize public demon-strations against any perceived insult to their culture and religion, as in the case of the Rushdie affair, and they may ask either for separate schools or for adequate recognition of their religion and customs in the state schools. They may also seek to present their own literary and aesthetic culture in the public sphere. Thus what one may expect is the emergence of minority cultural movements pursued with varying degrees of aggression and militancy.

The existence of movements such as these hardly threatens the national society. They can easily be tolerated. They become problematic only if they lead to overt political disloyalty. Such disloyalty or the suggestion of a prior loyalty to some other state has been advocated by a few extreme Muslim organizations in Britain. It is also the case that there are groups which advocate violence and terrorism in their homeland and are prepared to use the migrant community as a base for organizations. It is bound to be the case that national governments will do whatever they can to repress such activities.

What we are concerned with in this paper is the nature of ethnicity in the project of migration. What we have seen is that such ethnicity is not primarily concerned with the project of nationalism. It is concerned with the mainten-ance of a transnational community in which economic advantages can be pursued. It also has to come to terms with modernizing national societies and is usually easily able to do so. Mainly what one may expect in any particular country of settlement is the emergence of cultural movements trying to strengthen adherence to the culture and enlarge its area of operation. The existence of such movements can easily be tolerated and negotiated with as part and parcel of the working of a democratic society. The most important problems arise in connection with those movements which deliberately foster political disloyalty or which engage in violent and terrorist politics on an international scale. It is to be expected that any such movements and activities will be suppressed in a nation state. On the other hand it would be wrong to assume that they are typical of ethnic minority communities and their political culture.

We should remember here, however, that immigrant ethnic minority groups do not normally simply have to face the problem of fitting in to a society committed to multiculturalism. Even in the societies in which such a policy is professed there will be many individuals and often political movements who are hostile to or suspicious of ethnic minority communities and their cultures. Where this is the case, ethnic minority movements will not simply be concerned with the preservation of their culture and networks, but will pursue active policies against racism and racial discrimination. Not surprisingly in Britain there is a dispute between those in the ethnic minority communities who fight primarily for multiculturalism and those in more radical movements who see their main task as fighting racism.

It has been assumed in this paper that ethnic minority communities may have a more or less permanent existence on an international basis. This may well be true in some cases. In other cases, however, ethnic minority organizations and movements may be of a more transitional kind. They may exist for a few generations while there is still a need to fight for equality and for cultural respect. But after that what may remain, given religious tolerance, is a purely symbolic ethnicity involving such things as festivals and special occasions as well as some attempt at preservation of the minority language. Such purely symbolic ethnicity is something which troubles nobody and is usually regarded by an indigenous population merely as an exotic enrichment of their own culture.

Going beyond such purely symbolic ethnicity, however, neither the maintenance of the transnational migrant community nor the development of defensive community organizations are really incompatible with the maintenance of the institutions of a modernizing national state. It is very important, therefore, that what has been called here the second project of ethnicity should not be confused with nationalist projects. What has been happening in the former Yugoslavia holds no lessons relevant to the way in which blacks and Asians in Britain or Turks and Maghrebians in various parts of Europe have to be treated by their host societies. The real focus of the problematic of nationalism in these cases has to be in the majority nationalism of the host societies.

REFERENCES

Barth, F. (1959), *Political Leadership amongst the Swat Pathans*, London School of Economics Monographs in Anthropology, No. 19.
Barth, F. (1969), *Ethnic Groups and Boundaries*, London, Allen and Unwin.
Geertz, C. (1963), *Old Societies and New States: The Quest for Modernity in Asia and*

Africa, Glencoe, Illinois, Free Press.

Gellner, E. (1983), *Nations and Nationalism*, Oxford, Blackwell.

Marshall, T. (1950), *Citizenship and Social Class*, Cambridge, Cambridge University Press.

Rex, J. (1995), 'Ethnic identity and the nation state: The political sociology of multi-cultural societies', *Social Identities: Journal for the Study of Race, Nationality and Culture*, Vol. 1, No. 1.

Rex, J. and Drury, B. (eds) (1995), *Ethnic Mobilisation in a Multi-Cultural Europe*, Aldershot, Avebury.

Roosens, E. (1989), *Creating Ethnicity*, London, Sage.

Smith, A. (1986), *The Ethnic Origins of Nationalism*, Oxford, Blackwell.

Williams, R. (1961), *The Long Revolution*, London, Chatto and Windus.

Diasporas
JAMES CLIFFORD

An unruly crowd of descriptive/interpretive terms now jostle and converse in an effort to characterize the contact zones of nations, cultures and regions: terms such as 'border', 'travel', 'creolization', 'transculturation', 'hybridity' and 'diasporas' (as well as the looser 'diasporic'). Important new journals, such as *Public Culture* and *Diaspora* (or the revived *Transition*), are devoted to the history and current production of transnational cultures. In his editorial preface to the first issue of *Diaspora*, Khachig Tölölian writes, 'Diasporas are the exemplary communities of the transnational moment.' But he adds that diaspora will not be privileged in the new *Journal of Transnational Studies* and that 'the term that once described Jewish, Greek, and Armenian dispersion now shares meanings with a larger semantic domain that includes words like immigrant, expatriate, refugee, guest-worker, exile community, overseas community, ethnic community' (Tölölian 1991: 4-5). This is the domain of shared and discrepant meanings, adjacent maps and histories, that we need to sort out and specify as we work our way into comparative, intercultural studies [. . .].

When I speak of the need to sort our paradigms and maintain historical specificity, I do not mean the imposition of strict meanings and authenticity tests. The quintessential borderland is El Paso/Juárez. Or is it Tijuana/San Diego? Can *la ligna* be displaced to Redwood City, or to Mexican American neighbourhoods of Chicago? William Safran's essay in the first issue of *Diaspora*, 'Diasporas in Modern Societies: Myths of Homeland and Return' (1991), seems, at times, to be engaged in such an operation. His undertaking and the problems it encounters may help us to see what is involved in identifying the range of phenomena we are prepared to call 'diasporic'.

Safran discusses a variety of collective experiences in terms of their similarity and difference from a defining model. He defines diasporas as follows: 'expatriate minority communities' (1) that are dispersed from an original 'centre' to at least two 'peripheral' places; (2) that maintain a 'memory, vision, or myth about their original homeland'; (3) that 'believe they are not – and perhaps cannot be – fully accepted by their host country'; (4) that see the ancestral home as a place of eventual return, when the time is right; (5) that are committed to the maintenance or restoration of this homeland; and (6) whose consciousness and solidarity as a group are 'importantly defined' by this continuing relationship with the homeland (Safran 1991: 83-4). These, then, are the main features of diaspora: a history of dispersal, myths/memories of the homeland, alienation in the host (bad host?) country, desire for eventual return, ongoing support of the homeland, and a collective identity importantly defined by this relationship.

'In terms of that definition,' Safran writes, 'we may legitimately speak of the Armenian, Maghrebi, Turkish, Palestinian, Cuban, Greek, and perhaps Chinese diasporas at present and of the Polish diaspora of the past, although none of them fully conforms to the "ideal type" of the Jewish diaspora' (Safran 1991: 84). Perhaps a hesitation is expressed by the quotes surrounding 'ideal type', a sense of the danger in constructing a definition, here at the outset of an important comparative project, that identifies the diasporic phenomenon too closely with one group. Indeed, large segments of Jewish historical experience do not meet the test of Safran's last three criteria: a strong attachment to and desire for literal return to a well-preserved homeland. Safran himself later notes that the notion of return for Jews is often an eschatological or utopian projection in response to a present dystopia. And there is little room in his definition for the principled *ambivalence* about physical return and attachment to land which has characterized much Jewish diasporic consciousness, from biblical times on. Jewish anti-Zionist critiques of teleologies of return are also excluded.

It is certainly debatable whether the cosmopolitan Jewish societies of the eleventh- to thirteenth-century Mediterranean (and Indian Ocean), the *geniza world* documented by the great historian of transnational cultures, S. D. Goitein, was oriented as a community or collection of communities, primarily through attachments to a lost homeland (Goitein 1967–93). This sprawling social world was linked through cultural forms, kinship relations, business circuits and travel trajectories as well as through loyalty to the religious centres of the diaspora (in Babylon, Palestine and Egypt). The attachment to specific cities (sometimes superseding ties of religion and ethnicity) characteristic of Goitein's medieval world casts doubt on any definition that would 'centre' the Jewish diaspora in a single land. Among Sephardim after 1492, the longing for 'home' could be focused on a city in Spain at the same time as on the Holy Land. Indeed, as Jonathan Boyarin has pointed out, Jewish experience often entails 'multiple experiences of rediasporisation, which do not necessarily *succeed* each other in historical memory but echo back and forth' (Boyarin 1993).

As a multiply centred diaspora network, the medieval Jewish Mediterranean may be juxtaposed with the modern 'black Atlantic' described by Paul Gilroy (Gilroy 1993a). While the economic and political bases of the two networks may differ – the former commercially self-sustaining, the latter caught up in colonial/neo-colonial forces – the cultural forms sustaining and connecting the two scattered 'peoples' are comparable within the range of diasporic phenomena. In Safran's prefiguration of a comparative field – especially in his 'centred' diaspora model, oriented by continuous cultural connections to a source and by a teleology of 'return' – African American/Caribbean/British cultures do not qualify. These histories of displacement fall into a category of quasi-diasporas, showing only some diasporic features or moments. Similarly, the South Asian diaspora – which, as Amitav Ghosh has argued (1989), is not so much oriented to roots in a specific place and a desire for return as around an ability to re-create a culture in diverse locations – falls outside the strict definition.

Safran is right to focus attention on defining 'diaspora'. What is the range of experiences covered by the term? Where does it begin to lose definition? His comparative approach is certainly the best way to specify a complex discursive and historical field. Moreover his juxtapositions are often very enlightening, and he does not, in practice, strictly enforce his definitional checklist. But we should be wary of constructing our working definition of a term like diaspora by recourse to an 'ideal type', with the consequence that groups become identified as more or less diasporic, having only two, or three, or four of the basic six features. Even the 'pure' forms, I've suggested, are ambivalent, even embattled, over basic features. Moreover at different times in their history, societies may wax and wane in diasporism, depending on changing possibilities – obstacles, openings, antagonisms and connections – in their host countries and transnationally.

We should be able to recognize the strong entailment of Jewish history on the language of diaspora without making that history a definitive model. Jewish (and Greek and Armenian) diasporas can be taken as non-normative starting-points for a discourse that is travelling or hybridizing in new global conditions. For better or worse, diaspora discourse is being widely appropriated. It is loose in the world, for reasons having to do with decolonization, increased immigration, global communications and transport – a whole range of phenomena that encourage multi-locale attachments, dwelling and travelling within and across nations. A more polythetic definition (Needham 1975) than Safran's might retain his six features, along with others. I have already stressed, for example, that the transnational connections linking diasporas need not be articulated primarily through a real or symbolic homeland – at least not to the degree that Safran implies. Decentred, lateral connections may be as important as those formed around a teleology of origin/return. And a shared, ongoing history of displacement, suffering, adaptation or resistance may be as important as the projection of a specific origin.

Whatever the working list of diasporic features, no society can be expected to qualify on all counts, throughout its history. And the discourse of diaspora will necessarily be modified as it is translated and adopted. For example, the Chinese diaspora is now being explicitly discussed. How will this history, this articulation of travels, homes, memories and transnational connections, appropriate and shift diaspora discourse? Different diasporic maps of displacement and connection can be compared on the basis of family resemblance, of shared elements, no subset of which is defined as essential to the discourse. A polythetic field would seem most conducive to tracking (rather than policing) the contemporary range of diasporic forms.

DIASPORA'S BORDERS

The nation state, as common territory and time, is traversed and, to varying degrees, subverted by diasporic attachments. Diasporic populations do not come from elsewhere in the same way that 'immigrants' do. In assimilationist national ideologies such as those of the United States, immigrants may experience loss and nostalgia, but only *en route* to a whole new home in a new place. Such narratives are designed to integrate immigrants, not people in diasporas. Whether the national narrative is one of common origins or of gathered populations, it cannot assimilate groups that maintain important allegiances and practical connections to a homeland or a dispersed community located elsewhere. Peoples whose sense of identity is centrally defined by collective histories of displacement and violent loss cannot be 'cured' by merging into a new national community. This is especially true when they are the victims of ongoing, structural prejudice. Positive articulations of diaspora identity reach outside the normative territory and temporality (myth-history) of the nation state.

But are diaspora cultures consistently anti-nationalist? What about their own national aspirations? Resistance to assimilation can take the form of reclaiming another nation that has been lost, elsewhere in space and time, but powerful as a political formation here and now. There are, of course, anti-nationalist nationalisms, and I do not want to suggest that diasporic cultural politics are somehow innocent of nationalist aims or chauvinist agendas. Indeed, some of the most violent articulations of purity and racial exclusivism come from diaspora populations. But such discourses are usually weapons of the (relatively) weak. It is important to distinguish nationalist critical longing, and nostalgic or eschatological visions, from actual nation building – with the help of armies, schools, police and mass media. Nation and nation state are not identical. A certain prescriptive anti-nationalism, now intensely focused by the

Bosnian horror, need not blind us to differences between dominant and subaltern claims. Diasporas have rarely founded nation states: Israel is the prime example. And such 'homecomings' are, by definition, the negation of diaspora.

Whatever their ideologies of purity, diasporic cultural forms can never, in practice, be exclusively nationalist. They are deployed in transnational networks built from multiple attachments and they encode practices of accommodation with, as well as resistance to, host countries and their norms. Diaspora is different from travel (though it works through travel practices) in that it is not temporary. It involves dwelling, maintaining communities, having collective homes away from home (and in this it is different from exile, with its frequently individualistic focus). Diaspora discourse articulates, or bends together, both roots *and* routes to construct what Gilroy describes as alternate public spheres (1987), forms of community consciousness and solidarity that maintain identifications outside the national time/space in order to live inside, with a difference. Diaspora cultures are not separatist, though they may have separatist or irredentist moments. This history of Jewish diaspora communities shows selective accommodation with the political, cultural, commercial and everyday life forms of 'host' societies. And the black diaspora culture currently being articulated in post-colonial Britain is concerned to struggle for different ways to be 'British' – ways to stay and be different, to be British *and something else* complexly related to Africa and the Americas, to shared histories of enslavement, racist subordination, cultural survival, hybridization, resistance and political rebellion. Thus the term diaspora is a signifier, not simply of transnationality and movement, but of political struggles to define the local, as distinctive community, in historical contexts of displacement. The simultaneous strategies of community maintenance and interaction combine the discourses and skills of what Vijay Mishra has termed 'diasporas of exclusivism' and 'diasporas of the border' (1994).

The specific cosmopolitanisms articulated by diaspora discourses are in constitutive tension with nation-state/assimilationist ideologies. They are also in tension with indigenous, and especially autochthonous, claims. These challenge the hegemony of modern nation states in a different way. Tribal or 'Fourth World' assertions of sovereignty and 'first nationhood' do not feature histories of travel and settlement, though these may be part of the indigenous historical experience. They stress continuity of habitation, aboriginality, and often a 'natural' connection to the land. Diaspora cultures, constituted by displacement, may resist such appeals on political principle – as in anti-Zionist Jewish writing, or in black injunctions to 'stand' and 'chant down Babylon'. And they may be structured around a tension between return and deferral: 'religion of the land'/'religion of the book' in Jewish tradition; or 'roots'/'cut 'n' mix' aesthetics in black vernacular cultures.

Diaspora exists in practical, and at times principled, tension with nativist identity formations. The essay by Daniel and Jonathan Boyarin (1993) makes a diasporist critique of autochthonous ('natural') but not indigenous ('historical') formulations. When claims to 'natural' or 'original' identity with the land are joined to an irredentist project and the coercive power of an exclusivist state, the results can be profoundly ambivalent and violent, as in the Jewish state of Israel. Indeed, claims of a primary link with 'the homeland' usually must override conflicting rights and the history of others in the land. Even ancient homelands have seldom been pure or discrete. Moreover, what are the historical and/or indigenous rights of *relative* newcomers – fourth-generation Indians in Fiji, or even Mexicans in the south-western United States since the sixteenth century? How long does it take to become 'indigenous'? Lines too strictly drawn between 'original' inhabitants (who often themselves replaced prior populations) and subsequent immigrants risk ahistoricism. With all these qualifications, however, it is clear that the claims to political legitimacy made by peoples who have inhabited a territory since before recorded history and those who arrived by steamboat or aeroplane will be founded on very different principles.

Diasporist and autochthonist histories, the aspirations of migrants and natives, do come into direct political antagonism: the clearest current example is Fiji. But when, as is often the case, both function as 'minority' claims against a hegemonic/assimilationist state, the antagonism may be muted. Indeed there are significant areas of overlap. 'Tribal' predicaments, in certain historical circumstances, are diasporic. For example, inasmuch as diasporas are dispersed networks of peoples who share common historical experiences of dispossession, displacement, adaptation, and so forth, the kinds of transnational alliances currently being forged by Fourth World peoples contain diasporic elements. United by similar claims to 'firstness' on the land and by common histories of decimation and marginality, these alliances often deploy diasporist visions of return to an original place – a land commonly articulated in visions of nature, divinity, mother earth and the ancestors.

Dispersed tribal peoples, those who have been dispossessed of their lands or who must leave reduced reserves to find work, may claim diasporic identities. Inasmuch as their distinctive sense of themselves is oriented towards a lost or alienated home defined as aboriginal (and thus 'outside' the surrounding nation state), we can speak of a diasporic dimension of contemporary tribal life. Indeed, recognition of this dimension has been important in disputes about tribal membership. The category tribe, which was developed in US law to distinguish settled Indians from roving, dangerous 'bands', places a premium on localism and rootedness. Tribes with too many members living away from the homeland may have difficulty asserting their political/cultural status: This was the case for the Mashpee who, in 1978, failed to establish continuous 'tribal' identity in court (Clifford 1988: 277–346).

Thus, when it becomes important to assert the existence of a dispersed people, the language of diaspora comes into play, as a moment or dimension of tribal life. All communities, even the most locally rooted, maintain structured travel circuits, linking members 'at home' and 'away'. Under changing conditions of mass communication, globalization, post- and neo-colonialism, these circuits are selectively restructured and re-routed according to *internal and external* dynamics. Within the diverse array of contemporary diasporic cultural forms, tribal displacements and networks are distinctive. For in claiming both autochthony and a specific, transregional worldliness, new tribal forms bypass many visions of modernization seen as the inevitable destruction of autochthonous attachments by global forces. Tribal groups have, of course, never been simply 'local': they have always been rooted and routed in particular landscapes, regional and interregional networks. What may be distinctively *modern*, however, is the relentless assault on indigenous sovereignty by colonial powers, transnational capital and emerging nation states. If tribal groups survive, it is now frequently in artificially reduced and displaced conditions, with segments of their populations living in cities away from the land, temporarily or even permanently. In these conditions, the older forms of tribal cosmopolitanism (practices of travel, spiritual quest, trade, exploration, warfare, labour migrancy, visiting and political alliance) are supplemented by more properly diasporic forms (practices of long-term dwelling away from home). The permanence of this dwelling, the frequency of returns or visits to homelands, and the degree of estrangement between urban and landed populations vary considerably. But the specificity of tribal diasporas, increasingly crucial *dimensions* of collective life, lies in the relative proximity and frequency of connection with land-based communities claiming autochthonous status.

I have been using the term 'tribal' loosely to designate peoples who claim natural or 'first-nation' sovereignty. They occupy the autochthonous end of a spectrum of indigenous attachments: peoples who deeply 'belong' in a place by dint of continuous occupancy over an extended period. (Precisely how long it takes to *become* indigenous is always a political question.) Tribal cultures are not diasporas; their sense of rootedness in the land is precisely what diasporic peoples have lost. And yet, as we have seen, the tribal-diasporic opposition is not absolute. Like diaspora's other defining border with hegemonic nationalism, the opposition is a zone of relational contrast, including similarity and entangled difference. In the late twentieth century, all or most communities have diasporic dimensions (moments, tactics, practices, articulations). Some are more diasporic than others. I have suggested that it is not possible to define diaspora sharply, either by recourse to essential features or to privative oppositions. But it is possible to perceive a loosely coherent, adaptive constellation of responses to dwelling-in-displacement. The currency of these responses is inescapable.

REFERENCES

Boyarin, Daniel and Jonathan Boyarin (1993) 'Diaspora: Generational Ground of Jewish Identity', *Critical Inquiry* 19(4): 693–725.
Clifford, James (1988) *The Predicament of Culture*. Cambridge: Harvard University Press.
Clifford, James (1992) 'Travelling Cultures', in *Cultural Studies*, ed. Lawrence Grossberg, Cary Nelson and Paula Treichler, New York: Routledge, pp. 96–116.
Ghosh, Amitav (1989) 'The Diaspora in Indian Culture', *Public Culture* 1(1): 73–8.
Gilroy, Paul (1987) *There Ain't No Black in the Union Jack: The Cultural Politics of Race and Nation*. London: Hutchinson.
Gilroy, Paul (1993a) *The Black Atlantic: Double Consciousness and Modernity*. Cambridge: Harvard University Press.
Goitein, Solomon Dob Fritz (1967–93) *A Mediterranean Society: The Jewish Communities of the Arab World as Portrayed in the Documents of the Cairo Ceniza*. Six volumes. Berkeley: University of California Press.
Mishra, Vijay (1994) '"The Familiar Temporariness" (V. S. Naipaul): Theorizing the Literature of the Indian Diaspora', Paper presented at the Centre for Cultural Studies, University of California, Santa Cruz, 2 February.
Needham, Rodney (1975) 'Polythetic Classification', *Man* 10: 349–69.
Safran, William (1991) 'Diasporas in Modern Societies: Myths of Homeland and Return', *Diaspora* 1(1): 83–99.
Tölölian, Khachig (1991) 'The Nation State and its Others: In Lieu of a Preface', *Diaspora* 1(1): 3–7.

8 Racism and Xenophobia

Racism in Europe: unity and diversity
MICHEL WIEVIORKA

Observing growing racist tendencies that affect most European countries, an increasing number of scholars feel an urgent need for a comparative reflection that may bring answers to a central question: over and beyond the empirical evidence of differences, is there not a certain unity in contemporary racism in Europe? Is it not possible to elaborate a reasoned set of hypotheses that could account for most national racist experiences in Europe, while shedding some light on their specificities?

European unification, in so far as it exists, and the growth of racism are obviously distinct phenomena, and it would be artificial to try and connect them too directly. The most usual frame of reference for any research about racism and race relations remains national. And even the vocabulary or, more deeply, the analytical and cultural categories that we use when dealing with this issue vary so widely from one country to another that we meet considerable difficulties when trying to translate precise terms. There may be large differences in language, and words with negative connotations in one country will have positive ones in another. Nobody in France, for instance, would use the expression *relations de race*, which would be regarded as racist, although it is commonly employed in the United Kingdom.

The key preliminary task, therefore, is not to contribute direct empirical knowledge about the various expressions of racism in Europe, as can be found, for instance, in the important survey of 'Racism and xenophobia' published in 1989 by the European Community (CCE 1989). Nor is the initial task to compare elementary forms of racism, such as harassment, stereotypes, discrimination or political racism in a certain number of countries, in order to prove that they are more or less similar, or that they follow a similar evolution.

Rather the problem is primarily conceptual. If we want to test the idea of a certain unity of contemporary racism in Europe, we must elaborate sociological and historical hypotheses, and then apply them to the facts that we are able to collect. Thus the most difficult aspect of a comparative approach is not to find data, but to organize it with well-thought-out hypotheses.

My own hypotheses can be formulated in two different ways, one of which is relatively abstract and the other more concrete.

RACISM AND MODERNITY

An initial formulation of the problematic, in effect, consists in the construction of a global argument enabling us to demonstrate that racism is inseparable from modernity, as the latter developed from European origins, and from its present crisis (Wieviorka 1992a). Racism, both as a set of ideologies and specious scientific doctrines, and as a set of concrete manifestations of violence, humiliation and discrimination, really gathered momentum in the context of the immense changes of which Europe was the centre after the Renaissance. It developed further in modern times, with the huge migrations, the extension of trading relationships, the industrialization of Western society and colonization. But racism, in its links with modernity, cannot be reduced to a single logic, and even seems to correspond to processes which are sometimes so distinct that numerous demands are made for the discussion of racisms in the plural. This in fact gives rise to a debate the terms of which are badly posed. It is effectively possible to set up an integrated, global argument in which the various forms of racism, including anti-semitism, find their theoretical place, and which goes in the direction of a sociological, even anthropological, unity of racism. One can also consider each of these forms in its historical specificity, which goes in the opposite direction. Both approaches are legitimate and complementary, but since we are thinking here about the unity of contemporary forms of racism in Europe, it is clear that we should privilege the former. This leads us to distinguish four main lines of argument which cross the space of racism in its relation to modernity.

In the first instance, as the companion of modernity triumphant, racism is universalist, denouncing, crushing and despising different identities – hence the apparition of inferior 'races' as an obstacle to the process of expansion, in particular colonial expansion, or destined to be exploited in the name of their supposed inferiority.

Next, linked to processes of downward social mobility, or exclusion, racism is the expression, as well as the refusal, of a situation in which the actor positively values modernity, but lives, or is afraid he/she will be exposed to a form of expulsion which will marginalize him/her. The actor then assumes a reflex or an attitude of 'poor white', particularly common in contexts of economic crises or of retraction from the labour market. Racism here is a perversion of a demand to participate in modernity and an opposition to the effective modalities of its functioning.

A third line of argument corresponds not to a positive valorization of modernity, the rise of which must be ensured, or from which one refuses to be excluded, but to appeals to identity or to tradition which are opposed to modernity. The nation, religion and the community then act as markers of identity, thus giving rise to a racism which attacks those who are assumed to be the vectors of a detested modernity. The Jews are often the incarnation of these vectors, as are, in some circumstances, those Asian minorities who are perceived as being particularly economically active. Finally, racism can correspond to anti- or non-modern positions, which are displayed not against groups incarnating modernity, but against groups defined themselves by an identity without any reference to modernity. It expresses, or is an extension of, intercultural, intercommunity, interethnic or similar tensions.

It is therefore possible to represent the space of racism around four cardinal points:

Modernity against identities

Identities against identities   Identities against modernity

Modernity against modernity

In a space of this type, the racist actors do not necessarily occupy one single position, and their speech and their behaviour are frequently syncretic and vary over time. There are even sometimes paradoxical mixtures of these various positions, when people, for instance, reproach a racialized group with symbolizing at the same time modernity and traditional values which they consider deny modernity: in the past, but also today, Jews, in many cases, fulfil this double function (Wieviorka 1992b). They are hated in the name of their supposed identification with political power, money, the mass media and a cosmopolitan internationalism, but also because of their difference, their visibility, their nationalism and support or belonging to the state of Israel, or because they flaunt their cultural traditions or their religion.

This theoretical construction of the space of racism may help us to answer our question. In effect, it enables us to read the European experience, and above all its recent evolution. The latter has long been dominated, on the one hand, by a racism of the universalist, colonial type and, on the other hand, by oppositions to modernity which have assumed the form of anti-semitism; today, much more than previously, it is directed by the fear or reality of exclusion and downward social mobility, and on the other by tensions around identity and vague fears of which the most decisive concern the question of belonging to the nation.

FORMATION AND RESTRUCTURATION OF THE EUROPEAN MODEL OF NATIONAL SOCIETIES

The argument outlined above can be completed by a much more concrete historical analysis of the recent evolution of most of the major western European countries. The latter, throughout this century, and up to the 1960s or 1970s, can be defined on the basis of a model which integrates three elements which are then weakened and destructured, reinvigorating the question of racism.

The era of integration

In most western European countries, racism, before the Second World War, was a spectacular and massive phenomenon, much more widespread than today. Colonial racism postulated the inferiority of colonized people of 'races', and modern anti-semitism gave a new and active dimension to former anti-Judaism. This is why we must introduce a sense of relativity into our perceptions of contemporary racism. This is why we must also think in terms of periods, with the idea of a certain unity in time for the phenomenon that we are discussing. This idea means not that there is no continuity in racist doctrines, ideologies, prejudice or more concrete expressions, but that a new era in the history of racism began with the retreat, as Elazar Barkan (1992) says, of scientific racism, the end of decolonization, and, above all, the 'economic crisis' that has in fact meant the beginning of the decline of industrial societies.

Until that time, i.e. the 1960s and 1970s, most European countries had succeeded, to a greater or a lesser extent, depending on the country, in integrating three basic components of their collective life: *an industrial society, an egalitarian state* and *a national identity*.

Most European countries have been industrial societies: that is, they have had a set of social relations rooted in industrial labour and organization. From this point of view, they have been characterized by a structural conflict, which opposed the working-class movement and the masters of industry, but which extended far beyond workshops and factories. This conflict gave the middle classes a possibility to define themselves by either a positive or negative relationship towards the working-class movement. It brought to unemployed people the hope and sometimes the reality of being helped by this movement. It was also the source of important political debates dealing with the 'social question'. Furthermore, it influenced intellectual and cultural life profoundly, and acted as a point of reference for many actors, in the city, in universities, in religious movements and elsewhere.

European countries, and this is the second basic component of our model of analysis, have also been able to create and develop institutions which aimed at ensuring that egalitarian treatment was imparted to all citizens as individuals.

The state has generally taken over various aspects of social welfare and security. It has become a welfare state. The state also introduced or defended a distance between religion and politics. Although countries such as Spain, Portugal and Greece have recently experienced dictatorial regimes, states in Europe have generally behaved, since the Second World War, as warrants for democracy.

Lastly, most European countries have given a central importance to their national identity. This identity has usually included two different aspects, sometimes contradictory, sometimes complementary. On one hand, the idea of a nation has corresponded to the assertion of a culture, a language, a historical past and traditions, with some tendencies to emphasize primordial ties and call for a biological definition loaded with racism, xenophobia and anti-semitism. On the other hand, the nation has also been defined in a more positive way, as bound to the general progress of mankind and to universal values that could be defined in economic, political or ethical terms. In this last perspective, a nation is related to reason, progress, democracy of human rights.

Industrial society, *state* and *nation*: these three basic elements have never been consonant with their highest theoretical image. One can easily show the weakness of the working-class movement in some countries, or its constant subordination to political forces, the limits of the welfare state everywhere in the past, and the domination of the reactionary and xenophobic aspects of nationalism in many circumstances. Moreover, some European countries have defined themselves as bi- or plurinational. But since we recognize these limits, and since we recognize many differences between countries, we can admit, without the danger of creating a myth, that our three basic elements are typical of European countries until the 1960s and 1970s. Not only have they characterized three countries, but they have also been relatively strongly articulated, so much so that various terms are used to express this articulation: for instance, integration, nation state and national society. We must be very cautious and avoid developing the artificial or mythical image of countries perfectly suited to the triple and integrated figure of an industrial society, a two-dimensional national and a modern and egalitarian state. But our representation of the past is useful in considering the evolution of the last twenty or thirty years, an evolution which is no doubt dominated by the growing weakness and dissociation of our three basic elements.

The era of destructuration

All European countries are experiencing today a huge transformation which affects the three components of our reflection, and defines what I have called, in the case of France, *'une grande mutation'* (Wieviorka 1992c).

Industrial societies are living their historical decline, and this phenomenon should not be reduced to the spectacular closing of workshops and factories. More important in our perspective is the decay of the working-class movement as a social movement. In the past, the working-class movement was, to various degrees, capable of incorporating in a single action collective behaviour corresponding to three major levels. There could be limited demands, struggles based on the professional defence of political demands, dealt with by the institutional system, and, at the highest level of its project, orientations challenging the control and the direction of progress and of industry. These orientations are quite out of place today: the working-class movement is breaking up, and this decomposition produces various effects (Touraine *et al.* 1987). Among workers, there is a strengthening of tendencies towards corporatism and selfishness – those workers who still have a certain capacity of action, because of their skill or their strategic position in their firm, develop struggles in the name of their own interests, and not in the name of more general or universal ones.

Sometimes workers' demands can no longer be taken up by the trade unions, which have been considerably weakened. This can result in violent forms of behaviour, or in spontaneous forms of organization, such as the recent 'co-ordinations' in France, which are easily infiltrated by extremist ideologies.

In such a context, the middle classes no longer have to define themselves by reference to class conflicts, and they tend to oscillate between, on the one hand, unrestrained individualism and, on the other, populism or national populism, the latter being particularly strong among those who experience downward mobility or social exclusion. These two distinct phenomena are closely related to social and economic dualization. In the past, most people could have a strong feeling of belonging to a society, 'down' as workers, or 'up' as elites or middle classes. Today, a good number of people are 'in', and constitute a large middle class, including those workers who have access to jobs, consumption, health or education for their children, while a growing proportion of people are 'out', excluded and marginalized.

Such an evolution may lead to renewed expressions of racism. Those who are 'out', or fear to be, have a feeling of injustice and loss of previous social identity. They think the government and the politicians are responsible for their situation, and may develop populist discourses and attitudes in which anti-migrant or ethnic minorities racism can take place. They then impute their misfortune to migrants, even if these migrants share the same experience. And those who are 'in' may develop more subtle forms of racism, trying to secure themselves with a colour bar or by individual or collective behaviours that create social and racial segregation and build symbolic but also real barriers. Furthermore, the logic of segregation, particularly at the political level, is always likely to become indistinguishable from a national and populist form of discourse which amalgamates the fears, anger and frustrations of the excluded and the social self-centredness of those who wish to defend their status and their way of life. This merging therefore gives a result which is only paradoxical in appearance, since it results in an identical form of racism in those people who have experienced living with, or close to, immigrants or similar categories of people, and in those who have not actually done so, but who have heard about it through the mass media or from rumours.

A second element of destructuration deals with the state and public institutions, which encounter increasing difficulties in trying to respect egalitarian principles, or in acting as welfare states. Everywhere in Europe, the number of unemployed people has grown, creating not only a great many personal dramas, but also a fiscal crisis of the state. The problems of financing old-age pensions, the health-care system, state education and unemployment benefits are becoming increasingly acute, while at the same time there is a rising feeling of insecurity which is attributed, once again, to immigrants. The latter are then perceived in racist terms, accused not only of taking advantage of social institutions and using them to their own ends, but also of benefiting from too much attention from the state. At the same time, the ruling classes have been tempted since the 1970s by liberal policies which in fact ratify and reinforce exclusion and marginalization.

The crisis of the state and the institutions is a phenomenon which must be analytically distinguished from the decline of industrial society and the dualization which results from its decline. But the two phenomena are linked. Just as the welfare state owes a great deal, in its formation, to the social and political discussions which are inseparable from the history of the working class, which is particularly clear in the countries endowed with strong social democracy, so too the crisis of the welfare state and the institutions owes a great deal to the destructuration not only of these discussions and conflicts, but also of the principal actor which informed them, the working-class movement.

A third aspect of the recent evolution concerns the national issue, which becomes nodal – all the more so as social issues are not politically treated as such. In most European countries, political debates about nation, nationality and citizenship are activated. In such a context, nationalism loses its open and progressive dimensions, and its relationship with universal values, and is less and less linked with ideas such as progress, reason or democracy. National identity is increasingly loaded with xenophobia and racism. This tendency gains impetus with the emergence or growth of other identities among groups that are defined, or that define themselves, as communities, whether religious, ethnic, national or regional. There is a kind of spiral, a dialectic of identities, in which each affirmation of a specific identity involves other communitarian affirmations among other groups. Nationalism and, more generally speaking, communal identities do not necessarily mean racism. But as Etienne Balibar explains, racism is always a virtuality (Balibar and Wallerstein 1988).

This virtuality is not nurtured uniquely by the presence, at times exaggerated and fantasized, of a more or less visible immigration. It also owes a considerable amount to phenomena which may even have nothing to do with it. Thus national identity is reinforced in its most alarming aspects when national culture appears to be threatened by the superficial and hypermodern character of an international culture which originates primarily in America, by the political construction of Europe or, again, by the globalization of the economy.

At the same time, it becomes more and more difficult to assert that society, state and nation form an integrated whole. Those who call for universal values, human rights and equality, who believe that each individual should have equal opportunities to work, make money and then participate fully in cultural and political life – in other words, those who identify themselves with modernity – are less and less able to meet and even to understand those who have the feeling of being excluded from modern life, who fear for their participation in economic, cultural and political life, and who retire within their national identity. In extreme cases, social and economic participation are no longer linked with the feeling of belonging to a nation, the latter being what remains when the former becomes impossible. Reason, progress and development become divorced from nation, identity and subjectivity, and in this split, racism may easily develop.

In the past, industrial society often offered workers disastrous conditions of work and existence. But the working-class movement, as well as the rulers of industry, believed in progress and reason, and while they were opposed in a structural conflict, this was precisely because they both valorized the idea of progress through industrial production, and both claimed that they should direct it. The nation, and its state, as Ernest Gellner explains (1983) were supposed to be the best frame for modernization, and sometimes the state not only brought favourable conditions, but also claimed to be the main agent of development. Nationalism could be the ideology linked to that viewpoint, and not only a reactionary or traditionalist force. Today, waters divide. National-ism is mainly expressed by social and political groups frightened by the internationalization of the economy and culture. It is increasingly differentialist, and racism develops as social problems such as exclusion and downward mobility grow, and as anxiety develops in regard to national identity.

THE CATEGORIES OF THE SOCIOLOGICAL ANALYSIS OF RACISM

The argument outlined above is historical and sociologial in nature, but a closer examination of the contemporary phenomenon of racism requires explicitness in the instruments and, therefore, the categories of analysis of racism properly speaking (Wieviorka 1991).

The two logics of racism

Contemporary sociological literature increasingly insists on the idea of chang-ing forms of racism. Some scholars, relying on American studies, oppose the old 'flagrant' racism to the 'subtle' new versions (Pettigrew 1993). Others emphasize a crucial distinction, which could, in an extreme interpretation, lead to the idea of two distinct kinds of racism. Following authors such as Martin Barker or Pierre-André Taguieff, we should distinguish between a classical, inegalitarian racism and a new, differentialist one (Barker 1981; Taguieff 1988). The first kind considers the Other as an inferior being, who may find a place in society, but the lowest one. There is room for inferior people in this outlook, as long as they can be exploited and relegated to unpleasant and badly paid tasks. The second kind considers the Other as fundamentally different, which means that he/she has no place in society, that he/she is a danger, an invader, who should be kept at some distance, expelled or possibly destroyed. The point is that for many scholars the new racism, sometimes also referred to as cultural racism, is the main one in the contemporary world, while the inegalitarian one becomes secondary.

As long as this remark is intended as a statement of historical fact, based on the observation of empirical realities of present-day racism, it is acceptable. But it must not take the place of a general theory of racism. First, cultural or differentialist approaches to racism are not new. It is difficult to speak of Nazism, for instance, without introducing the idea that anti-semitism in the Third Reich was deeply informed by these approaches. Jews were said to corrupt Aryan culture and race, and the 'final solution' planned not to assign them to the lowest place in society, but to destroy them. Second, the opposition between the two main logics of racism should not conceal the main fact, which is that a purely cultural definition of the Other, as well as a purely social one, dissolves the idea of race. On one hand, Claude Lévi-Strauss is not a racist when he emphasizes cultural differentiation. One is a racist only when there is any reference to race in a cultural opposition, when beneath culture we can, explicitly or implicitly, find nature: that is, in an organicist or genetic representation of the Other as well as oneself. On the other hand, when the Other is defined only as socially inferior, exploited or marginalized, the reference to race may disappear or become, as William J. Wilson suggests (1978), less significant.

In fact, in most experiences of racism, the two logics co-exist, and racism appears as a combination of them both. There are not two racisms, but one, with various versions of the association of cultural differentialism and social inegalitarianism. The general analysis that has been presented for contemporary Europe helps us to refuse the idea of a pure, cultural racism, corresponding to a new paradigm that would have taken the place of an old one. The sources of European contemporary racism, as I have suggested, are in the crisis of national identities and in the dualization of societies, which favour a differentialist logic. But they are also connected with phenomena of downward social mobility and economic crisis, which lead to populism and exasperation and have an important dimension in appeals for an unequal treatment of migrants.

Two main levels

As I have indicated in my book *L'espace du racisme* (Wieviorka 1991), we may distinguish four levels in racism. The way that experiences of racism are articulated at the different levels where they act may change with their historical evolution. Our distinction is analytical, and should help us as a sociological tool.

A first level refers to weak and inarticulated forms of racism, whatever they may consist of: opinions and prejudice, which are more xenophobic and populist than, strictly speaking, racist; and diffuse violence, limited expression of institutional discrimination or diffusion of racial doctrines, etc. At this first level, racism is not a central issue and it is so limited, quantitatively and qualitatively, that I have chosen to use the term *infraracism* to characterize it.

We may speak of *split racism* at a second level, in reference to forms of racism which are still weak and inarticulate, but stronger and more obvious. At this stage, racism becomes a central issue, but does not give the image of a unified and integrated phenomenon, mainly because of the lack of a strong political expression.

We may speak of *political racism*, precisely, when political and intellectual debates and real political forces bring a dual principle of unity to the phenomenon. On one hand, they give it an ideological structure, so that all its expressions seem to converge and define a unique set of problems; on the other hand, they offer it practical forms of organization.

At the fourth level, we may call *total racism* those situations in which the state itself is based on racist principles. There is nowadays no real threat of total racism in our countries, and we may now simplify the distinction into four levels of racism by reducing them to two main ones, the *infrapolitical* level, including infra and split racisms, and the *political* one.

We can now come back to our general analysis of European contemporary racism and be more precise. This rise of the phenomenon, following what was previously said, is due to the evolution of three basic elements, and to their destructuration. We may add that it appears first at an infrapolitical level, and that it then ascends to the political level, with variations from one country to another.

In certain cases, a rather important political party appears and develops quickly, as in France with the *Front National*. In other cases, such a party appears but quickly declines, which means not that racism necessarily stays at the infrapolitical level, but that it informs political debates without being the flag of one precise strong organization – this could define the English experience. But above all, the analytical distinction into levels enables us to introduce a central question: is there not throughout Europe the same danger of seeing political actors capable of taking over and of directing infrapolitical racism?

On the one hand, we observe in several countries the growing influence of racist ideologies, but also of political organizations which are no longer small groups of activists and which may occupy an important space in political life. The French *Front National* appears as a leader in Europe, and sometimes as a model, but other parties or movements should be quoted too: the *Deutsche Volksunion* and the *Demokratische Partei Deutschlands* in Germany; the FPO (Freiheidlich Partei Österreich) in Austria, which gained 22.6 per cent of the votes in the November 1991 elections in Vienna; the *Vlaams Blok* in Flanders, with twelve members of Parliament since November 1991; and the Italian Leagues.

One must be careful, however, not to exaggerate. The more extreme-right parties occupy an important place, the more they appear as populist rather than purely racist. Racism, strictly speaking, is only one element, and sometimes a minor one, along with strong nationalism or regionalism. Moreover, political and electoral successes force these parties to look respectable, and avoid overtly flagrant expressions of racism.

On the other hand, racism appears in non-political contexts, when prejudice and hostile attitudes to migrants develop, when social and racial segregation is increasingly visible (which is the case in France, where the issue of racism is constantly related to the so-called urban crisis and 'the suburban problem'), when violent actions develop, sometimes with a terrorist aspect, when various institutions including the police have a responsibility for its growth, when discrimination is obvious (for instance, in relation to housing or employment), and when the media contribute to the extension of prejudice. In such a context, all the European democracies have to face the same problem. There is a growing opportunity for extreme-right forces to capitalize on fears, frustrations, unsatisfied social demands and feelings of threat to national identity. Even worse, there is a danger that these forces will introduce new elements into infrapolitical racism. This is the case in France, for instance, where popular racism is strongly hostile to migrants, to black people and to gypsies, rather than to Jews, and where the *Front National* tries constantly to instil anti-semitism.

More generally, there is still a real distance between infrapolitical and political racism, and this means that racism is not so much a widely extended ideology offering people a general framework in which to interpret their own lives and personal experiences, but rather a set of prejudices and practices that are rooted in these concrete lives and experiences, and which could possibly evolve.

In the present state of things, the development is dominated by a process of populist fusion in which popular affects and political discourse converge, but which, paradoxically, protects our societies from extreme and large-scale racist episodes. However, populism is never a stable phenomenon and is always potentially open to more frightening processes.

[. . .]

REFERENCES

Balibar, Etienne, and Wallerstein, Immanuel (1988), *Race, classe, nation*, Paris: La Découverte.

Barkan, Elazar (1992), *The Retreat of Scientific Racism*, Cambridge: Cambridge University Press.

Barker, Martin (1981), *The New Racism*, London: Junction Books.

CCE (1989) *Eurobaromètre: L'opinion publique dans la Communauté Européenne*, Brussels: Commission des Communautés Européennes.

Gellner, Ernest (1983), *Nations and Nationalism*, Oxford: Blackwell.

Pettigrew, Thomas, and Meertens, R. F. (1993), 'Le racisme voilé: Composants et mesure', in *Racisme et modernité* (under the direction of M. Wieviorka), Paris: La Découverte.

Taguieff, Pierre-André (1988), *La force du préjugé*, Paris: La Découverte.

Touraine, Alain, Wieviorka, Michel, and Dubet, François (1987), *The Working Class Movement*, Cambridge: Cambridge University Press.

Wieviorka, Michel (1991), *L'espace du racisme*, Paris: Seuil.

Wieviorka, Michel (1992a), 'Racism and modernity', paper presented at the Congress of the American Sociological Association, Pittsburgh.

Wieviorka, Michel (1992b), 'Analyse sociologique et historique de l'antésimitisme en Pologne', *Cahiers internationaux de sociologie*, vol. 93, pp. 237–49.

Wieviorka, Michel (ed.) (1992c), *La France raciste*, Paris: Seuil.

Wilson, William J. (1978), *The Declining Significance of Race*, Chicago: University of Chicago Press.

The liberal retreat from race since the Civil Rights Act
STEPHEN STEINBERG

Racial backlash was not an affliction only of the political right [in the USA]. As early as 1963, the *Atlantic Monthly* published an article entitled 'The White Liberal's Retreat'. Its author, Murray Friedman, observed that 'the liberal white is increasingly uneasy about the nature and consequences of the Negro revolt.' According to Friedman, a number of factors contributed to the white liberal retreat. For one thing, after school desegregation came to Northern cities, white liberals realized that the Negro was not just an abstraction, and not just a Southern problem. Second, the rise of black nationalism exacerbated tensions with white liberals, especially when they were ejected from civil rights organizations. Third, escalating tensions and violence tested the limit of liberal support. As Friedman wrote: 'In the final analysis, a liberal, white, middle-class society wants to have change, but without trouble' (Friedman 1963).

The liberal retreat also manifested itself in a rift between white intellectuals and blacks. As an example, Friedman cited Nathan Glazer's laudatory review of Nathaniel Weyl's *The Negro in American Civilization*. Weyl cited the results of IQ tests to argue that 'a large part of the American Negro population is seriously deficient in mental ability', and warned against the dangers of 'random race mixing without regard to learning ability'. According to Friedman, Glazer was critical of Weyl's biological determinism, particularly his reliance on African brain-size data, but nevertheless declared that Weyl 'is clearly free of any prejudice and deserves credit for having raised for public discussion crucial aspects of the Negro question which receive little discussion in academic and liberal circles, and which are usually left in the hands of bigots and incompetents' (quoted in Friedman 1963). Then Glazer posed the rhetorical question that leaves the answer to the racialized imagination: 'What are we to make of the high rates of [Negro] crime and delinquency, illegitimacy, family break-up and school dropout?'

As Friedman observed, there was nothing new in the tendency for white liberals to withdraw support from the liberation movement – essentially the same thing had happened during Reconstruction. In both cases, liberals demonstrated a failure of nerve, and nudged blacks into curbing their demands. Friedman described the situation in 1963 in these epigrammatic terms: 'to the Negro demand for "now," to which the Deep South has replied "never," many liberal whites are increasingly responding "later"' (Friedman 1963).

It did not take long for the intensifying backlash and the liberal retreat to manifest themselves politically. The critical turning-point was 1965, the year the civil rights movement reached its triumphant finale. The 1964 Civil Rights Act – passed after a decade of black insurgency – ended segregation in public accommodations and, at least in theory, proscribed discrimination in employment. The last remaining piece of civil rights legislation – the 1965 Voting Rights Act – was wending its way through Congress and, in the wake of Johnson's landslide victory, was assured of eventual passage. In a joint session of Congress on voting rights in March 1965 – the first such session on a domestic issue since 1946 – President Johnson had electrified the nation by proclaiming, in his Southern drawl, 'And we *shall* overcome.' As a senator from Texas, Johnson had voted against anti-lynching legislation. Now, in the midst of a crisis engineered by a grassroots protest movement, Johnson embraced the battle cry of that movement as he proposed legislation that would eliminate the last and most important vestige of official segregation.

In retrospect, Johnson's speech represented not the triumph of the civil rights movement, but its last hurrah. Now that its major legislative objectives had been achieved, not only the future of the movement, but also the constancy of liberal support, were thrown into question. By 1965, leaders and commentators, both inside and outside the movement, were asking, 'What's next?' However, this question had an ominous innuendo when it came from white liberals. In *Why We Can't Wait*, published in 1963, Martin Luther King provides this account of his appearance with Roy Wilkins on *Meet the Press*:

There were the usual questions about how much more the Negro wants, but there seemed to be a new undercurrent of implications related to the sturdy new strength of our movement. Without the courtly complexities, we were, in effect, being asked if we could be trusted to hold back the surging tides of discontent so that those on the shore would not be made too uncomfortable by the buffeting and onrushing waves. Some of the questions implied that our leadership would be judged in accordance with our capacity to 'keep the Negro from going too far.' The quotes are mine, but I think the phrase mirrors the thinking of the panelists as well as of many other white Americans (King 1963: 147).

By 1965 – even before Watts exploded – there was a growing awareness among black leaders that political rights did not go far enough to compensate for past wrongs. Whitney Young epitomized this when he wrote that 'there is little value in a Negro's obtaining the right to be admitted to hotels and restaurants if he has no cash in his pocket and no job' (Young 1963). As Rainwater and Yancey have suggested, 'The year 1965 may be known in history as the time when the civil rights movement discovered, in the sense of becoming explicitly aware, that abolishing legal racism would not produce Negro equality' (Rainwater and Yancey 1967: 77).

If laws alone would not produce equality, then the unavoidable conclusion was that some form of 'special effort' – to use Whitney Young's term – was necessary to compensate for the accumulated disadvantages of the past. By 1965 the words 'compensation', 'reparations' and 'preference' had already crept into the political discourse, and white liberals were beginning to display their disquiet with this troublesome turn of events. In *Why We Can't Wait* King observed: 'Whenever this issue of compensatory or preferential treatment for the Negro is raised, some of our friends recoil in horror. The Negro should be granted equality, they agree; but he should ask nothing more' (King 1963: 147).

[. . .]

In the spring of 1964 [there] was an early sign of the imminent breakup of the liberal coalition that had functioned as a bulwark of the civil rights movement. One faction would gravitate to the nascent neo-conservative movement. Another faction would remain in the liberal camp, committed in principle to both liberal reform and racial justice. This, however, was to prove a difficult balancing act, especially when confronted with an intensifying racial backlash. Even in the best of times, racial issues tended to exacerbate divisions in the liberal coalition on which Democratic electoral victories depended. As the polity swung to the right, liberals in the Democratic Party came under mounting pressure to downplay or sidestep racial issues.

Thus, the liberal retreat from race was rationalized in terms of *realpolitik*. The argument ran like this: America is too racist to support programmes targeted specifically for blacks, especially if these involve any form of preference which is anathema to most whites. Highlighting racial issues, therefore, only serves to drive a wedge in the liberal coalition, driving whites from the Democratic Party, and is ultimately self-defeating. That this reasoning amounted to a capitulation to the white backlash did not faze the political 'realists' since their motives were pure. Indeed, unlike the racial backlash on the right, the liberal backlash was *not* based on racial animus or retrograde politics. On the contrary, these dyed-in-the-wool liberals were convinced that the best or only way to help blacks was to help 'everybody'. Eliminate poverty, they said, and blacks, who count disproportionately among the poor, will be the winners. Achieve full employment, and black employment troubles will be resolved. The upshot, however, was that blacks were asked to subordinate their agenda to a larger movement for liberal reform. In practical terms, this meant forgoing the black protest movement and casting their lot with the Democratic Party.

Thus, after 1965 many white liberals who were erstwhile supporters of the civil rights movement placed a kiss of death on race-based politics and race-based public policy. They not only joined the general retreat from race in the society at large, but in fact cited the white backlash as reason for their own abandonment of race-based politics. In this sense, the liberal retreat from race can be said to represent the left wing of the backlash.

THE HOWARD ADDRESS: A CASE OF 'SEMANTIC INFILTRATION'

The ideological cleavage that would split the liberal camp was foreshadowed in a commencement address that President Johnson delivered at Howard University on 4 June 1965. The speech, written by Richard Goodwin and Daniel Patrick Moynihan, was riddled with contradiction, and for this very reason epitomizes the political limbo that existed in 1965, as well as the emerging lines of ideological and political division within the liberal camp (Moynihan 1986; Rainwater and Yancey 1967).

The speech, aptly entitled 'To Fulfill these Rights', began with the most radical vision on race that has ever been enunciated by a president of the United States. After reviewing the series of civil rights acts that secured full civil rights for African Americans, Johnson declared: 'But freedom is not enough.' He continued:

> You do not take a person who, for years, has been hobbled by chains and liberate him, bring him up to the starting line of a race and then say, 'you are free to compete with all the others,' and still justly believe that you have been completely fair. Thus it is not enough just to open the gates of opportunity. All our citizens must have the ability to walk through those gates.

Johnson's oratory went a critical step further:

> This is the next and more profound stage of the battle for civil rights. We seek not just freedom but opportunity – not just legal equity but human ability – *not just equality as a right and a theory but equality as a fact and as a result.*

With these last words, Johnson adopted the logic and the language of those arguing for compensatory programmes that would redress past wrongs. Equality, not liberty, would be the defining principle of 'the next and more profound stage' in the liberation struggle.

So far so good. Johnson's speech then took an abrupt detour away from politics to sociology, reflecting the unmistakable imprint of Daniel Patrick Moynihan, who only a month earlier had completed an internal report focusing on problems of the black family. Johnson said:

> . . . equal opportunity is essential, but not enough. Men and women of all races are born with the same range of abilities. But ability is not just the product of birth. Ability is stretched or stunted by the family you live with, and the neighborhoods you live in, by the school you go to and the poverty or the richness of your surroundings. It is the product of a hundred unseen forces playing upon the infant, the child, and the man.

Compare the language and logic of this passage with the one that follows:

> Overt job discrimination is only one of the important hurdles which must be overcome before color can disappear as a determining factor in the lives and fortunes of men. . . . The prevailing view among social scientists holds that there are no significant differences among groups as to the distribution of innate aptitudes or at most very slight differences. On the other hand, differences among individuals are very substantial. The extent to which an individual is able to develop his aptitudes will largely depend upon the circumstances present in the family within which he grows up and the opportunities which he encounters at school and in the larger community (Rainwater and Yancey 1967:125–32).

This latter passage comes from a 1956 book, *The Negro Potential*, by Eli Ginzberg, who was a leading liberal economist of that period. My point is not that Johnson's speechwriters were guilty of plagiarism. Rather it is to take note of their Machiavellian genius. With a rhetorical sleight of hand, Goodwin and Moynihan shifted the discourse away from the radical vision of 'equal results' that emanated from the black protest movement of the 1960s back to the standard liberal cant of the 1950s which held that the black child is stunted by 'circumstances present in the family within which he grows up'. The conceptual groundwork was being laid for a drastic policy reversal: the focus would no longer be on white racism, but rather on the deficiencies of blacks themselves.

[. . .]

The significance of the Howard address was that it drew a line in the political sands marking how far the Johnson administration would go in supporting the escalating demands of the protest movement. In throwing his support behind the Voting Rights Act, Johnson had gone further than any of his predecessors in jeopardizing the Solid South. The rhetoric of 'equal results' also threatened to antagonize blue-collar workers, Jews and other elements of the Democratic coalition. The covert message in the Howard speech was that, as far as the Democratic Party was concerned, the impending Voting Rights Act marked the end of the Civil Rights Revolution ('the end of the beginning', Johnson said disingenuously, quoting Churchill). If blacks were 'to fulfil these rights', they would have to get their own house in order. Literally!

Thus, behind the equivocal language in Johnson's address was a key policy issue concerning the role of the state in the era following the Civil Rights Act. Would future progress depend on an expansion of anti-racist policies – aimed not only at forms of intentional discrimination but also at the insidious forces of institutionalized racism that have excluded blacks categorically from whole job sectors and other opportunity structures? Or would future progress depend on programmes of social uplift that contemplate 'the gradual absorption of deserving Negroes one by one into white society'?

These alternative policy options were predicated on vastly different assumptions about the nature and sources of racism. The one located the problem within 'white' society and its major institutions, and called for policies to rapidly integrate blacks into jobs, schools and other institutional sectors from which they had historically been excluded. The other assumed that racism was waning, but that blacks generally lacked the requisite education and skills to avail themselves of expanding opportunities. This latter school included both traditional liberals who supported government programmes that 'help blacks to help themselves', and conservatives, including a new genre of black conservatives, who adamantly opposed government intervention, insisting that blacks had to summon the personal and group resources to overcome disabilities of race and class.

[. . .]

FROM INFILTRATION TO SUBVERSION: THE MOYNIHAN REPORT

The polarity between anti-racism and social uplift became even more sharply defined by the controversy surrounding the publication of the Moynihan Report three months after Johnson's address at Howard University. Officially titled: 'The Negro Family: The Case for National Action', the report presented a mound of statistics showing high rates of divorce, illegitimacy and female-headed households. Although Moynihan paid lip-service to the argument that unemployment and low wages contributed to family breakdown, he was practically obsessed with a single statistic showing that Aid to Families with Dependent Children (AFDC) continued to increase between 1962 and 1964, despite the fact that unemployment was decreasing. On this meagre empirical basis, Moynihan concluded that poverty was 'feeding upon itself', and that the 'disintegration of the Negro family' had assumed a dynamic all its own, independent of joblessness and poverty. In yet another leap of faith, he asserted that family breakdown was the *source* of most of the problems that afflict black America. In Moynihan's own words: '. . . at the center of the tangle of pathology is the weakness of the family structure. Once or twice removed, it will be found to be the principal source of most of the aberrant, inadequate, or antisocial behavior that did not establish, but now serves to perpetuate the cycle of poverty and deprivation' (Moynihan 1967a).

Moynihan's critics accused him of inverting cause and effect, and, in doing so, shifting the focus of blame away from societal institutions onto blacks themselves.

[. . .]

Notwithstanding the efforts of a number of writers, including Moynihan himself, to portray the controversy over the Moynihan Report as fruitless and even counterproductive, it proved to be one of the most formative debates in modern social science. The debate crystallized issues, exposed the conservative assumptions and racial biases that lurked behind mainstream social science, and prompted critics of the report to formulate other positions that challenged the prevailing wisdom about race in America. The principal counterposition – encapsulated in William Ryan's ingenious term 'blaming the victim' – blew the whistle on the tendency of social science to reduce social phenomena to an individual level of analysis, thereby shifting attention away from the structures of inequality and focusing on the behavioural responses of the individuals suffering the effects of these structures. The controversy also stimulated a large body of research – the most notable example is Herbert Gutman's now classic study of *The Black Family in Slavery and Freedom* (1976). This study demolished the myth that 'slavery destroyed the black family' – a liberal myth that allowed social scientists and policy-makers to blame 'history' for the problems in the black family, thus deflecting attention away from the factors in the here and now that tear families apart.

Yet leading liberals today contend that Moynihan was the victim of unfair ideological attack. Moynihan set the tone for this construction of history in an article that he published in *Commentary* under the title: 'The President and the Negro: The Moment Lost'. Again, Moynihan begins on the threshold of truth: 'For the second time in their history, the great task of liberation has been left only half-accomplished. It appears that the nation may be in the process of reproducing the tragic events of the Reconstruction: giving to Negroes the forms of legal equality, but withholding the economic and political resources which are the bases of social equality.' Moynihan goes on to argue, as I have here, that 1965 represented a moment of opportunity: 'The moment came when, as it were, the nation had the resources, and the leadership, and the will to make a *total* as against a partial commitment to the cause of Negro equality. It did not do so.'

Why was the opportunity missed? According to Moynihan, the blame lies not with the forces of racism and reaction, and certainly not with himself, but with 'the liberal Left' who opposed his initiative to address problems in the black family. Specifically, opposition emanated:

> . . . from Negro leaders unable to comprehend their opportunity; from civil-rights militants, Negro and white, caught up in a frenzy of arrogance and nihilism; and from white liberals unwilling to expend a jot of prestige to do a difficult but dangerous job that had to be done, and could have been done. But was not. (Moynihan 1967b:)

Thus, in Moynihan's recapitulation of events, it was his political enemies who, in 'a frenzy of arrogance and nihilism', had aborted the next stage in the Negro revolution that Moynihan had engineered as an influential adviser to the President.

[. . .]

In recent years there have been attempts to rehabilitate Moynihan, and to portray him as the hapless victim of the ideological excesses of the 1960s. For example, in *The Undeserving Poor* – a book that traces the poverty debates since that decade – Michael Katz asserts that 'because most critics distorted the report, the debate generated more passion than insight.' One result of the attack on Moynihan, he adds mournfully, 'was to accelerate the burial of the culture of poverty as an acceptable concept in liberal reform' (Katz 1989: 24). William Julius Wilson goes even further in suggesting that 'the controversy surrounding the Moynihan report had the effect of curtailing serious research on minority problems in the inner city for over a decade' (Wilson 1987: 4). Yet thanks to Wilson and others, Moynihan's theoretical and political positions would be given new life in the 1980s.

[. . .]

Wilson struck a number of themes that were at the heart of Moynihan's political analysis in 1965: that blacks had their political rights, thanks to landmark civil rights legislation; that there was 'a widening gulf' between the black middle class, which was reaping the benefits of an improved climate of tolerance, and the black lower class, which was as destitute and isolated as ever; that blacks were arriving in the nation's cities at a time when employment opportunities, especially in the manufacturing sector, were declining; and that future progress would depend less on tearing down racist barriers than on raising the level of education and skills among poor blacks. The underlying assumption in both cases was that the civil rights revolution was a watershed that more or less resolved the issue of 'race', but that left unaddressed the vexing problems of 'class'. By 'class', however, neither Moynihan nor Wilson was advancing a radical theory that challenged structures of inequality, or that envisioned a restructuring of major political and economic institutions. All they meant was that lower-class blacks needed to acquire the education and skills that are a prerequisite for mobility and that explain the success of the black middle class.

In *The Truly Disadvantaged*, published in 1987, Wilson spelled out the implications of his 'declining significance' thesis for politics and public policy. Again, he arrived at a position that Moynihan had articulated in 1965: that there was no political constituency for policies targeted specifically for blacks, and therefore 'we have to declare that we are doing it for everybody.' [. . .]

Originally Wilson intended to have 'The Hidden Agenda' as the title of *The Truly Disadvantaged*. Instead he used this as the title for chapter 7, in which he contended that, because there is no political constituency for policies targeted for blacks, it becomes necessary to 'hide' such programmes behind universal programmes 'to which the more advantaged groups of all races and class backgrounds can positively relate'. [. . .] The notion of a 'hidden agenda' also contradicts Wilson's claim that racism is of 'declining significance'. Indeed, it is *because* of racism that Wilson feels compelled to 'hide' his agenda in the first place. The underlying premise is that America is *so* racist – so utterly indifferent to the plight of black America, so implacably opposed to any indemnification for three centuries of racial oppression – that it becomes necessary to camouflage policies intended for blacks behind policies that offer benefits to the white majority.

At first blush it might appear odd to portray Wilson as a political clone of Moynihan. Wilson, after all, is an ivory-tower scholar and a political outsider who has described himself as a Social Democrat. Moynihan gave up any pretence of political chastity to become a major player within the Democratic Party. On closer scrutiny, however, Wilson is far from a detached intellectual. In two national elections he has gone on record, via op-ed pieces in the *New York Times*, to advocate race-neutral politics in order to enhance Democratic electoral prospects. And he has quietly served as President Clinton's exculpation for the administration's failure to develop policies to deal with the plight of the nation's ghettos. Whenever Clinton is confronted with this issue, his stock answer is to defend his do-nothing policy by invoking the name of 'the famous African-American sociologist William Julius Wilson', explaining how profoundly influenced he was by his book *The Truly Disadvantaged*, and ending with glowing projections about how blacks stand to benefit from his economic policies. [. . .]

Thus, whatever differences exist between Moynihan and Wilson, the factor of overriding importance is that both repudiated race-based politics and race-based public policy. Here we come to the delicate but unavoidable issue concerning the role that the race of a social theorist plays in determining what Alvin Gouldner (1970) refers to as 'the *social* career of a theory'. Not only was Moynihan white, but he wrote at a time of heightened racial consciousness and mobilization, both inside and outside the university. As a white, he was susceptible to charges of racism and of resorting to stereotypes in his depiction of black families. Even the voluble Moynihan was reduced to silence when it came to parrying the charges levelled against him by black scholars and activists.

Wilson, too, has had his critics, but at least he has been immune to charges of 'racism'. Furthermore, Wilson appeared on the stage of history at a time when racial militancy was ebbing. The nation, including the academic establishment, had grown weary of racial conflict, and was eager, like the Democratic Party, to 'get beyond race'. Wilson, clearly, was the right person in the right place and the right time, and, as if this were not enough, his book *The Declining Significance of Race* had the right title – one that satisfied the nation's yearning to put race behind, to pretend that racism was no longer the problem it had been in times past.

[. . .]

CORNEL WEST: THE LEFT WING OF THE BACKLASH

If books could be judged by their titles, one would think that a book entitled *Race Matters* (West 1993) would be the antithesis of a book entitled *The Declining Significance of Race*. But then again, one must beware of semantic infiltration, and the possibility that titles are subversive of meaning.

[. . .]

Two of West's essays serve as the basis of the following discussion: 'Nihilism in Black America' and 'Beyond Affirmative Action: Equality and Identity'.

The term 'nihilism' invites semantic confusion. Invoked by a professor of philosophy, the term conjures up hoary philosophical debates concerning the nature of existence and the possibility of objective knowledge. West surely is not claiming that the ghetto is an enactment of some dubious philosophical doctrine. Invoked by a political activist, 'nihilism' calls up associations with Russian revolutionaries who believed that the old order must be utterly eradicated to make way for the new. Again, it is doubtful that West, the political activist, is imputing these motives to ghetto youth. Nor does his use of 'nihilism' suggest the angst and denial of meaning that are often viewed as endemic to modernity. No doubt West could expound on all of these themes, but in describing the urban ghetto, he uses the word specifically to refer to destructive and self-destructive behaviour that is unconstrained by legal or moral norms. But this meaning comes dangerously close to the prevailing view of ghetto youth as driven by aberrant and anti-social tendencies. Alas, does 'nihilism' merely provide an intellectual gloss for ordinary assumptions and claims?

Any such doubts are seemingly dissipated by the book's opening sentence: 'What happened in Los Angeles in April of 1992 was neither a race riot nor a class rebellion. Rather, this monumental upheaval was a multiracial, trans-class, and largely male display of justified social rage.' With this manifesto, West establishes his credentials as a person on the left. By the end of the same paragraph, however, West says that 'race was the visible catalyst, not the underlying cause.' Already the reader is left to wonder: does race matter or doesn't it?

In the next paragraph West assumes the rhetorical stance that pervades his book: his is the voice of reason and moderation between liberals and conservatives, each of which is allegedly trapped in rigid orthodoxies that leave us 'intellectually debilitated, morally disempowered, and personally depressed'. Liberals, West avers, are burdened with a simplistic faith in the ability of government to solve our racial problems. Conservatives, on the other hand, blame the problems on blacks and ignore 'public responsibility for the immoral circumstances that haunt our fellow citizens.' Both treat blacks as 'a problem people'. West thus presents himself as mediator between ideological extremes. He is a leftist who does not resort to a crude economic determinism that denies human freedom and that relieves the poor of moral responsibility for their actions. And he is a theologian who does not use morality to evade public responsibility for social wrongs.

[. . .]

According to West, despite the tribulations going back to slavery, blacks have always been endowed with 'cultural armor to beat back the demons of hopelessness, meaningless, lovelessness'. He points out that until the 1970s the rate of suicide was comparatively low among blacks, but today young blacks have one of the highest rates of suicide. Thus for West the question becomes: what has happened to 'the cultural structures that once sustained black life in America' and 'are no longer able to fend off the nihilistic threat?' His answer focuses on two factors:

1 *The saturation of market forces and market moralities in black life.* By this West means that blacks have succumbed to the materialism and hedonism that pervade American culture and that 'edge out nonmarket values – love, care, service to others – handed down by preceding generations'. If blacks are more

susceptible to these corrupting influences than others, it is because the poor have 'a limited capacity to ward off self-contempt and self-hatred'.

2 *The crisis in black leadership.* Here West bemoans the failure of black leaders to carry on a tradition of leadership that was at once aggressive and inspirational. One reason for this failure is the corruption of the new middle class by their immersion into mass culture.

But another reason that 'quality leadership is on the wane' has to do with 'the gross deterioration of personal, familial, and communal relations among African-Americans'. With families in decline and communities in shambles, the basis for effective leadership is lost.

Thus, West harks back to the halcyon days when there was 'a vital community bound by its ethical ideals'. Unfortunately, oppression does not always produce such pleasing outcomes, and the victims of oppression are not always ennobled by their experience and an inspiration to the rest of us.

West's problem, to repeat, is not that he discusses crime, violence, drugs and the other notorious ills of ghetto life. Rather the problem is that he presents social breakdown and cultural disintegration as a problem *sui generis*, with an existence and momentum independent of the forces that gave rise to it in the first place. Moynihan, too, had held that centuries of injustice had 'brought about deep-seated structural distortions in the life of the Negro American'. But he added a remarkable addendum: 'At this point, the present pathology is capable of perpetuating itself without assistance from the white world' (Moynihan 1967b: 93). Similarly, West traces nihilism to centuries of injustice, but goes on to claim that nihilism is so embedded in the life of the ghetto that it assumes a life all its own. At least this is what West implies when he writes that 'culture is as much a structure as the economy or politics.' Indeed, the whole point of West's critique of 'liberal structuralism' is that nihilism is not reducible to political economy. It is precisely because nihilism is so deeply embedded that this 'cultural structure' must be addressed as a force in its own right.

It takes hairsplitting distinctions that do not bear close scrutiny to maintain that West's view of nihilism is different from the conservative view of ghetto culture as deeply pathological, and as the chief source of the problems that beset African Americans. Despite his frequent caveats, West has succeeded in shifting the focus of blame onto the black community. The affliction is *theirs* – something we shall call 'nihilism'.

It is also theirs to resolve. As with the Moynihan Report, the regressive implications of West's theory become clear when one examines his praxis. West asks: 'What is to be done about this nihilistic threat?' But his answer is sadly deficient. He calls for 'a politics of conversion' – a frail attempt to use radical vernacular as a cover for ideas that are anything but radical. 'Like alcoholism and drug addiction,' West explains, 'nihilism is a disease of the soul.' How does one cure a disease of the soul? West's prescription (to paraphrase Jencks) is to change the nihilist, not the system. To quote West again:

> Nihilism is not overcome by arguments or analysis; it is tamed by love and care. Any disease of the soul must be conquered by a turning of one's soul. This turning is done through one's own affirmation of one's worth – an affirmation fueled by the concern of others. A love ethic must be at the center of a politics of conversion (West 1993: 19).

Here, alas, is the reason for the acclaim that has been heaped on *Race Matters*. The cure for the nihilism that so frightens white America is not a resumption of the war on poverty. Nor is it a resumption of the movement against racism. West, of course, would endorse both, but he has also been explicit in saying that 'liberal structuralism' is not equipped to deal with 'the self-destructive and inhumane actions of black people'.

One can almost hear the national sigh of relief from those who feared that expensive new programmes of social reconstruction and a renewed commitment to affirmative action might become necessary to control the disorder emanating from the ghettos of America. Instead we have an inexpensive palliative: a crusade against nihilism to be waged from within the black community. So much the better that this proposal is advanced not by another black conservative whose politics might be suspect, but by a self-proclaimed Socialist. [. . .]

One cannot fault West for trying to bridge the chasm between religion and politics. However, he has not placed himself in the tradition of Martin Luther King, who invoked religious symbols and appealed to spiritual values in order to mobilize popular support behind a political movement. King did not believe that a love ethic could ever serve as an antidote to spiritual breakdown. The only remedy was a political transformation that eliminated the conditions that eat away at the human spirit. West, on the other hand, offers no political framework for his so-called politics of conversion. Indeed, he explicitly divorces nihilism from political economy, thus implying that moral redemption is to be achieved through some mysterious 'turning of one's soul'.

West cannot escape the retrograde implications of his position with disclaimers that 'unlike conservative behaviorists, the politics of conversion situates these actions within inhuman circumstances.' He ignores his own admonition that 'to call on black people to be agents makes sense only if we also examine the dynamics of this victimization against which their agency will, in part, be exercised.' And while he is guided by 'a vision of moral regeneration and political insurgency for the purpose of fundamental social change for all who suffer from socially induced misery', he fails to translate this prophetic ideal into a political praxis. The practical implication of West's position is to substitute a vapid and utterly inconsequential 'politics of conversion' for a genuine political solution – one that would call upon the power and resources of the national government for what is at bottom a national problem and a national disgrace.

It should come as no surprise that the most prominent convert to West's politics of conversion is President Clinton. In a speech delivered to a Memphis church in 1993, Clinton practically echoed West in asserting that there is a crisis of the spirit. The ramifications for public policy should have been predictable: 'Sometimes, there are no answers from the outside in. Sometimes, all of the answers have to come from the values and the stirrings and the voices that speak to us from within' (*New York Times* 14 November 1993). Thus are legitimate spiritual concerns used as a subterfuge for political and moral abdication. The irony is made still more bitter by the fact that Clinton gave his speech in the same Memphis church where Martin Luther King delivered his last sermon the night before his assassination in 1968.

Not only does West shift the focus of analysis and of blame away from the structures of racial oppression, but in his chapter entitled 'Beyond Affirmative Action' he undercuts the single policy that has gone a decisive step beyond equal rights in the direction of equal results. West is *not* opposed to affirmative action, but he engages in a tortuous reasoning that subverts the whole logic behind it. Thus, he begins on the one hand by declaring that in principle he favours a class-based affirmative action (as does William Julius Wilson). On the other hand, he knows that such a policy is politically unrealistic. He also knows that if affirmative action in its present form were abolished, then 'racial and sexual discrimination would return with a vengeance.' Why, then, all this hairsplitting? Even if a class-based affirmative action could be enacted, few of the benefits would filter down to African Americans who are not only most in need, but also have unique claims for compensatory treatment. Nor would working-class whites who become lawyers and doctors on the basis of affirmative action provide the black community with the professional talent that it sorely needs.

In short, affirmative action is meant to counteract the evils of caste, not of class. It is predicated on a realization that blacks have been victims of a system of oppression that goes far beyond the disabilities associated with class disadvantage, and therefore warrants a special remedy. West's equivocation with respect to race-based affirmative action is the clearest indication of how little race matters in his theoretical framework and in his agenda for change.

Reminiscent of Moynihan and Wilson, West's approach for helping blacks is to help 'everybody'. Like them, he provides a respectable liberal cover for evading the issue of race, and still worse, backing off from race-targeted policies like affirmative action, all in the name of getting 'beyond race'. West prides himself on steering 'a course between the Scylla of environmental determinism and the Charybdis of a blaming-the-victims perspective'. Unfortunately, he ends up in a political never-never land where, as Du Bois once said in his critique of historiography, 'nobody seems to have done wrong and everybody was right' (Du Bois 1935: 714). And nothing changes.

This nation's ruling elites need to be told that there is no exit from the current morass until they confront the legacy of slavery and resume the unfinished racial agenda. It is *their* nihilism that deserves our condemnation – the crime, the immorality, the self-destructive folly of tolerating racial ghettos and excluding yet another generation of black youth from the American Dream.

CONCLUSION

Martin Luther King's 'Letter from a Birmingham Jail' has become a part of this nation's political folklore. However, its specific contents have been all but expunged from our collective memory. The letter was not a condemnation of racism. Nor was it, like his celebrated 'I Have a Dream' oration – whose contents *are* remembered – an evocation of American ideals or a prophetic vision of better times ahead. King was responding to a letter signed by eight priests, rabbis and ministers that appeared in the *Birmingham News* while he was imprisoned. The letter spoke sympathetically of 'rights consistently denied', but criticized King's tactics as 'unwise and untimely' and called for a 'constructive and realistic approach', one that would substitute negotiation for confrontation. In his response King acknowledged their sincerity in seeking 'a better path', but explained why confrontation and crisis were necessary in order to shake white society out of its apathy and intransigence. Mincing no words, King issued the following indictment of the so-called moderate:

> I have almost reached the regrettable conclusion that the Negroes' great stumbling block in the stride toward freedom is not the White Citizens' 'Counciler' or the Ku Klux Klanner, but the white moderate who is more devoted to 'order' than to justice; who prefers a negative peace which is the absence of tension to a positive peace which is the presence of justice; who constantly says 'I agree with you in the goal you seek, but I can't agree with your methods of direct action'; who lives by the myth of time and who constantly advises the Negro to wait until 'a more convenient season' (King 1992: 91)

Was there hyperbole in King's assertion that the great stumbling block in the stride for freedom was not the Council or the Klan but those who seek a middle ground and would settle for a negative peace? Perhaps. As is often argued, liberals are not *the* enemy. However, the enemy depends on the so-called liberal to put a kinder and gentler face on racism; to subdue the rage of the oppressed; to raise false hopes that change is imminent; to modulate the demands for complete liberation; to divert protest; and to shift the onus of responsibility for America's greatest crime away from powerful institutions that *could* make a difference onto individuals who have been rendered powerless by these very institutions.

The liberal retreat from race since the civil rights movement is full of political paradox. When forced to confront the issue, the liberal will argue that in a racist society, race-based politics are not viable precisely because blacks are an isolated and despised minority. As with much race-think, this is upside-down and inside-out. It is precisely because blacks were an isolated and despised minority that they were forced to seek redress outside the framework of electoral politics. The civil rights movement was triumphant in part because it tapped the lode of revolutionary potential within the black community, and in part because it galvanized the support of political allies outside the black community, including white liberals. Furthermore, this movement not only achieved its immediate objectives, but also was the major catalyst for progressive change in the twentieth century. As Aldon Morris writes at the conclusion of *The Origins of the Civil Rights Movement*:

> ... the civil rights movement served as a training ground for many of the activists who later organized movements within their own communities. Indeed, the modern women's movement, student movement, farm workers' movement, and others of the period were triggered by the unprecedented scale of nontraditional politics in the civil rights movement (Morris 1984: 288).

A common refrain from the right is that advocates of affirmative action are guilty of the very thing that they say they are against – namely, treating blacks as a separate class. Again, this reasoning is upside-down and inside-out. The truth is that it is the *refusal* to see race – the wilful colour blindness of the liberal camp – that acquiesces to the racial status quo, and does so by consigning blacks to a twilight zone where they are politically invisible. In this way elements of the left unwittingly join the right in evading any reckoning with America's greatest crime – slavery – and its legacy in the present.

REFERENCES

Commentary (1964), 'Liberalism and the Negro: A Round-Table Discussion', *Commentary*, vol. 37, March.
Du Bois, W. E. B. (1935), *Black Reconstruction*, Harcourt Brace, New York.
Friedman, M. (1963), 'The White Liberal's Retreat', *Atlantic Monthly*, vol. 211, January.
Ginzberg, E (1956), *The Negro Potential*, Columbia University Press, New York.
Gouldner, A. (1970), *The Coming Crisis of Western Sociology*, Basic Books, New York.
Gutman, H. G. (1976), *The Black Family in Slavery and Freedom, 1750–1925*, Pantheon Books, New York.
Katz, M. B. (1989), *The Undeserving Poor*, Pantheon, New York.
King, M. L. Jr. (1963), *Why We Can't Wait*, Harper & Row, New York.
King, M. L. Jr. (1992), 'Letter from a Birmingham Jail', in *I have a Dream and Speeches that Changed the World*, Harper San Francisco, San Francisco.
Morris, A. (1984), *The Origins of the Civil Rights Movement*, Free Press, New York.
Moynihan, D. P. (1967a), *The Negro Family: The Case for National Action*, reproduced in full in Rainwater and Yancey, op. cit.
Moynihan, D. P. (1967b), 'The President and the Negro: The Moment Lost', *Commentary*, vol. 43, February.

Moynihan, D. P. (1986), *Family and Nation*, Harcourt Brace Jovanovich, New York.
New York Times (1993), 'Excerpts from Clinton's Speech to Black Ministers', *New York Times*, 14 November.
Rainwater, L., and Yancey, W. L. (1967), eds, *The Moynihan Report and the Politics of Controversy*, MIT Press, Cambridge, Mass.
West, C. (1993), *Race Matters*, Beacon Press, Boston.
Weyl, N. (1960), *The Negro in American Civilization*, Washington DC, Public Affairs Press.
Wilson, W. J. (1978), *The Declining Significance of Race*, University of Chicago Press, Chicago.
Wilson, W. J. (1987), *The Truly Disadvantaged*, Chicago University Press, Chicago.
Young, W. M. Jr. (1963), *To Be Equal*, McGraw-Hill, New York.

'Class racism'
ÉTIENNE BALIBAR

Academic analyses of racism, though according chief importance to the study of racist theories, none the less argue that 'sociological' racism is a popular phenomenon. Given this supposition, the development of racism within the working class (which, to committed socialists and communists, seems counter to the natural order of things) comes to be seen as the effect of a tendency allegedly inherent in the masses. Institutional racism finds itself projected into the very construction of that psycho-sociological category that is 'the masses'. We must therefore attempt to analyse the process of displacement which, moving from classes to masses, presents these latter both as the privileged *subjects* of racism and its favoured *objects*.

Can one say that a social class, by its situation and its ideology (not to mention its identity), is predisposed to racist attitudes and behaviour? This question has mainly been debated in connection with the rise of Nazism, first speculatively and then later by taking various empirical indicators (Aycoberry 1981). The result is quite paradoxical since there is hardly a social class on which suspicion has not fallen, though a marked predilection has been shown for the 'petty bourgeoisie'. But this is a notoriously ambiguous concept, which is more an expression of the aporias of a class analysis conceived as a dividing up of the population into mutually exclusive slices. As with every question of origins in which a political charge is concealed, it makes sense to turn the question around: not to look for the foundations of the racism which invades everyday life (or the movement which provides the vehicle for it) in the nature of the petty bourgeoisie, but to attempt to understand how the development of racism causes a 'petty bourgeois' mass to emerge out of a diversity of material situations. For the misconceived question of the class bases of racism, we shall thus substitute a more crucial and complex question, which that former question is in part intended to mask: that of the relations between racism, as a supplement to nationalism, and the irreducibility of class conflict in society. We shall find it necessary to ask how the development of racism displaces class conflict or, rather, in what way class conflict is always already transformed by a social relation in which there is an inbuilt tendency to racism; and also, conversely, how the fact that the nationalist alternative to the class struggle specifically takes the form of racism may be considered as the index of the irreconcilable character of that struggle. This does not of course mean that it is not crucial to examine how, in a given conjuncture, the class conditions [la *condition de classe*] (made up of the material conditions of existence and labour, though also of ideological traditions and practical relationships to politics) determine the effects of racism in society: the frequency and forms of the 'acting out' of racism, the discourse which expresses it and the membership of organized racist movements.

The traces of a constant overdetermination of racism by the class struggle are as universally detectable in its history as the nationalist determination, and everywhere they are connected with the core of meaning of its phantasies and practices. This suffices to demonstrate that we are dealing here with a determination that is much more concrete and decisive than the generalities dear to the sociologists of 'modernity'. It is wholly inadequate to see racism (or the nationalism–racism dyad) either as one of the paradoxical expressions of the individualism or egalitarianism which are supposed to characterize modern societies (following the old dichotomy of 'closed', 'hierarchical' societies and 'open', 'mobile' societies) or a defensive reaction against that individualism, seen as expressing nostalgia for a social order based on the existence of a 'community' (Popper 1966; Dumont 1986). Individualism exists only in the concrete forms of market competition (including the competition between labour powers) in unstable equilibrium with association between individuals under the constraints of the class struggle. Egalitarianism only exists in the contradictory forms of political democracy (where that democracy exists), the 'welfare state' (where that exists), the polarization of conditions of existence, cultural segregation and reformist or revolutionary utopias. It is these determinations, and not mere anthropological figures, which confer an 'economic' dimension upon racism.

Nevertheless, the *heterogeneity* of the historical forms of the relationship between racism and the class struggle poses a problem. This ranges from the way in which anti-semitism developed into a bogus 'anti-capitalism' around the theme of 'Jewish money' to the way in which racial stigma and class hatred are combined today in the category of immigration. Each of these configurations is irreducible (as are the corresponding conjunctures), which make it impossible to define any simple relationship of 'expression' (or, equally, of substitution) between racism and class struggle.

In the manipulation of anti-semitism as an anti-capitalist delusion, which chiefly occurred between 1870 and 1945 (which is, we should note, the key period of confrontation between the European bourgeois states and organized proletarian internationalism), we find not only the designation of a scapegoat as an object of proletarian revolt, the exploitation of divisions within the proletariat and the projective representation of the ills of an abstract social system through the imaginary personification of those who control it (even though this mechanism is essential to the functioning of racism).[1] We also find the 'fusion' of the two historical narratives which are capable of acting as metaphors for each other: on the one hand, the narrative of the formation of nations at the expense of the lost unity of 'Christian Europe' and, on the other, that of the conflict between national independence and the internationalization of capitalist economic relations, which brought with it the attendant threat of an internationalization of the class struggle. This is why the Jew, as an internally excluded element common to all nations but also, negatively, by virtue of the theological hatred to which he is subject, as witness to the love that is supposed to unite the 'Christian peoples', may, in the imaginary, be identified with the 'cosmopolitanism of capital' which threatens the national independence of every country while at the same time reactivating the trace of the lost unity.[2]

The figure is quite different when anti-immigrant racism achieves a maximum of identification between class situation and ethnic origin (the real bases for which have always existed in the interregional, international or intercontinental mobility of the working class; this has at times been a mass phenomenon, at times residual, but it has never been eliminated and is one of the specifically proletarian characteristics of its condition). Racism combines this identification with a deliberate confusion of antagonistic social functions: thus the themes of the 'invasion' of French society by North Africans or of immigration being responsible for unemployment are connected with that of the money of the oil sheikhs who are buying up 'our' businesses, 'our' housing stock or 'our' seaside resorts. And this partly explains why the Algerians, Tunisians or Moroccans have to be referred to generically as 'Arab' (not to mention the fact that this signifier, which functions as a veritable 'switch word', also connects together these themes and those of terrorism, Islam and so on). Other configurations should not, however, be forgotten, including those which are the product of an inversion of terms: for example, the theme of the 'proletarian nation', which was perhaps invented in the 1920s by Japanese nationalism (Anderson 1983: 92–3) and was destined to play a crucial role in the crystallization of Nazism, which cannot be left out of consideration when one looks at the ways in which it has recently reappeared.

The complexity of these configurations also explains why it is impossible to hold purely and simply to the idea of racism *being used* against 'class consciousness' (as though this latter would necessarily emerge naturally from the class condition, *unless* it were blocked, misappropriated or de-natured by racism), whereas we accept as an indispensable working hypothesis that 'class' and 'race' constitute the two antinomic poles of a permanent dialectic, which is at the heart of modern representations of history. Moreover, we suspect that the instrumentalist, conspiracy-theory visions of racism within the labour movement or among its theorists (we know what high price was to be paid for these: it is tremendously to the credit of Wilhelm Reich that he was one of the first to foresee this), along with the mechanistic visions which see in racism the 'reflection' of a particular class condition, have also largely the function of denying the presence of nationalism in the working class and its organizations or, in other words, denying the internal conflict between nationalism and class ideology on which the mass struggle against racism (as well as the revolutionary struggle against capitalism) depends. It is the evolution of this internal conflict I should like to illustrate by discussing here some historical aspects of 'class racism'.

Several historians of racism (e.g. Poliakov 1974; Duchet and Rebérioux 1969; Guillaumin 1972; Williams 1944 on modern slavery) have laid emphasis upon the fact that the modern notion of race, in so far as it is invested in a discourse of contempt and discrimination and serves to split humanity up into a 'super-humanity' and a 'sub-humanity', did not initially have a national (or ethnic), but a class signification or rather (since the point is to represent the inequality of social classes as inequalities of nature) a caste signification. From this point of view, it has a twofold origin: first, in the aristocratic representation of the hereditary nobility as a superior 'race' (that is, in fact, the mythic narrative by which an aristocracy, whose domination is already coming under threat, assures itself of the legitimacy of its political privileges and idealizes the dubious continuity of its genealogy); and second, in the slave owners' representation of those populations subject to the slave trade as inferior 'races', ever predestined for servitude and incapable of producing an autonomous civilization. Hence the discourse of blood, skin colour and cross-breeding. It is only retrospectively that the notion of race was 'ethnicized', so that it could be integrated into the nationalist complex, the jumping-off point for its successive subsequent metamorphoses. Thus it is clear that, from the very outset, racist representations of history stand in relation to the class struggle. But this fact takes on its full significance only if we examine the way in which the notion of race has evolved, and the impact of nationalism upon it from the earliest figures of 'class racism' onwards – in other words, if we examine its political determination.

The aristocracy did not initially conceive and present itself in terms of the category of 'race': this is discourse which developed at a late stage,[3] the function of which is clearly defensive (as can be seen from the example of France with the myth of 'blue blood' and the 'Frankish' or 'Germanic' origin of the hereditary nobility), and which developed when the absolute monarchy centralized the state at the expense of the feudal lords and began to 'create' within its bosom a new administrative and financial aristocracy which was bourgeois in origin, thus marking a decisive step in the formation of the nation state. Even more interesting is the case of Spain in the Classical Age, as analysed by Poliakov: the persecution of the Jews after the *Reconquista*, one of the indispensable mechanisms in the establishment of Catholicism as state religion, is also the trace of the 'multinational' culture against which Hispanization (or rather Castilianization) was carried out. It is therefore intimately linked to the formation of this prototype of European nationalism. Yet it took on an even more ambivalent meaning when it gave rise to the 'statutes of the purity of the blood' (*limpieza de sangre*) which the whole discourse of European and American racism was to inherit: a product of the disavowal of the original interbreeding with the Moors and the Jews, the hereditary definition of the *raza* (and the corresponding procedures for establishing who could be accorded a certificate of purity) serves in effect both to isolate an internal aristocracy and to confer upon the whole of the 'Spanish people' a fictive nobility, to make it a 'people of masters' at the point when, by terror, genocide, slavery and enforced Christianization, it was conquering and dominating the largest of the colonial empires. In this exemplary line of development, class racism was already transformed into nationalist racism, though it did not, in the process, disappear (Poliakov 1974, vol. 2: 222–32).

What is, however, much more decisive for the matter in hand is the overturning of values we see occurring from the first half of the nineteenth century onwards. Aristocratic racism (the prototype of what analysts today call 'self-referential racism', which begins by elevating the group which controls the discourse to the status of a 'race' – hence the importance of its imperialist legacy in the colonial context: however lowly their origins and no matter how vulgar their interests or their manners, the British in India and the French in Africa would all see themselves as members of a modern nobility) is already indirectly related to the primitive accumulation of capital, if only by its function in the colonizing nations. The industrial revolution, at the same time as it creates specifically capitalist relations of production, gives rise to the *new racism* of the bourgeois era (historically speaking, the first 'neo-racism'): the one which has as its target the *proletariat* in its dual status as exploited population (one might even say super-exploited, before the beginnings of the social state) and politically threatening population.

Louis Chevalier (1973) has described the relevant network of significations in detail. It is at this point, with regard to the 'race of labourers' that the notion of race becomes detached from its historico-theological connotations to enter the field of equivalences between sociology, psychology, imaginary biology and the pathology of the 'social body'. The reader will recognize here the obsessive themes of police/detective, medical and philanthropic literature, and hence of literature in general (of which it is one of the fundamental dramatic mechanisms and one of the political keys of social 'realism'). For the first time those aspects typical of every procedure of racialization of a social group right down to our own day are condensed in a single discourse: material and spiritual poverty, criminality, congenital vice (alcoholism, drugs), physical and moral defects, dirtiness, sexual promiscuity and the specific diseases which threaten humanity with 'degeneracy'. And there is a characteristic oscillation in the presentation of these themes: either the workers themselves constitute a degenerate race or it is their presence and contact with them or indeed their condition itself which constitute a crucible of degeneracy for the 'race' of citizens and nationals. Through these themes, there forms the phantasmatic equation of 'labouring classes' with 'dangerous classes', the fusion of a socio-economic category with an anthropological and moral category, which will serve to underpin all the variants of socio-biological (and also psychiatric) determinism, by taking psuedo-scientific credentials from the Darwinian theory of evolution, comparative anatomy and crowd psychology, but particularly by becoming invested in a tightly knit network of institutions of social surveillance and control (Netchine 1978; Murard and Zylberman 1976).

Now this class racism is indissociable from fundamental historical processes which have developed unequally right down to the present day. I can mention these only briefly here. First, class racism is connected with a political problem that is crucial for the constitution of the nation state. The 'bourgeois revolutions' – and in particular the French Revolution, by its radical juridical egalitarianism – had raised the question of the political rights of the masses in an irreversible manner. This was to be the object of one and a half centuries of social struggles. The idea of a *difference in nature* between individuals had become juridically and morally contradictory, if not inconceivable. It was, however, politically indispensable, so long as the 'dangerous classes' (who posed a threat to the established social order, property and the power of the 'elites') had to be excluded by force and by legal means from political 'competence' and confined to the margins of the polity – as long, that is, as it was important to *deny them citizenship* by showing, and by being oneself persuaded, that they constitutionally 'lacked' the qualities of fully fledged or normal humanity. Two anthropologies clashed here: that of equality of birth and that of a hereditary inequality which made it possible to re-naturalize social antagonisms.

Now, this operation was overdetermined from the start by national ideology. Disraeli (who showed himself, elsewhere, to be a surprising imperialist theorist of the 'superiority of the Jews' over the Anglo-Saxon 'superior race' itself; Arendt 1986: 68; Pourkov 1974, vol. 3: 328–37; Polanyi 1957: 290ff.) admirably summed this up when he explained that the problem of contemporary states was the tendency for a single social formation to split into 'two nations'. In so doing, he indicated the path which might be taken by the dominant classes when confronted with the progressive organization of the class struggle: first divide the mass of the 'poor' (in particular by according the qualities of national authenticity, sound health, morality and racial integrity, which were precisely the opposite of the industrial pathology, to the peasants and the 'traditional' artisans); then progressively displace the markers of dangerousness and heredity from the 'labouring classes' as a whole on to

foreigners, and in particular immigrants and colonial subjects, at the same time
as the introduction of universal suffrage is moving the boundary line between
'citizens' and 'subjects' to the frontiers of nationality. In this process, however,
there was always a characteristic lag between what was supposed to happen and
the actual situation (even in countries like France, where the national population was not institutionally segregated and was subject to no original apartheid,
except if one extends one's purview to take in the whole of the imperial
territory): class racism against the popular classes continued to exist (and, at the
same time, these classes remained particularly susceptible to racial stigmatization, and remained extremely ambivalent in their attitude towards racism).
Which brings us to another permanent aspect of class racism.

I am referring to what must properly be called the *institutional racialization
of manual labour*. It would be easy to find distant origins for this, origins as old
as class society itself. In this regard, there is no significant difference between
the way contempt for work and the manual worker was expressed among the
philosophical elites of slave-owning Greece and the way a man like Taylor
could, in 1909, describe the natural predisposition of certain individuals for the
exhausting, dirty, repetitive tasks which required physical strength, but no
intelligence or initiative (the 'man of the type of the ox' of the *Principles of
Scientific Management*: paradoxically, an inveterate propensity for 'systematic
soldiering' is also attributed to this same man: this is why he needs a 'man to
stand over him' before he can work in conformity with his nature; Linhart
1976; Coriat 1979; Balibar 1983). However, the industrial revolution and
capitalist wage labour here effect a displacement. What is now the object of
contempt – and in turn fuels fears – is no longer manual labour pure and simple
(we shall, by contrast, see this theoretically idealized – in the context of
paternalistic, archaizing ideologies – in the form of 'craft work'), but *mechan-
ized* physical work, which has become 'the appendage of the machine' and
therefore subject to a violence that is both physical and symbolic without
immediate precedent (which we know, moreover, does not disappear with the
new phases of the industrial revolution, but is rather perpetuated both in
'modernized' and 'intellectualized' forms – as well as in 'archaic' forms in a
great many sectors of production).

This process modifies the status of the human body (the human status of the
body): it creates *body-men*, men whose body is a machine-body, that is
fragmented and dominated, and used to perform one isolable function or
gesture, being both destroyed in its integrity *and* fetishized, atrophied *and*
hypertrophied in its 'useful' organs. Like all violence, this is inseparable from
a resistance and also from a sense of guilt. The quantity of 'normal' work can
be recognized and extracted from the worker's body only retrospectively, once
its limits have been fixed by struggle: the rule is overexploitation, the tendential
destruction of the organism (which will be metaphorized as 'degeneracy') and,
at the very least, excess in the repression of the intellectual functions involved
in work. This is an unbearable process for the worker, but one which is no more

'acceptable', without ideological and phantasmatic elaboration, for the worker's masters: the fact that there are body-men means that there are *men without bodies*. That the body-men are men with fragmented and mutilated bodies (if only by their 'separation' from intelligence) means that the individuals of each of these types has to be equipped with a *superbody*, and that sport and ostentatious virility have to be developed, if the threat hanging over the human race if to be fended off . . .[4]

Only this historical situation, these specific social relations make it possible fully to understand the process of aestheticization (and therefore of sexualization, in fetishist mode) of the body which characterizes all the variants of modern racism, by giving rise either to the stigmatization of the 'physical marks' of racial inferiority or to the idealization of the 'human type' of the superior race. They cast light upon the true meaning of the recourse to biology in the history of racist theories, which has nothing whatever to do with the influence of scientific discoveries, but is, rather, a metaphor for – and an idealization of – the somatic phantasm. Academic biology, and many other theoretical discourses, can fulfil this function, provided they are articulated to the visibility of the body, its ways of being and behaving, its limbs and its emblematic organs. We should here, in accordance with the hypotheses formulated elsewhere regarding neo-racism and its link with the recent ways in which intellectual labour has been broken down into isolated operations, extend the investigation by describing the 'somatization' of intellectual capacities, and hence their racialization, a process visible everywhere – from the instrumentalization of IQ to the aestheticization of the executive as decision-maker, intellectual and athlete.

But there is yet another determining aspect in the constitution of class racism. The working class is a population that is both heterogeneous and fluctuating, its 'boundaries' being by definition imprecise, since they depend on ceaseless transformations of the labour process and movements of capital. Unlike aristocratic castes, or even the leading fractions of the bourgeoisie, it is not a social caste. What class racism (and, *a fortiori*, nationalist class racism, as in the case of immigrants) tends to produce is, however, the equivalent of a caste closure at least for one part of the working class. More precisely, it is maximum possible closure where social mobility is concerned, combined with maximum possible openness as regards the flows of proletarianization.

Let us put things another way. The logic of capitalist accumulation involves *two* contradictory aspects here: on the one hand, mobilizing or permanently destabilizing the conditions of life and work, in such a way as to ensure competition on the labour market, draw new labour power continually from the 'industrial reserve army' and maintain a relative overpopulation; on the other hand, stabilizing collectivities of workers over long periods (over several generations), to 'educate' them for work and 'bond' them to companies (and also to bring into play the mechanism of correspondence between a 'paternalist' political hegemony and a worker 'familialism'). On the one hand, class condition, which relates purely to the wage relation, has nothing to do with antecedents or descendants; ultimately, even the notion of 'class belonging' is devoid of any practical meaning; all that counts is class situation, *hic et nunc*. On the other hand, at least some of the workers have to be the sons of workers, a *social heredity* has to be created.[5] But with this, in practice, the capacities for resistance and organization also increase.

It was in response to these contradictory demands that the demographic and immigration policies and policies of urban segregation, which were set in place both by employers and the state from the middle of the nineteenth century onwards – policies which D. Bertaux (1977) has termed 'anthroponomic', practices – were born. These have two sides to them: a paternalistic aspect (itself closely connected to nationalist propaganda) and a disciplinary aspect, an aspect of 'social warfare' against the savage masses and an aspect of 'civilizing' (in all senses of the term) these same masses. This dual nature we can still see perfectly illustrated today in the combined social and police approach to the 'suburbs' and 'ghettos'. It is not by chance that the current racist complex grafts itself on to the 'population problem' (with its series of connotations: birth rate, depopulation and overpopulation, 'interbreeding', urbanization, social housing, public health, unemployment) and focuses preferentially on the question of the *second generation* of what are here improperly called 'immigrants' with the object of finding out whether they will carry on as the previous generation (the 'immigrant workers' properly so-called) – the danger being that they will develop a much greater degree of social combativeness, combining class demands with cultural demands; or whether they will add to the number of 'declassed' individuals, occupying an unstable position between sub-proletarianization and 'exit' from the working class. This is the main issue for class racism, both for the dominant class and for the popular classes themselves: to mark with generic signs populations which are collectively destined for capitalist exploitation – or which have to be held in reserve for it – at the very moment when the economic process is tearing them away from the direct control of the system (or, quite simply, by mass unemployment, is rendering the previous controls inoperative). The problem is to keep 'in their place', from generation to generation, those who have no fixed place; and for this, it is necessary that they have a genealogy. And also to unify in the imaginary the contradictory imperatives of nomadism and social heredity, the domestication of generations and the disqualification of resistances.

If these remarks are well founded, then they may throw some light on what are themselves the contradictory aspects of what I shall not hesitate to call the 'self-racialization' of the working class. There is here a whole spectrum of social experiences and ideological forms we might mention: from the organization of collectivities of workers around symbols of ethnic or national origin to the way in which a certain workerism, centred on criteria of class origins (and, consequently, on the institution of the working-class family, on the bond which only the family establishes between the 'individual' and 'his class') and the over-valorization of work (and, consequently, the virility which it alone confers), reproduces, within the ambit of 'class consciousness', some part of the set of representations of the 'race of workers' (Noiriel 1985; Duroux 1982; Frémontier 1980). Admittedly, the radical forms of workerism, at least in France, were produced more by intellectuals and political apparatuses aiming to 'represent' the working class (from Proudhon down to the Communist Party) than by the workers themselves. The fact remains that they correspond to a tendency on the part of the working class to form itself into a closed 'body', to preserve gains that have been made and traditions of struggle and to turn back against bourgeois society, the signifiers of class racism. It is from this reactive origin that the ambivalence characterizing workerism derives: the desire to escape from the condition of exploitation and the rejection of the contempt to which it is subject. Absolutely nowhere is this ambivalence more evident than in its relation to nationalism and to xenophobia. To the extent that in practice they reject official nationalism (when they do reject it), the workers produce in outline a political alternative to the perversion of class struggles. To the extent, however, that they project on to foreigners their fears and resentment, despair and defiance, it is not only that they are *fighting competition*; in addition, and much more profoundly, they are trying to escape their own exploitation. It is a hatred of *themselves*, as proletarians – in so far as they are in danger of being drawn back into the mill of proletarianization – that they are showing.

To sum up, just as there is a constant relation of reciprocal determination between nationalism and racism, there is a relation of reciprocal determination between 'class racism' and 'ethnic racism' and *these two determinations are not independent*. Each produces its effects, to some extent, in the field of the other and under constraints imposed by the other. Have we, in retracing this overdetermination in its broad outline (and in trying to show how it illuminates the concrete manifestations of racism and the constitution of its theoretical discourse), answered the questions we posed at the beginning of this essay? It would be more accurate to say that we have reformulated them. What has elsewhere been called the excess which, by comparison with nationalism, is constitutive of racism turns out at the same time to be a shortfall as far as the class struggle is concerned. But, though that excess is linked to the fact that nationalism is formed in opposition to the class struggle (even though it utilizes its dynamic), and that shortfall is linked to the fact that the class struggle finds itself repressed by nationalism, *the two do not compensate one another*; their effects tend, rather, to be combined. The important thing is not to decide whether nationalism is first and foremost a means of imagining and pursuing the unity of state and society, which then runs up against the contradictions of the class struggle, or whether it is primarily a reaction to the obstacles which the class struggle puts in the way of national unity. By contrast, it is crucially important to note that, in the historical field where *both* an unbridgeable gap between state and nation and endlessly re-emerging class antagonisms are to be found, nationalism necessarily takes the form of racism, at times in competition with other forms (linguistic nationalism, for example) and at times in combination with them, and that it thus becomes engaged in a perpetual headlong flight forward. Even when racism remains latent, or present only in a minority of individual consciousnesses, it is already that internal excess of nationalism which betrays, in both senses of the word, its articulation to the class struggle. Hence the ever-recurring paradox of nationalism: the regressive imagining of a nation state where the individuals would by their nature be 'at home', because they would be 'among their own' (their own kind), and the rendering of that state uninhabitable; the endeavour to produce a unified community in the face of 'external' enemies and the endless rediscovery that the enemy is 'within', identifiable by signs which are merely the phantasmatic elaboration of *its* divisions. Such a society is in a real sense a politically alienated society. But are not all contemporary societies, to some degree, grappling with their own political alienation?

NOTES

1 The personification of capital, a social relation, begins with the very figure of the *capitalist*. But this is never sufficient in itself for arousing an emotional reaction. This is why, following the logic of 'excess' other real-imaginary traits accumulate: lifestyle, lineage (the '200 families'), foreign origins, secret strategies, racial plots (the Jewish plan for 'world domination'), etc. The fact that, specifically in the case of the Jews, this personification is worked up in combination with a process of fetishization of money is clearly not accidental.

2 Matters are further complicated by the fact that the lost unity of 'Christian Europe', a mythic figuration of the 'origins of its civilization', is thus represented in the register of race at the point when the same Europe is embarking on its mission of 'civilizing the world', i.e. submitting the world to its domination, by way of fierce competition between nations.

3 And one which substitutes itself, in the French case, for the 'ideology of the three orders' a basically theological and juridical ideology, which is, by contrast, expressive of the organic place occupied by the nobility in the building of the State ('feudalism' properly so-called).

4 Clearly, the 'bestiality' of the slave has been a continual problem, from Aristotle and his contemporaries down to the modern slave trade (the hypersexualization to which it is subject is a sufficient indication of this); but the industrial revolution brought about a new paradox: the 'bestial' body of the worker is increasingly *animal* and increasingly technicized and therefore humanized. It is the panic fear of a *super-humanization* of man (in his body and his intelligence which is 'objectivized' by cognitive sciences and the corresponding techniques of selection and training), rather than his *sub-humanization* – or, in any case, the reversibility of these two – which discharges itself in phantasies of animality, and these are projected for preference on to the worker whose status as an 'outsider' [*étranger*] confers upon him at the same time the attributes of an 'other male', a 'rival'.

5 Not only in the sense of individual filiation, but in the sense of a 'population' tending towards the practice of endogamy; not only in the sense of a transmission of skills (mediated by schooling, apprenticeship and industrial discipline) but in the sense of a 'collective ethic' constructed in institutions and through subjective identification.

REFERENCES

Anderson, B. (1983), *Imagined Communities*, Verso, London.
Arendt, H. (1986), *The Origins of Totalitarianism*: Part One, 'Antisemitism', André Deutsch, London.
Aycoberry, P. (1981), *The Nazi Question: An Essay on the Interpretation of National Socialism*, translated by R. Hurley, Routledge and Kegan Paul, London.
Balibar, E. (1983), 'Sur le concept de la division du travail manuel et intellectuel', in J. Belkhir *et al.* (ed.), *L'Intellectuel, l'intelligentsia et les manuels*, Anthropos, Paris.
Bertaux, D. (1977), *Destins personnels et structure de classe*, PUF, Paris.
Chevalier, L. (1973), *Labouring Classes and Dangerous Classes in Paris during the First Half of the Nineteenth Century*, translated by F. Jellinek, Routledge and Kegan Paul, London.
Coriat, B. (1979), *L'Atelier et le chronomètre*, Christian Bourgeois, Paris.
Duchet, M. and Rebérioux, M. (1969), 'Préhistoire et histoire du racisme', in P. de Commarond and C. Duchet (eds), *Racisme et société*, Maspero, Paris.
Dumont, L. (1986), *Essays on Individualism: Modern Ideology in Anthropological Perspective*, University of Chicago Press, Chicago.
Duroux, F. (1982), *La Famille des ouvriers: Mythe ou politique?*, unpublished thesis, University of Paris VII.
Frémontier, J. (1980), *La Vie en bleu: Voyage en culture ouvrière*, Fayard, Paris.
Guillaumin, C. (1972), *L'Idéologie raciste: Genèse et langage actuel*, Mouton, Paris and The Hague.
Linhart, R. (1976), *Lénine, les paysans, Taylor*, Seuil, Paris.
Murard, L. and Zylberman, P. (1976), *Le petit Travailleur infatigable ou le prolétaire régénéré: Villes-usines, habitat et imtimités au XIXe siècle*, Éditions Recherches, Fontenay-sous-Bois.
Netchine, G. (1978), 'L'Individuel et le collectif dans les réprésentations psychologiques de la diversité des êtres humaines au XIXe siècle', in L. Poliakov (ed.), *Ni juif ni grec: Entretiens sur le racisme (II)*, Mouton, Paris and The Hague.
Noiriel, C. (1985), *Longwy: Immigrés et prolétaires 1880–1980*, PUF, Paris.
Polanyi, K. (1957), 'Appendix II: Disraeli's "Two Nations" and the Problem of colored races' in *The Great Transformation*, Beacon Press, Boston, pp. 290–4.
Poliakov, L. (1974), *The History of Anti-Semitism*, translated by R. Howard, 4 volumes, Routledge and Kegan Paul, London.
Popper, K. (1966), *The Open Society and its Enemies*, 5th edn, 2 volumes, Routledge and Kegan Paul, London.
Taylor, F. Winslow ([1911], 1993), *Principles of Scientific Management*, Routledge, London.
Williams, E. (1944), *Capitalism and Slavery*, University of North Carolina Press, Chapel Hill, NC.

Index

public/private: liberalism and 248–9; and multicultural society 208–19, 255, 280
Puerto Ricans 237, 242, 244
Pujol, Jordi 134, 140–1, 143–52

Quebec 6, 9, 73, 82, 89, 152, 170–85, 237; identity 10

race 10, 34–5; caste signification of 321–8; ethnic groups and 2, 15–17, 21; liberalism and, since Civil Rights Act 302–17; and nationality 26, 140, 149; and plural society 224
racial desegregation in USA 237–9
racial discrimination/inequality 206, 207, 281, 282
racism 9, 11, 34–5, 133, 227, 238, 279, 280, 281, 282; American Indians and 242–3; and class 11, 318–28; European 291–301; four levels of 300; *see also* anti-racism
Radcliffe-Brown, A. 209
Reformation 47, 49
refugees 10, 93, 123, 275
regionalism 78, 149, 151, 152
Reich, Wilhelm 321
religion: ethnic groups and 23, 252, 271, 277; multicultural society and 214–15, 217, 218, 219, 279, 280, 281; and nationality 24, 273
religious groups 2
Renan, E. 44
republicanism 270, 279
revolution 74, 75
Rex, J. 7, 8
Ribó, R. 141–2
Riesman, D. 33
right-wing political parties and racism 300–1
rights *see* individual human rights; minority rights
Roma 4
Romania 70, 237
Romantic movement 5
Roosevelt, F. D. 195
Rovira, Carod 142
Russia, Russians 70–1, 91, 94, 95, 237, 275
Rwanda 96

Safran, W. 283–5
Sami 4, 39, 40
Scotland 6, 73, 176, 232; and devolution 10, 154–70
Scottish National Party 162–8 *passim*
Scottish nationalism 78

self-determination 6, 10
self-government: Indian tribes 196; national minorities 230–1, 242–3, 244, 245
separatism, explosion of, after 1989 69–79
Serbs, Serbia 24, 39, 70, 88, 95, 96, 97, 122–32 *passim*, 237, 269
sexual relations: ethnic groups 24; and race 15–17
Shils, E. 220–1, 222
Sikhs 40; migration 275–7
Sinn Féin 103, 108–19 *passim*
situational ethnicity 7, 270–2
Slovaks, Slovakia 70, 237
Slovenes, Slovenia 70, 121, 124–31 *passim*
Smith, Adam 58
Smith, Anthony 81–2, 135, 272
Smith, M. G. 208, 223–5, 226, 227
Snyder, J. 85, 87, 89, 97, 98
social anthropology 33–4
social circles (Weber) 3, 17, 19
social cohesion 5, 145, 147, 225
social democracy 9, 143, 270
social democratic welfare state in Germany 248–56
social division of labour 54
social reproduction 61–6
social science 270; value orientations 205–7; *see also* social anthropology; sociology
social work, in multicultural society 216
socialism 9; in Catalonia 140, 141, 142
socialization 209, 216, 219, 271; ethnic 29
society 173, 209
sociology: American 11; classical 2–3, 33; plural, multicultural society 207–10; of racism 298–301
Somalia 81
South Africa 208
sovereignty, sovereignty association: First Nations of USA 190, 192; indigenous peoples 289; Quebec 170, 171, 177–84 *passim*
Soviet Union 6, 50–1, 69, 71–3, 75, 82, 83, 85, 88, 90, 91, 94, 274; *see also* Russia
Spain 73, 162, 322; Autonomous Communities System 137, 138–40, 141, 142, 147–9, 150, 151; Catalonia's relationship with 147–9, 151 (*see also* Catalonia); Constitution of 1978 135, 136–7, 147; Francoist regime 133, 135–6, 137, 138, 143, 146, 151